DISCUSSION, CONFERENCE, AND GROUP PROCESS

SECOND EDITION

DISCUSSION, CONFERENCE, and GROUP PROCESS

SECOND EDITION

Halbert E. Gulley

Colorado State University

Holt, Rinehart and Winston, Inc.

New York   Chicago   San Francisco   Atlanta   Dallas
Montreal   Toronto   London

PREFACE

Wide participation in decision-making, long characteristic of democracy, has in recent years become important as well in business and industry, labor unions, schools and colleges, churches, and virtually all organizations where people work together or socialize. Increasing interdependence in a complex society means more reliance on group decisions and fewer instances where the individual can go his isolated way. This extensive need for wise group action justifies the courses and books on group discussion and conference leadership.

This book proposes to help students better understand how groups function and how individuals become effective discussion-leaders and participants. Primary emphasis is on decision-making in small groups, although some attention is given to information-sharing, public, and large-group discussion.

Almost everyone receives frequent practice in group discussion but much of it is of poor quality. Since interaction involves complex relationships, reaching effective group decisions is not easy, nor does communication skill in group situations develop by accident. Effective leaders and participants are made, not born.

Discussion looks easy because it is a common experience, yet the conscientious group member will not underestimate the need for thorough education in its intelligent use. Some people feel that able individuals naturally possess the capacity to talk with others, to understand how groups function, and to lead discussion; or that such aptitude develops through exposure and casual experience. While native ability, intelligence, and experience contribute to effectiveness, study and directed practice are essential.

Endeavoring to improve as a communicator in small-group situations is exciting but demanding. As one student wrote on an examination, with only slight exaggeration: "To have a good discussion and to be a good discussion leader, you should have the understanding of a social psychologist, the knowledge of a professor, the enthusiasm of a sorority girl, and the tact and patience of a saint!"

The chapters in this second edition have been reorganized and the whole work almost totally rewritten. When it appeared in 1960, the book combined the traditional approach to teaching discussion procedures with the contemporary research results of social psychology, sociology, and speech that illuminate the operation of discussion groups. The best elements have been retained and, hopefully, strengthened. The present edition makes even more use of experimental evidence to help explain discussion effectiveness. Additional examples improve clarity and usefulness. A new appendix offers cases for discussion.

Perhaps the most important change is a softening of viewpoint—a lessened rigidity about definitions, categories, and procedures. There is a clearer recognition that effective discussion may be approached in many different ways. The nature of controversy in discussion is given a fuller treatment, for example. There is greater emphasis on the role of the individual as proponent of his own views as well as participant in a group effort.

Part One explains the nature of discussion, its meanings, uses, limitations, and types. Part Two turns at once to preparation for discussion practice: planning; preparing to use information, reasoning, language, and communication; and understanding attitudes, ethical obligations, and other responsibilities of participation.

Part Three discusses leadership. Four chapters devoted to this subject underline the importance of leadership to high-quality discussion.

The fourth part focuses on the study of interaction. Chapter 14 introduces the elements of group process and Chapter 15 the intermediate interactional processes affecting decision-making. The evaluation of discussion is explored in Chapter 16. Some instructors may prefer to assign Part Four before turning to discussion practice and leadership as treated in Parts Two and Three.

Part Five deals with public discussion and discussion in large groups.

It is a pleasure to acknowledge the influence and help of many persons in the preparation of both the first and second editions. I am grateful to the authors and publishers who have allowed quotation from their works, and to Daniel Fitzpatrick and the St. Louis *Post-Dispatch* for permission to use a Fitzpatrick editorial cartoon. My indebtedness is great to those colleagues who have generously given constructive criticism, especially Dr. Wayne E. Brockriede and Dr. Ted J. Barnes. I wish also to express my gratitude to my students for their spontaneous appraisal of these ideas; and to my wife, Nadine, for editorial assistance and for forbearance.

Halbert E. Gulley

Fort Collins, Colorado
February 2, 1968

TABLE OF CONTENTS

PART ONE

THE NATURE
OF DISCUSSION

Chapter 1

AN APPROACH
TO DISCUSSION

This book is concerned with effective communication in discussion, especially decision-making discussion in small-group situations. Its intent is to help the reader become a more effective discussion leader and participant. Hopefully this will be achieved through guided practice and systematic study of communication in group situations as well as the study of group process itself.

We are surrounded, almost inundated, by enormous amounts of communication. Some of it we ourselves initiate. Thus each of us must be effective communicators and alert listeners. Political speaking vitally influences our national success and survival, and advertising our consumption. Our own expressive skills affect our ability to achieve the goals we set for ourselves, as well as the contribution we can make to the organizations and groups to which we give our allegiance. Hence it is essential that we become serious and lifelong students of the process of communication.

Discussion is one important use of talk, one that has multiplied enormously as institutions and organizations have become more complex and our society more interdependent.

When an individual accepts or seeks a relationship with others because he cannot satisfy particular needs alone, or satisfy them as well or as efficiently, he commits himself to a complex set of interactions. This involves much talk and many opportunities for misunderstanding and waste, on the one hand, and satisfying achievement on the other. In the family, the legislative committee, the board of directors, the town council, the corporation executive committee, the staff meeting, the student council, and similar situations, a group usually attempts to bring to bear on common problems the collective talents of all or of many. In these attempts, a vital vehicle affecting success or failure is the oral communication occurring during the group's discussion—the sharing of information and insights, weighing, considering, and deciding. The subject for study in this book is this oral discussion, together with those elements of the group and its operation that determine the group's productivity and harmony.

REASONS FOR STUDYING DISCUSSION

The study of discussion is vital for several reasons. Democracy itself depends on intelligent participation by many in decision-making. The distinguishing characteristic of democracy is that the group members themselves decide what is in the best interests of all. In a dictatorship or oligarchy, one man or a few exercise arbitrary control over many.

A democratic society, in contrast, places a great premium on wise group decisions. Of course, not all members of the larger democratic group take advantage of their opportunities to participate in decision-making. In fact, many decisions are influenced by a few powerful pressure groups, which do not have all citizens as members. This abdication of the right to participate, however, does not alter the fact that each has the privilege of taking part. If individuals fail to exercise their rights, ambitious and crafty persons may move in to fill the vacuum. The fact remains: decisions are made collectively and whether or not citizens make themselves part of the collectivity is a matter of their free choice.

Group participation in decision-making is obviously not confined to political government. Democratic groups function in many other fields: business and industry, labor, education, religion, social welfare, agriculture, and so forth. The same virtues that mark the superiority of group effort in political affairs are apparent when the method is applied elsewhere. Thus the person who studies discussion should find it possible to increase his contribution to group effort in his future vocation as well as in community and social affairs.

In addition to its usefulness as a tool widely used in government, on the job, and in the community, discussion study has the virtue of developing the individual's abilities to seek out information, to analyze problems, and to think reflectively. The habits of careful inquiry and rational thinking so characteristic of good discussion are valuable in many other situations as well.

The study of discussion also helps people to appreciate the frequent need for withholding judgment, avoiding hasty generalization, and offering statements tentatively. This willingness to be tentative—openness to modification—is one of the characteristics that distinguishes the discusser from the debater or advocate. The discusser has usually not made up his mind finally when he participates in decision-making discussion. He is searching for a decision more acceptable than any yet suggested. The advocate, on the other hand, has often decided firmly what in his opinion is the wisest policy. His aim, through persuasive speaking, is to convince others that his proposal should be accepted. He has passed the stage of tentativeness and has become a partisan of a particular course of action.

Another value of discussion study comes from the additional development of the individual as a communicator. Often the most successful person is one who communicates effectively in all the kinds of situations requiring expressive talent, as speaker, presiding officer, and parliamentary chairman as well as discussion leader and participant. To study discussion broadens the individual's education as a communicator. As organizations and institutions— governmental, industrial, educational, etc.—become more and more complex, it is possible that most persons will not work as individuals but as parts of teams and groups. In such circumstances, the influence of the person skilled in communicating within the group situation will be enhanced.

DEFINITION OF DISCUSSION

It is important to specify at the outset the kind of oral communication activity that is here being labeled discussion. This term is used loosely. Bob reports a street-corner visit with John where they discussed the weather. Another student says his history teacher led a class discussion yesterday. Are these instances of discussion?

Not all talk in groups is *discussion*, as the term is used in this book.

For our purposes we can say that *discussion occurs when a group of persons assemble in a face-to-face situation and through oral interaction exchange information or attempt to reach a decision on shared problems.*

We will give primary attention to decision-making in small groups. When the end is a decision, members usually proceed in a more or less orderly manner to *define and analyze the problem, evaluate possible solutions, and attempt to agree upon a high-quality decision to which all or the majority will be committed.*

Discussion involves a group. To have discussion, two or more persons must be involved. The individual talking to himself, introspecting, or thinking aloud is not participating in discussion.

Although we will be primarily interested in the small group, ideally five to seven, what we say should apply also to larger groups and to groups more highly organized and rigidly structured than the ideal. Further, while groups are used advantageously for therapy and many other purposes, we will concentrate on groups seeking solutions to social, economic, political, educational, and cultural problems.

Discussion is oral. This requirement is obvious. The emphasis in this book is on discussion in which members are physically present together in the same room. They are part of the same group, and communicate with each other directly and orally. It would be possible to carry on a discussion, which meets the other requirements, with members communicating in writing. A group of deaf mutes could engage in discussion. These situations would introduce some new dimensions, however, and would alter many of the aspects of greatest interest here. Hence, this treatment is confined to discussion where oral communication and language skills are of great importance.

Discussion involves interaction. To call an activity discussion, all or most members of the group must participate. Free participation means that there is communicative interaction among members; that members are free to talk and others to respond with facial expressiveness and further talk, in a circular communicative pattern. Otherwise, members are not likely to achieve a meeting of minds. The lecture in which communication flows in only one direction, from speaker to listeners, is not discussion. Discussion may follow the lecture if members of the audience and the speaker communicate with and respond to each other, that is, interact.

Note that easy interaction requires freedom for each member to initiate and react to contributions. Such freedom will not exist unless there is an atmosphere of permissiveness created within the group. Permissiveness means simply that each person is permitted to interact freely with the others, with minimum fear of censure, ridicule, or ostracism from the group.

Interaction is usually informal and conversational although in some situations involving larger numbers there may be some more or less formal speeches.

Discussion is usually purposeful. Members of a discussion group usually have a specific purpose that brings them together on a particular occasion. If the purpose is obscure, success will be impaired. A committee or conference group meets to solve concrete problems; a study group, which uses discussion for information sharing, comes together with commonly accepted aims in mind.

Casual social conversation in the living room, coffee break talk, idle or polite interchange on the street corner, and the after-hours bull session in the fraternity house are not instances of discussion as the term is used here largely because the talk employed is not purposeful. Discussion may take place during the coffee break or social conversation, assuming that other requirements of discussion are met, if the group decides that consideration of a specific problem would be worthwhile and proceeds to discuss the limited problem purposefully.

Discussion usually follows some orderly development. This is another reason for not considering casual social conversation and idle talk discussion. Talk in the unstructured social situation usually flits from subject to subject— from the weather to the ball game to women's hats to the political situation, etc. In contrast, decision-making discussion usually begins with a limited problem and moves more or less systematically toward questions about decision or action.

The kinds of groups we will study may or may not have a designated leader but they will usually have some kind of leadership. It is in contributing to orderly forward movement that leadership becomes vital. A group without leadership of any kind tends to proceed in many directions at once or to meander or to move in circles, or to remain in one place.

In discussion, members usually share an interest in some problem or in other ways accept some common goals. Most of the time it is this acceptance of common goals that brings the group together.

An important feature of most discussion is that participants proceed according to what is in the best interests of all or of most members. Methods and ends considered appropriate are determined by the attitudes, values, and objectives of the group rather than by those of one or a few. Of course a group is composed of individuals and there are group goals only in the sense that the members embrace some goals in common.

Deutsch has used the term *promotively interdependent* to describe the interrelationships of persons who accept goals in common in the cooperative social situation. The interrelationships of those in a competitive social situation are competitively interdependent. He says, "the members of a basketball team may be cooperatively interrelated (and be promotively interdependent) with respect to winning the game, but competitively interrelated with respect to being the 'star' of the team."[1] In discussion, the ideal situation would be one of promotive interdependence. A group member who strives to be the star of the discussion and to promote his own ends rather than to further the goal of a high-quality group outcome may endanger the success of the whole enterprise.

In informational discussion, members usually share a desire to understand a problem, pursuing the investigation wherever it may lead. If some members or a leader try to steer the exploration away from an aspect that may jeopardize their own pet beliefs, the discussion may suffer. Hence classroom discussion is often quite different from other kinds of informational discussion because a teacher usually guides contributions in a predetermined direction, so that students will be exposed to certain essential subject matter. This is not to say that there is anything wrong with this type of classroom discussion; it is often a very effective teaching method. But it is different from the kind of discussion where participants themselves are free to explore whatever avenues the members themselves want to investigate.

In decision-making discussion, members usually share a willingness to seek a solution that will be best for everyone or for as many as possible. During the discussion participants for the most part are willing to listen considerately to the views of others.

The implications of this mutual acceptance of goals are far-reaching. For example, acceptance of cooperative interrelationships means that members show some degree of respect for each other. Such acceptance contributes to a more permissive atmosphere, easier communicative interaction, and increased cohesiveness of the group as a functioning unit.

Discussion and Conference

The word *conference* has been added to the title of this book because it is a popular term that is used to label many group activities that are discussions. Discussion is the more general and perhaps more obscure term.

---

[1] Morton Deutsch, "The Effects of Cooperation and Competition Upon Group Process," Dorwin Cartwright, and Alvin Zander, *Group Dynamics: Research and Theory*, sec. ed., New York: Harper & Row, 1960, pp. 414–48.

Most conferences are types of discussions. Almost all conferences use discussion, at least some of the time. Not all discussions are conferences, although it must be admitted that the word *conference* is applied popularly to many varieties of group meetings.

The term *conference* is used most frequently to designate two types of activities. One type resembles a committee meeting—the group is usually small and the discussion private—but members represent two or more parent organizations with a mutual problem. The two houses of Congress, when they pass different versions of a bill, send representatives to a joint conference, which tries to reconcile differences. In this kind of meeting, the discussion is usually an informal, conversational interchange, just as committee discussion usually is. This book deals primarily with such private, informal, directly conversational committee-and-conference type of discussion.

The second most common meaning of the word *conference* designates a large meeting sometimes referred to as a convention or workshop. World scientists may gather for a conference on atomic energy or teachers of history may meet in a nationwide, annual conference or convention. Much use is made of discussion. Some sessions will be large with all registrants attending. At times, small-group discussions may be held, with members choosing among many programs occurring simultaneously in different rooms. To some sessions, the public may be invited. Thus there is a wide range of activities taking place, all under the omnibus label—conference.

Assuming that we have established the meaning and importance of discussion as a subject for study, as well as its general nature, we can now turn to its historical beginnings. Examination of the developments influencing its study should further clarify the nature of this method of inquiry and decision-making.

STREAMS OF INFLUENCE

At least three major developments have influenced the contemporary study of discussion. The oldest of these is that of rhetoric and its counterpart, dialectic. Aristotle and Plato both took an interest in these two subjects and it was Socrates, of course, who used skillful questioning as a means of clarifying thought and eliciting precise answers during speculative discussions. Through the intervening centuries, rhetoric—the study of persuasion and the complex interrelationships among communicator, message, and the responses of receivers—has enjoyed more consistent favor. Rhetoric has been tarnished in some periods, however, through misuse by the sophists of early Greece and through distortion by the elocutionists of the nineteenth century in Britain and the United States. It has received emphasis in the twentieth century, being newly championed within departments of speech in America. Recently it has been revived as a respectable study within many departments of English in its full-bodied sense, rather than as only a truncated course satisfying the freshman composition requirement.

Departments of speech not only have sponsored courses in classical rhetoric but also have offered courses in persuasive speaking and have promoted extra-curricular debating activities where rhetorical principles again assumed importance. The rediscovery of dialectic has been slower and less direct.

The Greek sophists damaged the reputation of dialectic as well as rhetoric. Aristotle thought dialectic useful in developing skill in reasoning, defining, and in asking and answering questions; it offers a "process of criticism wherein lies the path to the principles of all inquiries." For Plato, dialectic was even more valuable, being a disciplined path to truth including all of logic. Where the sophists used the method for logical hair-splitting and verbal gymnastics, Socrates employed it for serious inquiry. In Plato's *Republic*, Socrates advocates postponing the study of dialectic until the age of thirty because youngsters "when they first get the taste in their mouths, argue for amusement" and "like puppy-dogs, they rejoice in pulling and tearing at all who come near them. . . . But when a man begins to get older, he will no longer be guilty of such insanity; he will imitate the dialectician who is seeking for truth, and not the sophist, who is contradicting for the sake of amusement."

The respectability of dialectic was not helped at all by the scholars of the Middle Ages who had more time on their hands than facts with which to speculate about the realm of the spirit and the number of angels who could dance on the head of a pin. Neither has the word recovered from its use by Karl Marx in his conception of dialectical materialism.

Nevertheless, contemporary interest in group discussion has some of its roots in dialectic, since the method has been used by some persons in the past as a serious and orderly process of inquiry; "It is concerned with every phase of thought: with the establishment of definitions; the examination of hypotheses in the light of their presuppositions or consequences; the formulation of inferences and proofs; the resolution of dilemmas arising from opposition in thought."[2] The same departments of speech who gave a new birth to rhetoric began in the 1930s to introduce courses in discussion. At the University of Illinois in 1936, L. S. Judson produced a paperback *Manual of Group Discussion*, and in 1939 from the School of Speech, Northwestern University, came a textbook published nationally for use in college courses.

Democratic Participation

A second major historical influence has been the spread of democratic decision-making. Popular participation in political affairs has been fostered by community enterprises ranging from the earliest New England town meetings to the Great Books discussions of the last two decades. In the 1930s the

---

[2] "Dialectic," *The Great Ideas: A Syntopicon of Great Books of the World*, Chicago: Encyclopedia Britannica, 1952, p. 347.

Des Moines public forum movement gave this kind of civic meeting a new boost.

Many of the characteristics of political democracy coincide with the requisites for effective small-group discussion. Discussion by a limited number of persons face to face in a serious inquiry has many similarities to the process by which a democratic nation involves its citizens in the freedom to decide. Here the individual and his views become a matter of central importance; he is listened to and taken into account because the individual person matters. Members of the group accept the others as equals; participation by all is invited and expected as a matter of right, not as a matter of birth or station or wealth. After consideration of all views, decision is reached by consensus or by voting, whichever is sensible or possible, and the majority view is accepted as the wise outcome. In the same spirit with which the minority accepts the majority view as representative of the greater group good, those who prevail at the moment respect those in the minority. Because this kind of group consideration makes maximum use of the collective talents of all and at the same time produces maximum harmony in the group, the method of democratic discussion has spread beyond political affairs into business and industry, education, labor unions, and many other institutions where people must work together cooperatively. Today discussion courses are found in such colleges as commerce and education as well as within the liberal arts.

Small-Group Theory

A third major influence has occurred since World War II with the development of interest in the process of communication, the study of communication theory, and a tremendously accelerated pace of experimental research on small groups by psychologists, sociologists, and speech experts. This expanding body of knowledge has been immediately applicable to the teaching of discussion courses.

Out of communication theory has come the impetus to explain the operation of communication in any human situation. A helpful way to describe the ever changing process of persons in communication is to present a schematic model of the process. It will then be possible to suggest the unique features of discussion as one form of oral communication.

A MODEL OF COMMUNICATION PROCESS

Communication means literally to "make common"—that is, to create in a receiver's mind an idea or image similar to the one in the mind of the sender. If by some procedure not now known we could attach an electrode to a speaker's brain and connect it by wires to an electrode in a listener's brain, so that images could be transferred directly, we could eliminate many troublesome communication breakdowns. Delivering meaning to another person is not so simple. Meaning must be transmitted, not transferred. The sender must translate his thought or image into language symbols in a code familiar to both parties; then he must transmit these symbols and hope they will be intercepted and received by their destination. In between there are many excellent opportunities for mishap. The model should suggest some of the possibilities for error.

Of course, there is some danger in presenting a model of the process; we are tempted to think of it as static whereas it is extremely dynamic and continuously changing. To speculate about what happens, we must freeze the event into a still photograph of what is actually a motion picture; we can justify this exercise only for analytical purposes.

If a communicative act has a beginning, it begins when a source initiates a statement. Before he can say anything, however, he has had to perceive the world outside himself, interpret what he has observed, translate his interpretations into words that can be expressed and that can be understood by the receiver, and finally to commit himself to a statement he is willing to deliver.

Hopefully the receiver of the communication is attending to the statement delivered by the source. Then he, too, must perceive the transmission, interpret it through his view of the world outside himself, and decide how to respond. Some portion of his response will serve as feedback cues for the source, who can then attenuate for error when he delivers future statements. Other portions of the receiver's response may become statements initiated; thus the receiver becomes a source who transmits, the two reverse roles, and the former source is now the receiver, responding and providing feedback cues.

These two elements, source and receiver, are not connected by electrodes and wires. They can be related only by a signal or message that is transmitted in the way a radio station broadcasts a signal, even if source and receiver are two persons face to face in the same room. In this case the signal consists of sound waves and light waves carrying a message with a particular content, organized in certain structures, and worded in particular language, along with facial expressions and other visual cues of meaning.

This third element in the process, which connects source and receiver, is called a *signal* by engineers, a *channel* by communication theorists, and a *message* by rhetoricians. We thus can speak of multiple channels: seeing, hearing, etc. Engineers speak of noise in the signal. In face to face oral communication this "noise" may mean distractions competing for attention, the student next to you whispering in your ear, or some internal concern that keeps a listener from concentrating on the speaker's meaning, such as thinking about the week's unpaid room rent.

A fourth element in any communication event is the situation in which the event occurs. This can range from boy-girl whispering in the moonlight to the President addressing forty million Americans by television.

We should consider two additional matters about the source of a communication. The source communicates for certain purposes; and as a source he has

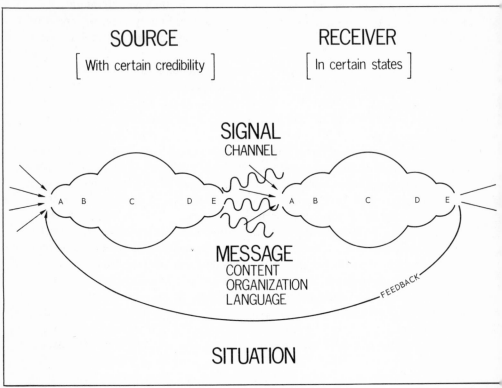

FIGURE 1–1 A SCHEMATIC MODEL OF THE PROCESS OF COMMUNI-
CATION *Communication occurs in a situation when a source with
certain credibility (A) responds to external stimuli (arrows) and,
for certain purposes, (B) decodes what he perceives, (C) scans his
"interpreter" for meanings and language he could communicate in
response, (D) begins to encode and (E) finally commits himself to
transmitting a signal, or message which, hopefully, the receiver
(who is in certain states) attends to, decodes, interprets, and responds
to (including some feedback responses) as, hopefully, the source
intended. This model is based in part on Wendell Johnson's article,
"The Spoken Word and the Great Unsaid,"* Quarterly Journal of
Speech, *37 (1951), pp. 419–29.*

certain credibility, or degrees of competence and trustworthiness, in the eyes of the receiver.

Finally we should consider one fact about the receiver. He is in certain conditions when he attends to the source's message. He already holds certain attitudes, has certain information, and sees the world in a particular way; at the time of transmission he may be alert, sleepy, hostile, or whatever; and for him the source is friend, stranger, foe, or something else.

ONE KIND OF ORAL COMMUNICATION

Much more could be said about this complex process, of course, but we have considered enough elements to specify some of the unique characteristics of discussion as one form of oral communication. Such a procedure will begin to open up the study of discussion as a form to be considered in detail throughout the book.

PURPOSE/ Participants and leaders in discussion may have similar or diverse purposes when discussion begins, or even when it ends. While some members may want to get busy with the assigned task, others may wish to socialize. If one member finds that he is a minority of one in the purpose he would most like to achieve, he can easily conceal this discovery simply by being silent. In fact, there are almost certainly some hidden agendas in most discussions.

The purpose of leader and participants may well be dissimilar. The leader may be more determined than the members to achieve efficient and high-quality productivity. One or two participants may even harbor an intent to compete with the chairman for the leadership role.

MULTIPLE SOURCES/ While almost all communication, in the familiar cliché, is a two-way street when, for example, an audience provides feedback cues to the public speaker, there is a uniqueness about small group discussion in the rapid-fire alternation of sources and receivers. In this kind of communicative interaction, receivers give a fair hearing in part to obtain a fair hearing for themselves. The sources of messages may be obscured in a rapid exchange of ideas and later the ideas may be dissociated from their sources; in some cases they may seem the common property of the group.

Because discussion involves multiple sources, there is an obvious gain from the years of experience and diversity of knowledge available for exploring the problem. There is a greater probability in a group that someone will have the key fact, can put into acceptable language the delicate agreement, or will think of the compromise that resolves a stubborn conflict. Of course, the procedure requires time and willingness to hear everyone's views.

SIGNAL/ In speaker-to-audience communication, and especially in the mass media, there is often a serious problem of noise in the signal. A listener fails to hear a key word or idea because the speaker spoke too softly or carelessly, or because the person next to him in the audience coughed or distracted him with conversation. The television viewer may miss the speaker's key sentence because of distractions in the home or because he is reading the newspaper at the same time. In small-group discussion, however, there is minimal difficulty with the signal. The members are face to face in the same room, often comfortably arranged around a table or in a circle. When they talk to each other they are separated only by a few feet. If a comment is missed, convention allows a member to ask the speaker to repeat it, as he usually cannot in the speaker–audience situation.

MESSAGES/ The nature of the messages in discussion is quite a different matter. The public speaker can prepare his remarks with care, paying attention to the logical unfolding of his arguments and planning the persuasiveness of his language. The discusser cannot. He may prepare meticulously but must communicate his ideas in short bursts, often of only a few seconds each. Rarely does he have an opportunity to speak without interruption for 2 or 3 minutes, but 3 minutes is a very long time in small group discussion. The usual pattern is for comments to be short. Such messages are difficult to organize and they may be delivered as part of a discussion that is itself disorganized.

Only by alert listening can members of a group detect fallacious or illogical or inconsistent reasoning in two related remarks separated by several minutes in time. Thus it is not surprising that a group sometimes recognizes its poor reasoning only after the meeting has ended. At the same time, there is the potential for superior reasoning through the combining of brain power if members are sufficiently alert as listeners to this kind of rapid interchange.

MULTIPLE RECEIVERS/ Speakers who address audiences have multiple receivers but in discussion there is an important difference—the discusser does not have the floor as does the speaker who has the center of the stage. The discusser is a speaker only in the most temporary sense. He must be much more alert to feedback cues and to the diversity of perceptions represented by his multiple listeners. He must take into account all that has been said earlier by all the others, what they are receiving and avoiding right now and what they are likely to accept or reject next.

COMMUNICATOR CREDIBILITY/ Many public speakers address a particular audience only once or at least infrequently. Their reputations precede them and their early remarks structure response to later remarks. In discussion, however, the communicator's credibility is likely to depend much more directly on the quality and style of his past performances within the group. Some groups exist over many meetings, perhaps extending over years, and even in groups existing for a single meeting, participants quickly build a credibility image for themselves based on their actions and contributions in this on-going situation.

SITUATION/ The uniqueness of discussion in terms of situation lies partially in the physical arrangements—the table or circle, the close proximity, the face to face directness and intimacy. More importantly, in most discussion situations, there is the addition of a leader or at least of leadership. Whereas in a public address situation there may be a presiding officer who introduces the speakers and chairs a question period, in discussion the style and quality of leadership may determine more than any other factor the nature of the discussion and its success.

Several careful studies of small-group interaction suggest that there are three vital factors operative in most discussion situations. One is that the individual members quite naturally want to be recognized, feel prominent, have their views taken into account, etc. A second factor is that most members, most of the time, recognize the importance of their task assignment and want to achieve the business at hand. The third factor is social—members react to each other as people, usually want harmonious relationships, want to avoid unpleasant conflict if possible, etc.

The leadership, the situation, and the participants' various purposes can interact in such complex ways in relation to these three factors that discussions may vary unbelievably, even when similar groups take up the same subject under similar circumstances.

An authoritarian boss, for example, may meet with his staff for the ostensible purpose of having them decide on a policy that they know very well he has already decided. If he concentrates exclusively on the task with a no-nonsense attitude toward socialization, and if he squelches individual recognition by calling only upon those chief assistants whose automatic allegiance he can rely on, it is easy to predict the interaction that will occur. There will probably be limited communication, short messages, concealed feedback, unexpressed hostility, and an orderly but brief meeting.

Perhaps the operation of these elements and this example of the authoritarian boss illustrate the components of group discussion we will be concerned with as we begin our study.

Almost immediately, however, we are confronted by a controversy over point of view. Do we propose to study the individual communicator relating himself to and influencing the group during discussion, or shall we study the group as a unit, considering separate individuals only incidentally as contributors to a collective entity?

THE INDIVIDUAL VERSUS THE GROUP

Champions of the individual express concern about submission to "group-think" and the submergence of the brilliant mind in order to receive the comforting reassurances of group mediocrity, a leveling toward the average. They point to the dangers of conformity when the organization man suppresses his personality in the corporate image. Someone has called a conference the "modern substitute for the martyrdom of individual responsibility and the loneliness of thought."

This view sometimes seems to make cooperation in groups almost an abdication of personal responsibility. "Surrender to the group" seems to holders of this view a repudiation of free choice and individualism. Within this faction, of course, are some social scientists who see a serious retreat from reality among persons who hide their weaknesses within a collectivity; but our interest at the moment is not with maladjustment or social irresponsibility.

One question that has stirred up the individualists is, "Is there such a thing as a group mind?" This question led some wag to contribute a facetious definition of a group. When six individuals in a room each rise and leave one at a time, he said, a group is what is left in the room after they are all gone.

Those concerned about suppression of individualism look upon the study of discussion as somewhat suspect. They want students to concentrate on debate and persuasive speaking, with heavy emphasis on logic and audience adaptation.

Those who champion groups take an opposite view. Some extremists, discovering small groups in action, have almost pronounced them the salvation of man. The world's ills will be magically cured, some of them are tempted to declare, if only men will learn to work together harmoniously in cohesive groups. Well, in a sense this is true. To work together harmoniously, men must become brothers and genuine world-wide brotherhood would lead to the elimination of most of the world's ills. But notice that the concept *group* here is used in a broad, sociological sense, referring to large, even national groupings of men rather than to small discussion groups. It may be sound to assert that world tensions will be lessened when men learn to work together harmoniously, but it does not follow that every small-group discussion is a step toward world salvation. Nor does it follow that men need only get together and talk things over, and anything at all can be worked out. Nor is it fair to say that anyone who persists in disagreeing with the magical group is therefore standing in the way of world reform and siding with unenlightened barbarism.

It is not sensible to think of groups or of group discussion as magical open Sesames unlocking new forces hitherto fettered because individuals were not together. Neither the small group nor group discussion is new, and any recent innovation such as brainstorming or the buzz group is a minor modification. It is true that group discussion is being used more now than ever before, and it is also true that groups have some unique powers. To exaggerate the virtues of group decisions or to claim a therapeutic bonus with every agreement, however, is to invite misunderstanding and distrust. One prominent teacher said sardonically in a paper given at a national convention that some speech teachers, failing to find a satisfying subject matter in rhetoric, "forsook controversy and took refuge in togetherness through discussion." This vague notion of companionable togetherness is not the aim of discussion. Its objectives are to reach high-quality outcomes to which the members are committed, and usually to maintain the group as a group, not for sensuous enjoyment but to develop a better team for more efficient future productivity.

Nor does discussion outlaw controversy. Here is another damaging misconception. Somehow the notion is widely current that anyone using discussion expects participants to be so spinelessly sweet that they would accept anything rather than be out of step. This misconception is ridiculous. In the first place, conflict is natural and inevitable in discussion. If members never disagree, they probably do not have any convictions, or they are examining the question superficially, or they are intellectual cowards. All three of these seem unattractive and unlikely possibilities. Moreover, disagreement is helpful in discussion; a clash is often the most efficient way to find fallacious reasoning and overlooked weaknesses.

It seems clear that neither the position of the individualist nor the group enthusiast is realistic in any extreme sense. The individual often has responsibility to influence others on a person-to-person, or person-to-group, or speaker-to-audience basis. The employee seeking a raise, the committee member with an exciting new proposal, and the senator crusading for re-election all need skill in persuasive speaking and direct advocacy. The same individuals, however, must participate also in group communication. It is virtually impossible to avoid group involvement. The society is too complex; there are too many complicated decisions to be made and too many persons to be taken into account. Thus it is misleading to suggest that people can choose whether or not they want to "take refuge in discussion;" they cannot get through a week without it!

With the statement of this middle position we can get down to cases as we approach the study of discussion. Shall we concentrate on the individual as a communicator, perhaps as an advocate within the group speaking for his own views as persuasively as he is able? Or shall we study the group, assuming that the individual must sublimate his views in order to seek an answer cooperatively as one among many? These questions sound complicated but the answer is simple: we can appropriately study both. The individual must be both spokesman for his own views and cooperative member of the group and neither in any extremist sense.

POINTS OF VIEW

The Individual

As we study discussion, we will be interested first in the individual as participant and leader. From his point of view, he is a single person. When he relates himself to a group he may be willing in some situations to work in harmony with the group, suppressing his individuality to group desires and goals. In other situations, he may press his own views, persuading members of the group if possible and upon failure, withdrawing from group participation figuratively or even literally.

Looking at discussion from the individual's view, we will be asking how he can learn to be an effective leader and a successful participant, contributing to the group's productivity and helping the group reach its goals while at the same time achieving his own purposes, to the extent possible. Some of the time, at least, his purposes and those of the group will coincide. As he views himself, however, the individual asks about his own success and effectiveness; he looks at the group from his own location as an individual.

Part Two of this book looks at discussion primarily from the individual's view. Chapter 4, Planning, asks what each student must understand in advance to make discussion successful. The next five chapters look at the individual's contributions to the group as information-bearer, reasoner, user of language and communication, and as participant displaying particular attitudes.

Part Three treats the problems of leadership from the individual's view as well as from the view of the group itself. The individual assigned a leadership responsibility will approach his task primarily in terms of what he must understand and do to contribute effective leadership.

The Group

A second major point of view in studying discussion is that of the group as a unit. While each person sees the world from inside himself, he must develop sensitivity to others. To understand himself in relation to others he must be perceptive about their ways of viewing. Thus he must understand the operation of the group by considering group process, procedures, and functions.

Parts One and Four take up the problems of studying the group and considering what the discussion group as a functioning unit is attempting to do, how it goes about its work, and how the components of group operation interact to determine success or failure. In Chapters 14 and 15 especially, the elements of group operation are explored.

The Larger Group and The Public

A third point of view is that of the larger organization and the whole society of which individuals and small groups are a part. Public discussion, in which participants in a small group address a listening audience, gives members an opportunity to stimulate large numbers of their fellow citizens to ponder problems of the day.

In Part Five we will be interested in ways a larger society makes up its mind through individual and group activity, and in ways of extending participation to many persons even though large numbers of people are involved. Specifically, Chapter 17 suggests some of the special problems introduced when discussion is presented before public audiences. Chapter 18 deals with the operation of discussion in large groups.

SUPPLEMENTARY READING

Berlo, David K., *The Process of Communication*, New York: Holt, Rinehart and Winston, 1960.

Braden, Waldo W., and Brandenburg, Earnest, *Oral Decision-Making*, New York: Harper & Row, 1955, Chapters 1, 8, and 9.

Cartwright, Dorwin, and Zander, Alvin, *Group Dynamics: Research and Theory*, sec. ed., New York: Harper & Row, 1960, pp. 33–5.

Hostettler, Gordon F., "Trends in the History of Rhetoric," Keith Brooks, ed., *The Communicative Arts and Sciences of Speech*, Columbus, Ohio: Charles E. Merrill Books, 1967, pp. 17–33.

Howell, William S., and Smith, Donald K., *Discussion*, New York: Crowell-Collier and Macmillan, 1956, pp. 7–9.

Johnson, Wendell, "The Spoken Word and the Great Unsaid," *Quarterly Journal of Speech*, 37 (1951), 419–29.

Wagner, Russell H., and Arnold, Carroll C., *Handbook of Group Discussion*, Chapter 1, Boston: Houghton Mifflin, 1950.

QUESTIONS AND EXERCISES

1. Write a paper or give an oral report in which you define discussion and specify its place and function within a democratic society.

2. Observe several discussions held as part of the meetings of your regular classes. Decide whether they are "discussions" as you would define the term.

3. Remo P. Fausti and Arno H. Luker, in an article entitled, "A Phenomenological Approach to Discussion," [*The Speech Teacher*, 14 (January, 1965), pp. 19–23] argue that discussion could be approached through phenomenology—through attempting "to understand behavior from the behaver's point of view." Read this article and respond to it by agreeing or disagreeing. Is the approach recommended here inconsistent with the approach treated in Chapter 1 of this book?

4. There are a number of perspectives from which to approach the problem of the individual versus the group. We frequently ask, "Is the individual or the group supreme?" Explain how this question might be approached from the vantage point of political science, sociology, social psychology, economics, history. What are the cultural determinants governing an answer to this question? How would the question be answered differently in the United States and in other parts of the world?

5. Do you agree with what has been said in Chapter 1 about the uniqueness of discussion as a form of communication? Would you point to other unique features?

6. Can you suggest definitions of discussion other than the one presented here?

Chapter 2

USES AND LIMITATIONS
OF DISCUSSION

Discussion is an ancient process, even though schools have offered courses about it and men have studied it systematically only in recent decades. It is possible that men met together to talk over at least some of their problems before they started recording their own history. The Bible reports a series of conferences which Moses and his brother Aaron held with the Egyptian Pharaoh; the question for discussion was: "Should the Children of Israel be released from bondage?" The uses of discussion in ancient times, however, probably resembled only partially those we see around us today. The number and diversity of discussions have been increased through the centuries by changes such as increasing population and its developing mobility, the growing complexity of societies and interdependence of peoples, improving methods of communication, and many others.

There are two major causes for the expanding use of discussion. First, through the centuries, power and control in a nation, society, group, or organization, have shifted from a single ruler or small clique of insiders to the larger group that makes up the nation, society, or organization. Obviously, such a shift meant that methods had to be developed for discovering what policies large numbers of group members favored. When many are involved in decision-making, talk and discussion are essential. Second, men have tended to substitute decision by talking it over for the barbaric methods of violence and war. Even the use of intrigue seems to have lessened over the long years, perhaps through the influence of ethical and religious thought and possibly even through the greater likelihood of exposure and wide condemnation by way of mass communication.

It is clear, of course, that these two are not completed causes; the evolution is still going on. There are many contemporary instances of rule by a single autocrat, both in nations and in smaller organizations such as industrial firms, churches, schools, or labor unions. Neither have we eliminated force, violence, war, and intrigue. Nevertheless, it would be difficult to deny that the world has moved and is still moving in the direction of distributing power among the many rather than the few, and of utilizing talk, negotiation, and compromise in place of violence and war. In the words of Herman Finer:

At last, the millennial writhing of the peoples for a principle of legitimacy—that is, an ultimate moral basis for deciding the values which are to rule societies and for making those values concretely supreme, by the use of force, if necessary—has gone through all the more vulnerable principles, monarchy, aristocracy, theocracy, oligarchy, ideocracy, and has arrived at the least (though still to some extent) vulnerable, *democracy*—that is, government by all, but in practice government by the majority, cognizant of the respect it owes to the minority. From this generalization the USSR and like polities are excluded, because they deny the capacity of the people to govern themselves for their own freely conceived purposes.[1]

It is also clear that these two causes are interrelated. If a group is willing to let all members participate in decision-making and then to abide by the decision, the need for violence and force is largely removed. In part, at least, that is the process through which law and order come to an untamed region. Each man in the Old West could quit carrying a gun only when the group as a whole cooperated in establishing justice, providing police protection, and settling controversy. It is likely that international war occurs when decisions within at least one of the combatant nations are made by the few rather than the many. Aggression would be less probable if the decision to initiate it had to be reached by all the citizens, including the soldiers. To say it this way is to oversimplify the problem, of course; the masses of the people would also have to be involved in all the decisions that led up to the crisis precipitating the war. Also, it is an oversimplification to suggest that all the people can participate in all decisions. Some power must be delegated to representatives; in large nations, mass deliberation on every action is a physical impossibility.

Extension of Participation

The historical development of these two interacting forces can be seen most clearly by looking at the part discussion has played in political affairs. John Stuart Mill, in his celebrated essay *On Liberty*, wrote that man early tried to secure the right to participate in government: "The struggle between Liberty and Authority is the most conspicuous feature in the portions of history with which we are earliest familiar, particularly in that of Greece, Rome, and England." To protect themselves from despotic tyranny, the people sought constitutional guarantees of political rights and restraints on autocratic power. Later they struggled for the right to choose and to remove their governmental representatives. When popular participation in government and the principle of majority will were finally recognized realities, said Mill, the crucial problem became that of protecting the minority from "the tyranny of the majority." In the whole process of this developing participation in governmental affairs, freedom of discussion has been central. According to Mill: "Liberty, as a principle, has no application to any state of things anterior to the time when mankind have become capable of being improved by free and equal discussion."

[1] Herman Finer, *Theory and Practice of Modern Government*, rev., New York: Holt, Rinehart and Winston, 1949, p. 14. Used with permission.

Pericles, in his celebrated speech praising Peloponnesian War heroes, also praised the citizens of Athens for their participation in civic affairs. He declared:

> We are called a democracy, for the administration is in the hands of the many and not of the few. . . . An Athenian citizen does not neglect the state because he takes care of his own household; and even those of us who are engaged in business have a very fair idea of politics. We alone regard a man who takes no interest in public affairs, not as a harmless, but as a useless character; and if few of us are originators, we are all sound judges of a policy. The great impediment to action is, in our opinion, not discussion, but the want of that knowledge which is gained by discussion preparatory to action.

The political freedom somewhat feebly and temporarily nurtured in Greece and Rome finally flowered, as everyone knows, in Britain and, by inheritance, in America. The rise of British parliamentary discussion during the English Renaissance has been traced by Karl Wallace. Both committees and conferences became important in parliamentary procedures during the seventeenth century:

> The reign of James I, 1603–1625, saw parliamentary discussion take on a sort of green, rather than ripe, maturity. . . . The chief sign of emerging parliamentary maturity is probably seen in the growth and stability of the committee, for it is in committee procedures that discussion rather than speechmaking controls decisions. . . . During [Francis] Bacon's time, the committees of the House of Commons took over the chief burden of discussion and deliberation. . . . Another kind of committee with which Bacon accumulated considerable experience during his parliamentary career was the joint or conference committee of the Lords and Commons.[2]

It was natural that discussion methods developed by the British were transplanted to the Congress and the legislatures of the United States. Here, too, the New England town meetings extended the use of discussion to all citizens. At regular meetings, residents assembled to deliberate and to establish town policy. From these kinds of beginnings in political affairs, discussion method has been elaborated and diffused into literally hundreds of thousands of different groups and situations today.

CONTEMPORARY USES OF DISCUSSION

It would be almost impossible to enumerate all the situations in which discussion is employed in the United States, or to estimate the number of committee sessions, conferences, round tables, public forums, and panels that occur on any given day. A political science textbook,[3] in suggesting the extent

[2] "Discussion in Parliament and Francis Bacon," *Quarterly Journal of Speech*, 43 (February, 1957), pp. 12–21. Used with permission.

[3] James M. Burns and J. W. Peltason, *Government by the People*, Englewood Cliffs, N.J.: Prentice-Hall, 1957, Chapter 10.

of political interest groups in the United States, observes that there are forty million family units, a quarter million local church congregations, more than fifteen million workers organized in labor unions, more than a million farmers belonging to agricultural organizations such as the Grange, Farm Bureau, and Farmers' Union, two thousand trade associations of businessmen, three thousand local business groups, and more than three million men who are members of veterans' organizations. Add to these the local branches of such national organizations as the National Education Association, American Association of University Professors, American Bar Association, American Medical Association, National Association for the Advancement of Colored People, League of Women Voters, Women's Christian Temperance Union, Lions, Kiwanis, Toastmasters, and Rotary International. The list could go on and on; and all these groups discuss.

Some notion of the number and diversity of the public conferences that occur and of the variety of labels given them can be gleaned from the following partial listing of the meetings indexed in a single volume of the *Reader's Guide to Periodical Literature*:

Conference for national cooperation in aquatics
Conference of eastern college librarians
Conference of foreign ministers
Governors' conference
Conference of international Catholic organizations
Conference of local airlines
Conference of mayors
Conference on church union
Conference on electronic instrumentation and nucleonics in medicine
Conference on higher education
Conference on medium energy nuclear physics
Conference on mental health
Conference on moral standards
Conference on religion in the age of science
Conference on scientific editorial problems
Writers' conference
Art education convention
Industrial arts clinic
Inter-American seminar on vocational education
U.S. assembly of youth
American youth congress

Instead of trying to enumerate the situations in which discussion occurs, it may be more illuminating to sketch some of the more important of them in order to suggest the complexity and extent of discussion in use.

Discussion in Political Affairs

Discussion of several kinds is employed by legislative bodies at all levels. On almost any campus, the student governing body uses committees to study problems, to reach decisions, and to make recommendations for action. In some cases, the student council or senate may be small enough to sit as a discussion group in its sessions where legislative policy is adopted. Where a governing body is large, of course, it must adopt more formalized rules of procedure and decide by majority vote. The nature of the discussion taking place is thereby modified. Such modified discussion occurs in the formal sessions of state legislatures, the Congress, and the General Assembly of the United Nations.[4] We are not primarily concerned in this book with the large parliamentary assembly. Vital to the operation of any legislative body, however, are many smaller group meetings, which clearly use the type of discussion and conference that concerns us here.

At the community and county level, city councils, park district boards, school boards, county boards of supervisors, public health boards, and similar groups make extensive use of discussion, both in their formal meetings and in their subgroups and committees. State legislatures and the Congress accomplish their purposes through standing and special committees, which conduct studies, hold hearings, deliberate, and recommend. Some states also have political party caucuses which meet to discuss pending legislation. Official state boards and commissions, and a large number of agencies at the national level, such as the Interstate Commerce Commission, Federal Communications Commission, Federal Power Commission, Civil Aeronautics Board, and the Securities and Exchange Commission, are other governmental groups that use discussion method. The United Nations has its Security Council, Trusteeship Council, Social and Economic Council, and many other agencies that strive for agreement through collective talk.

In addition to those of official bodies, there are other functions of government that require group deliberation. Among the most interesting of these at the international level are diplomatic and political negotiations. The Korean Armistice signed in 1953 involved some three hundred negotiating sessions spread over two years, and the Austrian peace treaty of 1954 required four hundred sessions. One estimate is that the total number of international conferences of all types has now passed two thousand annually.[5]

Discussion in Business and Industry

Discussion is also in general use in a substantial proportion of business and industrial organizations. Many firms have found that spreading participation in decision-making results in better decisions and greater commitment in carrying them out. *Business Week* magazine,[6] in looking back over a quarter century of business management, observed that industrial organizations have

[4] Clark M. Eichelberger, "Discussion in the United Nations," *Adult Education Bulletin*, 13 (1949) pp. 88–90.
[5] Paul W. Keller, "The Study of Face-to-Face International Decision-Making," *Journal of Communication*, 13 (June, 1963) pp. 67–76.
[6] September 4, 1954, pp. 79–82.

FIGURE 2–1 TEST OF DIPLOMACY *A Daniel Fitzpatrick editorial cartoon from the October 18, 1954, edition of the* St. Louis Post-Dispatch; *reprinted with the permission of Mr. Fitzpatrick and the* Post-Dispatch *through the courtesy of Robert Lasch, Editor of the editorial page.*

become so complex that "the executive job has simply outgrown the ability of a single decision-making, administering head." Herryman Maurer in *Fortune* traces the trend since the turn of the century from "strong-man" direction toward group management: "As soon as a manager is forced by the growth of his company, the variety or complexity of its products, or the simple geographic separation of its plants to establish broad policies, chart high strategy, and review operations—then the manager finds himself in conference with his peers."[7]

[7] "Management by Committee," *Fortune*, 47 (April, 1953), pp. 145–7.

Even in firms managed by a single "strong-man," Mr. Maurer feels that informal committees operate. Of course, different corporations have organized their internal decision-making machinery in diverse ways, adapted to particular circumstances. Some use spontaneous, informal meetings of executives, while others have carefully structured groups with specified membership and meeting times. Maurer reports, for example, that General Motors and du Pont have complex committee systems, that Union Carbide and American Can Company have decision-making committees, and that Jersey Standard has developed an intricate committee system, including an executive group that meets daily and an inside board of directors that meets weekly. He says, "The formal committee system, with *de facto* power entrusted to the committee itself, is increasingly the practice of many corporations."

One example of spreading participation is described by Charles P. Mc-Cormick, President of McCormick and Company, the world's largest producers of spices and extracts, in his book, *The Power of People: Multiple Management Up to Date*. This firm was established in 1889 by his uncle, Willoughby M. McCormick, and was operated for its first forty-three years by authoritarian methods:

> When it came to taking advice from others, my uncle was likewise an industrialist of the old school. He behaved like a proud father who was loath to believe that his children could grow up. He resented what he considered "impertinent attempts at intervention" from well-meaning employees and supervisors and his only too plainly expressed attitude could be summed up: "You do your jobs and I'll make the decisions." As a result of his authoritative manner, as well as thrice-yearly seasonal layoffs and other poor employment practices, employee morale was low.

When he took over the firm in 1932, the young Mr. McCormick instituted what he called *multiple management*:

> I had taken stock of myself and had arrived at the conviction that I possessed neither the ability nor the inclination to be a one-man manager of a multimillion-dollar business. I told the directors that I appreciated the value of their individual experience, mature judgment, and collective wisdom, but thought we should exhaust every source of ideas and information. To accomplish this, I suggested the formation of a Junior Board of Directors, to be chosen from among assistant department managers and others who had shown special zeal in their work. The purpose of the Junior Board then, as it is now, would be not to bypass the judgment of the more mature men, but to supplement that judgment with new ideas.
>
> The original seventeen-man Junior Board was appointed by me; since then, the Junior Board members themselves have held the elections. From the start, the board elected its own officers, wrote its own constitution and bylaws and governed itself without outside interference. The only checks upon it were that all proposals had to be passed unanimously before any action could be taken and that all major suggestions had to be sent to the Senior Board for approval. . . .[8]

Later were added a Factory Board, representing factory employees, and a Sales Board, with members from the sales, advertising, and merchandising departments. Almost a thousand other firms have studied the operation of multiple management at McCormick and Company and have adopted some of these methods.

These brief insights into the use of discussion in business and industry relate only to the active management of the firm. In addition, executives engage in many other types of discussion in sales promotion meetings, in national and district conferences involving representatives from other branches of their own corporation, in conventions on new developments and the like conducted for related companies in the same trade association, and in similar situations. Top executives and middle-management men in one chemical firm estimated that they were spending from 10 percent to 50 percent of their working hours in meetings.[9]

Discussion in Other Situations

These same tendencies toward widespread use of discussion have become characteristic in most other kinds of organizations. As Herman Finer has pointed out in another context:

> Within a nation, or any society for that matter, many groupings of human beings abound. . . . Non-state social-groups—like churches, business associations, labor unions, civic reform societies, professional guilds, athletic clubs, philatelic and other hobby organizations—all these, numbering thousands in modern nations, have characteristics shared by the state. For example, they have a hierarchy of authorities; they have rules of procedure; and their activities are marked by purpose. . . .[10]

We may observe that these groups also share with democratic government the practices of disseminating information to all and of distributing decision-making power among members, often through group discussion. In the club on the campus, in many local church congregations, in the labor union, in the farmers' organization, in the teachers' association, and in the medical society, committee discussion is a normal part of the group's functioning, and not infrequently information is exchanged and policies determined by discussion during general meetings of the whole organization.

Most religious leaders participate regularly in study groups and problem-solving discussions within their churches and often take part in interchurch meetings within ministerial associations, ecumenical conferences, and the like. Labor union officers engage in group sharing of information and in deliberation within their unions and also in labor–management negotiations involving

---

[8] New York: Harper & Row, 1949, pp. 9–13. Used with permission.

[9] "Reform in the Conference Room," *Dun's Review and Modern Industry*, 69 (March, 1957), p. 64.

[10] Finer, pp. 12–14.

working conditions, workers' grievances, and employment contracts.[11] Farmers are involved in numerous meetings where they discuss new agricultural methods and agree on policy in relation to legislation that affects them. Teachers are familiar with committee work and with informational and decision-making meetings at both departmental and school or college level, as well as with discussion groups at their regional, state, and national professional conventions. Medical societies use group methods to exchange ideas about new developments and to reach decisions on matters of public health and their professional interests.

Discussion procedures are commonplace on a campus among both student and faculty groups. Student government organizations and housing associations use committees and executive boards to make policy and regulate activities, as do the religious foundations, the YM–YWCA, student interest clubs, and dozens of other groupings. Faculties have their committees on courses and curricula, discipline, educational policy, athletics, etc., along with councils of department chairmen and deans, faculty senates, and similar policy-making bodies.

Lawyers, too, use discussion. The frequency of out-of-court settlements appears to be increasing; the oral discussions that result in a settlement are sometimes held in the judge's chamber. One indication of the trend is the use of arbitration to settle disputes not involving points of law. The method is to have the disputing parties agree on arbitrators whose decision, after talking over the problem, is binding. At first, attorneys were reluctant to participate in arbitration proceedings; now they appear in 91 percent of such cases, according to E. M. Marshall.[12] An indirect suggestion of growing awareness of discussion in the legal field is contained in a survey of law school deans and administrators of undergraduate colleges offering prelaw training. It showed that 95 percent of the officials replying thought lawyers could benefit from discussion training.[13]

Discussion is used frequently in social group work and group psychotherapy. Here role playing, sociodrama, and psychodrama are prominent procedures.[14]

STRENGTHS OF GROUP DISCUSSION

Discussion has been employed in wide-ranging activities and diverse groups because it has some obvious strengths. In many situations there are valuable

[11] Neil W. Chamberlain, "Group Discussion and Collective Bargaining," *Adult Education Bulletin*, 13 (1949), pp. 77–84.

[12] E. M. Marshall, "Lawsuits Can Be Avoided," *American Mercury*, 80 (June, 1955), pp. 139–40.

[13] Donald E. Williams, "Group Discussion and Argumentation in Legal Education," *Quarterly Journal of Speech*, 48 (December, 1955), p. 399.

[14] Dorwin Cartwright and Alvin Zander, *Group Dynamics: Research and Theory*, rev. ed., New York: Harper & Row, 1960, pp. 12–16.

outcomes accruing from group deliberation. In surveying these values, of course, we must be careful not to overstate the case.

As we have noted, some enthusiasts for group procedures have made exaggerated claims for the beneficial outcomes of togetherness. On the other hand, some critics of group action, recognizing the exaggeration of the over-enthusiastic, have failed to see the very real virtues that can result from group interaction in many situations. The student of discussion must make a realistic appraisal of the strengths as well as the limitations of group effort in decision-making as contrasted with the work of the individual executive.

Cartwright and Zander offer a sensible and cautious framework from which to approach such a realistic appraisal. First, they say that "groups are inevitable and ubiquitous." Groups seem to form wherever there is human activity. Second, "groups mobilize powerful forces which produce effects of utmost importance to individuals." It is meaningful to the individuals to be included, and the group may help to make him the kind of person he is. Third, "groups may produce both good and bad consequences." It is unrealistic to think that groups would be ideally productive or completely inefficient. Fourth, "a correct understanding of group dynamics (obtainable from research) permits the possibility that desirable consequences from groups can be deliberately enhanced."[15]

We must keep in mind while considering the strengths and limitations of discussion that groups and the individuals who make up groups differ from each other in an amazing variety of ways. Generalizations of any kind must be treated with extreme caution. One group may be composed of five highly gifted individuals and a brilliant leader whom the other five are willing and eager to follow. If we give this group a specific, limited question on which they are already well informed and which they are motivated to discuss, we will not be surprised when the group is highly productive. These same individuals would also be impressively productive if they worked on the problem separately. If we give these same five talented persons a dull, uninformed leader who creates a hostile climate during the discussion, and also a complex problem on which information is not readily available, they might well be more productive working separately than in the group. No doubt in many situations a brilliant, highly motivated individual would produce better decisions than some groups of mediocre, unmotivated, or hostile participants.

Our problem, then, is to understand the conditions under which groups are productive and efficient. Under what conditions is there a gain from group interaction? What kinds of tasks need group discussion? What kinds of leadership, participation, member attitudes, situations, etc., enhance productivity? What are the limitations and exceptions? Under what conditions are group productivity and harmony lessened? While we have some experimental evidence and much careful observation to suggest answers to questions such as

[15] Cartwright and Zander, pp. 34–5.

these, every statement we make must be approached tentatively and cautiously.

Groups May Produce Better Decisions

In most situations, groups apparently produce higher quality decisions than could an equal number of equally able individuals working separately. Lorge and his coauthors, after surveying a large number of experimental studies comparing individual and group productivity, concluded:

> In general, in the evaluation of the relative quality of the products produced by groups in contrast to the products produced by individuals, the group is superior. The superiority of the group, however, all too frequently, is not as great as would be expected from an interactional theory. In many studies, the product of the "best" individual is superior to that of the "best" group.[16]

Some of the experimental evidence on group versus individual productivity is derived from performance on tasks such as guessing the number of beans in a bottle or working simple arithmetic problems in the presence of other people, tasks rather far removed from decision-making on important political, social, economic, or business problems. However, there is now enough evidence involving complex discussion topics to suggest that there often is gain from the interaction of group members. Barnlund, for example, tested students on their ability to select a valid conclusion from a set of statements after studying supporting premises. Students were first tested individually. Several weeks later, some of the students were formed into discussion groups and asked to reach a group decision about the valid conclusion in each set of statements. Others were again tested individually. The discussion groups were superior to the best individuals working separately. The interacting groups also reached better decisions than did groups who arrived at a decision by combining individual judgments and taking a majority vote.[17]

The gain from group interaction is explained by many diverse factors. Some tasks and situations lend themselves to group discussion while other problems can be better solved by the individual executive. Then, too, in many situations there is no alternative to group action and hence comparison with individual productivity becomes meaningless. A single star cannot play a basketball game by himself; moving the ball down the court requires a team functioning as a coordinated unit. In the same sense, many manufacturing operations today are too complex for a single executive to know and perform all the tasks required. Thus a group interaction of production engineer, design specialist, sales manager, financial consultant, tax expert, and personnel director is

---

[16] I. Lorge, D. Fox, J. Davitz, and M. Brenner, "A Survey of Studies Contrasting the Quality of Group Performance and Individual Performance, 1920–1957," *Psychological Bulletin*, 55 (1958), pp. 337–72.

[17] Dean C. Barnlund, "Comparative Study of Individual, Majority and Group Judgment," *Journal of Abnormal and Social Psychology*, 58 (1959), pp. 55–60.

mandatory. In these situations the question is not whether executive action would be more efficient than group discussion but how to make the executive committee of the plant work smoothly in spite of the difficulties encountered in interaction.

Groups have more resources than individuals have. Since each person's background, experience, and exposures to knowledge are uniquely different from those of every other person, a group has access to more information, and their combined thinking results in some new insights for everyone. A pooling of experience and information means that someone is more likely to think of the breakthrough idea at the moment it is needed.

Collins and Guetzkow have contributed an excellent book synthesizing the experimental research in social psychology that is relevant to group processes for decision-making. They find support for the proposition that "for tasks which involve creating ideas or remembering information, there is a greater probability that one of several persons will produce the information than that a single individual will produce it by himself."[18] Kelley and Thibaut, in an earlier review of the literature, suggested the general superiority of group decision. They speculate on the possibilities that solutions may be improved through the social influence of others in the group; that motivation to complete a task successfully may be different in the presence of others; that the necessity for communicating with others may result in "sharpening and refining" of ideas; and that individual proposals in the group situation, being subjected to processes of "compliance, concession, compromise, and rejection," are thereby "combined and weighted in a complicated way in arriving at the group product."[19]

Groups are more productive when the task allows a division of labor. Most often groups discussing complex problems can bring to bear the unique talents of each member and also can take advantage of having several members by dividing up assignments both before and during discussion. In preparing for a particular discussion, members can divide responsibility for becoming informed.

The experimental evidence indicates that groups are usually no better than individuals on relatively routine tasks, or on simple assignments such as solving arithmetic problems. Groups tend to be superior, however, on tasks profiting from a wide range of possible solutions where much is to be gained by criticism and selectivity, and by originality and insight. A group can evaluate a wide range of solutions, but this will be a gain only if the task requires a large number of alternatives for arriving at a good outcome.

[18] Barry E. Collins and Harold Guetzkow, *A Social Psychology of Group Processes for Decision-Making*, New York: John Wiley & Sons, 1964, p. 20.

[19] Harold H. Kelley and J. Thibaut, "Experimental Studies of Group Problem-Solving and Process," Gardner Lindzey, ed., *Handbook of Social Psychology*, Reading, Mass.: Addison-Wesley, 1954, pp. 735–85.

A group assigned a task involving quantitative judgments can be more accurate than individuals working separately, perhaps because pooling of judgments reduces random error.

Through interaction members can improve on the thinking of other members, censoring out poor ideas, discovering fallacious reasoning, and in other ways taking advantage of their combined intelligence, experience, and information.

The group benefits most from division of talent and responsibility when members are heterogeneous. If all have had almost the same backgrounds and have similar ideas and convictions, the gain from unique contributions will be much less. On the other hand, a group may suffer from too much disparity in background and talent. In this case there may be conflict in goals and methods as well as interpersonal friction.

Perhaps the most important gain from division of labor comes in the acquisition and utilization of information. An individual is limited in the reading he has been able to do, the experiences he has happened to encounter, the observations he has been in a position to make. In a group, however, he can learn vicariously and efficiently what each of the others knows that is relevant to solving the problem at hand.

Members are often stimulated by the presence of others. In the discussion situation members of a group may be motivated by social stimulation to strive harder to contribute and to help the group succeed. It is possible that members will be stimulated to think of ideas that otherwise would not have occurred to them and perhaps to recall long suppressed information and insights. Brainstorming uses group pressure to promote "creative ideation"; members "hitchhike" and improve on the remarks of others.

In the Barnlund study mentioned earlier, "membership in the experimental groups produced a higher level of interest in the successful completion of the task." At the same time the social situation also had an inhibiting effect. "Knowledge that one's opinions were to be shared publicly made group members more cautious and deliberate in their own thinking."

Most likely members feel that helpful contributions to group effort will lead to social approval. As Collins and Guetzkow observe, high productivity tends to be socially rewarded although the stimulation effect of the presence of other persons may be temporary.

LIMITATIONS AND EXCEPTIONS/ Under some conditions, individuals are superior to groups. Group productivity varies enormously, depending on the nature of the task and situation, quality of leadership, abilities of individual members, availability and quality of information, and other factors. Thus it is unrealistic to expect that groups will always be superior to individuals in efficiency and quality of decisions. Since individuals working alone also differ in capacity, motivation, etc., it is equally clear that individuals are superior to groups only under certain conditions.

Individuals working separately seem able to produce a larger quantity of alternative suggestions for action than will a group, although the group has more potential ideas than can be expressed in a limited period of group interaction. Separate individuals do not have the benefit of criticism and group judgment leading to selecting the best alternative, nor do those working alone have any way of combining or pooling alternatives.

On some routine tasks, or on tasks where only one person can work at a time—such as writing a report or investigating facts or doing research—an individual effort is no doubt better than group action. An executive may be better equipped to make day-to-day decisions in managing an organization than could an executive committee even if it were in continuous session. If the group needs a report written or a matter investigated, it usually should refer the task to an individual or two, or to a subgroup such as a committee. The group can then conserve its time by being required only to consider whether to accept or to modify the finished product.

A group can best establish policies and evaluate the efficiency of appointed administrators, but an executive can make better decisions about purchasing typewriters and hiring secretaries. The board of directors might profitably discuss these matters only if the annual cost of typewriters became an unreasonable drain on the company's resources, or if a rapid turnover of secretarial employees was seriously interfering with worker morale. A group that finds itself spending time each month deliberating on such problems as the quantities and brands of typewriters is probably not using its discussion time intelligently.

Francis Bacon recognized three stages in public deliberation on a problem: "preparation, the debate or examination, and the perfection." While many can appropriately be involved in the middle stage, Bacon felt, the first and third parts are "best undertaken by relatively few persons." What Bacon proposes as a division of specialization between committee work and the parliamentary session can be extended to the small group and its delegation of responsibility to individuals. The more demanding the preparation and perfection stages, the fewer the number of persons who can work at them efficiently, especially in the early period of each stage.

An illustration of this division of responsibility can be seen in extreme form during a war. The joint chiefs of staff may discuss objectives, strategy, and general policy, but individual officers must exercise command over minute-by-minute operations in the field. As Macaulay observed, no successful army can be managed by a debating society.

We all have suffered the experience of the unproductive discussion group. Since everyone is permitted and encouraged to contribute, it is not unusual for a bright, well-informed member to be caught in a meeting where he must listen to two or three lengthy repetitions of points already established. Even when the desired outcome is imminent, it may be necessary to allow several additional minutes of communication. Unless the member is willing to risk offending the garrulous ones, or unless the situation is saved by a sensitive and skilled leader, patience is the only avenue open.

Collins and Guetzkow call attention to data which suggests that in many conferences "one or two of the group members could have solved the problem without the aid of the rest of the group. These skilled members even may have been slowed down by the necessity of listening to the inferior contributions of other members." If the organization knew in advance, of course, that an individual or two could deal with the problem more productively, these individuals would be asked to do so, unless there were other reasons for having everyone involved in the discussion. When everyone is included in order to seek group solidarity there will be occasions when the quality of group interaction is limited to the abilities of the weakest members.

The reader who would become an effective contributor to group discussion must study leadership, the orderly development of ideas during a discussion, sound reasoning in the group situation, and careful use of language and oral communication, along with other matters.

The problems of supporting ideas logically and communicating them clearly and effectively are especially vital in group decision-making. Collins and Guetzkow emphasize the limitations forced upon the group by the fact that some ideas and information will be excluded because each can recall and report only part of what he knows, and each fails to assimilate part of what he has heard. The information must be presented persuasively and documented carefully; ideas must be supported. The communication loss resulting from inept handling of information, language, ideas, and supporting documentation can compound the other difficulties inherent in the interactional situation.

While there is gain for the group from social stimulation, there are also possible dampening influences brought about by the presence of others. Members may find other persons a distracting influence. They may be made defensive or self-conscious, especially if another member of the group is a superior. As Hare summarizes the effect of the social situation, "the presence of others may change the content of an individual's activity from personal to group-oriented, it may increase his activity if he is spurred on by the implied competition, or it may depress his activity through distraction, conformity to norms, or group resistance to the task."[20]

Groups can use social pressure also to set goals of production lower than could be achieved by individuals separately. This behavior has been reported in industrial settings. Women sewing machine operators in one situation established through informal group interaction a comfortable rate of production for an eight-hour shift; individuals exceeding the acceptable norm were punished by group hostility. It is possible, also, for group productivity to

[20] A. Paul Hare, *Handbook of Small Group Research*, New York: The Free Press, 1962, pp. 352–3.

decline because of too much interaction, if the group talk becomes an enjoyable end in itself.

Group Members May Feel Stronger Commitment

There is normally a stronger allegiance to a decision when those affected have participated in its formulation. A single administrator can make a policy decision, but rarely can he carry it out alone. Those who must translate it into action feel more satisfied with the decision, more involved in it, and more willing to work for its execution if they have helped hammer it out.

Anyone can confirm this tendency by noticing that he is more sensitive to praise or criticism of one of his own statements than he is to reactions related to statements of others. In the opposite way, it is easier to feel indifferent or resistant to edicts forced upon him by another. This is the essential difference that makes democracy superior to dictatorship; while a dictator can decide and act more quickly and efficiently, he is eventually undone because others are not so committed to his ideas as he is.

There is some experimental support for this hypothesis. The study often cited is Kurt Lewin's experience with changing food-using habits of housewives during World War II. The purpose was to increase consumption of beef hearts, sweetbreads, and kidneys. A persuasive lecture induced only 3 percent of the women to serve one of these unpopular meats, whereas an amazing 32 percent served one of them after participating in discussion, where they talked about the practices of "housewives like themselves," the obstacles to overcoming husbands' dislikes, and so on.[21] Another study involved industrial workers. When they were transferred from one job to another, they experienced frustration, low motivation, and loss of efficiency. Recovery rate to former productivity levels was usually slow, and in one group of transfers, 62 percent remained substandard operators permanently or quit their jobs during the retraining period. In a search for an explanation, "an experiment was designed employing three degrees of participation in handling groups to be transferred. The first variation involved *no participation* by employees in planning the changes, though an explanation was given to them. The second variation involved *participation through representation* of the workers in designing the changes to be made in the jobs. The third variation consisted of *total participation* by all members of the group in designing the changes."

The results clearly showed the value of member participation during the group meetings. Recovery rates were more rapid and there was higher morale and fewer labor-management conflicts under the participation conditions; total participation led to the best results of all.[22]

21 "Group Decision and Social Change," in G. E. Swanson, *et al*, ed., *Readings in Social Psychology*, rev. edition, New York: Holt, Rinehart and Winston, 1952, pp. 459–73.

22 Lester Coch and John R. P. French, Jr., "Overcoming Resistance to Change," *Ibid.*, pp. 474–91.

Maier describes a study by Bavelas with similar results. Workers established production goals in three brief weekly meetings with the plant psychologist. They decided to produce eighty-four units per hour within five days, although up to that time sixty had been the standard and seventy-five considered the ceiling. They attained the goal of eighty-four within the time limit.

Participation in some group situations apparently can cause individuals to restructure their own goals and attitudes. It also may develop a feeling of loyalty to other group members, causing individuals to make sacrifices and to give extra energy to fulfillment of common objectives.

Persons who have interacted during some intense emotional experience such as the Great Blizzard of 1888 or a war-time battle or the great New York blackout exemplify the kind of group cohesiveness that may develop from more ordinary discussion in on-going groups.

LIMITATIONS AND EXCEPTIONS/ It must not be assumed that stronger commitment always results from interaction. Hostility may be heightened instead of being reduced. It may be a group discussion experience that causes an individual finally to withdraw from membership rather than to have his loyalty increased. Whether commitment to group decision is won depends on a complexity of factors.

Later replications of the studies involving industrial workers have not always shown a simple relationship between group participation in production quotas and increased effort. Sometimes other factors of leadership, worker morale, etc., have interfered, as we would expect. In general, however, individuals like to be involved in problems affecting their vital interests. Involvement through discussion participation frequently means stronger allegiance to policy than would otherwise be the case. A teacher who had once been a member of the executive committee of his department expressed in these words the involvement feeling coming from participation in decision-making: "I miss being on the inside of events before they happen."

Participation May Lead to Increased Understanding

Participants hopefully gain increased understanding of themselves, of others in the group, and of group operation. After exposure to many experiences, conscientious members should have greater insights into the reactions, attitudes and sensitivities of their fellows. Observing at close range the positions, hostilities, obstinacies, arbitrariness, and ineptitudes of others as participants and leaders may cause the individual to re-examine himself. Discussion may also contribute to the individual's ability in reflective thinking as a member of a group. He may gain a better understanding of approaches to problems in a general sense and of ways a group can approach specific tasks rationally rather than emotionally and in a systematic rather than a disorganized manner.

LIMITATIONS AND EXCEPTIONS/ "A little learning is a dangerous thing," however. The student who has had one course in discussion or social psychology is not thereby an expert on group process and discussion leadership.

If practice in discussion leads to increased understanding, this gain is a bonus. Such a happy outcome will not always result, unfortunately, and the individual must be forever humble in estimating what he knows about human behavior.

Group Participation May Promote Citizenship

There is at least one other possible value of discussion training and participation. Experienced participants may become more effective citizens. Members learn about collective responsibility and irresponsibility, group action and inaction, and similar matters. In many ways, the small, interacting group represents in microcosm the larger democratic society. Much of the experience in one transfers directly to understanding and operating in the other.

Since our contemporary society is becoming more complex, and people in our culture more interdependent, there is increasing pressure to have more people involved in decision-making and in each decision. Talking it over is necessary. The rugged individualist who wants to make his own decisions finds himself operating in increasingly restricted areas. If it is difficult to avoid participating in discussion, it seems wise for group members to operate as competently as possible.

OTHER LIMITATIONS

Discussion Is Unsuited to Some Tasks

Not all problems lend themselves to group solution. Some metaphysical questions could never be settled by interaction, just as some questions cannot be answered empirically. Questions asking, "Is God dead?" and "How many angels can dance on the head of a pin?" are not matters where persons can expect to come up with an answer by talking around a table. If the group benefits from such interaction, it will be for reasons other than learning the group's answer to the question.

A group should not waste its time considering trivial matters, such as those of taste or personal preference. A board of busy persons once spent an hour debating the wording of a sentence in a report. Some preferred one wording, while others liked different language choices. The composition of the sentence was not directly related to the purpose of the report, so their deliberation was not particularly constructive. If a minor point could be decided one way as well as another, the group should let an executive decide, or decide quickly by majority vote.

Discussion Takes Time

Discussion almost always requires substantial amounts of time. Autocratic decisions are speedy by comparison. If problems are complex and controversial, there are rarely short cuts to thorough understanding and deliberation. An executive group, for example, may find it necessary to meet for an hour or more daily as the price for better decisions and increased commitment through collective action. A committee may need to meet for longer periods and to hold more meetings than members had anticipated if they are determined to take all views into account.

Discussion cannot often be used fairly when members are in a hurry for a decision. For the leader to say, after two or three persons have spoken, "We don't have time to talk about this fully, but would you all agree that we should do so and so?" is to stampede the members. They are in no position to disagree without being disagreeable. Only if the proposal is so outrageous that all the members spontaneously howl out their disgust is the stampede likely to be stopped. Whether the proposal expresses the will of the group when they are silent after such a plea from the leader, no one can know. To find out requires additional communication from them.

Discussion Can Be Wasteful

Group discussion is not only time consuming, but also it often wastes some of the time it requires. Unless a group has unusually able leadership, members spend some of their time in false starts and unproductive byways. Discussers may talk at length, for instance, before they wake up to the fact that they have no power to do anything about the problem, or that they do not need an answer. The result for the person who places a high value on efficiency may be frustration or even disgust for the method.

Jacques Barzun tells of a discussion in a committee of college professors during the Second World War on "how to insure in war time the survival of permanent human values." One of the members pointed out "that if the human values were really permanent the college might let them shift for themselves. This broke up the meeting, but there is no reason to believe that the other committeemen were properly grateful."[23]

Members may at least feel that their time has been wasted when participating in a group that does not understand how to use discussion, or one where members do not yet have enough information to understand the problem. Occasionally a group must mark time while a very complex but essential matter is explained in words of one syllable to a dull member. If the group wants a unanimous decision it must wait until the slow member understands.

To communicate clearly and effectively is not a simple assignment nor a talent easily mastered. Some persons in particular find it difficult to express their meanings and contribute their information within reasonable time limits and with pleasing efficiency. It is thus not unusual for their articulate colleagues to find themselves waiting during labored explanations and obscure statements of opinion. The participant for the most part must take group members as they come although a few bitter experiences may lead him to favor additional study of the speech and communication arts.

Discussion may waste time if the group gets off on the wrong question. An

[23] *Teacher in America*, Boston: Little, Brown, 1945.

instance of this kind occurred when a student–faculty discipline committee was considering the case of a freshman girl accused by a merchant of passing a bad check. The merchant did not show up at the meeting to press charges; a member had heard a rumor that the girl's father had rushed to town and paid the merchant. The committee chairman should have asked, "Do we want to pursue this case and get some more information, or do we want to forget the whole thing unless the merchant shows up?" Instead the group spent a happy but irrelevant half-hour talking about a question it did not need to answer: "What makes parents so overprotective that they teach their youngsters false values?"

Another instance of waste in discussion may occur when the available participants are not really qualified to take part. If members of a staff, for example, are so new to the plant that they know almost nothing yet about its operation, it is usually foolish to ask them to make group decisions. When there is such a wide discrepancy between the knowledge of the plant manager, perhaps, and the new staff, it is usually better for him simply to tell them what is expected of them, and let them gather knowledge until the time when they can help with decisions. If the group attempts to use discussion under these conditions, members will be forced to spend most of the communication time asking the plant manager for information and his opinions, and they will almost inevitably conclude by doing what he recommends anyway. When there is rapid turnover in a staff, there may be situations in which discussion has limited usefulness.

Discussion Can Suppress Convictions

Social pressure and fear of disapproval may cause the suppression of convictions, valid objections, and helpful criticism. There is danger in discussion that members will conform to the apparently popular view rather than risk censure from others present. Group forces such as conformity pressures, which result from fear of expressing dissent, in the words of Kurt Back, "are likely to be dangerous and should be used sparingly, like dangerous drugs."[24] Discussion can only be used wisely by those who understand such forces and who can achieve permissive expression of all points of view.

Discussion Can Substitute Talk for Action

Division of responsibility among group members sometimes encourages the substitution of talk for constructive action and decision-making. Most group members find it easy and pleasant to talk, and there is a danger that visiting together will become an end in itself. It may appear that what is occurring is worthwhile, since it seemingly is sanctioned by the group, when in actuality what is happening is not constructive at all. Many unnecessary meetings and not a few unnecessary organizations are perpetuated primarily because talking together is a pleasurable habit. There is nothing wrong with enjoyable com-

[24] "Group Addiction . . . Its Cause and Cure," *Adult Leadership*, 3 (1954), p. 31.

munication in congenial groups, of course; most social events involve such activity. What is deplorable is pointless, meandering talk disguised as constructive discussion. As Barzun says of some contemporary committee discussion:

> The goal seems to be not so much to transact business as to stagnate in friendly feelings. These apparently forbid one to contradict, to argue concisely, or to recall any speaker to the point. Under these conditions, if the minutes of the meeting show any signs of consecutiveness, it is because the secretary has a good head and writes them up at home.[25]

Groups in some situations may tend to be indecisive. Since no one person is directly responsible for action, all often do nothing. No one member of a committee, for example, can be singled out as the source of delay, and consequently the group may spend much longer than it should in making up its mind. A chairman may quite properly claim that his hands are tied until the members choose to act. The net result may appear as inefficiency to an outsider waiting for a decision; he may say he is being given the run around. A humorist long ago observed incisively: "If Moses had been a committee, the children of Israel would still be in Egypt!"

An organization should not allow itself to become so dependent on group decision-making that it is immobilized when the group temporarily cannot meet. Congress can adjourn for several months, but the executive branch of government knows what it must do to carry out the policies already established. In the same way, a responsible group will agree on general policies, which will free it from remaining in constant session.

Discussion May Be Ineffective in Large Groups

Direct, conversational interaction will not work easily and effectively in large groups. In many situations, the greatest values of group interaction are not realized when more than twelve or fifteen are involved. Of course, there are types of discussion that can be used in large groups, but discussion makes its most unique contribution as a method of deliberation in small groups.

An alternative to discussion when time is short and the group is large is to use parliamentary methods (see Chapter 18).

Groups Are Individuals

Here, then, are some of the strengths and weaknesses of discussion. It is clear that discussion is often a powerful tool for good. The times call for much collective action, and to use discussion ably is a positive virtue. Group action and group efficiency are important considerations in our culture and in many others. Groups, however, have no substance apart from the individual human beings who compose them. A group has no hands except those of its members. The individuals while interacting thereby react differently and contribute

[25] *Teacher in America*, 179–81.

something through group action which they could not accomplish as individuals alone. Nevertheless, a group has no magical powers. It can do nothing that its members are unable to do, since the group consists only of its individual members interacting collectively. The strengths of group discussion can be applauded and put to constructive use even while recognizing realistically its limitations.

A group should do nothing that its individual members are unwilling or ashamed to do. Instead, members should strive to discuss as competently as they are able, and to serve expertly and faithfully as leaders whenever a group depends upon them to do so. By having a thorough understanding of group process and of discussion, and by attaining educated skill in participation and leadership, individuals can contribute immeasurably to the work that must be done in their chosen vocation, and to the democratic society of which they have the good fortune to be a part.

SUPPLEMENTARY READING

Anderson, Martin P., "Discussion in Agriculture," *Quarterly Journal of Speech*, 37 (December, 1951), pp. 463–8.

Barnlund, Dean C., and Haiman, Franklyn S., *The Dynamics of Discussion*, Boston: Houghton Mifflin, 1960, Chapter 15.

Bode, Carl, *The American Lyceum: Town Meeting of the Mind*, New York: Oxford University Press, 1956.

Bunn, Charles, "How Lawyers Use Speech," *The Speech Teacher*, 13 (1964), pp. 6–9.

Busch, Henry M., *Conference Method In Industry*, New York: Harper & Row, 1949.

Cartwright, Dorwin, and Zander, Alvin, *Group Dynamics: Research and Theory*, 2nd. ed., New York: Harper & Row, 1960, Chapters 1 and 2.

Chamberlain, Neil W., "Group Discussion and Collective Bargaining," *Adult Education Bulletin*, 13 (1949), pp. 77–84.

Collins, Barry E., and Guetzkow, Harold, *A Social Psychology of Group Processes for Decision-Making*, New York: John Wiley & Sons, 1964, Chapters 2, 4, and 5.

Eichelberger, Clark M., "Discussion in the United Nations," *Adult Education Bulletin*, 13 (1949), pp. 88–90.

Hare, A. Paul, *Handbook of Small Group Research*, New York: The Free Press, 1962, Chapter 12.

Joy, C. Turner, *How Communists Negotiate*, New York: Crowell-Collier and Macmillan, 1955.

Kriesberg, M., and Guetzkow, H., "The Use of Conferences in the Administrative Process," *Public Administration Review*, 10 (1950), pp. 93–98.

Maier, Norman R. F., *Problem-Solving Discussions and Conferences*, New York: McGraw-Hill, 1963.

Mill, John Stuart, *On Liberty*, Boston: Ticknor and Fields, 1863.

Nicholson, Harold, *The Evolution of Diplomatic Method*, New York: Crowell-Collier and Macmillan, 1954.

Williams, Donald E., "Group Discussion and Argumentation in Legal Education," *Quarterly Journal of Speech*, 48 (December, 1955), p. 399.

QUESTIONS AND EXERCISES

1. To obtain an idea of how extensively discussion is used today, go through two consecutive issues of a metropolitan daily newspaper and record a description of each meeting that could involve discussion. Attempt to estimate how discussion is being used in each.

2. Study in detail the way discussion is used in a single industrial plant, school, business organization, or similar unit. Be prepared to report on what you learn from observation, interview, and study of records.

3. Prepare an extensive bibliography and a written report on current uses of discussion for one of the following purposes:
   a. enlightenment, learning, or information-sharing;
   b. mental therapy;
   c. school or college training of speakers;
   d. decision-making.

4. Write a paper or give an oral report on how discussion is used today in:
   a. a campus organization, such as a student government;
   b. your state legislature;
   c. a local city council;
   d. the U.S. Congress;
   e. The United Nations;
   f. a town meeting;
   g. an agricultural organization;
   h. an organization for teachers;
   i. international negotiations;
   j. legal conferences;
   k. a business firm;
   l. an industrial organization;
   m. labor-management negotiations;
   n. the armed forces;
   o. a community forum.

5. Write a paper or give an oral report on the history of the use of discussion method in one of the organizations listed under exercise 4 above.

6. Observe a number of discussions of a city council, school board, student council committee, church board, or similar group. Make a careful analysis of the instances in which these groups exemplify (a) the strengths, and (b) the limitations of discussion as treated in this chapter. Be prepared to agree or disagree with the analyses in this book.

Chapter 3

TYPES
OF DISCUSSION

Discussion is used in a variety of ways, as we have suggested in Chapter 2. Different kinds of discussion are appropriate in various situations and circumstances. In order to have a consistent terminology in studying differences it will be helpful to consider ways of classifying the types of discussion used. We can then specify also the types that will be of greatest interest to us in this book.

To establish a reasonable classification system is no simple task because such activities, situations, and circumstances are so variable. It seems plausible, nevertheless, to describe differences introduced by variations in purpose, the presence of nonparticipants, the communication format, formality, authority, and leadership.

PURPOSE

Discussion is most often employed to achieve one of two basic purposes, information-sharing or decision-making, or some combination of these two.

Participants in informational discussion exchange data, insights, and ideas for the purpose of learning. The outcome, hopefully, is increased understanding. In decision-making, or problem-solving, or policy-determining discussion, a group is attempting to decide what to do or to believe. The outcome is a decision or a policy. Obviously these purposes are often combined in the same discussion; a group usually must exchange information preparatory to deciding; a staff of workers at the regular weekly meeting may engage on one occasion in simple informational discussion and on another may share information and also reach decisions on items of business.

Information-Sharing

Discussion for information-sharing is used in many different kinds of situations, as the following examples indicate.

STUDY GROUP/ Here members meet together to study some subject of common interest. All the women's organizations in one local church took as the study theme for a particular year the operation of Christian missions in Japan. At their meetings they heard talks or book reviews on the subject and

then discussed what they had heard in small groups to help each participant understand more adequately the scope, objectives, and effectiveness of
missionary work with the Japanese.

Students in a classroom may use study-group discussion. If the study is
group-centered, the process may be discussion. If the teacher supplies most
of the information, or if the communication pattern consists of teacher question, student answer, this may not be discussion as we have defined it.

WORKSHOP/ The label "study group" is usually given to informational
discussion used by a group that meets regularly or at regular intervals over a
period of time. When such study is concentrated within a session of a few
hours or days, a more common designation is a workshop. The purposes,
activities, objectives, and methods are similar to those of a study group.

Some confusion is introduced by this term, since at times it has been used
to refer to a convention or large conference.

STAFF MEETING/ The president of a firm, the principal of a school, the
mayor of a city, or the head of any complex organization may call his staff
together for the purpose only of sharing information. The communication
pattern may take several forms: the leader may do all the talking, explaining
policies, new developments, or accomplishments; if so, discussion is not taking
place. After the leader's explanations, there may be questioning and contributing of information by those present. Or the whole meeting may be conducted
as an interchange of information among members of the staff. Obviously, such
a staff at other moments may also employ decision-making discussion.

BRIEFING SESSION/ Another variation similar to the staff meeting is the
briefing session. Here information is needed by a group whose members are
ready to undertake a common task. Before departure on a bombing mission,
crews of military airplanes are given information on targets, routes, weather,
etc. Again, the procedure will not usually be discussion unless participants
question and exchange communications.

ROUND TABLE/ The term *round table* has been applied to so many different sorts of activities that it is perhaps meaningless to include it in any list. It
is a widely known label, however, and can be serviceable if a specific meaning
is assigned to it.

The activity that can best be identified as a round table is a discussion in
which participants with a common problem talk together "around a table"
(not often a round table) for the purpose of learning from each other. We
could also use this term to designate a study group. It is this overlapping of
possible meanings which contributes to the confusion in classification.

When high school teachers attend a state-wide meeting, for example, all
those who are instructors of American history may meet in one room to
discuss ways of improving instruction in this subject. Each may report on his
approaches, materials, and successes. The others gain new insights into their
own methods from the exchange of ideas. One name for this type of discussion
is a round table.

Decision-Making

Decision-making, problem-solving, or policy determination is most often the purpose of committees, conferences, and boards.

COMMITTEE/ The committee is usually a decision-making group. It is a subgroup of a parent organization, and ordinarily a recommendation group, since its decisions may or may not be adopted by the parent organization. A legislature's committee responsible for agricultural policy studies current conditions and drafts proposed legislation for consideration by the whole house.

Often a committee is assigned a specific task by the parent group and ordered to report its recommendations. The parent body has full control over its committees; it may discharge them and it may reject their recommendations without necessary embarrassment either to the whole house or to members of the committee.

CONFERENCE/ As was noted in Chapter 1, the word *conference* may be applied to various activities. Here the reference is to a relatively small-group meeting, which is private and whose purpose is decision-making.

In most such conferences, two or more persons representing different parent organizations meet together to work out a policy or reach a decision on a problem of common concern. Governors of adjacent states may meet to establish a common policy in regard to navigation on rivers and waterways. Automobile manufacturers may send delegates to a meeting for the purpose of agreeing on industry-wide policy; these representatives may decide, for example, that automobile advertising campaigns should emphasize safety rather than power or speed. These meetings are conferences.

Conferences, in most cases, are recommendation groups. An international agreement reached at a foreign ministers' conference must usually be ratified or approved by the heads of states and the parliaments of the member nations. When parent organizations send representatives to such a conference, however, the resulting recommendations tend to be morally binding on the parent bodies. The parent group still has the power to refuse to abide by the decision; but it cannot usually do so without embarrassment. If the decision seems acceptable to most of the other groups represented, and especially in cases where mass publicity given to the conference indicates a favorable response in the publics involved, a parent body usually finds it difficult not to ratify the policy.

These distinctions can be seen clearly in the Congress. The House of Representatives and the Senate each have an extensive set of committees that study and recommend legislation. Each house then passes bills. If similar bills on the same matter contain somewhat different provisions as passed by the representatives and senators, each house designates delegates to a joint conference committee, which attempts to work out a compromise. This amalgamated version must go back to each house separately for passage in the new form. At this point, either house may refuse to concur. Usually, however, the joint conference recommendation carries great weight.

Boards and Councils. There are many other varieties of decision-making discussions. The board of directors of a corporation usually reaches decisions during private sessions. In some matters the board will have power to act; in others they may serve as a recommendation group to the stockholders. Governing councils, such as a city council, may proceed in a similar manner; ultimately the council members may be responsible to the citizens they represent, but in many areas they have authority to decide and act.

Governing boards with decision-making power are found in many other instances. The Central States Speech Association, a professional organization of teachers of speech, has an executive committee. Members are the president, two vice-presidents, the executive secretary who is also the treasurer, and the editor of the Association's journal. Officers are elected by the members of the Association. The executive committee has power to set the place and time of annual conventions and in other ways to control policy, within the limits prescribed by the full membership.

Hybrids

Some situations involve a combination of informational and decision-making discussion. Almost any staff meeting, or meeting of a city council, officers' board, or board of directors involves during a single session both information-sharing and problem-solving discussion. At times during the meeting, members will exchange information on new developments within the organization. At other points on the agenda, the group will discuss problems and reach decisions. In order to decide whether the group is using informational or problem-solving discussion at a particular moment, it would be necessary to observe what was happening at that time.

This distinction is important only because participants should be aware of the differences between the two forms and should not confuse one kind of procedure with the other. When the group is striving to explain, to clarify, to share understanding, members should defer matters of policy to an appropriate stage in the meeting.

PRESENCE OF NONPARTICIPANTS

The most common type of discussion occurs when a small group meets face to face with only the group members present. All those in the room are participants and all communicate, or at least are expected to participate actively. This type of discussion is private, or closedgroup. Committees and conferences are most often closedgroup, as are most study groups, workshops, and other informational discussions.

In contrast, some discussions are public, and are held for the benefit of a listening audience. Participants must take other communicators into account as they do in private discussions, but, more importantly in the public situation, they must take the audience into account. Complex differences are introduced by the presence of nonparticipants. These differences will be explained more fully in Chapter 17, the only chapter in the book concerned with public discussion.

In public discussion the audience may be physically present in the same room or auditorium with the communicators, or the listeners may be hearing by radio or both hearing and seeing by television. Also, if the audience is physically present, they may become participants at some stage dictated by the format of the program.

In common with closedgroup discussion, public discussion may serve either of the two general purposes: to inform the audience or to stimulate listeners to decide what they believe a policy should be. In most cases, groups utilizing public discussion for policy-determination are recommendation groups. Some other body usually has the power to act on the problem.

A typical situation would be a publicly televised panel in which four or five prominent citizens, including perhaps a U.S. senator, discussed the question, "What should be United States foreign policy in the Middle East?" Power to act in this matter rests with the President and his advisers, primarily the Secretary of State, and, indirectly, the Congress. Any convictions reached as a result of this televised discussion could only be passed on to public officials for their consideration.

We should not be misled into concluding that public discussion is not particularly important because it cannot result in direct action. Public policy in a democratic society is formulated from the recommendations of hundreds and thousands of individuals and groups.

Public discussion may use many different formats and each may be employed either for information-sharing or decision-making. For example, a panel of school officials may explain to an audience of parents the various curricula available in the schools, or the same participants could discuss the desirability of passing a bond authorization to raise additional money for education.

PANEL/   In this type of public discussion, a small group of experts or well-informed persons discuss a problem for the benefit of an audience. The distinctive feature of the panel is the communication pattern. Participants engage in direct, conversational interchange of ideas. The communicative interchange is similar to that which is characteristic of the closedgroup committee, conference, or round table. Probably this format is the one most frequently used in public discussion.

DIALOG/   The dialog is similar to the panel, except that there are only two communicating participants. The interchange is directly conversational. Often one of them is an expert on the problem for discussion, and the other supplies more questions than information.

SYMPOSIUM/   Here, too, a small group of experts or well-informed persons discuss a problem for the benefit of an audience; the distinguishing characteristic is again the communicative pattern. Each participant delivers a relatively short speech without being interrupted, giving his view or explaining one aspect of the problem. Speakers follow each other in turn until all participants have been heard.

Usually the speakers are chosen because they represent a particular position on the problem or have special competence on a portion of the topic for discussion. On a college campus, participants in an information-sharing symposium conducted to familiarize new students with college customs might be the director of housing, who would explain housing regulations; the dean of women, who would describe rules governing coeds; the social director of the student union, who would tell about dating customs; and the president of the student body, who would explain campus traditions.

A nationally televised problem-solving symposium on the question, "What agricultural policy should the federal government adopt?" might use as speakers a representative of the Department of Agriculture who favors flexible price supports; a spokesman for a major political party who advocates price supports fixed at 90 percent of parity; a leader in the Farm Bureau who proposes that the federal government eliminate the price support program; and so on.

FORUM/ The term *forum* is used in three ways. The first is applied to participation by the listening audience after they have heard a public discussion or some other type of presentation. If the audience hears a panel discussion and is then invited to question and make contributions, this portion of the meeting is designated a *forum*. Thus, the whole discussion should properly be called a *panel-forum*. Similarly, there can be a *dialog-forum* or a *symposium-forum*.

Using the concept of forum to mean general audience participation after some type of presentation makes it possible to classify a *lecture-forum* as a type of public discussion. After the speaker delivers his lecture, an audience forum period follows. In the same way these other forms can be classified as public discussions: *debate-forum*, in which audience participation follows a set of formal debate speeches advocating affirmative and negative positions on a proposition; *film-forum*, where audience discussion concerns a motion picture that the group has just seen; and forums in which the vehicle for audience discussion is a radio or television broadcast heard by the whole group prior to the forum period. Obviously, any of these formats could be used either for enlightenment or problem-solving.

A second sense in which the term *forum* is used applies to a type of discussion in which members of the audience may participate from the beginning of the meeting. This form has at times been called an *open forum*. The entire meeting is devoted to discussion by the whole audience as participants. No formal presentation precedes audience participation. In effect, this type of forum is the same kind of discussion as the closedgroup type that we have called the round table. It is questionable whether this kind of forum is public discussion in our sense. The distinction here, if there is one, is unimportant.

The open forum, however, usually involves a much larger group than would be characteristic of the round table.

The third usage of the term forum designates a whole series of regular public discussions on related problems. Sometimes a group of people who want to meet regularly on common problems will call their organization and the activity a *community* forum.

Hybrids

A few discussions combine features of closedgroup and public discussion.

COMMITTEE HEARING/ One of the most important tasks of a committee is to investigate problems. Only on the basis of accurate information and thorough understanding can it make intelligent recommendations to the parent body. An effective device for acquiring understanding quickly is the committee hearing. Instead of sending out researchers to seek facts, important committees can invite well-informed persons to appear and offer information and opinions. Congressional committees even have the power to subpoena witnesses.

A committee's deliberation among its members is closedgroup, as we have seen. When a witness appears during a hearing, however, a new element has been added—the discussion is no longer private; the procedure takes on some of the characteristics of public discussion. At important Congressional committee hearings, reporters are usually present; often these hearings are open to the general public. Indeed, some have been televised on national networks. If, during an interval between hearing witnesses, the committee engages in procedural deliberation which under other circumstances would be closedgroup, but which now has press and nation overhearing, the committee discussion will certainly be altered. Members cannot communicate without taking the listeners into account in some sense.

CASE CONFERENCE/ Another closedgroup-public hybrid has been used as a learning device. Two or more participants engage in a conference in front of a listening audience. The participants are expected to proceed as if the conference were taking place in a real closedgroup situation. Often they are assigned roles; that is, they play the part of someone who would be involved in such a situation. The listening audience overhears for the purpose of learning from the procedures acted out by the participants.

Perhaps an illustration will make this type of case conference clearer. A class of forty labor union leaders are studying grievance handling. Three members of the class are assigned to hold two conferences for the benefit of the group. First, the worker will present his grievance to the student who is taking the role of the shop steward. Then the steward will present the grievance to the management representative. After the class has observed the way these three participants handle the grievance, members will discuss the strengths and weaknesses of the methods followed. This type of discussion has characteristics of both closedgroup and public discussion. The over-all situation involving the forty students is closedgroup; also the conferences are conducted as if they were closedgroup. But the demonstrators are communicating for the benefit of the audience, and their discussion will be altered because the observers are present. Hence there will be some elements of public discussion involved.

The term *case conference* has been applied to other forms of discussion. It is sometimes used to designate a closedgroup discussion by all members of a group about an actual case or situation. For example, a group interested in juvenile delinquency might discuss a particular case of a juvenile offender. His offense and treatment by the authorities would be described in detail; general discussion would follow. This type is similar to a closedgroup round table.

There are other discussions that combine features of private and public communication. A city council or school board holding open meetings where citizens may listen and on some occasions make comments is no longer conducting closedgroup discussion. When a board of governors of a university or a county board of supervisors is required to have open meetings where reporters are present, every member must take into account the fact that the public is listening.

COMMUNICATION FORMAT

Discussions vary in the kind of communicative interaction permitted and expected in the situation.

The most frequent kind is direct conversational interchange characteristic of committees, conferences, and public panels. Here participants speak up, usually without recognition, when they feel moved to make a comment, interrupt each other, and in other ways talk much as they would in conversation. Each individual alternates as speaker and listener, usually with some rapidity; comments from one person lasting as long as two minutes are uncharacteristic.

In some discussions, such as a symposium, participants deliver uninterrupted speeches as part of the meeting. Some public panel discussions will have a symposium feature where members explain their view in a formal speech before participants interact conversationally as a panel.

As we noted, the audience is sometimes invited to participate after a symposium or panel. This forum period involves impromptu speeches from the floor consisting of questions or comments.

FORMALITY

The degree of formality in a discussion situation does not indicate whether it is closedgroup or public, informational or decision-making. Any kind of discussion may be conducted in a formal or an informal, even casual, manner.

This dimension is worth noting, however, because it may help to explain the way the discussion is carried on, as well as its success in the minds of those involved.

A student committee assembled to talk about the next organization dance may, if it wishes, conduct itself with severe formality, and it may definitely do so if the group is large and if there are other considerations, such as the presence of a faculty adviser or the dean of students. On the other hand, heads of states, meeting in international conference to decide the fate of nations, may, if the participants wish, conduct their meeting with cordial and relaxed informality.

Formality varies with the kinds of persons involved, and especially with the personality of those providing leadership. A tense, anxious chairman may conduct a meeting of a social committee with a rigidity and seriousness considered inappropriate by others. The presence of an extremely influential person tends to increase formality, especially if other participants have had little experience in meetings with powerful people.

It varies also with the nature of the task and the type of group. In general, the more important the subject for discussion, the more formal are the proceedings. For similar reasons, a discussion in a meeting on the job is usually conducted more formally than is a meeting of a recreational or social club.

There are other causes for variation in this regard. When time is short, for example, formality of the meeting almost always increases. Further, when numbers are large one of the changes introduced into discussion is greater formality. It becomes necessary to call on speakers more positively in order to designate clearly who has the floor. Members become more conscious of the length of time they are speaking and are more polite to each other. Parliamentary procedures forced upon a group by the pressures of large numbers are simply rules designed to direct discussion in a more formal and efficient manner.

AUTHORITY

Some discussion groups have authority to decide and to translate their decisions into action. A city council, for example, has power to act on parking regulations, police and fire protection policies, and many other matters. In contrast, many discussions are held in groups with authority only to recommend action to other bodies. Committees and many conferences are thus types of recommendation groups.

When students in a college classroom discuss U.S. policy toward Red China, the outcome of their discussion is a recommendation to the President and the Secretary of State, who are actively responsible for U.S. foreign policy; these student members are a recommendation group. Their discussion is just as realistic and utilizes the same methods as would be the case if they were considering a problem where their group does have power to act.

LEADERSHIP

Discussion can be classified in another sense according to the amount of control or direction exercised in the group. Many discussions have a designated leader. Others may be leaderless: the group may be organized so informally or members may know the problem so thoroughly that they can conduct the discussion without any one person being in charge.

Still another arrangement sometimes used is one in which leadership functions are distributed among various participants.

We must be careful in studying groups not to confuse leaderless and leadershipless discussion. While a group may have effective discussion without one person being designated as the leader, a group where no one is supplying any leadership at all is not likely to be productive nor to have satisfied participants.

We see, then, that discussions cannot be classified into any tight table of categories although it is helpful to recognize the dimensions that may in general differentiate one type from another. Each of these dimensions is worthy of serious study. The student of discussion must become a careful observer of their operation in various situations.

In this book we will concentrate primarily on discussion theory and procedures in the closed small group concerned with decision-making, usually under the guidance of a designated leader. Thus our major interest will be in communicative interaction that is directly and informally conversational.

SUPPLEMENTARY READING

Braden, Waldo W., and Brandenburg, E., *Oral Decision-Making*, New York: Harper & Row, 1955, Chapter 14.

Howell, William S., and Smith, D., *Discussion*, New York: Crowell-Collier and Macmillan, 1956, Chapter 11.

McBurney, James H., and Hance, K., *Discussion in Human Affairs*, New York: Harper & Row, 1950, Part IV.

Phillips, Gerald M., *Communication and the Small Group*, Indianapolis: Bobbs-Merrill, 1966, pp. 52–66.

Wagner, Russell H., and Arnold, Carroll C., *Handbook of Group Discussion*, Boston: Houghton Mifflin, 1950, Chapter 9.

QUESTIONS AND EXERCISES

1. Do you consider conversation a type of discussion? Why or why not?
2. What are the essential differences between closedgroup and public discussion? Between informational and decision-making discussion?
3. Design, explain, and defend a system of classification of types of discussion other than the one presented in this chapter.

4. Observe a number of group discussions and classify them according to the dimensions suggested in this chapter. Do you observe characteristics not mentioned here that could be useful in describing types of discussion?
5. Watch a televised discussion and write a paper reporting on what you consider to be effects introduced into the discussion because it is public rather than private.
6. Observe a closedgroup business meeting of a relatively small group such as the executive board of a housing unit, fraternity, etc. Record the items taken up during the meeting and classify each into informational or decision-making discussion. If there are items you cannot classify, try to explain the difficulty.

PART TWO

PREPARING FOR DISCUSSION

Chapter 4

PLANNING

Good discussions are made in part on the drawing board. Careful planning for a specific discussion can often mean the difference between effective and haphazard decision-making.

In using the materials in this chapter, we face two hazards. This book is not a how-to-do-it manual but in planning there is a temptation to lay out the steps and say, "do it this way and succeed." We must resist the cookbook approach, however, because achieving good discussion is not as simple as cake baking. We must try to suggest the factors to be understood and taken into account in the planning stage and let those involved decide how to proceed on a particular occasion.

The second hazard is the temptation to address this chapter to a designated leader. The person in charge of a specific discussion seems to be the one who should be responsible for planning. What he does in advance is important, of course, but his efforts alone are not enough. Other members must help with planning. They must understand what advance preparation contributes and why it is vital. Furthermore, one advantage of group action, as we observed in Chapter 2, is that members can divide the labor of preparation.

In this chapter we must study two different but similar subjects: (1) planning for classroom participation in discussion for practice and learning; and (2) planning for discussions where actual groups engage in decision-making. One is an exercise for becoming effective in the other. What is said about each should be helpful in understanding the other.

PLANNING PRACTICE DISCUSSIONS

Analyzing Requirements

The initial step is to determine what is required for a productive discussion within the situation assigned. Demands are as varied as the types of discussion and kinds of circumstances.

Participants must be chosen and leadership responsibilities assigned to a designated leader or divided among members. After the type of discussion and situation are specified, a question must be selected and worded appropriately. Members must secure information and resource materials. The leader responsible for guiding the discussion will want to draw up an outline. Then the group must plan the physical arrangements and decide whether to hold pre-discussion meetings.

The class also will usually want to provide some kind of evaluation machinery for making an appraisal after the exercise is completed.

We can illustrate what is required in particular situations by supposing that a class wishes to practice three types of discussion: (1) closedgroup informational workshops; (2) closedgroup decision-making conferences; and (3) public panel-forums. In each case the class should be divided into small groups of five to seven. The assignments in these situations might be as follows:

Workshops

FORMAT: Each group, under the direction of a designated leader to be elected by the group, will discuss in front of the class an information-sharing question designed to increase our understanding of the subject. Class members, as observers, will overhear what is essentially closedgroup discussion. Each group will have 35 to 40 minutes for discussion, leaving a brief period at the end of the class meeting for evaluation by observers and the instructor.

EVALUATION: During the discussions each member of the class should take whatever notes he wishes. The class at a later meeting will evaluate each of the workshops. Observers will want to decide whether the group achieved its purposes; assess the contributions of individual participants; evaluate the contributions of leadership; and comment on the operation of the group as a group.

Conferences

FORMAT: Three representatives from each of two organizations will meet outside of class as committees to decide on the organizational position for the conference; then in front of the class the two subgroups will confer in an effort to reach a decision satisfactory to all the participants. (For example, three students may be a committee representing the independent men's association on campus and the other three a committee of the fraternity council. The two committees will then hold a conference during a class session to decide on a policy to be binding on all campus men in regard to the intramural sports program sponsored by the two men's organizations.) Class members will overhear what is essentially closedgroup decision-making. Each group will have 35 to 40 minutes for discussion, leaving a brief period at the end of the class meeting for evaluation by the observer team.

EVALUATION: Each conference will be evaluated by four members of an observer team to be appointed by the instructor. At the end of the discussion, the observers will have 2 minutes each to make brief evaluations of the aspect each has concentrated on: leadership, participation, quality of outcome, and group operation.

Panel-Forums

FORMAT: A panel of 4 or 5, under the direction of a leader designated by the instructor, will discuss for 30 minutes an important public problem with the class as listening audience. The problem must be a matter of public policy needing solution. After 30 minutes, the audience will be invited to question or comment.

EVALUATION: Each member of the audience will be asked to evaluate the panels he hears as listener (not as participant). He will make his own individual assessment in any way he chooses. At a later meeting after all panel-forums have been presented, the whole class will be asked to evaluate them during a class discussion.

For each of the assignments described, members will be required to choose participants, specify the leadership, select and word a question, collect information, plan a guiding outline, plan physical arrangements, and work out any prediscussion meetings. These matters are discussed in later sections of this chapter and in later chapters of the book. Special problems encountered in public discussion are explained in Chapter 17.

Assigning Participants and Leadership

Participants for classroom discussions are most easily selected by discovering clusters of students interested in a particular problem such as the United Nations, the grading system, regulation of student women's hours, capital punishment, etc. Certainly members should not be assigned to a group unless they are interested in the subject for discussion.

In assigning students to decision-making groups, it is important that there be some measure of disagreement in the attitudes of members toward the problem. If the question were whether the veto in the UN Security Council should be abolished and if all the participants believed before the discussion that the veto privilege is undesirable, the decision-making discussion will not be very exciting or even necessary. Similarly, a conference must embrace controversial points of view or be rather pointless.

Making leadership assignments is primarily a matter of giving class members as many opportunities as possible for different learning experiences within the class time available. Appointing one member a designated leader probably gives him the maximum of experience in the shortest time but students also need practice in dividing leadership among several participants.

SELECTING AND WORDING THE QUESTION

An early step in preparing for a particular discussion is agreeing upon the question.

To be productive, groups must discuss questions, not statements, single words, or phrases. Suppose, for example, that a classroom discussion is held on the general topic of juvenile crime. It is probable that each student participating, when preparing in advance and when contributing ideas early in the discussion itself, will have in mind a slightly different aspect of this general subject. One may think of the increasing crime rate. Another may concentrate on ways of preventing juvenile crime. Still another may be concerned with methods of punishing, or rehabilitating, or re-educating youthful criminals. A fourth may consider the failures of parents, schools, or churches in guiding youth. A fifth may see the problem as a breakdown in cultural organization. A sixth may view with alarm the moral deterioration that leads to crime. When this discussion gets underway, there may be a full half-hour of energetic talk before the members realize that they are not all talking about the same thing, except in a very general sense. At some point, the leader or some member must halt the proceedings and suggest that they determine the explicit question they wish to answer.

Even when the group seeks the real question, there are several possibilities and, if time is limited, a careful choice must be made. They might discuss any one of these questions: How can the juvenile crime rate be reduced? Should we recommend to the county court that juvenile offenders be given stiffer sentences? Should we recommend that parents be punished for the crimes of their minor children? Should we recommend that chronic offenders be placed in special schools? The point is that in a limited time, the group can discuss thoroughly only one, and not all, of these complex questions. If they attempt to consider them all at once, or to discuss the general topic, juvenile crime, the discussion will meander in great circles, doubling back time after time to the same ideas; it will not move forward efficiently and productively toward agreement on a specific outcome.

In publicizing a public discussion, of course, sponsors may wish to use a topic, statement, or phrase in a form attractive to the potential audience. Such wordings as these may have more public appeal than the formally worded question that will actually be discussed: *The China Crisis; Juvenile Crime and You; Capitalism versus Christianity; Social Drinking Among College Students.* Nevertheless, these are not suitable discussion questions. During the discussion, participants should consider a limited, specific, carefully worded question.

Sources of Questions

In seeking interesting and fruitful questions for classroom discussions, students can begin by making their own individual lists of problems. These lists can then be collated to find clusters of similar topics suggested by several members of the class. Questions for the interest list come from a number of sources.

INTERESTS OF THE GROUP/ If a particular section of discussion students share some common concerns, fruitful questions can emerge from these concerns. A number of class members, for example, may be majoring in teacher education and hence interested in discussing the grading system, the differences between high school and college teaching, federal aid to education, or other related matters.

The shared interest in studying discussion can also suggest topics: What are the possible leadership styles in discussion? To what extent should a designated leader exercise control over the group? What are the advantages of designating a leader in contrast to dividing leadership responsibilities? Should a designated leader prepare in advance a written outline for guiding a discussion?

INTEREST OF INDIVIDUALS/ Students may wish to suggest questions related to their individual interests and to their major fields of study. A student in liberal arts may want to discuss contributions of the Peace Corps to world peace or the standards for judging a man a success in our culture. A scientist or engineer may suggest: Are scientists responsible for the uses made of their technological creations? The premedical major may favor such questions as mercy killing and legalized abortion. The student in agriculture may be interested in parity prices and farm subsidies or world food supply in relation to population control.

CAMPUS AFFAIRS/ Perennial problems of the campus are always potential sources of discussion questions: To what extent should students have a voice in administering the college or university? To what extent do final examinations accomplish their stated purposes? Should the fraternity system be abandoned? Should all students be required to live in approved housing? Should students be allowed to operate automobiles? Should athletes be openly subsidized? Is the typical curriculum too specialized? What are the merits of year-round operation? What programs for study abroad have been tried in the United States? Is the student apathetic toward world problems? Do faculty members on this campus have academic freedom? Do students have academic freedom?

These questions have the advantage of immediacy of interest for all members of the class since all are involved. The examples given here could be extended to include dozens of similar topics.

CURRENT EDUCATIONAL, POLITICAL, ECONOMIC, OR SOCIAL PROBLEMS/ Contemporary conditions in politics, business, education, religion, and so on, may be sources of interesting discussion questions. Any particular discussion could be restricted to the problem at the local, state, national, or international level. Lists of such topics could be extended almost indefinitely since problems abound. In order to stimulate thinking of students who are drawing up their own list it will be helpful to suggest a number of examples.

Educational questions: To what extent does the federal government now give aid to education? Should prayers be allowed in public schools? What programs for the gifted elementary school child are now in operation? Should all high schools require a course on the history of communication? Is television damaging American children? What are the aims of education? How much freedom of speech should the instructor have in the classroom?

Political questions: Should this community fluoridate its water? Is city manager government the most desirable type of community government? Should this state adopt (abolish) a state tax on personal incomes? Should this state enact (abolish) a right-to-work law? What is the responsibility of the state for local schools? Should the United States depend on volunteers for an army? Should Congress be given power to reverse Supreme Court decisions? How secure is the United States against a surprise attack? Should the United States discontinue direct financial aid to foreign countries? What should be U.S. foreign policy toward Cuba? Should American food go to Iron Curtain countries? Should the United States recognize Red China? Should Red China be admitted to the United Nations? Should international agreements be reached only through the machinery of the United Nations?

Economic questions: Should all natural resources be controlled by the state? Should the United States nationalize industries vital to defense? Are labor unions helpful or harmful to the economy? Should local governments end reliance on property taxes as the primary source of school revenue? What are the symptoms of an economic recession? Should the United States allow trade with Red China? Should Congress establish an absolute maximum limit for the national debt? Should this state finance construction of public school buildings by issuing bonds? Should Congress require compulsory arbitration of labor–management disputes? Should workers in interstate commerce be required to join a labor union?

Social questions: Should the several states adopt uniform marriage and divorce laws? Is capital punishment justified? Should the United States provide other countries assistance with birth control problems? To what extent is morality declining in the United States? Are Americans less physically fit than they were a decade ago? What changes, if any, have taken place in American attitudes toward sex?

In considering questions such as these, we must note that topics worded here for decision-making may often suggest related information-sharing questions, and vice versa. The question, "Should the several states adopt uniform marriage and divorce laws?" asks for a policy decision. The general problem involved here also embraces a number of informational questions: To what extent do laws of the states vary in regard to marriage and divorce? What are the obstacles to establishing uniform laws in the several states? What efforts have been made in the past to achieve uniformity in marriage and divorce laws?

SPECIFIC EVENTS/ Another source of questions—and perhaps the most dramatic source of all—is the specific event or incident that touches the interests of the group. On campus a topic may be suggested when some decision of the college administration stirs controversy. Some international incident or local or regional catastrophe may suggest questions for classroom discussions. An example of such an event on the local level occurred when fifty men were killed in a mine explosion. In the wake of the disaster student groups were motivated to discuss whether safety precautions were adequate.

Kinds of Questions

Questions proposed for discussion can be of many kinds and it is helpful if participants are aware of the type of questions before undertaking their task. One especially useful differentiation among types is to distinguish among questions of fact, value, and policy.

QUESTIONS OF FACT/ These deal with truth and falsity. Is this so or is it not so? Does this characteristic exist or does it not? Is this happening? For example, the question, "Are we in a business recession?" is a question of fact.

Such questions vary from those easy to answer to those so difficult as to be unanswerable with present knowledge. The difference lies in the extent to which the problem is subject to empirical verification. Obviously we would not discuss questions of fact that could be answered by research, such as, "How many men in the United States are now unemployed?" However, a group might well discuss a question that can be partially answered by empirical methods but involves a judgment about the quality of the evidence. Examples are: "Is there a connection between cigarette smoking and lung cancer?" and "What evidence is there for a belief in flying saucers?"

The query, "Is there a God?" can be classified as a question of fact since either there is or there is not, but no amount of discussion could answer the question at the present time.

We should note that the answer to the question, "Are we in a business recession?" depends partially on what is meant by the word *recession*. Thus questions of fact that result in lively discussions are not so simple as they may seem at first glance.

QUESTIONS OF VALUE/ This type of question asks for judgments which involve the attitudes and feelings of participants: How good is *X*? How shall *X* be evaluated? Examples of value questions are: "Is fraternity hazing of new initiates a desirable practice?" and "Are present commercial television programs of satisfactory quality?" Here, again, part of the discussion must center on the meanings of *desirable practice* and *satisfactory quality*. Also, the question of value goes a step beyond the question of fact, but it must embrace information before the value question can be answered. We must agree on the kinds and extent of hazing practices before we can decide intelligently whether such practices violate what the group considers desirable activity. To say it another way, some members of the group may want to answer the question of fact, "Is hazing of new initiates actually practiced by fraternities on this campus?" prior to proceeding to the value question. Someone who denies its existence will not want to express a value judgment about desirability.

One can argue that questions of value are actually no different from questions of fact; that the question, "Is hazing desirable?" is a question of fact because it is either harmful or it is not. The distinction is not an important one except in pointing to the additional complexities introduced when a value judgment is required.

QUESTIONS OF POLICY/ These questions ask, "What action should be taken? How shall we proceed in the future? Often the word *should* appears in the question of policy: "Should youthful criminals be given stiffer punishment?" "Should the United States extend diplomatic recognition to Red China?"

Reaching a decision on a question of policy almost always involves questions of fact and of value. Two examples may make these relationships clearer.

Suppose we have some persons on the campus who want to eliminate compulsory physical education. The policy question is: "Should the college (university) abolish the physical education requirement?" Antecedent to reaching a decision are questions of fact such as, "Are students physically fit?" and questions of value, such as, "Is a physical fitness program a desirable part of a sound educational program at college level?" We may decide that students are not physically fit and that a fitness program is desirable; even so the answer to the policy question is not automatically that the present program should be retained. The group is free to decide that the present program should be abolished and a different method for guaranteeing fitness be put in its place. Thus all three kinds of questions are reasonable discussion tasks.

Another illustration could be encountered if a school were considering adopting an honor system for the administration of final examinations in place of providing proctors. A question of fact to be considered early may be: "Would an honor system for administering examinations work successfully on this campus?" A question of value would be: "Is an honor system a desirable thing?" Only after facing such questions as these could a group answer the decision-making question: "Should we recommend an honor system for this campus?"

Selecting the Question

As we have said, students should begin with their own interests in choosing questions for classroom discussions. In addition to discovering a question that the desired number of students are motivated to discuss, members will want to select a question they are competent to answer after study. Students can realistically discuss problems in areas where they have power to act, as in controlling many extracurricular activities, and in the case of other problems can recommend action to the faculty, such as changes in the grading system, or to public officials, such as changes in U.S. foreign policy. Also it is possible for groups holding practice discussions to select questions where they must play the roles of public officials or others.

Obviously groups must choose a question requiring the interaction of several minds and not one that could better be delegated to a single individual as a research assignment. Most problems of policy and especially those asking about changes in the way things are now done benefit from the thinking of several persons; many decisions require the assent or at least the good will of those involved. The question, "How many hours a week do students study?" is more properly a research than a discussion question, but a decision-making conference on the question, "Should compulsory study hours be established in the residence halls?" can profitably involve many persons in the discussion and in implementation of any decision.

Groups planning practice sessions will also wish to select questions for public discussion. For this purpose a question must not only meet all the other requirements but also should be chosen by taking into account current political, economic, and social affairs; and by considering carefully the nature of the listening audience.

In relation to public affairs, questions should be:

TIMELY/ It would be unwise to have a public discussion today on the question, "Should the United States levy a graduated income tax?" or "Should U.S. senators be elected by direct vote of the people?" although these were crucial issues at the beginning of this century. Public discussions, like public news broadcasts, must be current to be important.

SIGNIFICANT/ Another characteristic that makes the question important is that it concern a major, rather than a minor, problem. A topic may be timely and momentarily newsworthy without being worthy of public discussion. Sponsors must judge whether the problem is a significant one. Many audiences would not consider important the question: "Is comedian X an entertaining humorist?" However, they may want to hear a discussion on the question, "Are Americans changing their ideas about what is humorous?"

CONTROVERSIAL/ The question should involve sincere and healthy disagreement. The query, "Should women be given the vote?" is no longer in serious dispute. The question, "Should the United States defend itself against aggression?" would not be considered controversial by many. Further, the question to be satisfactory must be susceptible to rational deliberation. It would be difficult to make any substantial statements one way or another in response to such a question as, "Is man becoming more humanized?"

In relation to the potential listening audience, the question should be:

INTERESTING/ The question should be related to the interests of a large segment of the probable audience, and in the case of a policy question should stimulate their thinking on a problem vital to most of them.

WORTHWHILE/ The discussion resulting from the question should be worthy of the time and attention that listeners devote to it.

In relation to the communicating participants, the question should be one in which they have:

INVOLVEMENT/ It should be a question in which they have interest, one that matters to them. Most college students feel greater involvement in the question, "How can fraternities be improved?" than in the question, "In what ways should the rediscount rate be manipulated?"

COMPETENCE/ The question should be suited to their abilities, either because of experience and special knowledge acquired previously, or because of detailed study in preparation for this particular appearance. Few participants would be competent to discuss, "Under what conditions is it possible for man to survive on Mars?"

Note that the question to be selected must be one in which the interests of the participants and the listening audience coincide with the state of current affairs. A significant public problem that is interesting and worthwhile for the potential audience may not be one in which the available participants are competent or in which they feel involved.

Selecting the question, whether for closedgroup or public discussion, involves a careful judgment made with all these factors involved. In a situation, for example, where students are planning a closedgroup, decision-making conference involving representatives from student government, faculty, and administration on the crowded conditions caused by automobiles on campus, the following questions could be proposed by interested participants:

A. Should the parking problem in the campus area be solved?
B. Should student automobiles be barred from the campus area?
C. What should the university do about parking in the campus area?
D. What can be done to provide more parking spaces in the campus area?
E. Are there more automobiles than parking spaces in the campus area?

Proposal A would probably be rejected first since discussion of it is unnecessary; everyone would answer the question immediately in the same way. Proposal E is a matter for research; an individual could learn this fact and report it to the group as part of a discussion about a policy in regard to parking. The other three proposals are possible questions for profitable discussion and the selection will depend on the current situation and the extent to which the planners want to open up the whole problem. Proposal C is the broadest. It asks an open-ended question allowing consideration of a wide range of alternative solutions. Proposal B asks only about the wisdom of one limited solution to the problem, barring student cars. Proposal D also assumes that some decisions are unacceptable, such as keeping some or all automobiles away from campus, and asks only how to solve the problem of providing additional parking spaces.

Narrowing and Limiting

Questions selected must not be so broad that they encompass almost endless possibilities. Such questions as these are too broad: "What steps can be taken to promote interest of young people in world affairs?" "What additional services can the university provide for students?"

The question should be narrowed and limited to the time available for discussion. A good question is, "What steps, if any, should be taken to ease East-West tensions?" It would be possible, however, to spend months or even years discussing this question. Planners of a 40-minute discussion should limit themselves to a tiny portion of this larger problem. A narrower limitation would be, "Should the United States seek renewed relations with Cuba?" Even this question is complex for a short discussion. Perhaps a more realistic limitation for a short discussion would be: "Should the United States allow businesses to trade with Cuba?" Further narrowing could be achieved by limiting the question to trade in nonmilitary merchandise.

Also, the question should be limited to a single problem; it should not be double-barreled: "Should the United States nationalize the railroads and the coal mines?" It is difficult enough to discuss one complex problem at a time.

Wording the Question

A final requirement in planning for a discussion topic is wording of the question. The wording should be:

OPEN TO ALTERNATIVE ANSWERS/ Preferably, the question should be phrased so that it cannot be answered "yes" or "no." It is not always possible to avoid the "yes" or "no" phrasing, but the many-sided question is usually more satisfactory for discussion. Some questions are unacceptable because if taken literally they could be answered in one word and the discussion would be over: "Should students study more?" The answer is "yes." A better phrasing would be: "To what extent are students interested in academic achievement?" A "yes" or "no" question that is somewhat better is, "Is there a difference in the quality of undergraduate education offered by small colleges and large universities?"

Sponsors who phrase a "yes" or "no" question usually are interested in a much more complex answer than an affirmative or negative response. If a question were phrased, "Are examinations desirable?" the participants would probably discuss some such question as, "Under what conditions do examinations contribute to the educational development of students?" It is clear that it would be desirable to phrase the question this way in the first place.

Some questions, of course, can be phrased most directly as "yes" or "no" questions. For example, there is no desirable alternative to the kind of policy question that asks about a change in a particular law such as, "Should capital punishment be abolished?" In some situations this is also the best way to narrow a problem to manageable proportions. If a group does not have time to discuss the question, "What policy should be applied in cases of student dishonesty?" it may be wise to discuss the more limited "yes" or "no" question, "Should students be expelled for copying during final examinations?" Many closedgroups in real situations spend most of their time answering such specific questions rather than broader, more philosophical policy matters.

CLEAR/ A statement that persists among military men is that any order that can be misunderstood will be misunderstood. This statement can certainly be applied to discussion questions; if they can be misunderstood, someone in the group will misunderstand them. Questions should be worded clearly; vagueness must be avoided. What is meant by the question, "Should the United States adopt the policy of striking the enemy first?" Or this question: "Is the trend toward scientific education progress?" The wording here must be clarified or the discussion will be out of focus from the beginning. If the first question is asking about preventive war, it should be worded to ask: "Should the United States initiate immediately a preventive war against nation X?" As Wendell Johnson has said, "Human energy is never more extravagantly wasted than in the persistent effort to answer conclusively questions that are vague and meaningless."[1]

It is extremely important that the question be worded 'unambiguously. It should not be interpretable in two or more different ways. The question, "Should we elect a Democrat as our next President?" is satisfactory for discussion except that the word *Democrat* invites quibbling because of the "Democrat-democrat" possibility. This difficulty can be easily avoided by careful wording.

UNBIASED/ The question should be impartially worded. It should not suggest the bias of those who worded it: "Should the antilabor right-to-work laws be repealed?" Value judgments should be left to the participants; members should be given a fair wording at the beginning. Also, the wording should not suggest the hoped-for outcome: "Wouldn't you agree that University X is the best university in its conference?"

CONCISE/ Since participants and, in the case of public discussion, the listening audience need to grasp the question and keep it in mind throughout the discussion, it should be worded efficiently and succinctly. Doubtless this example is exaggerated, but certainly anyone involved would be discouraged with this wording: "Would a lowering of personal income taxes or of corporation taxes and a shift in the rediscount rate controlled by the Federal Reserve Board be effective deterrents for control of recessionary tendencies in our economy, or are these proposals just impractical measures which sound good superficially?" This question was actually proposed as a subject for discussion.

SECURING RESOURCE MATERIALS

It is essential that members of a discussion group be well informed and it is not enough that they have general knowledge and competence; they must understand thoroughly and have concrete, recent facts on the specific problem to be discussed. Thus members must produce a bibliography and read the sources vital to becoming informed.

One member may locate books on the subject, another magazine articles,

[1] Wendell Johnson, *People in Quandries*, New York: Harper & Row, 1946, p. 55.

and so on, although there are some sources that every member should read. Being well informed is so important that Chapter 5 is devoted to this aspect of preparing for discussion.

DRAWING UP A LEADER'S OUTLINE

Planners must draw up a satisfactory outline for guiding discussion on the problem. They must decide whether to distribute copies to all participants in advance. In some situations, it may be constructive to bring members together early in the planning stage and ask them to suggest questions for the outline. Most of the time, however, one or two members can put the outline into final form more efficiently.

Some designated leaders prefer to distribute in advance a rough draft or tentative skeleton of the outline, which can serve as a guide for study. Then, before the actual discussion, they revise the outline, insert more detailed questions, use fresh wordings, and in other ways produce a series of questions that will be new and stimulating, thus promoting more spontaneous discussion. One of the dangers of using a long-prepared, static outline is that leader and members will plod through it mechanically, stifling creative thinking.

Drawing up a guiding outline is a vital phase in preparation. Further suggestions about this part of the leadership responsibility are offered in Chapter 12.

PLANNING PHYSICAL ARRANGEMENTS

Another planning responsibility is to arrange the physical surroundings in which the discussion will occur. Thought should be given to time of day, meeting room, and such obvious aspects of physical comfort as adequate light, heat, and ventilation. Some hours of the day are more conducive to active thinking than others, although some kinds of closedgroup informality can best be achieved around a luncheon or dinner table. Participants should be comfortable, but not extremely so; a group cannot do its most efficient thinking if, for example, members are given an open invitation to relax as they might if seated in soft, overstuffed lounge chairs. A comfortable straight-backed chair with padded seat is preferable. Members are usually more productive when seated at a table where they can take notes and have reference materials easily accessible.

As everyone knows, members should be seated facing each other. Ideally, every participant should be located so that he can look directly at each other person without turning his chair. This arrangement is not easy to achieve, and may explain the popularity of the round table notion, although round tables are not commonly available. When a group is seated at a rectangular table, persons located on the sides cannot face everyone at once:

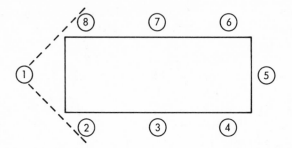

Member 3 cannot look at 2 and 4 at the same time. Nevertheless, he can turn from 2 to address 4 or 5 without turning his chair.

With this arrangement, the designated leader should seat himself at position number 1 or 5, since he can then face everyone directly, although he still cannot look every person in the eye at the same time. He can turn from number 8 to 2 with only about a 90° movement of his head; the shift to face any others is even less. Surprisingly, from the leader's position, the angle of shift is greater at a round table when he turns from the person on his right to the one on his left. The angle would approximate what it is in the diagram if the leader were seated at position 3. The disadvantage with a rectangular table is that only members 1 and 5 have a good view of everyone simultaneously. At a round table, every member has as direct a view of everyone else as it is possible to provide when there are more than three persons in the group.

For public discussion, participants should obviously be seated so that they face the listening audience directly:

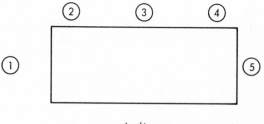

Audience

Here the designated leader will usually sit at position 3 in order to be in the center, and to keep the audience clearly in view. Some leaders prefer positions 1 or 5 so that they can directly face all their panel members at once, but a chairman at position 1 is required to turn his head almost 180° when he shifts his gaze from the audience to member 2. A better arrangement can be achieved by using two tables placed at an angle, with the chairman at the center:

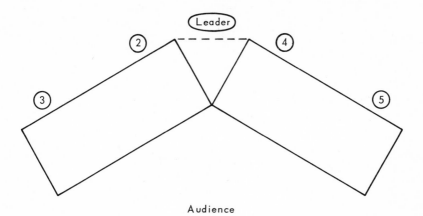

Audience

More important than such rather obvious matters as furniture arrangement and temperature control is the question of which members to place where, in relation to each other and the leader. One consideration is power structure within the group. Since the designated leader plays an influential role, it is usually undesirable to place the most powerful persons next to the leader. Such a concentration of highs will make it even harder for low-status persons to speak up or to disagree, especially if the highs seem to take similar positions. Another consideration is the talkativeness of members. A person known to be a high participator can be placed in the least desirable physical location and he will probably take an active part just the same, while the timid, shy, or reluctant communicator can be placed in a prominent position, such as one near the leader, where talking is easier.

Studies of physical arrangements in discussion indicate a relationship between seating position and communicative interaction. When members are seated in a circle they tend to talk more readily to those opposite than those next to them, at least in some kinds of situations. When a rectangular table is used, those who become high participators and who may emerge as leaders tend to choose the ends of the table or a central position. Those who talk least are inclined to take seats at the corners.[2]

DECIDING ON A PREDISCUSSION MEETING

Whether a prediscussion meeting will be necessary and fruitful obviously depends on many factors: time available, complexity of the problem, competencies of participants, and nature and importance of the discussion, among others. Those responsible for planning should at least consider a prediscus-

[2] A. Paul Hare and Robert F. Bales, "Seating Position and Small Group Interaction," Hare, Borgatta, and Bales, *Small Groups: Studies in Social Interaction*, rev. ed., New York: Alfred A. Knopf, 1965, pp. 427–33.

sion meeting. It is usually more necessary for public than for closedgroup discussions.

A word of caution is necessary here. Members may profitably meet, in most cases, to get acquainted, share bibliographical information, suggest questions for the outline, and in other ways discuss preparations, but they must not hold a rehearsal as actors rehearse a play. Even for public discussion, a trial run produced precisely as it is to be offered later will result in stereotyped, uninspired, unstimulating interaction.

PLANNING IN ACTUAL SITUATIONS

What has been said about preparing for classroom discussion could for the most part be applied to planning in real closedgroup situations. The stages can be repeated here in order to emphasize matters especially important in actual circumstances outside the classroom.

Analyzing Requirements

If a closedgroup is to face multiple problems, as will usually be the case, an agenda is needed. This will list the problems to come up and the order of considering them. For an item of great importance, participants and leadership must be taken into account, the question recognized and stated, resource material secured, guiding outline drawn up, physical arrangements planned, and any prediscussion meetings arranged.

The care and extent of advanced planning required will be determined by a number of factors, such as the nature of the group and the persons involved, the nature of the task, and the situation. If an executive committee responsible for a manufacturing plant meets every two or three days and handles largely routine decisions, little planning may be required for a particular meeting. Members are familiar with each other and each participant is an expert in the area he represents as a decision-maker, whether in sales, engineering, production, or finance.

In contrast, a special conference of executive vice presidents from the company's plants located throughout the country may require meticulous planning for success. If an executive is designated as leader for the conference he must also decide to what extent he should involve other participants in the preparation stages.

Identifying Participants and Leadership

The membership of most real groups is predetermined, and planners are not responsible for choosing and inviting persons to participate. For some closedgroup discussions, however, selecting the participants is necessary. They will be chosen for knowledge of and interest in the problem, and for special competence in communication and discussion.

The mayors of two adjoining cities could plan a conference to iron out some jurisdictional disputes in the areas of their common border. They must decide who in addition to themselves should attend. Which officials were included would depend on the nature of the disputes and their individual competencies. If the disputes involved enforcing traffic regulations on streets dividing the cities, they would obviously consider their chiefs of police and perhaps their city engineers and directors of traffic. Among the available officers who could be invited, however, they may choose participants according to competence. Perhaps the police chiefs could not be gracefully excluded, but any others might be added only if they could be expected to make a particularly helpful contribution.

It is difficult to suggest more specific criteria of participant selection but two others may be of some use to planners. In general, invited participants should not be persons who have identical views and backgrounds. If they already agree, or if they say much the same things in explaining the situation, then the discussion will be of minimum value and perhaps is unnecessary or useless. Certainly there will be little stimulation for participants. A second suggestion more or less balances this one: neither should those chosen disagree so violently or hold such rigid opinions that they find it difficult even to listen to other views.

Usually continuing closedgroups have a designated leader, but often a group meeting for one or two sessions will elect a leader from among the participants after they assemble. In this event, however, the person chosen will be handicapped in having almost no time for advanced planning.

IDENTIFYING AND WORDING THE QUESTION

In real groups, problems usually arise from the functioning of the group; are internal to the operation, task, or responsibility of the group; or grow out of social, economic, or political circumstances or specific events outside the group that are related to its interests and functions. Here the challenge is to recognize what is the real question for discussion. A group may lose much time in a discussion unless it recognizes the question that must be answered. Prior to the discussion, preferably, or certainly early in the discussion, the group must identify the real question.

Suppose that a board of directors has just learned during a meeting that the night before, burglars, probably youngsters, broke into the plant and poured motor oil over machinery and office equipment. The board has a problem and much lively talk will result. A fascinating half-hour may be consumed in considering any one of these questions: What is wrong with our youngsters these days? Have the American people lost all respect for property rights? What satisfaction do people get from doing malicious damage? Don't the schools train young people to know right from wrong? Why can't parents keep their children out of mischief? Why can't the police lock up all the burglars? These questions are interesting, but only indirectly related to the board's problem. The discussion will be of minimum value unless the group concentrates on a question or questions directly relevant to the group. Members can weigh the relevancy of questions by applying tests such as these:

Does this group need an answer to this question? Questions to be fruitful must be related to the group's interests and functions. The board of directors may be curious about the role of parents, schools, and police in preventing juvenile crime, but these matters are of indirect concern. Of more immediate concern to the board are questions such as these: What changes, if any, should be made in present arrangements for protecting the plant at night? Should additional men be assigned to the night watch crew?

Is this group competent to answer this question? Groups can waste happy hours considering questions that they cannot be expected to answer. The matter of police efficiency in locking up burglars is a problem for penologists and sociologists. The question, "What satisfaction do people get from doing malicious damage?" must be answered, if it can be answered, by psychologists and psychiatrists. The board of directors cannot profitably spend time discussing such questions.

Does this group have power to act upon the decisions agreed upon, or is it in a position to recommend to a group that does have power to act? The board of directors should not spend time discussing whether the police department should try harder to apprehend burglars and how policemen should be deployed to achieve increased vigilance. Rather, the board should consider whether it should recommend to the police department that it provide increased protection. This board cannot profitably decide what parents, schools, or other agencies should do since it is in a position only to recommend policy to other groups. Similarly, the National Security Council of the United Nations should not discuss, "What should be Russian foreign policy toward Hungary?" This group cannot set Russian policy nor would the Kremlin be influenced by this group's recommendations.

Is this question one that requires collective thinking and interaction of the group, or could it be answered more adequately by research or by a single executive? The board's discussion will be inefficient if it asks, "Was the watchman asleep last night?" or "How did the burglars get inside the plant?" These questions must be answered by investigation, and usually such queries can most efficiently be pursued by a single individual. Probably the board would direct an executive to investigate and recommend an answer to a question such as, "Should the chief of the night crew be replaced?"

Can the group answer this question in the time available? The requirements here are obvious. If the question is crucial, additional sessions must be scheduled, or a subgroup must be made responsible, or the question must be divided into more limited components, or some other method must be found for deciding.

Wording the Question

Phrasing and wording the question that must be answered requires the same kind of care already considered in connection with planning classroom discussions. The biggest difference comes in the amount of time available for planning. Sometimes a real group can announce its agenda in advance. A college executive committee, for example, can announce that at its next meeting it will decide whether to adopt a pass-fail grading system. Much of the time, however, questions that must be answered emerge from the discussion. Whoever is responsible for leadership must recognize and state the question on a moment's notice. If a designated leader words the question ambiguously or unclearly, he will waste the group's time.

Securing Resource Materials

Even experts who work constantly on a general subject must often read and prepare carefully for maximum contribution to a particular discussion. A designated leader of a closedgroup such as an executive committee or board of directors may distribute prior to a vital discussion a bibliography of recommended sources or a limited number of books and pamphlets on the problem.

If a board is to discuss the annual report, to take a limited example, it is important that each member read it carefully in advance; much time can be consumed at the meeting reading it orally or answering questions about its content.

Other Planning

The remaining preparation tasks faced by planners of discussions in actual groups are quite similar to those already explained for classroom practice sessions. For a particular meeting, the designated leader should draw up an agenda of all matters to come up as well as a guiding outline for those problems complex enough to require extensive discussion. Physical arrangements must be planned and prediscussion meetings held when one or more would be helpful. When participants are not well acquainted with each other, an informal get-together in advance, perhaps at a coffee session, can decrease tension, increase confidence, change attitudes toward the importance of the forthcoming discussion, and contribute to the development of later cohesiveness.

Whether a particular discussion is a classroom exercise or an international conference involving war or peace, careful planning is important to a successful outcome. Invariable rules cannot be supplied but those responsible are wise to give these matters of preparation their close attention, making whatever adaptations seem desirable in a particular situation. Later chapters of this book hopefully will contribute to further understanding of these procedures.

SUPPLEMENTARY READING

Barnlund, Dean C., and Haiman, Franklyn S., *The Dynamics of Discussion*, Boston: Houghton Mifflin, 1960, Chapter 4.

Braden, Waldo W., and Brandenburg, Earnest, *Oral Decision-Making*, New York: Harper & Row, 1955, pp. 38–46.

Collins, Barry E. and Guetzkow, Harold, *A Social Psychology of Group Processes for Decision-Making*, New York: John Wiley & Sons, 1964, pp. 88–106.

Maier, Norman R. F., *Problem-Solving Discussions and Conferences*, New York: McGraw-Hill, 1963, Chapter 3.

QUESTIONS AND EXERCISES

1. Write a paper in which you explain the differences you would expect to encounter in planning for a closedgroup as contrasted with a public discussion.
2. What are the arguments for and against holding prediscussion meetings?
3. Explain how you would take into account in planning a particular discussion the fact that two participants are extremely influential and powerful while three others are new members of the group who feel inadequate.
4. Under what conditions would you advise the designated leader of an actual group such as the City Council to write out a guiding outline for discussion of a particular problem. Be specific.
5. Go through all the examples of discussion questions mentioned in this chapter. Classify each one into (a) those concerned with problems at local, state, national, or international level; and (b) those that are political, economic, social, or educational in nature. Then rewrite each question to change it from a decision-making to an informational question, or vice versa.
6. The following questions have been proposed for discussion by a panel of college students; the type of discussion is to be problem-solving and the program is to be televised regionally. Each discussion is to be 45 minutes in length. Some of these questions are satisfactory and some are not. Evaluate them by applying the requirements for adequate discussion questions.
   a. The federal government should provide help, through legislation, to meet future demands for more and better educational facilities.
   b. Should students in this college with an "A" in a course prior to the final examination be exempted from the final examination?

    c. Does Russia fit into the picture of world affairs?

    d. Should the university committee on student affairs be so dominated by the faculty?

    e. What should be done to secure peace?

    f. What action, if any, should be taken to alleviate the parking problem on this campus?

    g. Should there be high taxes on economy?

    h. How can the United States best promote friendly relations with the newer nations of Africa?

7. For a Northwestern *Reviewing Stand* broadcast, the general discussion question was "Should Married Women Work?" The moderator, Dean James H. McBurney, began the program by explaining that several complaints had been received about the wording of the question. One was that the wording implied that some married women do not work. Dean McBurney asked if the group's primary concern was with "married women who are working outside the home." One participant wanted it narrowed even more because some wives have young children, others are the sole supporters of dependents where the husband is not present or is unable to work, etc., and each set of circumstances poses a different problem. Suggest a rewording of this general question that is more concrete and less ambiguous; defend your wording. Compose a number of subquestions that will elicit discussion of the major aspects of the problem.

8. Suppose that the president of the university or college has called you, as a campus leader, to his office. He explains to you his great concern with the symptoms of poor student attitude toward education: student enthusiasm for carnivals, stunt shows, dances, and similar nonacademic pursuits, and student disinterest in classwork, library study, and special honors for distinguished academic achievement; student interest in grade-point averages without particular interest in the acquisition of knowledge and understanding. The president asks you to plan and lead a closedgroup, problem-solving discussion using both faculty and student participants; he specifies that he wants from this group specific recommendations for improving the situation.

    a. Frame a satisfactory question for this discussion.

    b. Defend the question you propose and its wording in light of the characteristics of a satisfactory discussion question.

9. Bring to class three questions for discussion on problems of public concern at each of the following levels: (*a*) local, (*b*) state, (*c*) national, and (*d*) international.

10. Propose some satisfactory and some unsatisfactory questions for discussion and explain why they do or do not meet the tests of good questions.

11. Choose a discussion program regularly broadcast by radio or television

and listen to it for a period of time. Write a paper in which you evaluate the series of questions selected for discussion.

12. Prepare a 3-minute speech telling the class what, in your opinion, is the greatest single problem faced by the people of the United States today. From this general question or problem, suggest specific questions for group discussion.

13. Examples of discussion questions can be seen in these topics for symposium-panel-forum discussions. Hold a series of discussion programs utilizing each of these topics. A speaker talks on each of the subquestions for a specified time. Then all participants (five plus a chairman) sit around a table and hold a panel discussion on the general question, attempting to reconcile divergent views expressed in the symposium speeches. Finally the audience is invited to take part.

A. In what ways should the quality of American public high schools be improved?
   1. Should the quality of our teachers be improved?
   2. Should the quality of our curricula be improved?
   3. Should the quality of our physical plants be improved?
   4. Should the essential features of the British educational system be adopted?
   5. Should the essential features of the Russian educational system be adopted?

B. In what ways should we as a nation deal with unemployment?
   1. Should the states improve their unemployment compensation programs?
   2. Should the federal government supplement state unemployment compensation payments?
   3. Should the federal government reduce individual and corporate income taxes to stimulate the economy?
   4. Should state and federal governments plan large public-works expenditures to coincide with periods of increased unemployment?
   5. Should the federal government rely upon the manipulation of interest and rediscount rates by the Federal Reserve Board as the method of maintaining economic balance?

C. In what ways should we deal with the problem of crimes committed by children under twenty?
   1. Should parents be punished for the crimes of their minor children?
   2. Should high school students who are chronic and serious disciplinary problems be placed in special schools?
   3. Should the state legislatures require every county to employ an adequate psychiatric staff to counsel youthful criminals?

4. Should newspapers print the names of juvenile offenders as a deterrent to themselves and others?

5. Should youthful offenders be given stiffer punishment?

D. What initiative should the United States take to ease East-West tensions?

1. Should the United States negotiate directly with Russia?

2. Should the United States and the major western countries press for an immediate summit conference?

3. Should the United States invite the world's neutral nations to mediate East-West disagreements?

4. Should the United States attempt to reduce East-West tensions primarily through United Nation's machinery?

5. Should the United States extend diplomatic recognition to Communist China?

Chapter 5
SECURING AND USING INFORMATION

Discussion should not be a pooling of ignorance. Nothing constructive can result simply from collective group thought if the thinking consists of unsupported opinions. An uninformed group will achieve a worthless product; an uninformed individual will contribute to an equally worthless product, and a discussion under these conditions is a waste of time.

Occasionally, such a remark as this is overheard: "It's only a discussion, so we won't have to prepare for it." Some individuals feel they can hide their ignorance within the group, that they can participate even though empty-headed, and that something worthwhile will somehow emerge because there are several people sharing responsibility. It is hard to explain why the security of numbers furnishes a comfortable feeling of irresponsibility, when the same individual, if invited to make a speech at the meeting, would be terrified at the thought of appearing without careful preparation.

Whatever the source of this misleading notion, it should be stated emphatically that careful and thorough preparation is absolutely essential to fruitful discussion. Without relevant facts and specific information, the outcome will not be sound nor will it be respected and accepted by others outside the group who are interested in it. Without facts the group will not often make satisfactory progress toward agreement. Each individual in the group must take upon himself the responsibility for becoming well informed prior to the discussion.

A study conducted at the University of Michigan[1] suggests that the use of facts may be even more important in some discussion situations than in others. It involved careful observation and ratings of seventy-two decision-making conferences in business and government groups of five to twenty participants and a designated chairman. Measures were made of two kinds of conflict: substantive conflict, consisting of the number of supportive comments made contrasted with the number of disagreements expressed; and affective conflict, defined as the extent to which trained observers noted member frustrations or interpersonal clashes. Estimates also were made of the amount of consensus resulting from the discussion.

---

[1] Reported in Barry E. Collins and H. Guetzkow, *A Social Psychology of Group Processes for Decision-Making*, New York: John Wiley & Sons, 1964, pp. 106–19.

For groups in substantive conflict, the groups having more factual knowledge available and those making more extensive use of the facts and the background experience of participants were more likely to resolve their conflicts and reach consensus. Significantly, also, the chairmen of groups that experienced high substantive conflict but went on to reach consensus worked much harder at the task of making use of information than did chairmen where groups did not reach agreement. The chairmen who achieved consensus made three times as many attempts to elicit factual information from participants.

Use of facts did not give the same results for groups in affective, or interpersonal conflict. In these groups, consensus was related to partial withdrawal from the total task by concentrating on simpler agenda items, to lack of personal interest in the outcome, and other factors.

There were many other important matters investigated in this Michigan study and we will again refer to it in later chapters. What we should note from this careful field study is the confirmation of the observations all of us have made: when we disagree about a policy, we sometimes can resolve our differences by looking at the facts. Certainly in cases where information is clearly needed, we cannot progress beyond our differences until we obtain the information.

SOURCES OF INFORMATION

The college student is already familiar with the basic sources of information and we should not in this kind of book take time for a complete treatment of research methods. On the other hand, members of a discussion group have a collective responsibility to become thoroughly informed and hence should overlook no possible sources of increased understanding. What we will do in this chapter, then, is to review the basic sources of information in order to help members check on every possibility. Then we can treat more directly the process of securing information on particular discussion problems before turning to the intelligent use of facts.

Personal Knowledge

Most discussions, and especially those which take place in closedgroups, concern problems with which the member participating has had some acquaintance and knowledge. A member of a committee that must plan this semester's house dance should recall the plans for and the successful features of last year's dance. The problem here is to recall accurately the relevant facts. It is wise for the member, as part of his preparation, to write out systematically on separate cards or sheets the items of his personal knowledge that will help the group to answer the essential questions.

When the participant can bring to bear upon a problem some of his own experiences of the past, he will talk with enthusiasm and involvement. It is also likely that each member's background has been unique and thus for a member to overlook any past experience that would be helpful is to deprive the group of a bit of information that can come only from this one source.

Observation

In preparation for discussion on some topics, members may be able to make a special observation of relevant conditions. In this event, too, there is gain from the member's feeling that he has become personally involved in the problem. He will usually report on his observations with enthusiasm and for him the problem has become more vivid. Of course, personal observation is limited to certain kinds of problems. If the discussion concerns the campus parking problem, members will benefit from seeing the crowded conditions for themselves and perhaps even visiting parking lots at certain times to count vacant spaces. However, members must resist the temptation to organize a large-scale research project. It would be possible to make such thorough observations of all the parking areas and use up so much time that other aspects of preparation would be neglected.

A good decision will involve much more than can be learned through observation of the physical surroundings. Observations should be confined to the search for information that can be learned most readily and swiftly in this way. If extensive observation would be required, it would be better to interview an expert who had been observing the parking situation over a long period of time.

If the group feels it will benefit from making personal observations, members must keep in mind three requirements for acceptable investigation. The first is seeing accurately. The observer must place himself in a position to observe and spend sufficient time on the scene to see exactly what is there. Another essential is reporting accurately. This requisite involves exact use of words. The observer must be able to report so precisely that listeners who did not see will understand what was witnessed. A third requirement is reporting fairly. The observer must attempt to describe what he saw without regard to whether he liked what he saw. If he favors federal aid to education and if he has observed the operation of a federal program in the local schools, he must be careful not to make his report sound more favorable than the conditions warrant. After he has reported on the situation accurately and fairly, of course, he is free to draw any conclusions from the facts just as other members can introduce their own opinions in response.

Interview

A very valuable source of information for many discussion groups is the interview with persons who are in a position to know pertinent facts. Students preparing for a discussion on penalties for violations of automobile regulations probably would gather most of their information by talking with the director of traffic and parking, members of the discipline committee, and students who had violated the regulations.

A number of cautions must be kept in mind in connection with interviewing. Not every person in an official position knows enough about a particular problem to be worth the time and thought required for a good interview. Also a person in a position to know may not have been on that particular job long enough to answer the questions. In learning about parking violations, for example, the investigator may go to the chief of police and find that he only carries out instructions for issuing tickets and knows nothing about reasons for policy. The director of traffic and parking may be responsible for policy but may be so new in the job that he has not yet learned why the regulations are as they are. Thus the investigator should make some discreet inquiries about who knows the most about what before he uses up investigation time.

Another caution is that the interview should be planned carefully in order to be courteous and also productive. The interviewer should ask for an appointment at a convenient time, specify the nature of his visit, and respect time limits established in advance. He should plan his questions carefully and should not waste time by probing outside the authority's competence. Questions should deal directly with the area of expert knowledge. Especially important is to avoid asking for information that can be obtained by reading what the authority has written or that is readily available in printed sources.

A special kind of pencil and paper interview is the public opinion poll or survey. If a group is discussing academic study habits or conditions, it may be useful to ask members of a housing group to fill out a survey giving the hours they study, the places they study, and similar information. It must be remembered that formulating opinion questions and sampling questionnaires is a high-level skill and the student may need expert guidance in the use of this technique. Sometimes the investigator determines the outcome of a poll by careless wording of questions.

General Reading

The ideal discussion participant is the person who is well informed in a general sense. He reads one or two good newspapers every day and perhaps a weekly news magazine, too. In an industrial setting, he is the executive who reads carefully the publications of the company and materials in his field as they cross his desk. While preparing for a particular discussion, he will be able to find quickly up-to-date printed materials that are relevant and which he recalls from his general reading.

Listening

In the same sense that the alert person reads widely, the discusser should profit from his general listening. Public programs broadcast by radio or television, lectures and meetings, and conversations with informed friends will supply information that may be useful in future discussions.

Library Research

The most important single source of information, of course, is the library. The discusser must be proficient in locating materials of many different kinds.

Unless the problem is of recent origin he should begin by searching for books in the card catalog. This index of all books housed in the library lists each book in three different places, by author, book title, and subject. The discusser usually begins with a topic and thus will start by looking at subject cards. For instance, if the question is, "Should youthful criminals be given stiffer punishment?" he should look for such subjects as "Juvenile Crime," "Juvenile Delinquency," "Courts, Juvenile," and "Punishment." After the last card in one of such a series of cards, will sometimes be this entry: "See also: "Street Corner Gangs"; "Reform Schools"; etc.

Imagination must be used in thinking of specific headings that may lead to books on the topic. The precise wording of the key phrase in a discussion question may not be one that is indexed in the card catalog. The library will have a book or more on almost any subject that has existed for any length of time. The problem is to search imaginatively.

In searching for books it is important to conserve time and thus to examine with some care each card in the card catalog that looks promising. The card will often list a partial table of contents or the primary section headings of the book. When the researcher has time only to examine a limited number of books, he can frequently identify the best ones at this stage without having to check all of them out of the library.

The card catalog is not the only guide to books on a discussion question. In reading articles or books on the subject the alert researcher will see references to other books that may prove even more valuable than those he located on his own. From this source he can tell that the books are directly relevant and often he can learn something of their content.

REFERENCE WORKS/ Useful as sources of general information are encyclopedias such as the *Britannica* or the *Americana* and their annual yearbook supplements. To begin learning about treatment of juvenile offenders, for example, the discusser may read first a general article in a good encyclopedia on juvenile courts or children's courts. At the end of a major article there usually is a short list of excellent references on the subject.

Even more valuable for many purposes are special reference works such as the *Encyclopedia of the Social Sciences*; encyclopedias on religions, education, and other special subjects; and dictionaries, specialized yearbooks, and atlases.

Biographical information is at times important to the discusser. *Who's Who* and *Who's Who in America* are familiar. There are also numerous biographical dictionaries for well-known persons in a particular state or region, and in specialized fields such as those listed in *American Men of Science, Leaders in Education, Directory of American Scholars,* and *Who's Who in Engineering.* When a discussion group is evaluating a proposal by some authority it is helpful to know who he is and what his qualifications are. For some kinds of subjects especially the opinions of experts form the best guides for judgment by a group. If a group were discussing questions such as, "What evidence is there for a belief in flying saucers?" or "Can life as we know it exist on Mars?" expert opinion would be the controlling information; in such cases the group should learn about the background of each alleged expert.

MAGAZINES/ Since most discussions deal with current problems, magazine articles are often the best sources of up-to-the-minute information. To locate helpful articles quickly, the researcher must use indexes to periodicals.

Magazine articles appearing in large-circulation magazines such as *Time, Atlantic Monthly*, and *The Saturday Evening Post*, are indexed by author and subject in the *Reader's Guide to Periodical Literature*. Magazine articles in specialized fields, which appear in journals for that specialty, are indexed in such publications as *Agricultural Index, Education Index*, and *Industrial Arts Index*. When preparing for discussion of a particular topic, it is efficient first to check *Reader's Guide* for possible articles of a general nature, and then to find out whether there is a specialized index for the field from which the question is drawn. If there is none, it may be possible to locate specialized magazines for that field; the periodicals themselves are likely to have an index appearing once or twice a year.

Periodical indexes are issued once a month and then combined into annual volumes. Older magazine articles are listed in *Poole's Index* and *Nineteenth Century Reader's Guide*. There are also specialized indexes to periodical materials such as *Biological Abstracts, Business Periodicals Index, Engineering Index*, and *Psychological Abstracts*. Some of these, as the names suggest, contain abstracted information as well as references to articles.

PAMPHLETS/ Pamphlet materials are somewhat harder to locate than are books and magazine articles. However, there are two dependable indexes listing many of these publications. *Public Affairs Information Service* lists publications of all kinds, including pamphlets, that deal with current problems in public affairs. H. W. Wilson Company's *Vertical File* also indexes pamphlets. The difficulty comes in finding these ephemeral materials in a particular library or in having time to order copies. The indexes give names and addresses of organizations that have published each pamphlet, along with the price if a charge is made. Cost is usually nominal and many are supplied free upon request to the sponsoring organization.

Special interest groups publish materials on many topics. Names and addresses of such organizations can be obtained from directories such as the *Guide to Public Affairs Organizations*, the *World Almanac*, and the U.S. Department of Commerce publication, *Trade and Professional Associations of the United States*. If a group were discussing hospitalization insurance, for instance, an inquiry to the American Medical Association would probably bring a supply of relevant pamphlet materials.

The discusser must be a careful reader of such materials. They are almost always published to promote the interests of the organization paying the printing bill and must be evaluated in that light. However, they often contain much accurate and useful information. The reader must separate the helpful facts from the special interest pleadings.

GOVERNMENT PUBLICATIONS/ Official publications prepared by government officials can sometimes be valuable sources of information. The researcher should be especially familiar with the *Congressional Record*, which contains official proceedings and speeches in both houses of Congress and an amazing accumulation of articles in the appendix. Committees of the two houses hold extensive hearings on a large variety of subjects; published transcripts of committee hearings are storehouses of information, expert testimony, and opinion.

Other government publications can be located through a monthly catalog of *United States Government Publications.*

STATISTICAL INFORMATION/ Facts in the form of statistical tables can be vital in some discussions. Fortunately this kind of information is readily available in many different places. The U.S. Department of Commerce issues an *Abstract of the Census* and the *Statistical Abstract of the United States*, which contain a variety of facts on population, education, business, and so on. This department also publishes information on domestic and foreign trade in its monthly *Survey of Current Business*. The Department of Labor has a similar publication, *Monthly Labor Review*, giving facts on employment and similar matters. Statistical data of various kinds appear in such popular periodicals as *World Almanac* and *Information Please Almanac*. *Statesman's Year Book* supplies much statistical information on the nations of the world.

These are the major types of printed materials available in libraries. The careful group preparing for a discussion will check this list and make sure that no fruitful source is overlooked. Members must not only be familiar with the kinds of information to be gleaned from each of these sources, but also they must know where such materials are located in their particular library and be able to use them quickly, with a minimum of wasted effort.

SEARCHING FOR INFORMATION

A discussion group is often faced with the task of becoming well informed on a complex problem in a short time. Unfortunately, the shortage of time seems to be almost a universal characteristic in discussion. The parent group asks a committee to have a report in two weeks; a city council meets every Monday evening and considers several complicated matters each time—and in between members are busy making a living. A public discussion is held while the problem is current. Preparation time for discussion is nearly always shorter than the members would wish.

Compensating somewhat for this handicap is the gain from a group's opportunity to divide the labor of collecting information. To mention this approach is not to suggest that any member can thereby abdicate his responsibility for becoming informed. However, a division of labor can eliminate unnecessary duplication of effort and make preparation more efficient. It should be emphasized that all members must be informed and that there are certain sources that all should consult, so there will be a basis for common understanding of the problem.

If members have time to do so, one possibility for proceeding would be for the group to meet early and agree on the most promising sources of information. One person could be assigned the task of making a personal observation of particularly relevant conditions. Another member or two might agree to interview persons with pertinent knowledge. Others could divide up the various library sources; they could pool the bibliography items they discover from consulting the various indexes.

Ideally, at this point, the group should meet again and with the collective bibliography in hand, agree on the books and articles that every member of the group must read in common. At this meeting, those who observed and interviewed might distribute written reports of what they learned.

By sharing responsibility for research in this way, the group will be assured of having a core of understanding possessed by everyone and also of collecting a wider range of information than could be assembled by each working alone in the limited time available.

Collins and Guetzkow, basing their reasoning partially on the work of Donald T. Campbell, have explained what makes intellectual division of labor possible. Each member of a group has available to him information from three sources: (1) his own direct observation and research; (2) observations of the investigations of others; and (3) verbal contributions of other group members. "In terms of the final information (or acquired behavioral disposition as Campbell would call it), *knowledge and habits gained through* any *of the three sources can contribute to the group product*. . . . Although one group member must first 'learn' or observe on his own, the rest of the group can assimilate the same knowledge with less effort than was involved in the original learning. In short, the verbal statements of a single group member are an important and efficient source of knowledge for other group members." They go on to state a proposition recognized in essence by Aristotle and supported by recent experimental evidence: "The group is most likely to accept a member's contribution (a) when it is well supported by evidence, (b) when it is logically sound or internally consistent, and (c) when it is consistent with past experience."[2]

The benefits accruing from dividing up the labor of preparation must not be underestimated. A group that fails to take every advantage of the opportunities for sharing the load is not using all the resources resulting from group activity. A single individual can have firsthand knowledge of only a fraction of the matters he must discuss with some intelligence. The time he can give

[2] Collins and Guetzkow, pp. 37–9.

to research is limited. Moreover, most of us cannot fly to Europe or to some distant city in order to investigate problems personally. We must rely on the reports of others. In a real sense this is what we are reading in the library: the reports of observers who have recorded from other places and perhaps other centuries what they have investigated.

In relying on others, the important questions concern observer credibility. We want to know what observers on the spot have learned but which reports can we believe? Have they recorded the information we need or must we guess from indirect references they happen to make?

Reading Critically

The investigator must not accept uncritically everything he hears and reads. Rather he should read and listen skeptically and cautiously. Insofar as his convictions will allow he should begin with an open mind and not permit himself to decide prematurely. He should accept statements tentatively, retaining his flexibility and doubling back to cross-check and compare.

Deliberate lying and distortion do not occur too often in printed media although there are enough instances of fabrication to make the discerning reader wary. Biases and hidden interests of those controlling information releases can mislead the reader. Some amusing examples of this occur in television as well as publishing. Ford Motor Company once insisted on the deletion of a picture of the Chrysler building and a railroad sponsor took out a bit of dialogue from a program using the line, "I'd rather fly." A program on Andrew Carnegie had an uncomplimentary remark about John D. Rockefeller; the reference was deleted because a Rockefeller was on the board of the sponsoring corporation. Many newspapers have long been accused of trimming their editorial sails so as not to offend their advertisers.

Only occasionally, however, is there flagrant fabrication. One such incident occurred in Times Square when a white woman told police a Negro stranger forced his attentions on her and stabbed her husband. Later the wife admitted the stabbing was done by a white man, a former friend. She confessed that she and her husband made a whispered agreement to lie about the assailant's identity while the husband lay bleeding on the sidewalk. A more harmful instance was the disclosure a few years ago of rigged television quiz shows.

Much more troublesome to the investigator than intentional deception is the more common unintentional distortion. One cause is brevity. There is rarely enough space in the newspaper or magazine to report the whole truth. Something must be left out or condensed. The source must make a selection, and naturally he leaves out what suits him least. Thus another cause for inaccuracy is human bias and limitation. The inexperienced observer may not see the right things even though he was right on the scene. Given an experienced observer and adequate opportunity to observe, the reporter cannot tell someone else everything he saw and heard and felt. Also, time seems always to be short; the story is covered hastily, written up quickly, and printed hurriedly. The amazing thing is that a news magazine, for example, is as accurate and helpful as it is when it must appear every week and compete for the very latest in news coverage.

Still another obstacle to accuracy is that reports must be put into words, which are fragile vessels for saying precisely what the observer wants to say and nothing more. Even if the reporter has ample time for observation, ample media space for his report, and is completely honest and controls his biases, the language he uses may still admit unconscious slanting according to the way he looks at the world.

We have perhaps labored the point too long, but we must emphasize the importance of reading critically and cautiously. The group preparing for discussion will search diligently but will match its diligence with careful evaluation of sources. A skillful winnowing of the dependable from the specious may prevent members from accepting an unsound conclusion.

Evaluating Sources

How does the investigator check on the reliability of his sources? For one thing he does not depend on a single source but reads as widely as possible. For another, in addition to being analytical and tentative in his approach, he is cautious about interpreting the language of the report. Then, too, he asks some direct questions about information and about the observers responsible for the information:

1. Is the information accurate? Can it be confirmed by two or more sources?
2. Is the information recent? Conditions may have changed and the most recent information available is the kind needed in discussion. For this reason, the discusser will usually find books and general reference materials less helpful than current periodicals.
3. Is the information complete? Does the information collected describe only part of the picture? The only cure for incomplete information, of course, is to do additional research.

Questions testing the credibility of observers, authorities, and experts who have given testimony of interest to discussion groups must be somewhat broader. An authority may be an institution as well as an individual expert. A newspaper, a magazine, a church body, a labor union, a research organization, may express a collective opinion and this position may be cited as the basis for decision. Reports and opinions can be evaluated by asking about competence and trustworthiness.

1. Is the authority competent? In order to have confidence in authoritative testimony, the expert must be competent in general, that is, have special training, knowledge, and experience, and have a reputation for honesty and accuracy; in addition, he must have special competence in the particular subject matter on which he is testifying. It is failure to meet this latter test which often makes ridiculous testimony in current advertising—the expert baseball

player has no special competence to evaluate breakfast foods nor the movie star, cigarettes. Such advertising gains favorable attention for a product and its impact depends on the desire to be associated with prominent people, but such endorsements do not constitute authoritative testimony.

One of the requirements for special competence is that the authority have been in a position to observe the matters on which he can testify as an expert. A common violation of this requirement occurs when a person who has briefly visited a foreign country willingly evaluates conditions there. For an authority to give an expert opinion, not only would he need to spend sufficient time there to study the situation carefully, but also he would need to begin with special competence in the limited area of study. A trained economist could perform this function, but would be willing and qualified to testify only about economic conditions and would and could not make judgments about the problems of juvenile crime, for example.

The statement of an authority should not be confused with the testimony of a witness to a particular event. In court, any person who has general competence (for example, normal intelligence and eyesight) can testify to events he observed firsthand. Inferences can be based on statements made by such ordinary witnesses, but authoritative testimony is much broader and more important. A witness, for example, may establish the existence of an event, such as the presence of a suspect at the scene of a murder, but only an expert can be relied on for an opinion as to whether a particular gun fired the fatal shot.

These same tests may be applied to evaluate sources of information. A magazine or newspaper, for instance, must establish a reputation for general honesty and reliability, as well as for special competence in particular areas where its testimony carries authoritative weight. Otherwise, readers can have no confidence in inferences based on facts or opinions from such sources.

2. Is the authority unbiased? An authoritative statement is not just an ordinary opinion. In an election campaign, partisans on either side say, "In my opinion, candidate X is the man best qualified for this office," but these statements are not expert testimony. An authority weakens the weight of his opinion as an expert if he has a reason for bias; moreover, the expert is expected to be objective in his evaluations even if he does have a personal prejudice. A medical expert is expected to study the quality of medical care given patients under the British compulsory health-insurance system and give an authoritative opinion apart from his personal feelings about the wisdom of the system. If he is suspected of altering his judgment because he fears his favorable opinion would encourage adoption of the system in the United States, listeners would immediately discount his opinion. In fact, to be guilty of bias is to cease operating as an expert and to become a partisan.

The most convincing expert testimony is obtained when an authority offers an objective opinion in spite of the fact that he may have personal reasons for disliking what his judgment tells him is the case. A person in this position giving ordinary testimony is sometimes called a *reluctant witness,* and a similar designation might be given an authority who expresses an opinion contrary to his private interests.

Finding the Right Facts

Throughout our consideration of the search for and the evaluation of information, we have encountered the problem of deciding whether we are learning the whole story and whether the printed sources we have read have reported the things we want to know. The group preparing for discussion must be satisfied that members are finding the right facts for accurate understanding.

Collecting the right kinds of information depends upon asking the right kinds of questions about the problem to be discussed. In general, the question is: "What will we need to know in order to understand the problem thoroughly?" Specifically, however, the questions must concern the particular problem to be discussed. Perhaps the best way to illustrate the kinds of specific information needed is to suggest questions that should be asked and answered in advance by groups planning to discuss the following two topics.

A group wishing to discuss the question, "Should capital punishment be abolished in Illinois?" should seek in advance answers to these kinds of specific questions:

1. What is the history of this proposal in Illinois? What groups have proposed and opposed abolition of capital punishment, and what have been their reasons? Has a bill proposing abolition been presented to the state legislature? What was said for and against it? What was the outcome?

2. What states and nations have abolished or have considered abolishing capital punishment? What were the reasons for doing so or refusing to do so? What states and nations have abandoned the practice and then reinstituted it? Why did they return to it?

3. What are the conditions of crime and punishment in Illinois as compared with other states and nations that have abolished capital punishment? Are there special problems with capital crimes in a metropolitan area such as Chicago which are different from problems faced by other states and nations that have abolished capital punishment?

4. What are capital crime rates in Illinois as compared with the rates of capital crimes in states and nations that have abolished capital punishment?

5. What has been the success of prisoner rehabilitation in Illinois for those convicted of capital crimes, as compared with the success in states and nations that have abolished capital punishment?

6. For what kinds of crimes have courts in Illinois assessed the death penalty, as compared with courts in other states and nations?

7. What do authorities on crime and penology say about the purposes and effects of capital punishment and the absence of it?

A second example is drawn from a student group discussing the question, "What penalties should be imposed upon student violators of university automobile regulations?" In advance, members should seek answers to questions such as these:

1. What are present automobile regulations?
2. What kinds of violations occur: parking violations? failure to register cars? reckless driving? drunken driving? others?
3. What are present penalties assessed for these violations?
4. What group(s) assess present penalties?
5. What kinds of regulations and penalties are typical at other comparable universities?
6. What are the attitudes toward present regulations of the groups involved: the university administration? the discipline committee? the faculty? the students? the student government?

If members of these two groups can find satisfactory answers to these kinds of questions prior to the discussion, they will have an adequate basis for a wise decision on the over-all question they are discussing. With these kinds of specific questions before them, they can decide which sources will be the most helpful in providing answers and divide up specific assignments.

USING FACTS DURING DISCUSSION

What has been said in this chapter so far has concerned preparation that should occur prior to the discussion. It is important to add here a suggestion about the use of information during the discussion.

Much careful research can be wasted unless the information is contributed when the group needs it. When the group reaches a point in the discussion where it needs a specific kind of information, the discussion will be crippled unless the right facts are contributed at that very moment. Members must be well enough informed to supply the required information and if they fail to recognize what information is needed at a particular time but attempt to contribute it 5 minutes later, the efficiency of the group will be impaired. If the group needs certain information which no member can supply, it is often wise or necessary to adjourn the meeting and assemble again when the proper facts are obtained. A discussion simply cannot proceed properly without the right facts. Irving Lee has commented on the number of discussion situations in which "the speaking took fire almost in inverse ratio to the thinness of the argumentative fuel."[3]

The designated leader of a discussion should insist—patiently but firmly—that the relevant facts be brought out when they are needed by the group. He is attempting to help the group move forward in an orderly and systematic fashion; members should have faith, in most cases, that he has such a plan and they should supply the information he asks for when he asks for it. The leader should discourage members from expressing opinions on solutions, for

[3] *How To Talk With People*, New York: Harper & Row, 1952, p. xi.

example, while the group is trying to analyze by describing the present situation.

Notes can appropriately be brought to the discussion table but they should be used skillfully. It is ineffective to read long quotations or to give the group extensive statistics members have not specifically asked for. Visual aids may be helpful in such cases. The member wishing to report complex statistical tables can prepare a wall board containing the figures in large print so that the whole group can view them at a glance.

In contributing facts, members should remember that discussion is a cooperative, sharing enterprise. They should listen carefully to information presented by others and try to build upon it by adding relevant facts that further illuminate the situation. They should be eager to capitalize on the specialized knowledge and unique background experiences of other members. In these ways they demonstrate their understanding that facts do make a difference in the quality of the group product and at the same time make their maximum contribution to the group's knowledge of the total problem.

SUPPLEMENTARY READING

Braden, Waldo W., and Brandenburg, E., *Oral Decision-Making*, New York: Harper & Row, 1955, Chapter 4.

Collins, Barry E., and Guetzkow, H., *A Social Psychology of Group Processes for Decision-Making*, New York: John Wiley & Sons, 1964, pp. 106–119.

Eubank, Henry L., and Auer, J., *Discussion and Debate*, 2nd ed., New York: Appleton-Century-Crofts, 1951, Chapter 5.

QUESTIONS AND EXERCISES

1. Choose a discussion question of current importance. Assume that you are responsible for providing participants with a complete bibliography on the subject. Prepare an exhaustive list of the sources—library and non-library—to which you would send them.

2. Plan a discussion on a question of public concern. Begin the preparation of a cooperative bibliography; that is, assign to specific members of the group responsibility for securing relevant bibliographical items from each general category of reference sources. One member can be responsible for recent books, another for general reference works, a third for current magazine articles, and so on.
   a. When each person has secured his bibliographical entries, pool the lists and type copies of the combined bibliography for all members.
   b. Have each person give an oral report on his category, telling the others what to expect in each reference, discussing which articles everyone must read to be well informed, and so forth.

3. How much research must members of a group do before they are qualified

to discuss a problem? If members of a group admit that they are not as well informed on the subject as they would like to be, should they disqualify themselves from discussing the problem? Should problem-solving discussion be engaged in only by experts on a problem?

4. Lyman Bryson has said: "Properly speaking, discussion is controversy. It is talk in which opinions are contrasted and judged. It is controversy over judgments that belong properly in the realm of opinion. Discussion is not a means, except incidentally, for discovering facts. . . . Very few important questions can be settled by fact alone. When all the available facts are in, the important issues of life arise." Is he saying that persons need not seek facts before discussing? That discussion by nonexperts is futile? That facts are not important in discussion?

5. Have you discovered false reports in books, magazines, and newspapers? If so, where do you think the obligation for accuracy was violated? How did you discover the error?

Chapter 6

REASONING

Information is essential to successful discussion, but it is of little use until the pieces are put to work in some meaningful way. Facts must be interrelated and participants must draw valid inferences from them. This process of recognizing the interrelationships among data and of drawing inferences is the process of reasoning.

Students are often baffled by a formal presentation of the elements of reasoning. In particular, the syllogism and its many moods can be used to frighten the most stable and serious student. Consternation is not really necessary; people reason every waking hour and on the whole do so quite competently. Admittedly they encounter greater difficulties as they undertake to think their way through complex and unfamiliar problems, as is often necessary in discussion. The reasoning process employed under these circumstances, however, is essentially the same as that used in facing daily personal problems. There is little mystery or extreme complexity in the process itself. Most reasoning errors arise from ignorance of reasoning patterns and from mental carelessness. Discussers must examine patterns of inference and learn to recognize fallacies in reasoning, errors resulting at least in part from carelessness.

As observed in Chapter 5, members of groups accept the contributions of others more readily when they are supported by evidence. Part of this process, however, is the presenting of information in logical, reasonable form so that the contribution as a whole is rational and sounds convincing. We now have some experimental evidence that high-quality thinking is important just as observation has suggested. A study by Pyron, for example, showed that participants ranked by other members as high or medium in usefulness to the discussion made significantly higher scores on a test of reflective thinking ability; those ranked low in usefulness were clearly poorer in thinking skills. Groups tested were "adult decision-making groups from business, industrial, professional, and educational environments, meeting to solve real problems."[1]

To help the student become a useful participant proficient in reasoning, we must consider the thinking process, including the nature of reflective thinking, the bases of belief, and the traditional forms of support; the familiar patterns and tests of reasoning; and the special problems of using reasoning in group situations.

[1] H. Charles Pyron, "An Experimental Study of the Role of Reflective Thinking in Business and Professional Conferences and Discussions," *Speech Monographs*, 33 (1964), pp. 157–61.

HOW WE THINK

John Dewey's book, *How We Think*,[2] has been influential in explaining to several generations of students the nature of the thinking process. His analysis is an especially good beginning point for the student of discussion since he emphasizes reflective thinking, "the kind of thinking that consists in turning a subject over in the mind and giving it serious and consecutive consideration." This is exactly what discussion groups usually attempt to do—think seriously together through a period of time in an attempt to reach a reasoned outcome based on reflection rather than passion or power. This is not to say that discussers are completely rational. Members of discussion groups are influenced by their emotions; they sometimes pursue nonrational arguments and accept outcomes based on power rather than reasoning. In most situations, however, most members of groups would like to reason together and base their decision on reflective thought.

Reflective thinking, Dewey says, is "active, persistent, and careful consideration of any belief or supposed form of knowledge in the light of the grounds that support it and the further conclusions to which it tends." Thus evidence and observations based on the nature of things become grounds for belief. Reflection causes us to accept statements, not on their own direct account, "but through something else which stands as witness, evidence, proof, voucher, warrant; that is, as ground of belief."

A discussion group if it is going to be reflective does not, then, decide only by bargaining or weighing power blocs. A conference involving mayors and councilmen of two towns would not be concluded by one mayor proposing: "We have 6000 people and you have 4000 people; therefore we should get our way in three of these disputes and you can have your way in two." Instead the conference would proceed to bring forth the relevant considerations and to think through the grounds for reaching one conclusion rather than another on each point of dispute.

Reflective thinking starts with a "state of doubt, hesitation, perplexity," and moves to searching and inquiring for ways to resolve the perplexity. Attitudes conducive to inquiry, according to Dewey, are open-mindedness, whole-heartedness, and enthusiastic absorption in the task, willingness to accept responsibility for the consequences of our beliefs, curiosity, and an orderly consecutiveness of thinking moving toward a conclusion. Rational thought is thus purposefully intellectual rather than emotional, orderly rather than random, inquisitive and curious rather than closed and combative, responsible rather than careless, and tentative rather than hastily decisive.

The group reasoning together about political, social, and economic problems can learn from the thinking characteristic of the scientific method. The

---

[2] Rev. ed., Boston: D. C. Heath, 1933.

scientist attempts to maintain an objective view by keeping himself and his feelings completely outside the problem. His measurements are precise as well as objective and his definitions operational. He collects information exhaustively and suspends judgment until the facts are in. Even then he accepts conclusions tentatively, being the first to insist on revising his own findings in light of newer data. He does not merely guess about the way nature may be ordered, although he does not reject the use of hunches, intuition, and creative conjecture. What he does do is state a hypothesis carefully and then test it experimentally or by controlled observation. He then restates it with more confidence or he forgets it and tries something else. He does not keep pushing it because it was his idea or because he likes the sound of its expression. He moves forward by building on what has been learned before, one step at a time.

A discussion group cannot stop and run experiments, of course. But, members can emulate the scientist's rigor, his respect for facts, his care in checking on the reasoning process, his willingness to revise and to hold views tentatively, and his willingness to be reflective.

Bases for Decision

Assuming for the moment that they want to think reflectively and responsibly about their problem, how do the members of a group make up their minds? Out of the welter of facts, the cross-purposes, the emotional conflicts standing in the way, the expression of opinions, and the sometimes seemingly endless reports on past experience must come finally a decision, a conclusion, a meeting of separate minds. What kind of a process is this?

It must be admitted that members commonly experience confusion and frustration. The world is extremely complex, most of our problems are complicated, and people who must stand in the center of their problems are not simple organisms. It is exceptionally difficult for a single individual to think straight about a problem. It is much more demanding for a group to reason cogently together. All is not hopeless, however. There are some time-tested patterns of reasoning that offer help in organizing the welter of confusing pieces into a more recognizable whole. Once evidence and opinion are related in some integrated fabric, it becomes easier to decide whether the conclusion indicated is an acceptable one.

We are guided toward decision in a general way by the confluence of three sources of influence. The first, as we have seen, comes from the factual materials, observations, and reports of experiences growing out of our inquiry. This form of support for decision is sometimes called logical or rational proof. Some persons insist that it is the only kind of proof.

A second source of influence in making up our minds occurs in the statements made by authorities, experts, and persons whose views we respect, including other members of the group. We, in turn, influence them as a source of opinion and statement. This factor is credibility and the form of support is often called ethical proof or *ethos*. Its force depends on the respect of the receiver for the source's competence, trustworthiness, etc.

The third general source of influence lies within each of us as organisms interpreting the world in certain ways. We are influenced to decide in ways consistent with our attitudes, feelings, and motives. This form of support looked at from the view of the person trying to influence us has been called emotional proof, although this label is not clear or helpful. We do not like to admit that a speaker can "appeal to our emotions," but it is fairly clear that we decide about problems in part according to how we feel and how the outcome will relate to our well-being and our interests.

These three types of influence or proof have been accepted for a long time as important in explaining how men change their attitudes. Aristotle enumerated them explicitly in the *Rhetoric* as they apply to the persuasive speaker:

> Of the modes of persuasion furnished by the spoken word there are three kinds. The first kind depends on the personal character of the speaker; the second on putting the audience into a certain frame of mind; the third on the proof, or apparent proof, provided by the words of the speech itself. Persuasion is achieved by the speaker's personal character when the speech is so spoken as to make us think him credible. We believe good men more fully and more readily than others: this is true generally whatever the question is, and absolutely true where exact certainty is impossible and opinions are divided. This kind of persuasion, like the others, should be achieved by what the speaker says, not by what people think of his character before he begins to speak. It is not true, as some writers assume in their treatises on rhetoric, that the personal goodness revealed by the speaker contributes nothing to his power of persuasion; on the contrary, his character may almost be called the most effective means of persuasion he possesses. Secondly, persuasion may come through the hearers, when the speech stirs their emotions. Our judgments when we are pleased and friendly are not the same as when we are pained and hostile. . . . Thirdly, persuasion is effected through the speech itself when we have proved a truth or an apparent truth by means of the persuasive arguments suitable to the case in question (examples, enthymemes or syllogisms, etc.).[3]

Rational or demonstrative proofs are valuable in discussion, but so are the statements of credible persons. When all three of these forms come together, that is, when the group has factual and logical support for a conclusion, when this conclusion is supported by respected authorities, and when the same conclusion fits in with the motives and emotional interests of the members, therein exists a happy outcome for a discussion group.

PATTERNS OF REASONING

Now that we have considered some of the bases for proof and decision, we must turn to the specific mental processes involved in formulating and testing

[3] *Rhetorica*, W. Rhys Roberts, trans. Oxford: Clarendon Press, 1924, I, 2, 1356.

reflective thought. In so doing we will be looking at reasoning in an active, on-going sense. Between the introduction of facts and the final decision, there must be a myriad of propositions stated, proof brought to bear, fallacies caught, and false starts corrected. We need guidelines for following what happens in inference between fact and conclusion; and for detecting specious relationships. Then we need to look at the patterns of reasoning that help to organize pieces of evidence into manageable statements. Only then can we decide whether our reasoning is sound.

Inference

An inference is a mental leap from fact or data or statement (premise) to conclusion. The process can be thought of as a mental jump because the mind moves swiftly and because it crosses at one quick bound what was previously a gap blocked by insufficient access. Here are two simple examples. A student parks his car diagonally at the curb after a rainstorm. When he opens the door, he finds a pool of water under the car too wide to jump across. Then he suddenly sees that, by climbing from the front seat to the back seat, he can jump from the back door to a dry spot near the middle of the street. Now he can make the desired leap, literally. Mental inference is similar. Some facts are known, but their interrelationships are not clear—they form no evident pattern—no conclusion can be reached. Then a new fact is recognized which suddenly makes clear the relationships and a leap can be made to the conclusion.

Tom is fond of Betty. He has not been as ardent a suitor as have Jim and Ted, but he and Betty have dated occasionally. One day Tom asks Betty for a date and she says she is busy. Tom then notices that she is absent from the regular crowd gathered for cokes. He learns that Ted has also asked her for a date and has also been turned down. Tom is puzzled. Then, Betty shows up at the dance with Jim and she is wearing a diamond ring, third finger, left hand. "Aha!" he says, "Betty and Jim are engaged." All the facts now fit together. In a sense, inference is the "aha!" experience.

To emphasize that inference is an "aha" experience, of course, may cause the student to believe (infer) that every inference is dramatic, but this would be misleading. A dramatic inference which clears up a confusing situation suddenly can be called an *insight* and certainly this is a reasonably common experience. This type of inference has been illustrated here in an attempt to make the concept clearer. Most of the time, however, inferences do not supply excitement by clearing up mysterious situations. Nevertheless every inference involves this same kind of leap and can be described as an "aha" experience, even though it is a subdued one. The process goes on so commonly and continuously that we often take little notice. If an instructor gives a quiz and all the students in the class are unprepared and taken by surprise, we infer that the instructor is mistaken in claiming that he announced the test at a previous meeting. When in a discussion of the American automobile market, participants report that sales increased 5 percent and 8 percent in the last 2 years, we may infer that sales may increase next year.

Inferences can usually be made easily and often with minimum mental effort. Then, it may properly be asked, why is reasoning considered so difficult? The answer is fairly simple: reasoning occurs naturally and easily enough, but making certain that reasoning is sound is a more complicated matter. We must have some guidelines for proceeding.

Inferences are fallible. The mind is agile, as has been indicated; the leap of inference often comes easily. Unfortunately, however, inferences can be inaccurate. We can jump to an erroneous conclusion as readily as to a sound one. When the car owner climbs from the front to the rear seat of his car to jump across the pool of water, he may still get wet feet because he has underestimated the distance to the dry spot. Betty may not be engaged to Jim—he may be operating as a protector on behalf of a fiancé in another city. Automobile sales may decline next year. The conferees at Versailles after World War I must have felt that they were providing a sound basis for lasting peace in Europe. Later, U.S. senators, in rejecting membership in the League of Nations, concluded that our enlightened self-interest dictated aloofness from the affairs of Europe. World War II demonstrated the fallibility of these inferences.

Does fallibility mean that we should refuse to draw inferences? Not at all— we have no choice if we wish to reason. What fallibility forces upon us is caution. We must infer carefully and thoughtfully. We must slow down the process enough to examine critically the basis and direction of the leaps we make. We must be prepared to back up, to test, and to try again. While reaching isolated inferences is usually easy, reasoning about a problem of any difficulty involves a complicated network of inferences, and at any point of choice we may start in a misleading direction. The more complicated the problem, the more cautious and deliberate we must be in our reasoning.

Inferences can be disputed. Two equally sincere, intelligent, and well-informed persons can examine the same set of facts, data, circumstances, or premises and draw contradictory inferences. Part of the explanation for this apparent perversity lies in the difficulty of reasoning on complicated problems, and part lies in the fact that no two persons ever see exactly the same data.

We may think that reasoning is a hopeless morass of uncertainty; in a sense it is an uncertain process, but there is no cause for despair. Disagreement is inevitable—and healthy—but we are not helpless; we have some tested procedures to guide us. They will be examined presently.

What the controversial nature of inferences indicates to the discusser is that he must expect disagreement and that sometimes he will be wrong when others are right. A sober realization of this fact suggests that the discusser must suspend critical judgment at times. He must not dismiss arbitrarily the conclusions of others as irrational or idiotic. He must be willing to respect the inferences of others until all views have been considered dispassionately and thoroughly. A discusser who arrives quickly at an inference and insists upon its accuracy in the face of repeated questioning and testing is indeed a fool rushing in "where angels fear to tread."

In other words, the fallibility of inferences places upon a discussion group the responsibility for engaging in careful, reflective thinking. The wise discusser recognizes the complexities and uncertainties in the reasoning process; he proceeds cautiously and slowly; he holds convictions tentatively; he examines his own inferences as thoroughly as he does those of others.

Once we have a willingness to reason reflectively and a proper regard for the difficulties involved, we can proceed rationally to consider some more concrete guidelines for drawing and testing inferences. It is not necessary for us to depend on inferences that occur to us at random. As has been indicated, there are some established, tested aids to guide us. These consist of recognizing and following certain patterns of reasoning, which help us to organize data so that the resulting inferences are more likely to be valid; and of formulating questions that can be asked to test the soundness of inferences.

An inference drawn from a single, isolated fact is less likely to be sound than one drawn from many pieces of related data. The standard patterns of inference presented here help organize data into related groups. The discusser must learn to use these standard patterns both to improve his own reasoning and to evaluate the inferences of others. Organizing data into such patterns reduces the probability of error. After related data and the inferences they support are stated, there are tests by which to judge validity. Again, if the inferences meet the tests, chances are reduced that the conclusions are fallacious.

Specific Instances

In the method of specific instances, a generalization is reached after examining a number of specific cases, all having a common characteristic stated in the generalization. This pattern is also called the method of generalization, or example.

In a discussion on the question, "What steps, if any, should be taken to end alleged racial discrimination in organized houses on this campus?" the leader asked the specific question, "What evidence is there that racial discrimination is practiced in our organized houses?" One member reported that fraternities X and Y practice racial discrimination. Another said that his house, fraternity Z, refused to pledge Negroes. A third member had knowledge of racial barriers in sororities M and N. The group then agreed that there was widespread racial discrimination in organized houses on the campus. They had reached a generalization based on specific instances.

This kind of inference can be tested by asking questions such as these:

1. Have enough instances been examined to justify a generalization about all the members of the class of objects covered by the generalization? In the

illustration, the question is, Can the group safely generalize about all organized houses on campus from an examination of three fraternities and two sororities? If the answer is no, they have committed the fallacy of hasty generalization. This fallacy is common. If a student reports being short-changed in a campus store, his friends will obviously be skeptical if he generalizes: "All those campus businessmen are crooks." Their next question should be: "Do you know of any other stores in which students have been cheated?"

It is natural to wonder how many cases must be examined before a generalization is safe, and no one can answer this question precisely. Part of the answer lies in considering what proportion of all possible cases have been examined. If there are fifteen organized houses on the campus, a generalization based on five instances will be sounder than would be the case if there were sixty-five organized houses.

Such generalizations can be strengthened by applying statistical methods. If it is possible to report that a survey of all fifteen organized houses on campus revealed that twelve practice racial discrimination, the generalization that there is widespread racial discrimination in organized houses will be virtually unchallengeable. It can be attacked only by questioning whether the attributed racial discrimination is actually practiced or by questioning the meaning of *widespread*. Here, too, the method is that of specific instances. If all of the fifteen houses have been examined, this would be what is called a *perfect induction*; that is, a generalization is based on all the members of the class of objects covered by the generalization.

Statistical methods can be much more involved than this simple report of proportions, of course. Average test scores achieved by students taught by one method may be higher than the scores made by those subjected to another method. The significance of the difference may be discovered by using statistical method. The first set of scores may be significantly better than the second. Also it is possible to estimate the significance precisely. The statement may be that the difference is significant at the .01 (1 percent) level of confidence, which means that the difference discovered could probably happen by pure chance only once in 100 such comparisons of 2 sets of scores.

2. Are the instances examined typical or representative of all the members of the class of objects covered by the generalization? Obviously, if the claim is that what is true of five houses on campus is true of all or most, it is necessary to be reasonably certain that the five examined are typical of the rest. This test asks whether the sample is biased.

The problem of sampling is familiar in connection with public-opinion polling. The pollster wishes to select a random sample of the population. If he wants to know how much money Americans expect to invest in government bonds during the next year, he must avoid asking only bankers. The proportion of bankers interviewed must be similar to the proportion of bankers in the total population; included in the sample must be a proper proportion of all other socioeconomic groupings in the nation.

3. Are there negative instances? If, in' the survey of fraternities, three houses are located that have eliminated racial discrimination, observers will be reluctant to put faith in a generalization based on five cases. The reason here is obvious. The generalization based on five typical houses implies that if five other houses were examined, the same inference would be drawn; in the face of negative instances, however, it is as reasonable to expect the five new houses to be in the nondiscriminating category as in the discriminating category.

Causal Relationships

Causal relationships are perhaps the most pervasive of all the reasoning patterns; that is, the "if this, then that" relation is present in many inferential processes. The underlying notion of such relationships is that the universe is a logically ordered whole with an interlocking unity, and that nothing happens without an explainable cause. An event is the result of an earlier event, and it, in turn, leads to other consequences. Reasoning by causal relation involves breaking into this endless chain at some point in time.

If reasoners observe an event and look backward in time to the forces responsible, they are reasoning from effect *to* cause. When they go outdoors and find the ground wet, they infer that it has recently rained. They infer when a friend receives a failing grade in a course that he has limited ability, poor study habits, and/or low motivation. If the small foreign car captures a substantial proportion of the market this year, this event is an effect and they wish to discover the causes that explain the phenomenon. They may examine possible causative factors and infer that the most plausible are desire of buyers for economy, for a feeling of prestige resulting from owning a European product, and for satisfaction resulting from appearing to be a nonconformist. Notice the wording "most plausible." The inferential connection between effect and alleged causes is probably more tenuous than that involved in the method of specific instances. When it is found that five organized houses practice racial discrimination, it is certain that there is some discrimination on campus, even though the generalization that there is widespread discrimination is later proved to be untenable. In a complex effect-to-cause relationship, it is rarely possible to locate the true causes. Historians are still debating the causes of the American Civil War.

Cause-to-effect reasoning occurs when we recognize events in the present and reason that these causes will bring about future effects. Careless driving may lead to an accident; detected crime is followed by punishment; a lowered rediscount rate results in increased borrowing. We reason that production of a small American car will have the effect of reducing sales of imported models. Here the probability of error is even higher than in effect-to-cause reasoning. The inference is tenuous for the same reasons that effect-to-cause inferences are, and in addition we are usually predicting the future; a multitude of intervening causes may prevent the expected result. Foreign manufacturers may lower prices or introduce a dramatic innovation which increases the appeal of their automobiles; or import duties may be decreased, preventing American manufacturers from meeting the price competition.

A third causal relationship is effect-to-effect reasoning. Here we infer that one effect will be accompanied by another effect of the same cause. If lessened American demand for small foreign cars results in decreased imports, another effect will be lower profits for these foreign manufacturers and still another will be the collection of lessened import duties by the United States.

The questions usually asked to test causal relationships are:

1. Does the alleged causal relationship actually exist? If a superstitious person tells his friends he is having bad luck because he broke a mirror, they naturally question whether his misfortunes are related to the breakage. No such relationship has been established in past experience; other causal explanations for his bad luck can almost always be discovered.

To attribute an effect to an unrelated circumstance is to commit the fallacy of false cause. A common form of this error is labeled *post hoc ergo propter hoc* (literally: after this, therefore because of this). The postwar increase in juvenile delinquency was sometimes alleged to be an effect of World War II, but the mere fact that it followed the war does not establish that the war was responsible.

2. Is the alleged cause a sufficient explanation for the attributed effect? One of the gravest risks in employing causal reasoning is that of oversimplification. Rarely does a single cause explain a complex phenomenon. What was the cause of the great depression? Even when observers are wise enough to look for multiple causation, it is sometimes difficult to be sure that particular causes were alone influential enough to bring about the alleged effect.

3. Are there intervening causes which may prevent the alleged effect? In the example above, the actions of foreign-car manufacturers may intervene to alter what would otherwise be a reasonable cause-to-effect relationship.

Analogy

Reasoning from analogy, or resemblance, is a particularly useful inferential pattern for discussion. In analyzing problems, it is often desirable to know what has happened in other places under similar conditions. In evaluating a proposed solution, discussers properly ask, where has this proposal been tried and how successful was it? The analogical pattern is one in which we predict certain outcomes in the situation under discussion because these features emerged in a situation having similar characteristics, or involving similar relationships.

In any discussion of compulsory national health-insurance for the United

States, it would be desirable to examine carefully the operation of such a system in Great Britain. Those favoring the proposal here would infer that the beneficial effects in Britain should operate similarly in the United States because of the resemblance between the two countries, peoples, and medical systems.

There is only one crucial test of this reasoning pattern: are the situations being compared similar enough so that what resulted in one could reasonably be expected to occur in the other? The resemblance must not only exist generally; the two situations must be alike in those specific areas with which the assertion deals. In case of national health-insurance, for the analogy to be sound the medical problems, financial aspects of medical care, and attitudes of doctors and patients toward state-directed medical care in the two nations must be sufficiently similar. Those who oppose such a system in America would likely say that conditions in the two nations have too little resemblance for the analogy to carry much weight.

Authority

Another common inferential pattern is one in which we reason that a condition exists or a policy is wise because respected authorities—those who presumably understand them best—say so. Economists are asked to estimate the probability of a business decline; psychologists can explain personal behavior; educational experts can evaluate proposals for improving schools.

It must be observed at once that for many purposes argument from authority offers weak and unreliable inferences. Often as many respected authorities can be cited on one side of a controversy as on the other. As Shakespeare observed, "The devil can cite Scripture for his purpose." On the other hand, there are areas of investigation and controversy in which authority is the most fruitful and sometimes the only source of inference. Suppose discussers ask whether the United States should finance a project to send manned spacecraft beyond the moon. Citizens, that is, nonexperts who must pay the bills, can appropriately consider the question. In the analysis stage, they must ask whether man can survive on or near other planets. Who can answer this question? They must turn to experts and listen to their opinions; and at this point in time inferences can be only opinions. The fact is that most discussers cannot interpret data transmitted by rockets, and must rely on authoritative knowledge.

Tests for deciding when an authority has high credibility are the same as those applied in Chapter 5 to the sources of observer reports. We want to know about his competence, opportunity to observe, biases, and so on.

Sign and Circumstantial Detail

As has been said, inferences are based on pieces of data, or evidence. When interrelationships or organizational patterns begin to emerge, it is possible to draw inferences and to have increasing confidence in them. Two other kinds of patterns in which inferences are not usually drawn unless there are a number of interrelated pieces are sign and circumstantial detail.

A discussion of reasoning from sign is often omitted from current textbooks, perhaps because it can be considered in part as causal relationship and partially, at least, as argument from circumstantial detail. Both will be treated here because it is desirable to be familiar with these terms. Perhaps also such treatment will make the other forms clearer. Certainly the overlapping among patterns should not be a cause for concern; all the reasoning forms are interrelated.

Whereas the patterns discussed so far offer instances or comparisons or causes or authoritative statements on which inferences are directly based, a sign supplies only indirect evidence that a condition exists. A sign is a symptom or outward manifestation of a condition that cannot, at least at the moment, be directly determined. A doctor diagnoses disease by basing an inference on signs: fever, blood count, spots on the skin, nausea, and so forth.

Increasing unemployment and declining inventories may be signs of a business decline. Of course, these symptoms may also be considered effects of conditions which contribute to that decline. A racing fire engine is a sign of a fire, and indirectly its mission is the effect of the fire—the bell would not have rung and the chase begun without a fire report—but the clanging engine rushing by is not an effect of the fire in the same direct sense that property damage and financial loss are effects.

Whatever the overlapping with causal relation, reasoning from sign is useful in discussion because so often in complex problems causes and effects are not yet clearly identifiable. What are the causes of juvenile crime and what are the best methods for combatting it? Is such crime increasing? Concrete answers are scarce, but it is possible to study signs which suggest causes of improvement or failure where various solutions have been tried and it is possible to discover signs of increasing or decreasing criminal acts.

The argument from circumstantial detail also is based on indirect, or circumstantial evidence. From assorted bits and pieces emerges an interrelated picture that seems to make all the pieces fit together. Most familiar here is the use of circumstantial evidence in connection with criminal trials: There is no witness although the accused was seen emerging from the building at the approximate time of the murder; he had a motive; he owns a gun of the caliber used; he cannot account for his movements that day; and a coat button clutched in the victim's hand was similar to those on his coat. Similar reasoning is sometimes appropriate in discussion. In discussing admission of Red China to the United Nations a group should ask whether Communist China is an aggressor. It may be difficult to assemble direct evidence, but there are indirect circumstances which may add up to a composite picture. Signs are obviously fallible—there may be smoke but no fire, at least no unwanted fire—and the indirect nature of sign and circumstantial detail requires us to proceed with special caution in using these inferential patterns. Tests are also difficult to apply. There are two questions which provide some protection from error:

1. Are there a sufficient number of signs (and/or circumstantial details), all pointing toward the same conclusion, to make the inference seem reasonable? From an increase in unemployment alone a reasoner would hesitate to forecast a business decline; but the combination of a large number of indirect indications lends credence to an inference.

2. Is there corroboration for the inference suggested by signs (and/or circumstantial detail) from other kinds of reasoning? A confirming generalization based on specific instances, or an authoritative statement, for example, would do much to increase confidence in the conclusion.

Deductive Inference

Reasoning usually involves a complex chain of interlocking inferences. Viewed from one perspective, part of this chain consists of drawing, from pieces of evidence that form a related pattern, a conclusion, generalization, general statement, or general premise. This process of moving from the specific to the general is called *induction*. Once a generalization or general premise is established, it is possible to move again in a specific direction by applying the general statement to a particular instance. A deductive inference, then, moves from the general to the specific.

This induction-deduction dichotomy is often protested because it tends to oversimplify the reasoning process; it is also pointed out that the observer should not be concerned with identifying a particular step as inductive or deductive, but should concentrate on the validity of the inferences, whatever their type. This note of caution is reasonable, but for analytical purposes it is often helpful to isolate and identify a phase of a reasoning chain, even if some degree of artificiality is introduced. To do so is sometimes particularly valuable in testing inferences.

Deductive inference is customarily presented as a syllogism:

> All teachers are scholars;
> Jones is a teacher;
> Therefore Jones is a scholar.

There are here three statements: a major premise, or generalization, which has been established, perhaps inductively, by other reasoning methods; a minor premise, which asserts that a particular instance can be classified within the category of events covered by the generalization in the major premise; and a conclusion which follows inevitably from the first two statements.

The form here is crucial. Note that there are also three terms: the major term is *scholars*, the condition of existence that we are establishing in the particular case of Jones; the minor term is *Jones*, the particular instance about whom we are making a deduction; the middle term, *all teachers*, is most vital to the validity of the syllogism—in the major premise it includes any and every teacher within the category of teachers and in the minor premise it places Jones within this category. If every single example of teacher has the condition of being a scholar, and if Jones is indeed one of these instances of teacher, then it follows that he exhibits the characteristic common to everyone in the category, scholarship.

This deductive pattern is labeled a *categorical* syllogism because the major premise asserts categorically, that is, without exception, that all members of a class have a certain characteristic. This requirement suggests the first test of the categorical syllogism:

1. Does the middle term in the major premise include all members of the class? If the middle term is not "universally distributed," that is, not absolute and categorical, the deduction is invalid. A syllogism violating this requirement is:

> Some students study;
> John is a student;
> John studies.

Since there are two categories of students, those who study and those who do not, it cannot be determined from the statement to which group John belongs.

2. The second essential question asks, Does the instance named in the minor term of the minor premise, actually belong to the category named in the middle term? Is Jones a teacher and is John in truth a student? Unless the particular instance can be located within the class of objects having the common characteristic asserted, then the specific member named does not necessarily have this characteristic.

There are two other syllogistic forms which should be mentioned. A *hypothetical* syllogism expresses a condition in the major premise:

> If unemployment increases, there will be a business decline;
> Unemployment will increase;
> There will be a business decline.

The "if" clause is called the *antecedent*, the predicted result, the *consequent*. In such a syllogism, the minor premise may affirm the antecedent, as in the example just given: "Unemployment will increase." Or the minor premise may deny the consequent:

> If unemployment increases, there will be a business decline;
> There will not be a business decline;
> Unemployment will not increase.

Tests of validity follow from these requirements:

1. Does the minor premise affirm the antecedent? If the minor premise affirms the *consequent*, invalidity results:

If unemployment increases, there will be a business decline;
There will be a business decline;
Unemployment will increase.

A business decline can result from many causes other than decreasing employment.

2. Does the minor premise deny the consequent? If the minor premise denies the antecedent, no valid conclusion can be reached:

If unemployment increases, there will be a business decline;
Unemployment will not increase;
There will be no business decline.

Again, business may decline for any number of reasons.

A third form is the alternative, or disjunctive syllogism, in which the major premise presents two alternative possibilities in "either—or" form:

Either Germany must be unified or there will be war;
Germany will not be unified;
There will be war.

The minor premise denies one of the alternatives and the other is affirmed in the conclusion.

Tests of the disjunctive form are:

1. Does the minor premise deny one of the alternatives? If it affirms one of them, no valid conclusion is possible. In the example above, if the minor premise asserts that Germany will be unified, we cannot conclude there will not be war since war may result from some other cause.

2. Do the two alternatives exhaust the possibilities and must one or the other occur? Is it possible that Germany can remain divided and still that there will be no war? If there is a third possibility, the syllogism is invalid. You may remember from early American history the slogan, "54° 40′ or Fight." The United States wanted the northern boundary at this latitude or they wanted to fight, they said. The boundary was established elsewhere, but there was no war.

FALLACIES OF REASONING

In addition to fallacies arising from violations of the reasoning patterns discussed, errors of inference can result from inattention to language, and from the substitution of emotional for rational thinking. If language is used ambiguously or vaguely, inferences will be distorted and misunderstanding result. Using a word in two senses may create the fallacy of equivocation: "Crackers are better than nothing; nothing is better than ice cream; so crackers are better than ice cream." Discussers must stop often to define terms and make meanings precise.

There are also some common fallacies that arise when emotionalism is confused with rationality. Some persons are tempted to resort to emotional thinking when they are afraid that their rational arguments are too weak to prevail. Of course, emotionalism is not always intentional; every person is guilty of nonrational thinking at times.

One emotional argument is to attack the source rather than the idea. This fallacy is called *argumentum ad hominem,* or "poisoning the well." The attack is on the man rather than his argument. Another is to argue for acceptance of a policy because others have endorsed it. An idea must be judged on its merits; because it is approved "by millions," or because "everybody favors it," or because generations of ancestors believed in it cannot alone justify it. Discussion groups should be sensitive to the weaknesses in such thinking.

USING REASONING IN DISCUSSION

Now that the essential traditional syllogistic forms have been briefly explained—and there are almost endless complexities of form and mood that have not been touched here—there is a powerful temptation to say to the discusser that for him this material is nonsense and that he should proceed to forget it. This temptation, like most, should at least in part be resisted for two reasons: the reasoner cannot be educated without knowing the traditional dogma and technical terms; and these concepts are useful in testing reasoning—our own and others'—by reducing arguments to simple forms and looking for flaws. The inflexible traditional forms, however, have limited usefulness. To force reasoning into molds where it will not really fit sometimes can interfere with thinking.

The absolutism of traditional deductive forms rarely corresponds to the real world. All A is almost never B, and drawing neat circles cannot make it so. Discussers must try to decide such matters as what to do to reduce juvenile crime. The difficulty is that they cannot find many categorical major premises. Finish this premise with its universally distributed middle term in twenty-five words or less: "All juvenile delinquents are. . . ." No one can as yet establish universalities in human behavior, nor can experts ordinarily say in complex matters that either this or that must occur. The discusser is advised, then, to test his deductions carefully. He must not insist that a conclusion follows inevitably from a major premise in which the middle term is not in actuality universal.

Perhaps a sensible improvement for the discusser is to substitute probability for absolutism. He can make some general statements about complex matters if he is careful to make the proportion of certainty expressed correspond to his knowledge:

Invasion of another nation's territory has almost always led to war.
Most juvenile criminals have had minimal church affiliation.
Most students study.

A large increase in unemployment is probably a sign of a business decline. If juvenile offenders are encouraged to affiliate with a church, they will perhaps be deterred from further delinquency.

Deductions expressed in such qualified terms will not be as neat as syllogisms, and the conclusions are not certain, but they offer much more solid ground for the discusser:

Invasion of another nation's territory has almost always led to war;
General X proposes invasion of the Chinese mainland;
General X's proposal will probably lead to war.

For the discusser's purposes, another weakness of traditional forms is that the truth of the premises is considered irrelevant. If form alone is considered important, this ridiculous syllogism must be accepted as logically valid:

All airplanes fly the Atlantic under water;
Lindbergh's "Spirit of St. Louis" was an airplane;
Lindbergh flew the Atlantic under water.

Obviously discussers must be certain that all their statements are true, that is, accurately represent actual events in the real world. The wise discusser will be skeptical of a deduction that asserts that any outcome is absolutely certain, any association invariable, or any conclusion inevitable.

Anyone using language to communicate must understand the reasoning process, but it is particularly important for the discusser to have a thorough knowledge of reasoning patterns. Discussion typically consists of direct, conversational interchange and brief communications from each participant interspersed with the short contributions of others. Rarely in lively discussion does any member have the opportunity to present an extended, closely developed chain of reasoning. Rather, the pieces of evidence and inferences are contributed in bits by various members. Hence, each participant must recognize what is happening when the materials are fitted together for a conclusion. Otherwise, a member who is not following the reasoning will introduce an unrelated piece of evidence or opinion which leads in another direction; the result will take the group off on a tangent. The leader will then have two choices:

1. He may do nothing, in which case the group will proceed on the newly introduced tangent and the original development will be lost; or

2. He may bring the group back to the original reasoning under development, which will mean that the person introducing the new line of thought will be confused and frustrated. This second course is probably preferable, although either procedure results in some slight damage to group thinking, even if the leader explains to the naive participant what is happening. The undesirable possibilities point up the great importance of thorough understanding by all participants.

Another difficulty encountered in applying reasoning in a discussion situation stems from the fact that the reasoning patterns studied in isolation for analytical purposes do not often appear in pure form. Two or more forms when interrelated are more confusing to recognize, yet strengthen the soundness of conclusions. In fact, it may be unwise to attempt a sorting out of types—when all the evidence and inferences of various kinds fit together into a reasonable pattern our thinking is probably approaching validity. If a group first agrees that a causal relationship seems to exist between increasing unemployment and a business decline, the relationship will seem more plausible if someone describes a similar situation in the past—the method of analogy—in which a business decline apparently resulted from decreasing employment. Even greater weight will be added if collectively they can cite six examples of past recessions, supporting a tentative generalization—using the method of specific instances—that rising unemployment preceded a business decline. Finally, they may add authoritative testimony—a number of experts expressing the opinion that these two phenomena are causally connected.

It should be repeated that in lively discussion these corroborative patterns will not be presented in this orderly, one-step-at-a-time fashion. Different members with varied experiences and knowledge will contribute the pieces as they are recalled. At some point the designated leader or a member must review the contributions and summarize them in an integrated form.

Discussers should not hesitate to ask the group to halt temporarily and test their collective reasoning. Also, it is wise to ask, for example, whether an analogy is an isolated resemblance, or whether enough similar cases are known to expand the comparison to a generalization based on numerous specific instances; or whether authoritative opinion coincides with the inferences suggested by signs and circumstantial detail.

Still another difficulty encountered by members using reasoning in group situations is the pressure generated by group conformity. Often the person who is seeing most clearly the relationships among the facts presented over a period of many minutes will be the only one who at first analyzes the implications in the way he does. The discomfort that comes to a person when he is a minority of one may operate to discourage him from pressing his view. Yet his interpretation could well be the one the group will accept later or would have accepted had he shared his views with the group.

Social influence can help group productivity if it stimulates members to better thinking. As we have seen, the presence of several members means wider experience and more knowledge brought to bear. Several opinions may mean the better alternative will be chosen by the group judgment. When members conform or suppress their ideas merely to win group approval or to avoid being out of step, however, the group product is being damaged by social influence. Members must be willing to speak up even at the risk of some criticism. If the group has already created a permissive climate, of course, there is freedom to express a different or unpopular view.

Some persons apparently are so unsure of their own views that they are perfectly willing to go along with a group on almost any basis. They just assume that the group's reasoning will be sounder than their own. Such an assumption can be damaging to the group effort, obviously. As Collins and Guetzkow observe, "members can become so much in the habit of depending on other persons for knowledge and information that they cannot make contributions on their own."[4] Such dependence, especially in the case of reasoning, leads to unsound thinking. It may mean in some groups that one or two bold persons are doing almost all the real thinking for the group. It certainly reduces the contributions the conformists could make if they would become full participants.

Members who recognize unsound reasoning or fallacious thinking but who hesitate to point it out for fear of group disapproval are cancelling out one of the values of using group effort. Here, too, the group should create a climate of frankness and a direct "let's all look openly but not defensively" attitude toward exploring all aspects of the problem.

Using reasoning during the discussion, then, becomes an assignment in seeing the logical parts of the problem as a whole in spite of its disjointed presentation; of resisting conformity pressures; and most importantly of using reason clearly without becoming entangled in rigid complexities or syllogistic absolutism. It is extremely important, as we have said, to test reasoning for validity. But the traditional forms are discouraging, often unclear, and sometimes impossible to use in the rapid-fire communication of discussion. It is thus appropriate to close this chapter by suggesting a less rigid form for laying out arguments, both for expressing a line of reasoning quickly in the group situation and also for testing arguments others have advanced. This scheme seems particularly useful in discussion.

THE TOULMIN MODEL

This flexible format for laying out an argument has been proposed by Stephen Toulmin in his book, *The Uses of Argument*.[5] His model for recording the interrelationships of evidence and inference avoids the "allness" of the syllogism, allows for locating supporting statements, and adds some helpful concepts not suggested at all by traditional forms. For example, his scheme shows the assumptions that must be accepted before a connection between premise and conclusion will be recognized or accepted.

Logicians, Toulmin says, have tried to display arguments from all fields in a single, common form and hence have stressed symbolic relationships: All A is B. He finds a wide divergence "between the attitudes and methods of professional logicians and those of everyday arguers." What he proposes is a method for displaying a particular argument by stretching out its components

[4] Barry E. Collins and Harold Guetzkow, *A Social Psychology of Group Processes for Decision-Making*, New York: John Wiley & Sons, 1964, p. 42.

[5] Cambridge, England: Cambridge University Press, 1958. Also available in paperback.

before us as if it were an organism. Then we are able to see its gross "anatomy" or structure, and its finer "physiology." Its components, and the grounds that support them, can vary with the subject matter of that field, since the criteria for judging statements valid or established are different from field to field.

What we will do here is explain Toulmin's layout in simple form, argue that it is usefully applicable to discussion, and urge the student to look at Toulmin's book for further understanding.

We begin with an assertion: George is a student in this college. When we make this statement to someone we *Claim* it to be true. If our statement is challenged, we must attempt to produce the support we had for making it in the first place. If it is said, "How do you know for a fact that George is a student here?" we may respond, "he is attending one of my classes." This statement then is the *Datum* or fact that is the basis for our assertion. We can propose the first relationship between *Data* and *Claim*:

Datum ⟶ So Claim

George is a member
of one of my classes ⟶ So, he is a student ,
in this college.

Now the other person has a right to ask about the step from Data to Claim. Is there an appropriate and legitimate (logical!) connection? What is needed at this point, Toulmin says, "are general, hypothetical statements, which can act as bridges, and authorise the sort of step to which our particular argument commits us." He calls these connecting bridges *Warrants*. Persons who appear in a classroom and sit among other students listening to the instructor are presumed to be students. George has been coming to this classroom since the first day of the term and sitting among others known to be students; the widely accepted notion that those attending a class are students is authorization or warrant for our assertion that George is a student. We can represent these three elements schematically:

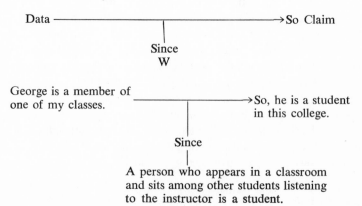

Data ⟶ So Claim

Since
W

George is a member of
one of my classes. ⟶ So, he is a student
in this college.

Since

A person who appears in a classroom
and sits among other students listening
to the instructor is a student.

The Warrant may seem incidental and obvious in some cases. Its task is to record explicitly the justifiability of the step involved from Data to Claim. It also is a more general statement than the pieces of Data; it may be authorization for a large number of specific Data–Claim relationships.

Now we can start to recognize the differences introduced by dealing with subjects from different fields. There are many kinds of Warrants. In some fields it is fairly easy to establish the validity of Warrants and see the Data–Claim relationships they authorize. There are simple ways of establishing that a person is enrolled as a student in a particular college. As we move into the political realm, however, and talk about invasion of another nation's territory leading to war, we cannot be certain that relationships are so invariable. Thus we must protect ourselves against making unreasonable Claims and offering Warrants that cannot establish an unvarying relationship. Some Warrants in some areas justify a Data–Claim step only if we are willing to allow for exceptions or to express some qualifications in making the statement. Toulmin thus adds a fourth element, a *Qualifier*, to the Data, Claim, and Warrant already introduced. Now we can qualify the step from Data to Claim and say that since George is a member of one of my classes, he is *probably* a student in this college, or *almost certainly* a student here, or *presumably* a student here.

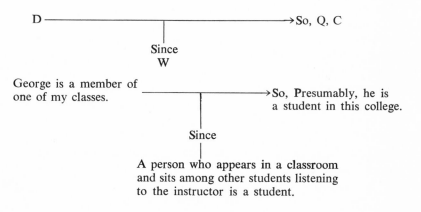

Also, the qualification step introduces the possibility of stating the *Reservation* or *Rebuttal*, as Toulmin calls it, that can be cited as recognition that the Data–Claim relationship may not hold. The Reservations indicate circumstances in which the Warrant would not be valid and would be set aside. It is possible that George is only masquerading as a student. If he is, the general Warrant that those who attend and listen are students will not hold in this case. The Toulmin layout enables us to foresee this possibility and allow for it. We are thus less likely to make a mistake in reasoning. We can also state our assertion less rigidly and positively; we are not forced into an all-or-nothing claim:

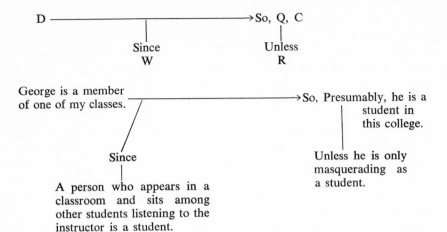

The final element in the layout is *Backing* for the Warrant. We must ask why a Warrant has authority, or why this particular Warrant is sound. Backing varies with the field, also. The kind of support needed to show that a person who attends a class is a student may be quite different from backing for the Warrant that invasion of any nation's territory will lead to war. To complete the Toulmin scheme we can represent our argument in this way:

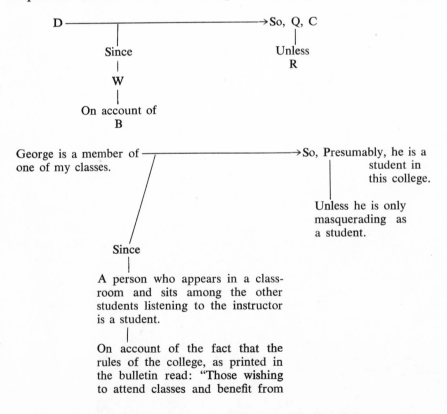

the instruction must be officially
admitted and must enroll as regular
students, paying fees of . . ."

It is in providing the Backing for Warrants that traditional inductive forms come into use. Support may be in the form of specific instances, examples, analogy, or any of the other kinds.

We should note that there can be more than one fact in the Data and that we could have several Data all related to the same Claim. We can allege, for example, that Mary, Sue, and Jim are students in the college by pointing to the same relationships already established. Likewise, there can be multiple Reservations and additional Backing. George may not be a student even though we have presumed he is one because he is actually another instructor sitting in the class to observe teaching technique, or a student from another college who is a visitor, or an alumnus of the college who has received permission to audit this one course. If someone questions whether our Backing for the Warrant is sufficient we may need to quote an authority such as the dean of the college to the effect that anyone attending classes is presumed to be a student.

We should be able now to lay out a more complex argument in this manner. Suppose we have asserted that the Russians are more likely than we are to first place men on other planets. Our reason for making this claim is that they have developed rockets with greater thrust (Data).

Russia has developed
rockets with greater thrust ————→ So ————→ Probably ——→ Russia will
than those of the   first place men
United States   on other planets.

Since tremendous thrust is needed to push a mammoth rocket to another planet.   Unless Russia has not perfected a reliable guidance system

                                        or

Because NASA estimates that a rocket large enough to carry two men to the nearest planet and back will require three times the thrust of present equipment.   The United States develops rockets with greater thrust

                                        or

And our foremost space engineer has said that developing engines with thrust is the key to travel to other planets.   Russia pursues other goals in rocketry.

This cause-to-effect relationship is reasonable, since it is recognized that tremendous thrust will be required to push to other planets the necessarily mammoth rocket (Warrant). This Warrant can be questioned and hence may require Backing. Even though the Claim may seem a reasonable inference from these Data, considering the Warrant with its Backing, Toulmin recognizes that it is wiser to talk about probability than certainty. Hence, between Data and Claim he supplies a Qualification, such as "presumably," "probably," "perhaps," "in 98 percent of the cases," or whatever seems supportable by the circumstances. Also, there is always the possibility that the outcome will be interfered with by intervening causes; hence, there is a place for Reservations; unless some other force prevents it, the Claim seems reasonable.

Ehninger and Brockriede, in their book, *Decision by Debate*,[6] have extended the Toulmin model to the reasoning process used by the debater. They illustrate its use in causal relation, generalization, and analogy. They also show how this same layout of argument can be used where the datum is a statement from a credible authority and where the argument is in the "emotional mode" of proof. These authors call this last form the use of *motivational* proofs. Finally they discuss fallacious reasoning in terms of the Toulmin system, explaining unwarranted claims, deficient warrants, ignored reservations, and overstated claims along with the more familiar kinds of fallacies. Since careful reasoning is as critical to the discusser as to the debater, the student seeking additional help in applying the Toulmin system is urged to consult the Ehninger and Brockriede book.

This Toulmin model is worthy of careful study. It enables the reasoner to be properly cautious, by qualifying his Claims. He avoids rash inferences pretending inevitability by noting the Reservations (that is, in Toulmin's terms, Rebuttal) that may alter his Claims. If his Data statement is questioned, he can make this statement a Claim and back up to construct a new model supporting it. Finally, it enables him to support Warrants. In the example given, he may back the Warrant by citing specific instances of rockets that required certain amounts of thrust; through analogy; with authoritative statements; or any combination of these and other inferential patterns.

The Toulmin scheme should also lend itself easily to discussion groups. While it may seem blunt to say, "I'm not sure that your reasoning is sound," it may be easier to say, "What were you considering the Warrant that connects your Data and Claim in this case?" A group approach should be possible in citing additional Data for a particular Claim, or Backing for a Warrant. Any system that promotes sound reasoning will certainly be a welcome contribution to the conscientious discussion group.

SUPPLEMENTARY READING

Baird, A. Craig., *Argumentation, Discussion, and Debate*, New York: McGraw-Hill, 1950, Chapters 8–15.

---

[6] Douglas Ehninger and Wayne Brockriede, *Decision by Debate*, New York: Dodd, Mead, 1963, Chapters 8–12.

Dewey, John, *How We Think*, rev. ed., Boston: D. C. Heath, 1933.
Ehninger, Douglas, and Brockriede, Wayne, *Decision by Debate*, New York: Dodd, Mead, 1963, Part III.
Toulmin, Stephen E., *The Uses of Argument*, Cambridge, England: Cambridge University Press, 1958, Chapter 3.
Werkmeister, W. H., *An Introduction to Critical Thinking*, Lincoln, Neb.: Johnson Publishing Co., 1948.

QUESTIONS AND EXERCISES

1. In his book, *How To Talk With People* (New York: Harper & Row, 1952, p. 3), the late Irving J. Lee points out that in discussion, "Trouble comes when somebody contradicts somebody else without seeing what the first man was talking about. The speaker says, 'You can't trust the Abibs.' The listener says, 'Yes, you can.' Then they go at it. When the speaker was asked to specify, he told about Samo and Har and Myri. And, of course, they were untrustworthy. When the listener specified, he told about Mil and Janx and Car. And without a doubt they could be trusted. If the contradictor had asked first, the contradictee might not have had his feelings hurt." Here are contradictory generalizations based on different, mutually exclusive sets of specific instances. What tests of inference will expose the weaknesses here? How common is this kind of reasoning in discussion?

2. Listen carefully to a number of discussions in order to discern whether you hear the kind of reasoning described in question 1, above.

3. What kinds of reasoning and/or additional facts will be needed to solve the following problem, reported in a student newspaper: "About eight hundred University of Illinois students became ill simultaneously early Sunday in two men's residence units, Forbes and Hopkins halls, calling for some diagnostic detective work by health agencies. The ailment was only a mild diarrhea. There was little nausea or vomiting, which differentiates it from usual cases of food poisoning. . . . An unusual aspect of the case is the fact that men living in Garner Hall, which is fed from the same kitchen, were not stricken. The students eat in separate dining rooms, serviced from a central kitchen. A factor pointing toward the food service, however, is that men who failed to eat dinner there Saturday night 'uniformly were exempted' from the illness, the health director said. Items of food served are undergoing analysis. . . ."

4. Werkmeister (see Supplementary Reading above) explains the propaganda devices of name calling, glittering generalities, tabloid thinking, testimonials, bifurcation, association, identification, band wagon, and card stacking. Study these propaganda devices; then give a report in which you discuss the similarities and dissimilarities between these propaganda devices and the kinds of errors in reasoning explained in this chapter. Can

the tests of reasoning suggested here be applied to the analysis of propaganda?

5. Of what importance to the participant in discussion is an understanding of errors in reasoning, and of propaganda devices?

6. Analyze a number of newspaper editorials and speeches from sources such as *Vital Speeches*. Write or give an oral report in which you:

   a. Cite examples of fallacious reasoning; and

   b. Identify as many types of reasoning as possible.

7. Record a number of statements as assertions making claims. Lay out each one as a complete argument following the Toulmin model. Try to find weaknesses in your examples after they are written out.

Chapter 7

LANGUAGE
AND COMMUNICATION

In evaluating the worth of a particular individual to a discussion group discussers may sometimes say: "He is a valuable participant because he knows so much about the problem." A little reflection will indicate that they mean much more than this statement includes. If he is in fact a valuable participant, then he has demonstrated an ability which goes beyond understanding the problem, being well informed, and reasoning validly. To know is only half enough; in addition, the effective discusser must be able to communicate that knowledge to others. It is possible to go further: if he is unable to communicate his grasp of the problem, others will have no awareness that he knows. Discussion, moreover, requires still another ability. It is not enough that he be able to communicate painstakingly in writing or haltingly through speaking, so that he gets the meaning through to us at last; he must be able to communicate both efficiently and effectively. To compliment the good discusser, others must say at least two things about him: he knows, that is, he is informed, he understands, he reasons well; and he is articulate.

The University of Michigan study of seventy-two decision-making conferences on business and government, referred to earlier, indicated that communication effectiveness is related to reaching consensus in high-conflict groups. This was true for groups in substantive as well as affective conflict. "The ability of the members to understand what each said led to agreement. When participants knew the vocabulary the others were using and talked on a common conceptual level, high conflict tended to end in consensus."[1]

To understand how the discusser becomes articulate, it is necessary to review the process of oral communication introduced in Chapter 1. The two primary agents in the situation are (a) the speaker as the source of a particular oral comment, and (b) the listeners in the discussion group who are the receivers, or destination, of the communication. Obviously in the conversational interaction characteristic of discussion, the direction of communication changes repeatedly as a particular individual is now speaker, now listener.

Look first at the speaker. Impinging upon him are literally hundreds of stimuli to which he could react: those in the immediate discussion situation, such as the persons present, the questions asked by the leader, and the com-

---

[1] Barry E. Collins and Harold Guetzkow, *A Social Psychology of Group Processes for Decision-Making*, New York: John Wiley & Sons, 1964, p. 111.

ments made by others and those in his memory, such as past experiences (both relevant and irrelevant) and information learned in the past, some of it perhaps read in specific preparation for this discussion. Some of these available stimuli he will perceive at a particular moment, but he cannot concentrate on all of them at once. From them he must select those stimuli to which he will react when he makes a comment. Also available to him are any number of ways in which he can translate into language what Wendell Johnson has called this silent *preverbal state*. Again he must select from the possible language choices the one configuration he wishes to use. Thus, he encodes in words some part of the total meaning he perceives. These words, now uttered, and accompanied by bodily and facial movements largely related to the words, are transmitted to the listener by sound and light waves called a *signal* or a *message*. It is only the signal, words, carried by sound waves, and such visual cues as facial expression, carried by light waves, which connects speaker and listener. Nothing of the complex perceptions of the speaker, what he feels he should say or wishes he could express, or of the language choices he might have made, are transmitted unless they are contained in the actual message finally broadcast. While the signal is in transmission, there can be noise which interferes with its reception: inaudibility, impreciseness of sound production, competing sound from coughs or scraping chairs or slamming doors or the whispering of one listener to another.

Now consider the destination, the other participants in the discussion. Each of them, too, is being subjected to many external and internal stimuli that compete with the speaker for attention. Each will perceive some of the signal being transmitted, and will decode the message in terms of what the words, the facial expressions, and so on mean to *him*. Part of the message as decoded may stimulate in a listener response that induces him to initiate an oral contribution, and the process as described again occurs.

This brief review of the oral communication process is presented for two purposes. First it emphasizes the hazards in communicating: consider the number of choice points at which a breakdown can occur. The speaker may not choose to concentrate on stimuli such as the facts of a situation, for example, which are adequately relevant to the discussion; he may make unwise language choices in encoding; he may produce inaudible or imprecise oral sounds; his signal may receive interference from outside events; the listener may not perceive in his message those aspects which are central, or may not decode the words with the same meanings intended by the speaker, or may respond in an irrelevant manner. Awareness of these types of hazards should give the discusser a proper respect for the difficulties of transmitting meaning precisely, and should encourage him to put his most cautious and careful efforts into his attempts to be articulate.

A second purpose of presenting this process is to make clear the points at which the individual can substantially improve his effectiveness as a communicator. There are three aspects on which he should concentrate: making his language choices reflect precisely his intended meaning; delivering the message effectively through the use of adequate speech skills; and being a perceptive listener.

LANGUAGE

Discussion flourishes best in an atmosphere of intellectualism. Discussers strive to express ideas calmly, rationally, and reflectively, yet precisely and efficiently. Unless participants can use language properly, the best thoughts can be lost. Language must facilitate rather than impede clear thinking, and is important because it is almost the only means of clarifying, informing, defining, and communicating insight into our feelings and attitudes. In discussion, words must carry almost the whole burden of communicating; such auxiliary means as gesture, facial expression, or pictorial representation can play only minor roles at best.

What Language Is

It is impossible to present here an elaborate treatment of such a highly technical matter as language; we can note only the essentials necessary for a basic understanding. To oversimplify, we can say that a language consists of a set of arbitrary signs understood by their users to symbolize or refer more or less to objects and events. To say that signs are arbitrary is to indicate that words mean only what we agree among ourselves—or that the molders of our language long before us agreed—that they are to mean. The meaning of a word is not part of the word; meaning exists only in the minds of users.

In the world external to our sensory perceptors there is a blooming plant, the flower of which has certain characteristic arrangements of petals, color, and fragrance, which we designate by the word *rose*. The word is only a combination of sounds produced in a certain way or it is a configuration of lines arranged on a piece of paper; the sound combination or the configuration "ROSE" by agreement becomes a *sign* of a rose. When a speaker says the word, he hopes a listener will be able to visualize this particular bloom, and if he asks him to pick some roses, he hopes the listener will not come back with chrysanthemums. But the word is not the rose; it only symbolizes, represents, or designates this particular bloom.

If discussers held discussions only on picking roses rather than violets, language would present little handicap. Difficulties set in when they must talk about democracy, capitalism, justice, freedom, equal protection of the laws, and similar concepts where the objects or events in the real world to which we refer are not as easy to identify. Lewis Carroll's Humpty Dumpty was not troubled by such limitations:

> "There's glory for you."
> "I don't know what you mean by 'glory,'" Alice said.
> Humpty Dumpty smiled contemptuously. "Of course you don't—till I tell you. I meant 'there's a nice knockdown argument for you.'"

"But 'glory' doesn't mean 'a nice knockdown argument,' " Alice objected.

"When I use a word," Humpty said in rather a scornful tone, "it means just what I choose it to mean—neither more nor less."

"The question is," said Alice, "whether you *can* make words mean so many different things."

"The question is," said Humpty Dumpty, "which is to be master—that's all."

But we are getting ahead of ourselves.

Referents

Signs, such as words, refer to objects or events in the world external to ourselves, and the object is called the *referent* of the word. A bloom having certain characteristics is the referent for the word *rose*. As long as both speaker and listener know exactly what the referent is when one uses a word, they can communicate without confusion. When one uses the words *Franklin D. Roosevelt* the other cannot mistake the designation of this sign because there is one and only one possible referent, a specific person. But suppose the speaker says, "Franklin D. Roosevelt was a great President." What is the referent of the word *great*? If the kinds of behavior, accomplishment, or contribution that one visualizes as the referent for great are considerably different from the other's conceptions, one may not understand what the other means. They may then proceed to disagree about the statement when in fact they disagree about the intended referent of great.

Levels of Abstraction

Part of the reason persons can point to the same bloom in response to the sign *rose*, but disagree about greatness is explainable in terms of abstraction. The referent for rose is concrete while the concept of greatness is more abstract or general.

Most students are familiar with the so-called abstraction ladder. In the external, physical world, the object we signify by the word *rose* is a mass of swirling electrons, etc. One step up the abstraction ladder, that is, a more abstract way of finding out in part about these electrons which we cannot see is to examine under a microscope the cells that make up the bloom. Another step up is the bloom that we can see with our eyes, or point to, or smell, or feel. Now we take a large step toward abstraction when we assign to this bloom the word *rose*. Whereas if we examine a petal under a microscope, we are considering part of a particular bit of a specific bloom, the word *rose* refers to any number of different varieties, kinds, and colors of blooms lumped together into a classification. When a speaker says "rose" a listener does not know whether he refers to an American Beauty or a Crimson Glory, to say nothing of the possible interpretations if the speaker says, "My love is a rose of Sharon." Even more abstract is a word that designates this kind of bloom and many others as well, the word *flowers*. It is possible to go on abstracting and to produce a simple example of one kind of abstraction ladder:

Things of beauty
↑
Decorative plants
↑
Flowers
↑
Roses
↑
All white roses
↑
A specific variety of white rose
↑
The only white bloom on the first rose bush
just outside the front door

Now we can return to the word *great*. This concept is an abstraction, corresponding to the words *things of beauty* in the illustration above. To what concrete objects or events in the real world does it refer? What is at the base of its abstraction ladder? Until the listener knows to what the speaker is referring when he uses the word, it is impossible to communicate meaning or reach agreement on the statement that Roosevelt was a great President.

The primary concern, then, is with the degree of correspondence between the words used and the objects or events, the referents, they are intended to signify.

It is through language that the object world is related to the sign world. Language enables persons to talk about concepts that are too complex or abstract to be communicated with a simpler system, such as pointing or drawing pictures. (Draw a picture of greatness!) It allows people to talk about the "not here," the "not now," and even the "not seen." As has so often been observed, such abstracting is largely a human capacity.

USING LANGUAGE IN DISCUSSION

These general concepts of language can now be applied directly to the problems of achieving effective, efficient language usage in discussion. Language must be clear, accurate, appropriate, and fair to others.

Language Must Be Clear
The discusser must above all strive to express his meanings clearly. If other participants are not certain what he means, confusion and misunderstanding are inevitable. Often disagreement evaporates when members finally make clear to each other what they mean.

Clarity depends upon the extent to which the meaning as interpreted by the listener coincides with that intended by the speaker. When a speaker uses a word, he presumably intends the word to signify a particular referent; if the listener in decoding the message can visualize the same or approximately the same referent, the speaker's intended meaning is clearly communicated. Suppose, however, a participant says, "We can probably agree that Senator Johns is a faithful legislator." What does he mean by *faithful*? Perhaps his referent is a man who keeps his campaign promises, honest or dishonest, and who looks out for his friends. A listener, on the other hand, may visualize as the referent a man who is consistent, unselfish, and strictly honest. For this listener, the speaker's comment will be unclear, perhaps incomprehensible, and disagreement will likely follow.

One form of unclarity is vagueness, which often results when a speaker says too little, and that perhaps imprecisely, to get the whole of his intended meaning across. What does the discusser mean if he says, "The Senator has rejected a slavish hyperdemocracy and favors a return to old-fashioned liberalism?"

Another kind is ambiguity, where there are two or more possible referents for a word and the message does not indicate which is intended. During World War II, British and American officers working together in a staff meeting exchanged some bitter words when a British officer moved to table a motion which the Americans wished desperately to adopt. Tension subsided only when the ambiguity of the motion to table became clear; by tabling the British meant to postpone consideration temporarily, perhaps for a few hours, while American practice had been virtually to forget about a proposal once tabled.

The careless use of slang expressions, or of ordinary words in an unconventional manner, can cause ambiguous interpretation by listeners. A newspaper reporter who watched a pilot bring an airplane to the ground at an airport wrote, "It was a *terrific* landing." Is it possible to visualize the landing from this description? Webster's *New International Dictionary* defines the word *terrific* as "exciting, or adapted to excite, great fear or dread; terrible; appalling . . . tremendous, extreme; excessive." What actually had happened was that the airplane's landing gear was working improperly and the pilot was required to land the plane without wheels. The pilot did so successfully, without injury to the passengers. The reporter, in calling the landing *terrific*, meant that the pilot had handled the craft skillfully and was to be commended. But the word he chose is misleading and inadequate to convey the whole message. Of course, the listener receives further clues to the intended meaning from the context of the other words used by the reporter, who also described the dangerous situation faced by pilot and passengers.

How can vagueness and ambiguity be avoided? The general principle to remember is that care and caution must be used in expressing complex ideas. The speaker must say enough to reveal his whole intent. Usually short, simple sentences are clearer than long, involved statements. A sentence that rambles on and on may be so difficult to follow that the listener loses the beginning of the thought before the end arrives. Complex sentences, those with modifying clauses and dependent elements, are much harder to follow when spoken than when written. The speaker must try to avoid extremely complicated sentences.

Of course, every statement in oral discourse cannot and should not be a simple sentence—subject-verb-object only—but sentences with several dependent clauses and modifiers will be less clear than those with simpler construction.

A minor source of confusion arises from inaccurate sentence structure. A pronoun used without a clear indication of its antecedent can be misleading. Recently a prominent newspaper columnist reported that she and the ladies who were her traveling companions flew to a certain city where the mayor presented her with the keys to the city. Then, she added, "We went to stay in a beautiful motel." The possible inclusion of the mayor as part of the antecedent of "we" suggests an unintended meaning which could have been avoided by more careful sentence construction. The misplaced modifier is another kind of confusing error: "Because they were having economic difficulties, the federal government was asked by the states to supply economic assistance." If the speaker means that the states were the ones with economic difficulties, he must place these two elements together in the sentence: "Because they were having economic difficulties, the states asked the federal government for financial assistance."

Most of the time, the concrete and the specific are clearer than the abstract and the general. The referent for the name *Yale* is more likely to be the same for speaker and listener than that for the word *school*. The discusser who talks about "the perimeter defenses of the United States" can increase the clarity of his communication by presenting concrete statements about missile bases and radar warning networks, for example. The Russians refer to the governments of the Eastern European nations as "people's democracies." A discussion by westerners of these governments, using the abstract term *democracies*, will be largely meaningless since our referents for this concept are almost wholly different from those of the Russians. We approve of democracy, yet only a few concrete statements about these people's democracies will quickly make clear the differences in meaning.

Methods of Definition

The discusser's most useful tool for dispelling vagueness and ambiguity is the process of definition. Participants in discussion should define terms often, completely, and carefully. Members should not hesitate to ask for a definition of words used. As Wendell Johnson writes, the key question in clarity is, "What do you mean?" Discussion groups should make this query habitual. At any phase of the deliberation, early or late, members should be willing to stop and ask, "What do we mean?" In fact, the participant should interrupt himself when he realizes he has used an abstraction which may be unclear and say, for example, "Let me explain what I mean by *perimeter defenses*." The good discusser will certainly understand thoroughly the methods of definition.

A definition of any complex concept must be regarded as a process rather than a finished product. Dictionary definitions are helpful for understanding standard verbal meanings of single words, but a dictionary cannot adequately define for a discussion group the "perimeter defenses of the United States."

Nor can this concept be defined in a general statement applicable for all the ages. Imagine what "perimeter defenses of the United States" consisted of in 1870 and contrast that with today! For that matter, there were no missile bases or radar warning networks when World War II began. This concept is constantly undergoing change—it is a process. As the general semanticists suggest, the discusser can when using the term be clearer if he designates what he is defining as "perimeter defenses$_{US1870}$" and "perimeter defenses$_{US \ today}$."

The general method of definition, of course, is first to locate a term within a class, or genus, and then to differentiate the particular term from all other members of that class. A "square" belongs to the general class of plane figures, and it is differentiated—by the *differentia* of the definition—from other members of that class by its four sides of equal length and four right angles. Democracy$_{US \ today}$ is a system of government; within this same classification is located the "people's democracy" of Czechoslovakia. To differentiate one from the other we must specify that the former is characterized by such features as free elections for choosing representatives to make and enforce laws, individual freedom and dignity, and legal protection from search and seizure.

A special method of definition sometimes useful to the discusser is to locate an abstract concept as a point along a continuum. It is usually an error to think that an object, event, or characteristic is either this or that—that a man is either rich or poor, that a nation is either democratic or else it is undemocratic. A man's wealth is relative; he may have sufficient material possessions to make him appear relatively wealthy as compared with those who are poverty-stricken. A nation such as Spain may be more democratic than Czechoslovakia, but less so than Britain. Placing a number of systems along a continuum makes clearer this relativity.

Defining by use of a continuum is simply illustrated in the color spectrum. The colors range from red at one end, through orange, yellow, green, blue, and indigo, to violet at the other end. We can define an ambiguous color by saying, for instance, that it is located between green and blue, with more greenness than blueness. We might similarly define the *democracy* in a particular nation. Of course, it is difficult to define all of democracy at the same time. We can be clearer if we concentrate on one concrete characteristic at a time. Thus, we might locate various nations in terms of the amount of personal freedom accorded the individual citizen:

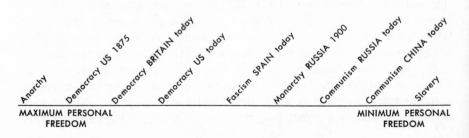

| MAXIMUM PERSONAL FREEDOM | MINIMUM PERSONAL FREEDOM |

Such a continuum does not eliminate all the difficulties, obviously; the location of each item relative to the others is subject to controversy, and there may be disagreement on what is meant by *personal freedom accorded the individual.* Nonetheless, the definitions resulting from considering a cluster of such continua are much less vague and ambiguous than would be an attempt to supply a generalized, dictionary-type definition expressed only in verbal terms.

Another method for increasing the preciseness of a definition is to supply concrete details about the object, event, or concept. Democracy$_{US\ today}$ can be clarified by explaining who may vote and when; who may be elected to office and how and why they may be removed from office; whether there is trial by jury, *habeas corpus,* and freedom from search and seizure of persons and property. With this procedure our kind of system and a dictatorship by whatever name are quickly differentiated.

The operational definition is one which recognizes that change is constant and that a concept is not fixed. Here discussers define by explaining how a system works, or operates. Defining the North Atlantic Treaty Organization (NATO) by this method requires members to explain such characteristics as the structure of the organization, the powers of its leadership, and the degree of autonomy and commitment of member nations. Here again it must be kept in mind that NATO today is not NATO$_{1948}$.

Terms may be defined by comparison and contrast. Capitalism and communism as economic systems may be differentiated by showing their similarities and differences.

Some concepts can best be defined by tracing their history. The Monroe Doctrine, for example, can hardly be understood except by relating its varying interpretations from the time of its first enunciation by President Monroe, through the wars of the twentieth century, and the recent extensions made by President Truman during the 1946 crisis in Greece and Turkey, by President Eisenhower during the Middle East turmoil in the 1950's, and by President Kennedy during the Cuban missile crisis.

Definition by authority should not be overlooked as a method. As has been noted, the dictionary can be helpful as a source of standard definition for single words. For some technical concepts, such as the nature of cosmic rays, the distinction between recession and depression, or the meaning of psychotic behavior, discussers can profit most from the definitions supplied by experts who thoroughly understand them.

Language Must Be Accurate

Although clarity and accuracy usually go hand in hand, it is possible for the speaker to communicate clearly his intended meaning without being accurate in his information. He may spell out precisely what he means by democracy and still be mistaken: the details he gives about democracy$_{US\ today}$ may not accurately reflect what is happening within our system of government.

The accuracy of language usage is the problem of semantics and concerns the extent to which our words refer to objects or events as these realities actually exist in the world external to our senses. Semantic difficulties arise when we fail to realize that words cannot express all of any reality, that words are not things, and that a particular black is not necessarily all black but may be partially gray. Words are necessarily incomplete—they cannot contain all of meaning. To express ideas words are put together within necessarily incomplete statements—that is, statements about anything cannot say all that could or should be said.

The discusser must thus treat language as the fragile instrument it is. He must use it with care and make every possible effort to choose words which will elicit from listeners only those images which correspond as explicitly as possible to reality. He will be aware that no matter how carefully he uses words he is placing his own values and interpretations upon everything he perceives and attempts to convey to others.

He will add overtly or covertly to all his statements, "At least this is the way this concept appears to me, as I see it." He will often qualify his statements: "This is *apparently* true," or "This *may* be the way it is," or "This is what will *probably* (or *possibly*) result." Absolute judgments, arbitrary positions, and unqualified statements rarely reflect the real world with accuracy, and are usually damaging to a discussion. *A* is not always all *A*. To use an extreme example, discussers should look with suspicion upon a declaration that "no person in our democracy has ever had his personal freedom interfered with" or that "citizens in the Czechoslovakian 'people's democracy' have no personal freedom." The truth almost always exists somewhere between such extremes. The conscientious discusser hesitates to generalize absolutely. He avoids exaggerated claims. Rather, he attempts to use words which have concrete referents, and to signify accurately conditions as they actually exist in the external world.

Language Must Be Appropriate

Language choices should be appropriate to the discussion situation, to the subject matter, to the other participants, and to the listening audience in public discussion.

Words and sentences can be less formal in some situations than in others. The use of slang expressions is an example of one type of informal language choice which may be appropriate in a student committee and wholly inappropriate in a foreign ministers conference. Subject matter, too, may affect language usage. An extremely complicated discussion problem may require more careful word choices, definition, and sentence construction than simpler subjects.

In public discussion adaptation to the other participants and to the listening audience is necessary because the listener must be led to identify precisely the referent intended if meaning is to be communicated. Technical words, obsolete expressions, provincialisms, and colloquialisms should be avoided if listeners are unfamiliar with them.

Language Must Be Fair to Others

It is often easy to tell when a discusser is talking nonsense or making extreme statements. It is more difficult at times to detect language choices that subtly color, slant, or distort concepts. The very complexity of the symbolizing process makes slanting easy to use and in many cases hard to identify. In fact, the speaker may or may not know when he is guilty of using "loaded" language. Obviously, reflective thinking and rational deliberation can be damaged severely by language which introduces unfair distortion, whether deliberately or naively.

The discusser must be sensitive to the distinction between denotation—the referent a word presumably designates, denotes—and the additional meanings that can be suggested by the word, called its *connotations*. A word differs in connotation for different persons because of varying past experiences with the word, and the attitudes and interests of the person reacting. Most of us react favorably to the word *capitalism*, while the leaders of Russia apparently relate it to starvation and oppression of captive workers. For most of us, the designation *Wall Street* is more or less a neutral concept, yet to the Russians it seems to suggest imperialism, war-mongering, or something worse. Officials of labor unions and management executives probably react quite differently to such terms as free enterprise, big business, profit motive, strike breaking, the slow-down, the speed-up, and yellow-dog contract.

Note the differences suggested by these words:

	Usually Neutral	*Probably Complimentary*	*Probably Derogatory*
Horse	Thoroughbred	Nag, plug
Lawyer	Counsellor	Shyster, Mouthpiece, Ambulance-chaser
Old (person)	Mature	Decrepit, Senile
Slender (girl)	Sylphlike	Skinny
Congressman	Statesman	Ward-heeler, Wire-puller
U.S. financial aid to foreign countries	Investment in democracy! Helping hand to valiant allies! Investment in enlightened self-interest	Handout! Underwriting of socialism! Pouring money down a rat-hole! Santa Claus to the ungrateful!

The discusser can make two errors when he uses words that may have unfavorable connotations. He may fail to communicate his meaning, and he may rupture interpersonal relations needlessly. If a person refers to his friend's favorite horse as a nag, he need not be surprised if the friend reacts unfavorably to the word and to him.

There are many ways to say approximately the same thing. A teacher can report that a student, after the class bell had rung, "entered quietly," or "sneaked in." A crackpot can also be described as a "champion of unorthodox views" and "a defender of nonconformity." A banker who espouses thrift may be considered stingy by his family. The "finest quality filet mignon" can be assigned the literal but unappetizing label, "first class piece of dead steer." A headline writer can report the results of a baseball game by writing, "Score: Cubs, 5; Giants, 3," or he can reveal his own feelings: "Cubs Trounce Giants 5–3." Equally revealing of the biases of the writers are the differences in the following three messages, each communicating approximately the same content:

Laudatory:
 He is a man of strong convictions and he works in concert with those who will guard our established traditions. His conduct of the Presidency should exemplify the highest type of statesmanlike leadership.
Derogatory:
 He is a creature of strong prejudices and belongs to the camp of reactionaries. His conduct of the Presidency portends a degeneration of that office into dictatorship.
More or Less Impartial Report:
 He is a man who seems to feel strongly about his views and he is apparently reluctant to see policies changed quickly. His term as President may be a period of change during which policies will be altered more slowly than in the preceding administration.

In discussion, unwise language choices can also serve to discourage other participants, shut off thinking, and prevent pursuance of promising lines of thought. A group of executives listed these examples of "idea killers":[2]

"Don't be ridiculous."
"We tried that before."
"It's too radical a change."
"That will make other equipment obsolete."
"We're too small for it."
"Not practical for operating people."
"Let's get back to reality."
"You're two years ahead of your time."
"Can't teach an old dog new tricks."
"We'll be the laughingstock."

---

[2] Quoted in Lester R. Bittel, "Brainstorming," *Factory Management and Maintenance,* 114 (1956), p. 107.

The objections contained in these statements may be quite valid in some situations. The fault lies in the words chosen to express the objection. Older persons can learn new ways of doing things. But the timeworn expression, "You can't teach an old dog new tricks" may connote that anyone who continues to pursue the new idea is a fool. In other words, the person who advanced the new idea may feel that he is being called a fool when, in reality, the speaker who objected may only have meant: "Adopting a new technique is made more difficult by the necessity of retraining workers." If this is what he meant, this is what he should have said. The reacting listener will be affected by what the words suggest as well as by what they denote.

OTHER SPEECH SKILLS

Using language effectively is an important aspect of communication in discussion, but in addition there are other vital elements of speaking skill. The discusser must also deliver oral messages effectively. Language usage will reappear here since words cannot be separated from the total process of communication.

Intelligibility

The discusser must make his speech intelligible, first of all by speaking audibly so that he can be easily heard. He also must have reasonably accurate and precise articulation and enunciation. Carelessness in making sounds distinctly may obscure the distinction between such words as *effect* and *affect*. Listeners may misunderstand when some sounds are omitted or distorted. They may not know whether a speaker who habitually slurs and slights sounds has said, "I c'n 'cept that," ("I can accept that") or "I c'n't 'cept that." ("I can't accept that.") The resultant misunderstanding may occasionally cause serious difficulty. Some discussers are also guilty of speaking too rapidly.

Naturalness

The speaker should sound as natural in discussion as he does in informal conversation. There is no reason for stilted, unnatural voice usage. He will be unnatural if he does not sound as if he were talking to these people in this room at this moment. If he sounds as if he is reciting words he has memorized earlier or as if he is reading without awareness of his listeners, then he is not speaking naturally.

The speaker must be aware of the meaning of his words as he delivers them. The story is told of a discusser who was interrupted and asked to repeat what he had just said; he replied, "I can't—I wasn't listening." This speaker was not speaking naturally—and he probably did not sound the way he would in conversation—because the words were not registering in his mind as he used them.

To be natural, also, the speaker will use facial expressiveness, bodily action, and gesture as he would in informal conversation with friends. His voice will vary naturally according to the meaning of the words.

Directness

Closely related to naturalness is directness. The discusser must face his listeners squarely and look at them directly if he is to hold their attention and communicate effectively.

Directness is easier to achieve during the conversational interaction of closedgroup discussion than in public discussion such as symposium, where the participant is in effect a public speaker. Even in public discussion, however, the speaker must communicate directly.

Interestingness

Intelligibility, naturalness, and directness are minimal requirements for the speaker. To be maximally effective, he must also speak interestingly, with enthusiasm and feeling. Before his listeners will react with attentiveness, he must himself sound interested. Further, he must speak with vocal variety; a communication delivered in a monotone is dull and difficult to listen to without strain and loss of attention.

Some Kinds of Communication Failures

To speak in most discussion situations seems deceptively easy, but it is possible for discussers to overestimate the success with which they are communicating. One kind of communication failure is to get across only part of the meaning. This can occur when the speaker fails to secure the attention of his listeners, has fuzzy ideas which are not clear even to him, or delivers his communication in a jumbled, disorganized, illogical sequence.

Another kind of breakdown occurs when the wrong or unintended meaning is transmitted. Since words have different meanings for different people, the speaker must adapt his message to the particular listeners he is addressing. He must watch his colleagues or his audience carefully for signs of misunderstanding, and try with other words to make his meanings clear.

The speaker must avoid misleading his listeners through inconsistency between his words and his voice and bodily action; meaning and manner of delivery must match. If a participant says, "I think this is a satisfactory solution," when his facial expression and vocal inflection seem to say, "I disapprove," or "I don't believe it will work very well," or "I am not very enthusiastic about it," the listeners will be confused.

LISTENING

All communication should be a two-way process, but in discussion a reciprocal relationship between a person who happens to be speaker at the moment and those listening is absolutely essential. The discussion participant must be a good listener.

Occasionally a person fails to listen because he is reciting or thinking to himself what he will say next, or because he is planning a defense of an idea of his own attacked earlier. He may need to do such thinking, but he must not become so preoccupied that he ignores the comments of others. The poor listener diverts the group to unrelated tangents, causes the group to repeat ideas already covered, limits his own understanding of what is happening, and misses opportunities to contribute to the outcome or to object if he disapproves.

Listening is more than hearing; it is an active mental process. The listener must consider alertly what the speaker is saying. Listening is made difficult in part because the mind can operate many times faster than the speaker can talk. While the speaker stumbles along at 140 words a minute, the listener's mind may go racing along thinking about a multitude of irrelevant distractions within himself or outside him in the total situation. The hearer gets lost when his mind hits upon something more fascinating than the discussion at hand, and he completely tunes out of the immediate situation. When he finally realizes that he has lost track of the discussion, the contributions have moved on.

The listener can train himself to combat the danger of tuning out by concentrating all his mental powers on what the speaker of the moment is saying. He should ask himself varied but closely related questions: Why is the speaker saying it this way? What does he mean? How does this relate to what was said earlier? Does his statement fit what I already know? Where is the group likely to move next? By keeping his mind busy on matters related to the communicative interchange, he will follow the discussion closely and make a maximum contribution when he comments.

SUPPLEMENTARY READING

Hayakawa, S. I., *Language in Thought and Action*, sec. ed., New York: Harcourt, Brace & World, 1963.

Johnson, Wendell, *People in Quandaries*, New York: Harper & Row, 1946, especially Part III.

————, "The Spoken Word and the Great Unsaid," *Quarterly Journal of Speech*, 37 (1951), pp. 419–429.

Lee, Irving J., *How to Talk with People*, New York: Harper & Row, 1952, especially Chapters 2 and 8.

Nichols, Ralph G., and Lewis, Thomas R., *Listening and Speaking*, Dubuque, Iowa: Wm. C. Brown, 1954, pp. 23–25, and Chapter 5.

Wagner, Russell H., and Arnold, Carroll C., *Handbook of Group Discussion*, Boston: Houghton Mifflin, 1950, Chapter 8.

QUESTIONS AND EXERCISES

1. Wendell Johnson (1951, above) writes: "We inevitably talk about our-selves, whatever else we may also strive to symbolize. What the speaker . . . directly symbolizes, what he turns into words or other symbols, are neurophysiological, or electrochemical, or, if you prefer, electronic goings-on inside his own body. His organism, in this sense, operates constantly as a kind of filter through which facts (in the sense of sensory impulses) must pass before they can become known to him and before they can be communicated by him to others in some symbolic form. . . . We often talk about the world outside, but when we do, we filter it through our inner states." Explain what he means. Explain also what this concept has to do with the problems of the participant in discussion.

2. Arthur Hadley, in his book, *Do I Make Myself Clear?* (New York: Holt, Rinehart and Winston, 1956) presents some amusing examples of polit-ical double talk. "I have no political ambitions. I consider it my duty to serve the nation in the job to which I have just been appointed and I will devote my life to this job I now hold." Translation: "I am running for Governor." The statement, "I am receiving information from businessmen and labor leaders all over the country that the provisions of this law have proved unfair," means, "My brother-in-law is in trouble." When a speaker says, "There can be no doubt that owing to the interplay of economic factors there were several sharp price fluctuations during the time of active government interest in this commodity," he may mean "The boys in the know made a killing." Collect similar examples of vague, ambiguous language from speeches and newspapers, and translate them into literal, denotative statements.

3. In his book, *Teacher in America* (Boston: Little, Brown, 1945, p. 136), Jacques Barzun says that "Words are not clothing for an idea, they are its incarnation." Explain and elaborate upon what he means.

4. Find an excerpt from a speech or newspaper editorial that consists almost wholly of abstractions without concrete referents. Attempt to supply referents for some of the terms.

5. Listen carefully to a public group discussion and prepare a report of your observations of one of the following:
   a. Use of abstract language in which the absence of clear referents ham-pered the communication.
   b. Instances of unclear, ambiguous language usage.
   c. Satisfactory and unsatisfactory uses of definition.
   d. Instances of accurate and inaccurate uses of language.
   e. Instances of appropriate and inappropriate uses of language.
   f. Fair and unfair uses of language.
   g. Evaluation of the use of speech skills by members.
   h. Evaluation of the listening skill of members.

Chapter 8

ATTITUDES
AND ETHICS

We have approached the study of discussion primarily from the view of the individual as participant or leader. In the last three chapters we have considered the problems of securing and using information, of reasoning in group situations, and of employing language and communication. Now we must ask about the individual's attitudes as he takes part in group decision-making. What should be his motives? Can he appropriately try to win a discussion as he would a debate or should he suppress his convictions for the good of the group? What are his ethical responsibilities in group situations?

These are important but difficult questions. In the final analysis only the individual can decide what his attitudes should be. The key question he must answer is this: To what extent am I willing to cooperate as part of a group effort and to what extent must I pursue my personal objectives? When he takes into account the group's welfare, he places upon himself some special responsibilities.

What the individual will consider appropriate varies with the group, the nature of the task, the situation, and other factors. All we can do here is to suggest some of the dimensions of the problem and leave to the individual the making of decisions about his own behavior in particular circumstances.

The individual is more willing to sacrifice for the collective good in some groups than in others. When the time comes for a family to decide where the first youngster will go to college, each member will usually take every other member's interests into account. Father will be concerned about cost and the vocational opportunities for his son after graduation, but most fathers will listen carefully to the motivations and aspirations of the boy. Mother may be interested in the prestige of the prospective college and the attractiveness of its campus although she will undoubtedly realize the importance of financial and vocational considerations. The son will be influenced in part by the college choices of his friends, by the academic demands of the school, and other factors. The younger brothers and sisters will look at the problems partially in terms of the effect on them when their turn comes to go away to school. In general, however, the family usually tries to decide as a cooperating unit, to arrive at what is best for the whole group. In doing so the members will display attitudes characteristic of cooperative group endeavor.

The family would find it easier to operate as a unified group in handling a simpler task. If they were planning a Sunday picnic, the family could choose a place which everyone could approve happily. A single veto of the beach as the site might cause that alternative to be rejected. Where more vital individual interests are at stake, especially those with long-term implications such as the choice of a college, it is more difficult for each member to accept a decision derived from composite group judgment.

Some groups, in contrast, do not have such cohesiveness. In these cases, individual motivations cannot be put aside for the greater group good, to the extent that they may be within the family, because the objectives of various members can be in direct conflict. If, for example, four major powers hold a foreign ministers' conference for the purpose of averting a threatened war, the representative of each nation must be extremely wary of placing the collective welfare above the nationalistic interests of his nation. The success of the conference will undoubtedly be related to the willingness of participants to consider the collective interests of all, but members cannot be expected automatically to sublimate their personal interests to group purposes.

Situations, tasks, and groups are not the only variables. We can refer to the illustration of the family choosing a college for the first youngster. Not all families would operate as a cooperative unit. The family is, ideally, a type of group that is highly cohesive but the decision-making there depends also on the personalities of members. In some families the father, for instance, is an authoritarian who expects any decision to please him first of all. Others attempt to achieve the outcome best for themselves within the limits of the decision the father will allow.

Stages in a Controversy

In the earliest stages of the emergence of a controversial problem, individuals usually find it easier to pursue the problem in cooperation with others in a group situation. A community, for example, may notice that the incidence of holdups and burglaries is increasing. Up to this time citizens may not have been particularly aware of the crime rate. Discussions may now take place in the Town Council, church boards, and civic clubs on the causes of the growing number of robberies and break-ins. At this early stage, discussion will likely be reasonably unemotional. Groups will agree easily on the essential facts. At some point, however, someone or some group will propose a course of action, such as adding ten policemen to the force at a cost of so many dollars. The conflict in such groups as the Town Council will now depend on the attitudes of individuals toward this specific proposal and the extent to which the financial interests of citizens are affected.

When the proposal of adding ten policemen is first made in the council, the members may well try to reach a consensus by defining and analyzing the crime problem; considering alternative solutions, such as adding the ten men to the police force; weighing of alternatives; and deciding on the best solution. We can represent the stages in the consideration of the problem in this way:

In the beginning stages, members will not have made up their minds about the solution. They will be seeking to understand the situation and searching for an answer. Thus they will likely be open to all kinds of information and ideas.

There is a good chance that the council will not reach a consensus quickly on the wisdom of adding ten policemen. It is more likely that some members who have been pressing for improved community services will start arguing for the proposal while those who are concerned with increasing costs of city government will oppose such an expensive solution. If such a controversy emerges and if it becomes intense, proponents of each view may become so firmly convinced that only their decision is wise that they become active advocates of their cause. In such instances, these individuals will find it increasingly difficult to look at the problem in terms of the group's interests.

The advocate of a particular proposal has a goal which he has not had earlier in the discussion. He is now trying to persuade the group that his view should be accepted by the others. The change in the participant is one of mental attitude or aim; from an attitude of searching with others for the best decision he has shifted to one of conviction that he has found the best one and his mission is to convince his colleagues.

It must be emphasized that there is nothing wrong with differences of opinion. When people differ, they have a right, even a duty, to speak persuasively, marshaling evidence to support the wisdom of their position. In many situations, a sensible policy will emerge more readily from sharp confrontation of candid differences than it will from overly cautious detachment and neutral statements. After members have given every view a full and fair hearing, however, the group must get on with the business at hand, which is reaching a decision. The advocacy of particular alternatives should not be an end in itself. The whole process of deliberation, including one or more periods of advocacy, could be represented as a deliberation continuum. The council considers the problem, weighs alternatives, concentrates on the pros and cons of a particular proposal, and proceeds to consider the wisest decision, perhaps by voting or perhaps by further discussion:

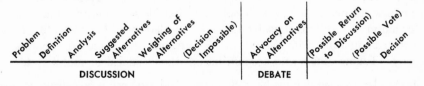

In the area of political deliberation, when the nation is electing a President, to take another example, limited groups in the two parties first discuss possible candidates. There are controversy and advocacy in many caucuses before the nominating convention. At the convention there is discussion in both official and unofficial meetings. The election campaign is a period of debate and persuasive speaking. Champions of the opposing candidates attempt to influence the voters. Finally there is a decision at the ballot box. The attitude of the individual participant in these proceedings changes with the stage of controversy. At some points he may give in on his personal preference in order to agree with the larger group on a candidate with the best chance to win. At other stages he will advocate the election of his party's choice without equivocation.

The Individual and the Collective Good

The individual participant in the group setting, then, will hold a mixture of attitudes that will change from situation to situation, group to group, task to task, and even from moment to moment within the same meeting. At times the achievement of his personal goals will be uppermost while at others he will put the group welfare ahead of his own interests. From moment to moment the individual tries to maintain a balance, or state of congruity, between his personal orientation and the collective good of the others involved.

As civilized members of an established community, from which we derive many benefits, most of us have a willingness to help maintain our political and cultural groups. In our vocational groups, such as the staff or executive committee which may be a part of our jobs, we see the importance of contributing to the team effort. It is as we recognize this loyalty to the collective welfare of those assembled that we sacrifice part of our selfish motives for the larger group. By contributing to the group effort we gain certain benefits that we could not obtain by ourselves. Beyond this, most persons on occasion are willing to make a completely selfless sacrifice for the greater good of others, or to give in to the group judgment in the belief that the majority is sometimes wiser. At the same time, we cannot fail to size up each situation from our own personal perspective.

Fausti and Luker have analyzed the congruity problem of the person engaged in problem-solving discussion. "The individual," they write, "seeks to maintain homeostasis or a state of equilibrium, which is never quite reached." He perceives the problem from his "private frame of reference," which is the only way open to him. "Privately he may develop an extreme preference for one of the possible solutions, but his selection of a final course of action must take into consideration another element in his perceptual field: his interrelationship with others, as he perceives the place he occupies in society." Taking others into account introduces an ethical or moral factor.

It must be assumed that the basic character of human need is essentially positive rather than negative; adequacy of the individual is inextricably interwoven with the society of which he is a part. Democracy assumes faith in our fellows—an interdependent society. No member of a society can exist alone. Each must work with, cooperate with, and associate with other members of the society whether he wants to or not.

In balancing these forces, according to these authorities, the individual chooses the line of action that best maintains his equilibrium and enhances his personality and self-adequacy.[1]

Perhaps we are now ready to suggest some guidelines for answering the question: What individual attitudes toward a discussion are appropriate under these widely varied conditions?

Specific answers, as we have indicated, will vary with the situation, group, task, persons, stages of controversy, and the need of the individual for equilibrium and the satisfying of self-oriented goals. Yet there are some general considerations that determine attitudes and ethical responsibilities under conditions where the participant wishes to discuss cooperatively and contribute to a collective effort.

OBJECTIVITY AND OPEN-MINDEDNESS

One way in which the individual can contribute to the group effort, at least in the early phases of discussion, is to maintain an attitude of tentativeness. He can withhold judgment until everyone has been heard and all the facts are in.

Most of the time, in most situations, the discusser is searching, inquiring, and engaging in reflective thinking—in company with others in the group. He must be willing to explore any area of investigation or any proposal that seems pertinent, even if it conflicts with, for example, his favorite myths, biases, political or social prejudices, or economic interest. This requirement does not mean that the discusser should not have convictions, that he should be indecisive, or that he should agree to anything the group wishes, just to be a good fellow and build harmony. Obviously, each participant must have convictions, or the group will not respect him; nor, incidentally, will he make much constructive contribution to the group. What it does mean is that the discusser refrains from prejudgment; he does not often enter discussion with a rigid mind-set about the best course of action and spend all his time arguing for it and refuting members who are exploring other possibilities. He may feel strongly about the advantages of some proposals and the disadvantages of others. He may express his convictions passionately. However, he must be willing to explore the convictions of others with vigor. In the process he may discover ways to improve the ideas he held previously.

The discusser's mental attitude toward the problem will often be one of objectivity–open-mindedness. He can be compared to an explorer who searches out and makes a map of new territory. He must look carefully at the

[1] Remo P. Fausti and Arno H. Luker, "A Phenomenological Approach to Discussion," *The Speech Teacher*, 14 (1965), pp. 20–1.

terrain from all aspects and must define and describe explicitly what he sees. He must approach his task with an open rather than a closed mind, resisting preconceived notions of what the new land will be like. His new map must not be made to conform to what he had hoped its shapes would be.

If the discusser is to achieve objectivity, he must have the ability to *examine objects and events in the world external to himself without allowing his internal biases, attitudes, and value system to distort his perception of these external objects and events.* Webster's *New International Dictionary*, in defining objectivity, quotes Sir W. Hamilton: "Objective means that which belongs to, or proceeds from, the object known, and not from the subject knowing."

Open-mindedness is receptivity to new concepts. After the discusser has explored, defined, and described all the new facts and ideas available, he must be willing to consider them, set them alongside notions already possessed and cherished, make comparisons and contrasts, and, perhaps, incorporate them into his thinking.

Open-mindedness both precedes and follows objectivity. The discusser must have an open mind or he will not be willing to examine the external world objectively. If he is already fully satisfied with his cherished notions, he will not look without bias at new concepts. After making an objective examination of outside events and objects, he must be open-minded if he is to consider carefully whether to incorporate these new concepts into his attitude and value systems.

Objectivity depends on the accuracy of perception. To be objective, the discusser must view the external world with detachment, with minimal involvement of his internal states. Open-mindedness depends on the flexibility of his internal attitude-value systems. If the discusser regards his presently held concepts as adequate, fixed, closed, and final, he has minimal open-mindedness.

Perhaps the operation of objectivity–open-mindedness can be illustrated if we imagine a Republican and a Democrat informally discussing the Presidential candidates of their respective political parties. Each must first be open-minded, and this state is indicated by willingness to compare the candidates and especially by willingness to talk with each other. Objectivity would then involve careful description of the strengths and weaknesses of the two men as presidential candidates. The Republican should describe the strengths of the Democratic candidate, and the Democrat should describe the strengths of the Republican candidate, just as readily and objectively as each describes the weaknesses of the opposition candidate. Suppose the Republican had held a political job that he had lost when the Democrats last took power, and that he and his father before him have never once voted for a Democrat. If this background prevents him from seeing a single good trait in the Democratic candidate, he is probably not looking at him objectively. Open-mindedness is also important following the objective description of the two candidates. The Republican and the Democrat will probably each remain convinced of the superiority of his own party's candidate. To be open-minded does not require a change in attitude. However, after a discussion in which both men are as objective as possible, each will probably see his candidate as not quite as good and the opposition candidate as not quite as bad as he had previously seen them.

Obstacles to objectivity–open-mindedness

A little thought will make clear that it is not easy to achieve objectivity–open-mindedness. Some persons find it easier than others, but it is not true that some persons are objective and open-minded at all times and that others never achieve these states. Objectivity–open-mindedness is a relative matter. Each of us is more objective and open-minded on some problems than on others, and at some times than at others. There are some serious obstacles that make objectivity–open-mindedness difficult at times for everyone.

PERCEPTUAL DIFFICULTIES/ When we observe, define, and describe, it is difficult not to see concepts in the external world in terms of our internal physical and mental states: needs, attitudes, values, past experiences. Even in physical, sensory perception, what we see when we look with our eyes may be altered by our internal states. Otto Klineberg, in his book, *Social Psychology*, says:

It is no longer possible to approach perception as a purely individual phenomenon, the nature of which is determined by the pattern of neurones which bring impulses from the outside world to the central nervous system. Although it is true that the process of vision is made possible by the impingement of certain vibrations on the optic nerve, and the transmission of the impulse through the optic thalamus to the occipital part of the cortex, there are aspects of vision which are determined by the previous experience of the individual, in connection with which group-membership plays an important part. Considerable evidence has accumulated which indicates that social factors must be considered if the phenomena of sense perception are properly to be understood.

Klineberg presents a number of examples, one of them involving the Trobriand Islanders:

Among the Trobrianders, the idea of resemblance between parents and offspring, or between children of the same parents, is controlled by strict social norms. These may at times go counter to the evidence of one's senses. In the first place, resemblance to the father is regarded as natural and proper, and such similarity is always assumed and affirmed to exist. It is a great offense to hint that the child resembles his mother or any of his maternal relatives . . . it is taken for granted that brothers do not resemble each other.

Klineberg observes:

It is difficult to know with certainty whether the sense perception has actually been interfered with, that is to say, whether the Trobrianders actually *see* the two brothers as different even though to us they would obviously resemble each other, or whether they are merely unwilling to acknowledge such a resemblance even when they do see it. It is probable, however, on the basis of our knowledge of the degree to which we see what we are looking for, that the Trobrianders fail to note any resemblance because they do not want or expect to find it.[2]

Sherif's studies on the autokinetic effect demonstrated that persons imagined the movement of a stationary point of light in a dark room, and that the extent of the movement perceived by individuals was influenced by the announced judgments of others viewing the light at the same time.[3] Asch found that some persons stated that two lines were of equal length even when their sense perception told them they were unequal, in the presence of a group of others who had agreed beforehand to announce an incorrect judgment, that is, one not confirmed by sensory perception.[4]

Wendell Johnson observes that our communication is a response to what we perceive in the external world, creating a "preverbal state of affairs within the organism." He then remarks that this preverbal state

is truly silent, or nonverbal [and] it is precisely this preverbal condition inside the organism that is transformed into words (or other symbols). This means— and these next few words one must read at a snail's pace and ponder long and fretfully—that, besides talking always to ourselves, although others may be listening more or less too, *we inevitably talk about ourselves*, whatever else we may also strive to symbolize. What the speaker (or painter, musical composer, actor, etc.) directly symbolizes, what he *turns into words* or other symbols, are neurophysiological, or electrochemical, or, if you prefer, electronic goings-on inside his own body. His organism, in this sense, operates constantly as a kind of filter through which facts (in the sense of sensory impulses) must pass before they can be *communicated* by him to others in some symbolic form. . . . The implication is not intended that we talk solely about our inner states. We often talk about the world outside, but when we do we filter it through our inner states. To the degree that our individual filters are standardized, are alike, we will agree in the statements we make about the world outside—allowing, of course, for differences in time, observational set, equipment, sensory acuity, perceptive skill, and manner of making verbal reports.[5]

All that has been said here concerns perception of physical objects. Committees, conferences, and boards do not often discuss questions involving only sensory perception: "Do these brothers resemble each other?" "How far does this light move?" "Are these lines of equal length?" Groups discuss complex social, political, and economic matters involving abstract concepts. When they switch from a reality that can be confirmed by sensory perception to

[2] Rev. ed., New York: Holt, Rinehart and Winston, 1954, pp. 204ff. Used with permission.

[3] Muzafer Sherif, "A Study of Some Social Factors in Perception," *Archives of Psychology*, No. 187, 1935.

[4] Solomon E. Asch, *Social Psychology*, Englewood Cliffs, N.J., Prentice-Hall, 1952, pp. 450–501.

[5] "The Spoken Word and the Great Unsaid," *Quarterly Journal of Speech*, 37 (1951), p. 422. Used with permission.

social reality—where correct responses are anchored only in what the group accepts—the obstacles to objectivity–open-mindedness are multiplied. It is obvious that members of a group may discuss the same problem and not perceive the facts in the same way.

It may be helpful to mention two examples of more complex perceptual difficulties where social reality is involved. Some persons have a tendency to operate with a "two-valued orientation." A solution is "right" or it is "wrong." The proposal is "wise" or it is "unwise." We must accept "all" of the proposal or "none." Persons who see involved social concepts in such "yes" or "no" pigeonholes find objectivity–open-mindedness more difficult. Another tendency is to oversimplify the world: to see part of it and to accept that as the whole of it. Persons who wish to simplify situations so that they are easier to understand often, in discussion, are willing to approach a solution with insufficient evidence.

EXPRESSIVE DIFFICULTIES/ Perceptual difficulties are only part of the problem of objectivity–open-mindedness. Even if we are objective and open-minded when we examine socially anchored concepts, it is difficult to express what we have observed precisely and fairly. Even with the best of intentions, it is hard to use language efficiently enough to express our meanings accurately and objectively. To this complication can be added the danger of introducing bias unconsciously through the particular words chosen. Then, of course, it is impossible to express all of our meaning or to say everything there is to say.

PERSONAL INVOLVEMENT IN THE PROBLEM/ Objectivity–open-mindedness is made even more difficult when the individual is deeply involved in the particular problem being discussed by the group. In fact, it is likely that objectivity–open-mindedness of the individual varies inversely with his involvement in the problem.

For example, a college student can be more objective–open-minded in discussing this question: "Should oil producers be granted an additional deduction in federal income taxes to compensate for the risk of exploring new oil fields?" than he can in discussing this question: "Should each student at this college be assessed an additional ten dollars a semester as an activity fee?" On the other hand, the difficulty of achieving objectivity–open-mindedness would be reversed for a Texas oil producer discussing the two questions.

The discusser must attempt to recognize his own "hidden agendas"—those motives and aspirations that he unconsciously hides, and that color his contributions.

He must not establish a feeling of proprietorship of his ideas so that others cannot trespass upon his property without emotional reaction from him. To be objective, he must be able to weigh his own ideas with almost the same detachment and calm judgment with which he evaluates those of others.

He must listen carefully and constructively to the ideas of others in the group. Rather than listening passively, he must think actively about the concepts introduced by others. He must be determined to understand precisely what others mean by each comment, for as Cardinal Newman observed: "When men understand each other's meaning, they see, for the most part, that controversy is either superfluous or hopeless."

He should ask, tactfully, for clarification when he fails to understand others, and hope that they will reciprocate by asking him to restate a point he fails to make clear.

The discusser who wishes to be objective should consider the ideas advanced by others on the merits of the ideas. An excellent idea may come from what an individual considers an unfavorable or unlikely source, and such a value judgment related to the holder of the idea should not interfere with the thoughtful weighing of the concept involved. Perhaps the opposite danger is even more common in discussion: accepting an idea which is not sound just because it comes from a source considered favorable, for example, from a person well liked or one with high prestige.

He should modify his own ideas if he hears better ones. It has often been observed that there are usually three ways to do things: the right way, the wrong way, and our way. Our way is usually somewhat right and somewhat wrong. The willingness to modify usually means encouraging everyone in the group to build on everyone else's ideas, including our own. He must not regard concepts as immutable, but as changing, and requiring constant re-examination.

ATTITUDES TOWARD OTHERS

The group task is vital in discussion, and open-mindedness in relation to the problem makes a contribution to group effort. Members must also be concerned with social function. If they are willing to contribute to a group product, they must be objective about and tolerant of other participants.

To be objective about other persons is to observe them and work with them without allowing our internal states to color our observations and reactions. Negatively, it means that we must not let our prejudices, likes or dislikes, or attitudes toward particular individuals or kinds of persons distort our judgment. Tolerance means that we treat them with dignity and respect.

Again, objectivity depends upon the accuracy of our perceptions: the ability to see others with detachment and to evaluate them dispassionately. Tolerance depends upon our internal value system. If we do not accept the premise that each person deserves our respect, then group interaction will be made more difficult.

Tolerance both precedes and follows objectivity. We must have forbearance in order to view others objectively. Without it, we would operate unquestioningly, according to our prejudices and stereotypes. Tolerance also follows our objective examination of others, and perhaps we are more willing to cooperate with them wholeheartedly if, after objective consideration, we find them more deserving of our respect than we had believed them to be.

Obstacles to Objectivity

Just as the discusser has difficulties in being objective and open-minded when he considers concepts, so he is confronted with obstacles in exhibiting objectivity and tolerance toward persons.

PERCEPTUAL DIFFICULTIES/ Here, too, there are difficulties in objective perception. Bruner and Tagiuri explain some of the distortions in judging others, three of which seem especially common in discussion. One is the halo effect: our general impressions of a person cause us to assume that each of the parts has the same characteristics as the whole. We think a person is a "good guy"; therefore, we are inclined not to examine critically a proposal he puts forth. Another is logical error: on the basis of past experience, we feel that certain traits go with certain other traits. Thus, if a member expresses himself fluently, we may jump to the conclusion that his summary of what the group decided should be accepted. The third is the leniency effect: we have a tendency, according to Bruner and Tagiuri, "to rate others (and also oneself) high in favorable traits and low in unfavorable traits." In discussion, we may tend to examine ideas (our own and others') less critically than we should; that is, to base a decision on careless thinking because we are too kind and tactful to others. We may give people credit for being much better reasoners than they actually are. Objectivity requires frank and careful judgment; tolerance for others and leniency in judging poor thinking ability must not be allowed to overbalance objectivity.[6]

PRIOR ASSOCIATION WITH OTHERS/ The involvement of the individual with the other members of the discussion group may make objectivity-tolerance more difficult. Previous acquaintance and interaction, favorable or unfavorable, can alter our efforts to assess others objectively.

Objectivity may be easier to achieve when discussing some problems with strangers, while for some other topics it may be easier with persons we know well. Members of momentary groups often report that interaction becomes less difficult as the discussion proceeds. This may suggest that as members feel more at ease with each other, objectivity becomes less difficult to achieve.

Even the presence of members of the opposite sex in the discussion group may make objectivity more difficult in some situations, and in the discussion of some topics.

POWER DISCREPANCIES/ It is obvious that extreme difference in power between two members of the group makes objectivity more difficult for each of them. The high may tend to discount the value of a low's ideas and find it difficult to be tactful in reacting to him. The low may tend to overestimate the soundness of the high's reasoning, and to be more tactful than he should be.

The discusser must learn to perceive and react to others objectively: he must try to consider every member of the group equal to every other as a

[6] Jerome S. Bruner and R. Tagiuri, "The Perception of People," Gardner Lindzey, (ed.), *Handbook of Social Psychology*, Cambridge, Mass.: Addison-Wesley, 1954, p. 641.

person and, therefore, entitled to the time to present his ideas. It does not mean that everyone's ideas will be equally meritorious, but that every person is equally meritorious of attention, being heard, and having any objections answered. Further, the discusser must learn to be equally objective in reacting to close friends and strangers.

ETHICAL RESPONSIBILITIES

In an interdependent society men must trust each other to fulfill their functions honestly and faithfully, at least most of the time. An airline passenger fastening his seat belt casually awaits the flight because he assumes that the pilot, whom he cannot see, is appropriately trained and properly concerned about passenger safety. A customer drinks coffee without wondering whether the waitress may have put poison in it. An engineer in a bridge-building crew assumes that the crane operator who is hoisting him a hundred feet into the air has checked his motor and cables and will deposit him safely on his high perch. In the same way, a discussion group proceeds on faith. Members usually assume that everyone is aware of the interests of others, that what a member says is approximately what he means, and that each is functioning as forthrightly as he appears to be. The honesty of each is more or less taken for granted until there is some reason to question it.

Students occasionally ask what virtue there is in honesty. They sometimes argue that human interaction should be judged only by behavioral results; if a method works, it must be acceptable. Honesty may be a positive good, they say, but it is irrelevant. What matters is effect. The weakness in this pragmatic position is that it stands too near the trunk to see the tree, and certainly it altogether obscures the forest. Causation is never so simple. An action cannot be judged by a single effect, since there are effects of effects of effects. Moreover, evil means can corrupt as surely as can evil ends. John Dewey argued, in fact, that "nothing can justify or condemn means except ends, results. But we have to include consequences impartially. . . . It is wilful folly to fasten upon some single end or consequence which is liked, and permit the view of that to blot from perception all other undesired and undesirable consequences."[7]

It is difficult to present a rational argument for a positive morality because each person develops his own value system, which is a private matter. The individual in a democratic society is as free to choose his own code of moral behavior as he is to embrace whatever political philosophy pleases him. His freedom is limited only when his choices infringe on the rights and freedoms of others, and these restrictions are largely specified by legal limitations.

In discussion, however, ethical problems go far beyond legality. To mislead

[7] *Human Nature and Conduct*, New York: Holt, Rinehart and Winston, 1922, pp. 228–9.

people is not often illegal, but it can bring chaos and disastrous consequences to the discussion group striving for consensus.

The challenge for the discussion participant is to think through his own reasons for ethical conduct. Some individuals do not always realize the implications of their behavior. Yet most of us would accept Thomas Nilsen's "concept of the *good* which characterizes our culture: *whatever develops, enlarges, enhances human personalities is good; whatever restricts, degrades, or injures human personalities is bad.*"[8] Respect for the worth of others carries with it some ethical obligations for the discusser.

Group Responsibility

If all are responsible for group action, is no one personally responsible? Occasionally a person asked to account for a group decision replies: "That was what the committee decided; don't blame me!" Apparently groups sometimes appoint a committee to make an unpleasant decision in order to protect individuals from the necessity of defending the action. The morality of this procedure should be examined carefully. It is defensible to spread the responsibility to several persons since a better decision usually results, and since the individual often finds it easier to justify a decision made by several competent persons than one made by himself alone. Nevertheless, the individual who participated in formulating policy cannot escape the responsibility for defending it. A decision reached collectively is still the product of individual action, collectively applied. In a committee of five, each participant is one-fifth responsible. The individual cannot hide within the mass of others, as part of a group entity which he feels exists apart from the individuals of which it is composed. He should not allow a group to take a stand with his acquiescence and in his name that he would repudiate as an individual. He should not pretend to agree and later denounce or work against the decision, or appear to accept the outcome—even through remaining silent—and then later refuse to accept responsibility for his part in it.

If a participant feels that he will be unable later to defend the group decision, he is responsible at the time for entering a minority report, or in some other way making clear that he will refuse to support the action, and that he dissociates himself from the outcome. Once a group decision is reached, with the apparent concurrence of all, then each member is individually and collectively responsible for it.

The Duty to Know

Information is indispensable in intelligent deliberation and groups assume that an individual who contributes facts knows what he is talking about. If a group had to verify independently every statement presented, the purpose and efficiency of meeting together would be defeated. Each individual is morally

[8] Thomas R. Nilsen, *Ethics of Speech Communication*, Indianapolis: Bobbs-Merrill, 1966, p. 9.

responsible for the accuracy of his contributions. To present a few facts as the whole story, tentative findings as firmly established conclusions, or partial understanding as authoritative is to mislead the group. The participant should not say, "I'm sure this is the way it is," when he means, "I think this is the way it is." Group members obviously should strive to report their observations or research results as objectively and clearly as possible.

Ideally, participants should understand the discussion problem thoroughly. It is dishonest to overstate understanding, to misrepresent facts, or to sound more positive than knowledge justifies. To avoid this risk, the good discusser exerts himself to find the facts; he knows for sure.

The Duty to Be Fair

Individuals who value democratic privileges will strive to guarantee to all a full and fair hearing. To do so requires more than passive noninterference when others talk. It means active encouragement and a seeking out of all views, even unpopular ones.

In order not to deceive others, participants must reveal their biases frankly. They should put on the record their sources of information, and any prejudices of such authorities, books, or organizations.

Definitions and other statements should be expressed in language that is as free as possible from distortion and that does not introduce unfair slanting. In presenting arguments, participants should use reasoning fairly. They should not use fallacious reasoning deliberately designed to short-circuit careful thinking.

ETHICAL LAPSES

Uninhibited lying, fabrication of evidence, inventing of sources, deliberate misquoting, and falsification of facts are obviously dishonest practices. Some ethical lapses are identified as easily as are these, but others are not so simply recognized, even by the person guilty of them. It is not always possible to tell when an authority has been quoted out of context, or a source inadequately identified. It is clear that these practices are unfair, however, and a participant with a sense of ethics will not omit part of a quotation in order to make it sound more favorable, or rush through the identification of a source because the reference would be received unfavorably if clearly identified.

Unfair Channeling of Talk

The ethical group member does not attempt to manipulate the talk unfairly so that his selfish ends are served and group wishes frustrated. For example, it is questionable practice for an individual or a leader to encourage profuse talk on matters about which he is indifferent but to divert discussion, hurry a decision, or assume a point settled with minimum comment when the discussion reaches an issue he hopes the group will decide in a way he has predetermined.

A group studying discussion methods once asked the instructor how they could lead a group to reach a decision they had predetermined, while at the same time make the group think that the members had decided of their own free will. Such a procedure is obviously manipulation. It is equally unfair for the leader to channel discussion by recognizing those who give approved answers and ignoring those who disagree.

Howell and Smith describe other instances of unfair channeling of talk. Members should not usurp leadership functions for personal aggrandizement, nor present summaries before the leader can, in order to push discussion in directions they favor. It is unfair to sabotage rivals in the group by slyly criticizing or undermining them; to gain personal advancement by monopolizing the talk, forming a two-man mutual admiration society, or taking an unpopular position for the purpose of demonstrating extreme reasonableness when becoming converted; and to obstruct discussion through diversion or "inaccurate restatement and pseudo-summary."[9]

Unfair Use of Language and Reasoning

The conscientious participant does not intentionally use loaded language to make concepts he favors appear laudatory and those he opposes appear unpleasant. He avoids name-calling, the attribution of guilt because of association, and other devices of the propagandist. He does not attempt to short-circuit thinking by offering hasty generalizations (labor leaders are racketeers; capitalists exploit workers), or by oversimplifying alternatives in "either . . . or" form when he knows there are other possible courses of action. He should not define a term in one manner and later deliberately use the word with a different meaning.

Communist Tactics in Negotiations

Extreme examples of unethical manipulation in discussion can be clearly seen in the negotiating methods used by the Communists in international conferences. Admiral C. Turner Joy, who served as Chief United Nations Delegate during the Korean Armistice negotiations with the Communists at Panmunjom, wrote a highly informative book, *How Communists Negotiate.* The Communists chose delegates who could exhibit "persistence and an unruffled demeanor in the face of logic. . . ." They attempted to dictate an agenda that specified part of the decisions in the statement of the problem. They staged incidents that would bolster their position at the bargaining table, and imposed tedious delays which they hoped would weaken the opposition. They introduced completely unacceptable red herrings which they offered to withdraw on the condition that the UN delegation grant unpalatable concessions.

[9] William S. Howell and Donald K. Smith, *Discussion,* New York: Crowell-Collier and Macmillan, 1956, Chapter 18.

Rather than face the truth, Admiral Joy wrote, the Reds either denied it flatly or more often tried to distort it: "The basic procedure is to select out of the whole truth certain parts, which, if put together in a particular way, produce a conclusion exactly contradictory of the whole truth." Offers of UN concessions aimed at compromise and progress were interpreted by the Communists as weakness calling for even further concessions.

The Communists at Panmunjom did not hesitate to repudiate agreement reached earlier or to insist on a new interpretation of written agreements. They tried to wear out the opposition with endless repetition of the same demands. In their discussion about prisoners of war, they engaged in the whole range of deceitful practices: "They lied; they blustered; they became vindictive; they welshed; they twisted, distorted, and denied truth; they delayed; they threatened."[10]

Fortunately, such extreme forms of evasion, obstinacy, and dishonesty are not often encountered in discussion, and certainly not among persons who have shared the benefits of a free society. These excesses may at least suggest, however, some of the kinds of obstacles that can impede discussion where ethical responsibilities are completely ignored by some participants.

SUPPLEMENTARY READING

Brameld, Theodore, "Ethics of Leadership," *Adult Education*, 4 (1955), pp. 5–8.

Bruner, Jerome S., and Tagiuri, R., "The Perception of People," in Lindzey, Gardner (ed.), *Handbook of Social Psychology*, Cambridge, Mass.: Addison-Wesley, 1954, p. 641.

Gulley, Halbert E., *Essentials of Discussion and Debate*, New York: Holt, Rinehart and Winston, 1955, Chapter 1.

Howell, William S., and Smith, Donald K., *Discussion*, New York: Crowell-Collier and Macmillan, 1956, Chapter 18.

Joy, C. Turner, *How Communists Negotiate*, New York: Crowell-Collier and Macmillan, 1955.

Nilsen, Thomas R., *Ethics of Speech Communication*, Indianapolis: Bobbs-Merrill, 1966.

Wallace, Karl R., "An Ethical Basis of Communication," *The Speech Teacher*, 4 (January, 1955), pp. 1–9.

QUESTIONS AND EXERCISES

1. Define scientific attitude. What are the similarities and differences between scientific attitude and attitudes appropriate to discussion? Can a consideration of public affairs be called scientific?

[10] New York: Crowell-Collier and Macmillan, 1955.

2. Divide the class into pairs of students. Each person should tell his partner what limited subject he feels equipped to discuss accurately and fully. Each student should then interview his partner in front of the class, eliciting information through a carefully planned series of questions. At the conclusion of the interview, the interviewer should summarize succinctly the information gained, and state objectively the precise views of his partner. Then the class should discuss the interviewer's objectivity, fairness, and skill as questioner and summarizer.

3. Listen to a group discussion involving no more than five persons. Observe each participant closely and make one of the following reports. (If it is desired to report on more than one of these aspects, then observe more than one discussion.)

    a. Record instances where individuals failed to display objectivity and open-mindedness toward the problem discussed.

    b. Record instances where individuals failed to display objectivity and tolerance toward the other participants.

    c. Rank the participants in the order in which you feel they succeeded in displaying appropriate attitudes. Write a paper in which you explain and defend your rankings.

    d. Select one of the participants and write a paper in which you report without bias or distortion the precise views he expressed.

4. Write a paper in which you explain to what extent you agree or disagree with the suggestions on ethical responsibilities made in this chapter.

5. What, in your opinion, is the responsibility of each individual to the democratic society of which he is a part?

6. Are groups in contemporary American society more or less ethical than they were fifty years ago? Defend your answer.

7. Listen carefully to a group discussion. On the basis of your observation, what are the clues, if any, to individual expressions of honesty or dishonesty?

8. What, if anything, would you do as a designated leader of a discussion if you suspected a member of your group of dishonest or unethical conduct?

Chapter 9

THE CHALLENGE
OF PARTICIPATION

Much of this book deals with preparation for effective participation in discussion and therefore some of the matters mentioned in this chapter are developed more fully elsewhere. It seems important, however, to focus attention on the specific requirements of participation. As the individual prepares to take part in a discussion, he is concerned with what will be expected of him.

One of the misconceptions about discussion is that the participant has an easy assignment and can perform it with minimal preparation and effort. Obviously, if something constructive is accomplished during a discussion, someone must do it. If each participant does nothing, who accomplishes it? A designated leader cannot make a collective decision by himself. What seems to happen in the mind of the weak participant is this: he assumes that because several others are present, something constructive will occur without any special effort on his part; or he assumes that the presence of others will inspire him in some magical way to contribute something worthwhile, more even than he was aware he knew.

It is nonsensical, of course, to dream of inspired, magical outpourings from empty heads, even from six empty heads gathered at the same round table. To carry his share of the responsibility an effective participant must have extensive knowledge of the problem. This comes from careful research and thought. During the discussion he must be capable of using a wide range of skills particularly important to efficient group productivity. To select for special emphasis the requirements that are stressed here is not to suggest that these are the only abilities needed by the good member. It is hoped that everything in this book has reasonable relevance in educating the alert participant; furthermore, one book cannot possibly say everything that could profitably be said. The attributes recommended here for special study by the participant are those that seem especially vital.

The effective participant should make a contribution to leadership, to group productivity, and to harmonious social relationships. We can organize our suggestions to the participant in these three categories.

HELPING WITH LEADERSHIP

It is difficult to generalize about giving effective support to the leadership of discussions because there are so many different kinds of situations and circumstances. In most discussions, however, there is a designated leader or else there are certain individuals who are responsible for the leadership functions. The challenge for the person who wants to be an effective participant is to help with the leadership rather than to oppose or ignore or compete with those assigned these functions.

At least when a designated leader is doing reasonably well, the cooperative participant is willing to follow. If the assigned leader fails to provide leadership, of course, members must step in to fulfill the essential functions, but this possible necessity does not license the ambitious member to usurp the leader's position for personal aggrandizement. Should this unfortunate situation arise, other participants must rally to the designated leader's defense.

Participants can help the weak leader by suggesting what might be done next. They can assist him in many ways with the difficult task of leadership without displacing him entirely. Members should be extremely patient; they must give him every chance to recover his position of authority before taking over guidance and control functions.

In many situations, of course, members cannot remove the designated leader, nor can they take over his duties. The chairman of the board, the mayor, or the chairman of a committee may be chosen by the parent group. If he is weak, the only reasonable choice of participants is to help him through suggestion, or to work outside this specific group for a change in leadership.

Respecting the Leader's Outline

In most decision-making situations a designated leader attempts to guide the group through analysis of the problem and toward agreement on what to decide. It is a responsibility of participants to try to recognize the outline the leader is following in directing the discussion, and to respect his leadership by helping the group move forward in the manner being suggested.

Imagine what would happen if six carpenters building a single house each worked from a different design; they could create a monstrosity with a kitchen in each corner. The outcome of a discussion can be monstrous, too, if each participant tries to move in a different direction. There must be coordinated, systematic forward movement. Each member must be aware of the essential ideas pursued at any moment, of the stage reached in the outline, and of the relationship between specific questions being asked and the over-all progress of the discussion. At any point during the discussion, he should understand what ground has already been covered, where the group is, and where it is likely to move next. He must recognize the key questions that need answers before the group can leave one area and proceed to another. Ideally, each should be able to think ahead, to anticipate the next step.

At the same time, the good participant does not force upon the group his notions of where they should move next. He is ready to respond, but he usually waits for the designated leader to request the new step forward. A member may properly suggest forward movement, of course, but he is wise not to do so as long as the leadership is reasonably efficient.

The important thing is that each member of the group be aware of and heed some unified developmental outline that leads in the appropriate direction.

Fostering Productivity

Group productivity is related to the nature and demands of the assignment. To reach a high-quality decision is more demanding than to exchange information only. Some problems are more complex than others. Some groups must face many vexing decisions on a variety of problems in a short time, while others may encounter only routine matters most of the time. As Collins and Guetzkow say,

> The group differs from a collection of individuals working separately in several ways. For instance, the interacting group will have a wider range of information and a greater critical facility. These factors can produce either the efficiency of division of labor or the wasted effort of duplication. The outcome depends on the nature of the task on which the group is working.[1]

Whatever the nature of the task a discussion group must accomplish, the effective participant will want to do what he can to foster this aspect of productivity.

Social climate also influences productivity. The presence of the others affects the performance and attitudes of each member. They may develop into a smoothly interacting and cooperating unit, remain an unintegrated collection of separate individuals, or reach some stage of integration in between these extremes. In most situations the participant will want to foster harmonious interpersonal relationships and integrated effort as a means of enhancing productivity.

ACCOMPLISHING THE GROUP TASK

It is clear from observing decision-making discussion that members derive satisfaction from the successful completion of the assigned task. Furthermore, data from experimental and field studies reviewed by Collins and Guetzkow[2] confirm these observations. There is evidence that members report high satisfaction when the discussion is thorough, when there is a good interchange of ideas and opinion, when much is accomplished, when the leader keeps the

---

[1] Barry E. Collins and Harold Guetzkow, *A Social Psychology of Group Processes for Decision-Making*, New York: John Wiley & Sons, 1964, p. 57.
[2] Collins and Guetzkow, pp. 196–9.

discussion in focus, when a large proportion of the agenda is completed, and when meetings are orderly, efficient, and reasonably brief. Satisfaction appears to be lowered when the group encounters difficult problems that elicit strong conflict and frustration.

If participants can contribute to efficient achievement of the group's task, they will increase member satisfaction and thus be viewed as helpful to the group. There are a number of ways to assist task productivity.

Being Mentally Alert

Good discussion requires intellectual alertness. Complex ideas are explained swiftly. Many different concepts are introduced, commented on, reacted to, and modified in a short period. The group strives to think collectively and systematically, and to progress in a purposeful direction. The individual participant must try to make his own contribution to the group effort and at the same time follow closely what others are saying and what the designated leader is doing. Unless he has mental agility, he is soon lost. It is disruptive if a group must constantly double back and repeat for a laggard thinker what has already transpired.

Answering the Question

In television versions of courtroom drama, the hard-driving prosecutor frequently barks at the witness: "Answer the question." When the squirming suspect is hesitant or evasive, the lawyer can appeal to the judge, who says: "The witness will answer the question." Although there is no comparable machinery in discussion, the participant often needs similar prodding. It is common for the leader to ask a question and to receive incomplete, evasive, or even irrelevant answers. To compound the tragedy, the leader sometimes does not even seem to realize that the question has remained unanswered, but proceeds blithely to another query.

Each participant is responsible for understanding the question, asking for clarification or definition if necessary, supplying whatever relevant responses he can, and helping the group stay with it until it is answered fully and directly. Failure to follow faithfully this simple and obvious advice leads to misunderstanding and chaos. If many questions are evaded or half-answered, the whole group is soon lost. The "tragedy" can quickly become a comedy of errors. If no one can answer the question, this fact must be faced squarely.

Don't change the subject. Answer the question.

Contributing Information When Needed

As Chapter 5 suggests, facts must be supplied at the moment the group needs them. Some participants are so eager to demonstrate that they have done research and have facts in their possession that they contribute them—all of them—the first time they talk. Others apparently are woolgathering when a relevant moment arrives, but realize later they have items of information which have not been presented. Then they insist on producing them; "No sense in letting them go to waste," they say.

In a real sense, such information is largely wasted in both these instances. Facts are maximally helpful only when they are relevant to the group's discussion at a particular moment. To jump ahead, or to back up and reconsider a situation that has once been described, is to be unsystematic and inefficient. Of course it is better to present facts late than never to introduce them, since the group is eager to take all related information into account, but progress will be smoother and productivity higher if information is made available at the appropriate time.

Checking for Fallacies

Most participants tend to accept uncritically everything said in a discussion. Often each statement is taken at face value, without challenge, even if it is misleading, questionable, inaccurate, or fallacious. Members apparently feel that they can add to, but never discount or take away.

One particularly damaging habit frequently observed consists of accepting a conclusion as established on the basis of one fact presented by a single member. The well-informed group should be able to produce several pieces of information supporting the same inference. It is especially important to discover whether there are facts that contradict what has been offered. Only if all the facts seem to agree is it wise to proceed. An inference based on a single fact, example, comparison, or authoritative statement may be invalid. The alert group will stop and test if it seems fallacious.

Perhaps the reluctance of members to challenge questionable reasoning stems from their desire to be cooperative, display helpful attitudes, and consider harmonious interpersonal relationships. If so, they misunderstand these concepts. If it were necessary to choose between straight thinking and cooperative, cordial social relationships, the group that wants a high-quality product would choose valid thinking. Of course, it is not necessary to choose. Valid reasoning is essential and should have the highest priority. It can be achieved within a cooperative group working collectively and considering the rights, feelings, and interests of all.

Reasoning must be tested. All statements must be examined critically. The member drawing a conclusion should be the first to suggest that it be checked for weaknesses. He should be eager to have others offer corroboration or contradiction. Fallacious thinking or unsupported assertions should be identified with complete candor. Poor reasoning should be abandoned without a backward glance. The participant who happens to initiate an inference that turns out to be unsound need not feel guilty or stupid. To refine the raw materials of thought into the pure metal of sound reasoning is a central justification for subjecting ideas to the smelting process of group interaction. It is an indication that members have achieved high-quality "groupness" when they can abandon unpromising lines of thought without anyone feeling defensive or even remembering particularly who was first responsible for them.

Building on Other's Reasoning

Rarely in discussion can one person present a series of inferences in orderly "if this and this, then this" sequence. Rather, as is observed in Chapter 6, conclusions are drawn from bits of evidence given at different times by various members. Each participant must understand reasoning patterns well enough to follow what inferences are being put together. He should not often expect to develop a complex chain of reasoning all by himself. Thinking in groups is a collective process, just as the whole discussion is a group effort.

Individual participants should advance the group's thinking by building upon the reasoning already established. The group moves forward together or it flounders. If individuals race ahead, the group must be allowed to catch up; otherwise there is confusion and division.

Listening "Behind the Statement"

A political reporter who writes about the resolutions passed by a nominating convention may also explain what is going on behind the scenes—who influenced what or why a plank in the platform is worded as it is. In much the same way, a discussion participant must be aware of what is going on behind the statements made by others. He listens to what they say, but he also listens for what is left unsaid. He is alert for clues to why contributions were phrased in certain words, and to attitudes, feelings, and responses, expressed and unexpressed.

The reasons are apparent: he can then understand better the bases of conflict, areas unsatisfactorily explored, and other factors that will help him to communicate more ably information and opinions that will help the group.

Being Clear

An important by-product of listening for what is behind the statements of others is that the participant learns whether his own contributions are clear. He discovers from others how they are responding to him. When he communicates, he must adapt to them. If they do not understand, or if their responses suggest reactions he did not intend to evoke, he must try again.

Above all, his comments must be clear. He must be able to convey his meaning without distortion or coloring. Clarity is a matter both of language usage and of speech skills. Words must be used precisely; intended meaning, vocal inflection, physical gesture, and facial expression must all match or distortion and misinterpretation result. These matters were treated more fully in Chapter 7.

Contributing Efficiently

It always seems that time is limited in discussion. Most members want to accomplish as much as they can in the shortest possible time. Perhaps this phenomenon is a cultural characteristic, but an explanation is of little consequence here. It is apparent that groups are impatient when participants spend 5 minutes communicating information that could be presented in 2. Each member should be capable of efficient communication.

Efficiency is also a matter of language usage and speech skills. Words must be chosen that will be clear the first time around; tiresome, time-consuming explanation and repetition may result from unwise and awkward initial language choices. The participant must speak fluently, without unnecessary pauses and hesitations.

In general, contributions made during interactional discussion should be brief. This kind of discussion is characterized by lively direct interchange. Members do not expect lengthy, involved speeches. What a member contributes is broken up into many short comments made at the most relevant and appropriate moments. If he is to be maximally helpful, he must be capable of presenting substantial amounts of information or opinion in each relatively brief communication.

Being Thorough

Many discussion participants give up too easily: they may settle for a quick solution to save time; they may quit because no satisfactory decision seems readily at hand; or they may accept the first proposal presented because no one bothers to scratch beneath the surface to its weaknesses.

The effective participant is thorough. He is tough, persistent, and firm. Even if more time or another meeting is required, he insists upon examining the problem with careful thoroughness. He wants the job done right the first time if possible. He is unwilling to settle for half measures.

RESISTING CONFORMITY PRESSURES

Groups tend to exert pressure on individual members to conform to standards of acceptable behavior, and discussion groups are no exception. Results of this pressure can be both beneficial and harmful. "The established orderliness stemming from pressures toward uniformity helps the group in its work. The standards reduce confusion and wasted effort, but at the same time they often cause uneasiness, inflexibility, and a reduction of creativeness among members."[3]

While the acceptance of group norms will contribute to social harmony and may make forward movement easier, members of discussion groups must be careful not to let conformity pressure prevent them from presenting unpopular ideas or objecting to unsound reasoning.

The valuable participant anticipates the pressure upon him to conform to the notions of others in the group. He knows it is more comfortable at times

[3] Dorwin Cartwright and Alvin Zander, *Group Dynamics: Research and Theory*, sec. ed., New York: Harper & Row, 1960, p. 179.

to go along with the crowd than to insist on a fuller examination or to call attention to error or to chastise the group for hasty, illogical thinking. To make a maximum contribution, however, he must resist the temptation to conform and he must encourage others also to resist. If each person in the group develops habits of independent thought and judgment, collectively they will have increased confidence in the soundness of their decision when their thinking converges in agreement. The quality of group thinking suffers when members hesitate to disagree or to express an unpopular view.

Displaying Enthusiasm

Discussion involves an exciting, collective search for understanding and for acceptable decisions. Interaction that is spirited and lively stimulates the kind of inquisitive thinking essential to high-quality productivity. Hence, effective discussion is stifled by members who appear bored or indifferent. The helpful participant is enthusiastic about the search and his opportunity to be part of it. He is excited about new discoveries, insights, agreements; about the clash of alert minds and the resolution of conflict. When he contributes, he does so with enthusiasm. Leaning forward eagerly in his chair is more characteristic of him than speaking from a slumping, overly relaxed position suggesting weariness, disinterest, or studied detachment. He is not a passive observer of discussion—he is actively engaged in making it what it is; he is a participant.

There is no intention here to suggest that discussion should be frantic and frenzied, or that participants must speak breathlessly. What has been recommended could be easily caricatured as animated frenzy and of course such excitement would be ridiculous as well as impossible to sustain. Interest, curiosity, enthusiasm, and excitement are desirable attributes in discussion, although perhaps the participant should be told to temper his enthusiasm with some degree of restraint.

Maintaining Objectivity

The effective participant approaches the task objectively. As Chapter 8 emphasizes, he considers ideas on their merits, apart from his emotional involvements in the problem. He accepts statements tentatively and views alternatives with an open mind.

Taking Constructive Roles

Many attempts have been made to suggest the kinds of role behaviors group members may exhibit. Some of these behaviors are helpful and others obstructive. Benne and Sheats, for example, examine functional roles open to participants in interacting groups. Those related to task accomplishment are the initiator–contributor, the information seeker, the opinion seeker, the information giver, the opinion giver, the elaborator, the coordinator, the orienter, the evaluator–critic, the energizer, the procedural technician, and the recorder.

Another set of roles, on the other hand, are taken to satisfy personal needs and may serve to obstruct progress toward a decision. These are the aggressor, the blocker, the recognition seeker, the playboy, the dominator, the help seeker, and the special interest pleader.

These authors recommend that during training sessions, students observe, identify, and analyze each of these roles which they see enacted during a group meeting. Members can then practice "enacting a wider range of required roles" and "role flexibility." Help can come from the group "in evaluating and improving the required skills."[4]

Any number of additional roles can be identified and labeled. McBurney and Hance present detailed characteristics of such personages in discussion as Mr. Pontifical, Mr. Parlor Pink, Mr. Doom, Mr. Smug, Mr. Milquetoast, Mr. Wordy, Mr. Lunatic Fringe, and Mr. Suspicious.[5] Among desirable roles identified by Sattler and Miller are those of organizer, fact finder, creator of ideas, critical tester, and questioner. Undesirable participants they point to are Mr. Orator, Mr. Fearful, Mr. Isolate, Mr. Contrary, and Mr. Emotional Antagonist, and persons who agree with almost anything, who know it all, and who have an executive complex.[6]

Guetzkow experimented with different kinds of communication networks in group interaction and found three types of roles based on the handling of information and messages. Some participants took a "keyman" role by receiving information, formulating a solution, and sending answers. The "endman" participant merely sent information the others did not have and later received answers from others. Some participants served in the relayer role, passing on missing information from others and relaying any answers received.[7] It is possible that similar differentiation of functions occur in many discussion situations.

There is a temptation to invent dozens of additional roles typical of discussion participants. It is easy to observe such types as the "compulsive interrupter," the "hasty summarizer," and other destructive communicators. It must be remembered, however, that categorizing can be overdone and can lead to oversimplification and distortion. One individual does not often exhibit the characteristics of a single role throughout a discussion, nor is a member restricted to a single, limited function. No one person, for example, can be the only initiator of new thoughts during a discussion, nor can he confine himself only to initiating. If participants think of role-taking in such

[4] Kenneth D. Benne and Paul Sheats, "Functional Roles of Group Members," *Journal of Social Issues*, 4 (1948), pp. 41–9.

[5] James H. McBurney and Kenneth Hance, *Discussion in Human Affairs*, New York: Harper & Row, 1950, Chapters 13 and 14, and pp. 259–65.

[6] William M. Sattler and N. Edd Miller, *Discussion and Conference*, Englewood Cliffs, N.J.: Prentice-Hall, 1954, Part IV.

[7] Harold Guetzkow, "Differentiation of Roles in Task-oriented Groups," in Cartwright and Zander, pp. 683–704.

restricted terms, their knowledge of roles may do them more harm than good. There is a danger, also, that members will classify each person in one of these neat pigeonholes and fail to appreciate the complexity of an individual's contributions. Roles can most profitably be identified because they give helpful insights into member behavior. They should not be oversimplified, nor should they be thought of as explaining all of behavior.

Participants should analyze their own habitual ways of contributing to the discussion to discover whether they exhibit any of these undesirable roles. Only constructive ones should be retained, and of course methods of contributing should vary with the needs of the group at a particular moment. Classifying behavior into these oversimplified categories is helpful only for training purposes. Students in an organized class can help each other by identifying the roles each takes in particular situations, deciding whether these are helpful or obstructive, and practicing the retention of desirable and the elimination of undesirable ones.

BUILDING HARMONIOUS RELATIONSHIPS

Group accomplishment of a task cannot be separated from the actions of the persons who make up the group and the interpersonal relationships that unify or fail to unite them. In reviewing the experimental literature, McGrath and Altman conclude: "Interpersonal attraction among members of a group seems to be consistently and positively associated with, and perhaps derived from, member perceptions of their own and each other's status, power, and attitudes. For example, perceptions of others' task-related abilities and others' social and task status bear a positive relationship to liking others." Members are attracted to those whom they perceive as liking them and who take an approach to task productivity similar to their own. One accompaniment of this state of attraction is increased communication rate, although the relationship between attraction and group performance is not yet clear.[8]

Individuals who work together in a group with persons they like and who also accept them tend to report satisfaction with the progress of the group as well as increased liking for the others. Sharing a common fate may also increase interpersonal attraction.[9] Congeniality will be easier when the group is efficiently productive and, conversely, goal achievement will make it easier to like the other participants, although we must be careful not to assume that these relationships are simple or automatic. These are tendencies and the actual outcomes vary with tasks, groups, situations, personalities and other factors, as we have seen in connection with variables considered earlier.

In addition to contributing to both task and social functions by communi-

[8] Joseph E. McGrath and Irwin Altman, *Small Group Research*, New York: Holt, Rinehart and Winston, 1966, pp. 60–1.
[9] Collins and Guetzkow, pp. 203–4.

cating freely and effectively, the participant must aid directly the development of harmonious social relationships by displaying sensitivity to others and by promoting cooperative interrelationships.

Being Sensitive to Others

The good participant is pleasant and likeable. Others enjoy interacting with him. They feel he is a valuable member of the team. Part of his personableness results from his sensitivity to others as fellow human beings. He respects them. He shows warm regard for their feelings and needs. He is sympathetic toward, rather than critical of, their shortcomings and weaknesses. He is curious about ways in which their information, insights, and values differ from his own. He is eager to learn more about their ways of thinking, not to embarrass them, refute them, or catch them in inconsistencies, but to achieve clearer collective understanding and reconciliation of views.

There are many facets to likeableness in interpersonal relationships, but three qualities which are especially important should be singled out.

TACT/ There are good reasons for disagreement in discussion, as in any other social relationship. To dodge the responsibility for disagreeing when conviction and intelligent reflection dictate it is to be an intellectual coward. Constructive discussion cannot be built upon sweet reasonableness alone; in fact, a group that reaches consensus without any sign of conflict usually has an extremely easy problem, feels uninvolved, or is considering it only superficially. Disagreement is healthy and necessary.

However, there are many different ways in which to express disagreement. The participant can state his opposition tactfully or rudely, just as he can make the choice in other social situations. In discussion, it is essential that the participant have the ability to disagree tactfully, without putting others on the defensive unnecessarily. Basically, this means evaluating a man's idea without in any way attacking him as a person for having expressed it. It is the difference between saying, "I see the basis for your conclusion, but I feel differently," and saying, "I don't think you can defend that position; here's the way it should be. . ."

Being tactful also involves ordinary courtesy. A simple rule of thumb might be to show others the kind of consideration a well-mannered person would give important, invited guests in his home.

SENSITIVITY TO THREAT/ The need for sensitivity to the feelings and reactions of others is increased when the participant or the problem being discussed represents a threat to the position, ego, or allegiances of the others involved. The good participant is one who is sensitively aware of such threats to others. He tries even harder to be objective, for example, when evaluating certain religious beliefs which happen to be accepted by a member of the group. A high-power figure in particular must be careful when responding to those with less influence within the group.

COOPERATIVENESS/ Some persons are rugged individualists. They find it restricting or even unmanly to work with others. They sometimes are impatient with time-consuming interaction. They may say frequently, "We're wasting time; let's get on with it." They may prefer to "go it alone" and are in groups under at least mild protest. Such persons must curb these impulses if they are to be effective discussion participants. Patient cooperativeness is essential. Discussion takes time and it is a collective, group effort. Unless the participant is willing to work cooperatively with others, discussion simply will not work well.

The qualities that should not be exhibited by the effective participant are indicated by the opposites of these desirable traits. He should not be dull, biased, disinterested, insensitive, tactless, and uncooperative. In addition, there are some other attributes he is advised not to display. He should avoid dogmatism. He has a right to his convictions, but he should not claim infallibility and refuse to budge, as a habitual pattern of response. He can justifiably express his views with confidence, but he should not keep coming back to a pet panacea already rejected by the group. He should neither monopolize the conversation nor be noticeably silent, moody, or irritable. The participant who talks too often and too long encounters resentment, and one who is "glum and mum" dampens the spirits of everyone.

A good participant does not disagree merely to be disagreeable. He does not say, "I disagree," without having reasons and constructive countersuggestions. He does not rush toward a solution, urging agreement on anything just to end the discussion. Nor is he a mere phrasemaker without solid information to contribute, trying to bluff his way by saying, "That's a good idea;" "I agree with that;" and "Why don't we agree on that?"

Taking Constructive Roles

Just as it is possible to suggest member behaviors that aid task achievement, we can categorize those who promote helpful social relationships. Benne and Sheats place in this category the encourager, the harmonizer, the compromiser, the gatekeeper and expediter, the standard setter, the group observer and commentator, and the follower.[10]

Cartwright and Zander also give examples of member behaviors related to the two functions, task and social. Goal achievement is aided by behavior that:

initiates action
keeps members' attention on the goal
clarifies the issue
develops a procedural plan
evaluates the quality of work done
makes expert information available.

[10] Benne and Sheats, pp. 41–9.

Group maintenance is aided by behavior that:

keeps interpersonal relations pleasant
arbitrates disputes
provides encouragement
gives the minority a chance to be heard
stimulates self-direction
increases the interdependence among members.[11]

These classifications of behavior are specific enough to suggest some of the kinds of roles participants take when they want to make a positive contribution to social relationships. Members must be cautious, however, in interpreting what specific roles mean. What is important is that the participant assess his own behavior in relation to the other members and in relation to his own goals as he decides how to operate within the group.

SUPPLEMENTARY READING

Baird, A. Craig, *Discussion: Principles and Types*, New York: McGraw-Hill, 1943, Chapter 8.

Benne, Kenneth D., and Sheats, Paul, "Functional Roles of Group Members," *Journal of Social Issues*, 4 (Spring, 1948), pp. 41–49.

Braden, Waldo W., and Brandenburg, Earnest, *Oral Decision-Making*, New York: Harper & Row, 1955, Chapter 12 and pp. 280–286.

Collins, Barry E., and Guetzkow, H., *A Social Psychology of Group Processes for Decision-Making*, New York: John Wiley & Sons, 1964, Chapter 10.

Sattler, William M., and Miller, N. Edd, *Discussion and Conference*, Englewood Cliffs, N.J.: Prentice-Hall, 1954, Part IV.

Wagner, Russell H., and Arnold, Carroll C., *Handbook of Group Discussion*, Boston: Houghton Mifflin, 1950, Chapter 7.

QUESTIONS AND EXERCISES

1. Does your observation of discussion confirm what Bales and Slater conclude from their study of role differentiation? They found that some members are more concerned with task accomplishment while others put social harmony above goal achievement. Do you consider this distinction valid?
2. Can the participant contribute to social relationships without helping the group along toward the achievement of its task and vice versa?
3. List some other ways in which the participant may help with leadership or interfere with it.
4. Write a paper in which you explain the gains and losses resulting from group conformity pressures.
5. Observe a number of discussions and attempt to invent some new partici-

[11] Cartwright and Zander, p. 496.

pant roles that could be used to categorize kinds of behaviors characteristic of various persons. Compare your list with those roles mentioned in this chapter.

6. Listen carefully to a discussion and prepare a report on the helpful and detrimental attributes exhibited by participants. Explain why each kind of action aided or thwarted (a) task achievement; and (b) social function.

7. Participate in a discussion before a classroom group and try to demonstrate the desirable qualities and abilities the good discussion participant should exhibit.

8. Plan and carry out a classroom discussion. Appoint listening teams to observe and evaluate the participation of each member of the demonstrating group. After the discussion, have the class discuss the extent to which each member succeeded in displaying desirable participant qualities and abilities.

PART THREE

LEADERSHIP

Chapter 10

NATURE
OF DISCUSSION
LEADERSHIP

Leadership in general means influencing others within a particular situation and social context in a way that induces them to follow, to be modified, to be directed. The person who influences may do so intentionally, or without deliberate intent, and if deliberately, his leadership attempt may be *direct*, open, obvious to all, or *indirect*, subtle, suggestive, at least partially hidden. Persons influenced may be aware or unaware of the leadership source that induced them to change.

There is a prodigious amount of literature on leadership in general, and the student has doubtlessly been exposed to some of it in other contexts. Much of it has little direct bearing on the problems of leadership in discussion and we can give it little attention here.

An important controversy has surrounded the question: Are there leaders and nonleaders or is leadership situationally determined? Much energy has been expended in efforts to identify the traits of the leader. Is he physically stronger and larger, more intelligent, dominant, aggressive? Does he have certain personality characteristics? Research along these lines has not been overly fruitful, and there is now fairly general agreement that there are no persons who are natural, born leaders in every situation, and others who are naturally followers. Rather, an individual seems to exercise leadership when his specific personal abilities, knowledge of a problem, and other qualifications interact fortuitously with a particular situation, and with other persons who are predisposed to accept his influence on this problem, in this situation, at this moment. Perhaps this statement is too cautious, but it seems clear that almost every person may be a leader in some situations and a follower in others. When the situation changes, the leadership may also shift.

Studies of leadership have ranged over a wide assortment of situations and tasks and probably in part for this reason many of the traits exhibited by leaders in one study have not shown up in others. Nevertheless there probably are some generalized traits that tend to characterize those who provide leadership in social groups. In surveying the available studies some years ago, Stogdill found five general characteristics that seemed to be associated with leadership in various situations:

1. Capacity (intelligence, alertness, verbal facility, originality, judgment).
2. Achievement (scholarship, knowledge, athletic accomplishment).
3. Responsibility (dependability, initiative, persistence, aggressiveness, self-confidence, desire to excel).
4. Participation (activity, sociability, cooperation, adaptability, humor).
5. Status (socioeconomic position, popularity).[1]

Stogdill calls attention to the fact that many of the research reports are contradictory, although there seems to be some agreement that leaders have higher intelligence, scholarship, dependability, social participation, and socioeconomic status.

Fiedler has suggested a different approach to the problem, arguing that the traits enabling a person to rise to a leadership position will not be the same as the leadership effectiveness traits he must exhibit once he holds such a position. He has studied the extent to which those providing leadership assume that their preferred co-workers are similar to themselves in personality traits. Somewhat surprisingly, leaders who had low assumed similarity scores and who maintained greater psychological distance were more effective in promoting task productivity than were those who developed a warmer, closer personal relationship with followers.[2] The groups studied varied from basketball teams and tank crews to workers in open hearth steel mills and surveying teams, but the implications for discussion leadership are clear. However, the results must still be interpreted cautiously. Even within Fiedler's studies, for example, the group's effectiveness under a leader with low assumed similarity could be predicted only for groups with a leader who had clear *de facto* power and authority, that is a single designated or elected leader.

As McGrath and Altman observe, much of the research on leadership traits has been conducted in leaderless group situations. This together with the fact that much of it involved group behavior in situations larger than group discussions, should add to our caution in making general statements about the characteristics of effective discussion leadership. The position taken by Hare after reviewing the literature seems to be a safe one: "The variety of traits which a leader may have is the same as that of any other group member, except that the leader is usually found to have a higher rating on each 'good' trait," such as intelligence, enthusiasm, dominance, self-confidence, social participation, and equalitarianism. He notes, however, that the person who emerges as leader must not be so extreme in these qualities that he is perceived as a deviate. For example, the individual who dominates the talk often

[1] R. M. Stogdill, "Personal Factors Associated with Leadership: A Survey of the Literature," *Journal of Psychology*, 25 (1948), pp. 35–71.

[2] Fred E. Fiedler, "The Leader's Psychological Distance and Group Effectiveness," in Dorwin Cartwright and Alvin Zander, *Group Dynamics: Research and Theory*, sec. ed., New York: Harper & Row, 1960, pp. 586–606.

becomes the leader "unless he talks so much that he antagonizes the other group members."[3]

Hare recognizes another reason for caution in generalizing about the qualities of leadership. The correlations between desirable traits and leadership-influenced productivity or group effectiveness tend to be positive but low, probably because so many other variables in the situation can intervene. Thus only a part of the variance explaining why one group outcome differs from another is accounted for by the qualities exhibited by those providing leadership.

In spite of the need for caution, we must say what we can about the nature of leadership in the discussion situation specifically. Norman Maier has underlined the great importance of leadership to decision-making groups. He observed conformity pressures based on fear of disapproval from the leader or boss and fear of disagreement with other participants. From studying many discussion groups he concluded that "disagreement can lead either to hard feelings or to innovation, depending on the discussion leadership." He has also demonstrated that training for the leader resulted in increased group satisfaction and a larger percentage of creative solutions reached.[4]

THE ASSIGNMENT OF LEADERSHIP

In discussion, it is wise to speak of leadership rather than the leader, so as not to suggest that one person is always to direct while others are to be pliable, yielding, and inert in terms of influencing the outcome of a discussion. Leadership may shift during a discussion for various reasons, and the responsibility for achieving results should be shared by the group as *a whole*. Leadership should not be the exclusive possession of one member. At the same time, it is proper to speak of the designated leader. He is a person who is assigned the primary responsibility for guiding the discussion. Most discussion groups have a designated leader: the chairman of the board or committee, the mayor, the chief officer of a staff or department, the professional moderator of a public discussion, the appointed arbitrator of a labor-management negotiating conference. He may be designated as leader by the group members themselves, as when a chairman is elected, or may preside because of his position, as when the mayor chairs city council meetings. When the word *leader* is used alone in this book, it usually refers to the person who is performing leadership functions at the moment, or to the designated leader.

The fact remains that leadership in a particular situation may or may not be supplied by the designated leader. He is responsible for exercising leader-

---

[3] A. Paul Hare, *Handbook of Small Group Research*, New York: The Free Press, 1962, p. 292.

[4] Norman R. F. Maier, *Problem-Solving Discussions and Conferences*, New York: McGraw-Hill, 1963, pp. 36–46 and pp. 244–6.

ship, and as long as he does so wisely and efficiently, his will probably be the strongest leadership influence. But leadership is not an all-or-nothing matter. Others will at times contribute to the total influence being exerted to guide the group. If the designated leader fails to function, others should and almost always do take over to supply the necessary influence. A group is in serious difficulty only when the designated leader fails, and others also fail to apply the needed guidance. In other words, a group may perform productively and be temporarily without a specific person as leader, but it will flounder if it is even temporarily without leadership.

We must be specific in our labels. We can speak of the leader when referring to a designated leader or to one who is carrying leadership responsibility at the moment. We can refer to a leaderless discussion as one without a designated leader where leadership is shifting from person to person as one or another becomes central in influencing direction, decision, etc.; or where the leadership functions have been divided up and assigned in advance to various members. Thus a leaderless discussion may be enjoying excellent leadership but there is no single designated leader or appointed chairman. A leadershipless discussion, in contrast, is one in which no leadership is being exercised. Such a group is directionless and will almost certainly be low in task productivity and member satisfaction.

"Without leadership," as Gibb says, "there is no focus about which a number of individuals may cluster to form a group." At the same time, he suggests an important distinction between leadership and "domination or mere headship." In some situations the boss or authority figure can require acquiescence and regulate group activity and decision-making simply by virtue of his role. Leadership, on the other hand, cannot be assigned as a right of proprietorship. It varies with the situation, with follower acceptance, with information possessed that propels a group toward a decision, and with other factors. A leader is not exercising leadership until he has followers in the specific situation of a moment.[5]

In general, then, leadership in discussion consists of performing functions that influence the group to achieve its objectives, and these duties are delegated directly or indirectly to certain individuals because it is in the best interests of the whole group to have guidance, direction, and some degree of control. In many cases, leadership functions are assigned by the direct voluntary action of members, as in the election of a chairman, and are subject to change when the needs of the whole group require it. In some cases, designated leaders are selected by persons outside the discussion group, as in a committee with a chairman appointed by the president of the parent organization. Here if the leader is skillful, members usually submit to influence and consider the guidance helpful rather than restrictive. At least it is clear that

[5] Cecil A. Gibb, "The Principles and Traits of Leadership," A. Paul Hare, E. F. Borgatta, and R. F. Bales, *Small Groups: Studies in Social Interaction*, rev. ed., New York: Alfred A. Knopf, 1965, pp. 87–95.

leadership in discussion must proceed according to the best interests of the whole group.

Influence of the Situation

Small closedgroup committees, conferences, round tables, study groups, and public panels are characterized by direct, conversational interchange. In these situations, the designated leader operates with the kind of influence the student probably first thinks of when discussion leadership is mentioned. This kind is informal and the interaction direct. In a public discussion situation calling for a symposium, however, the designated leader is exercising leadership functions which are quite different. Here he is operating as a presiding chairman, and his duties are similar to those of a presiding officer at any public meeting, whether or not discussion is involved. (See Chapter 17).

For another type of leadership, the parliamentary chairmanship, the chairman appears to have more power than he has in fact. There is usually machinery for his removal and replacement, and certainly the body can refuse to re-elect him at the end of his term. (See Chapter 18).

The Shifting of Leadership

Even with a recognized leader, the actual leadership being contributed at any moment can shift from person to person in the discussion group. In early stages of definition, orientation and analysis, guidance may be provided by the participant who has the most information, perhaps one in the best position to observe the problem being talked about or one with the longest experience. Later during the decision stage, a different member may be the dominant influence for a time. Some persons may emerge as leaders because they have a facility for expressing complex ideas or for mediating conflicts. Studies of leadership indicate that "leaders tend to give more information, ask for more information, and make more frequent interpretations about the situation than do the rest of the members."[6] When participants other than a designated leader can contribute these helpful behaviors, they tend to exert influence on the group at various moments.

Some groups are obviously more willing than others to have members share in leadership. One of the fundamental characteristics of democratic groups is that many persons are permitted to influence the group's goals and procedures, but some kinds of organizations and situations develop more rigid patterns of leadership acceptance. A military or industrial group, for instance, may not permit the sharing of functions with the appointed officer.

More extreme forms of acquiescence without shifting leadership could be observed in countries where groups are accustomed to authoritarian and autocratic control by ruling party or military leaders. In these cases, as Berkowitz notes, training in democratic leadership procedures would be of little value. Leadership procedures must be consistent with the group needs and expecta-

[6] Cartwright and Zander, p. 490.

tions.[7] Just to allow members to express their ideas, however, if the authoritarian leader is listening, introduces some elements of democratic sharing.

STYLES OF LEADERSHIP

There seem to be two fundamental categories of activity occurring during group discussion that have distinct characteristics of their own: the achievement of the task or assignment and interpersonal relationships. Members vary in the importance they attach to each kind of activity. In fact, the evidence suggests that for many groups a task-achievement leader emerges while a different member becomes the "social-emotional specialist."

The style of guidance contributed by a designated leader would naturally be affected if he considered one of these activities more important than the other. Some leaders press for efficient task productivity irrespective of personal feelings or harmony. Others prefer a warm, permissive atmosphere in the group even if decisions require more time or drastic compromises and revision of views. As we have said, each of these choices will be more appropriate under some conditions than others.

Another fundamental distinction suggested by the research studies affects leadership style. Apparently there are persons who are self-oriented and feel a need to have a place of importance in the center of a group's activities, while others are group-oriented and can work comfortably as part of the group, taking a follower role when this is helpful. Self-oriented persons tend to be authoritarian when in control while the group-centered person can be more equalitarian.[8]

A similar dichotomy may exist among teachers leading classroom discussion. The teacher-centered group preferred by some may be more demanding and may elicit more student hostility or withdrawal. In contrast, learner-centered discussions may be more permissive and may produce greater interaction and positive feeling. Whether students learn more in one or the other seems to be a function of the teacher's goals and the type of examination.[9]

Thus, styles of leadership are determined by the personalities of the individuals involved, by group preferences and even the culture or political structure of the society, by the nature of the situation and the task, and by other factors. While it is risky to offer generalizations about types of leadership in all the various circumstances, we should mention the styles that have been most often identified.

Authoritarian Leadership

Ralph White and Ronald Lippitt have summarized the research familiar to most students on authoritarian, democratic, and laissez-faire leadership styles.

[7] Leonard Berkowitz, "Sharing Leadership in Small, Decision-Making Groups," Hare, Borgatta, and Bales, p. 676.

[8] Hare, *Handbook of Small Group Research*, p. 293.

[9] Hare, p. 317.

These studies involved boys club meetings and activities over a period of months. In one study four trained, adult leaders shifted from group to group each six weeks, changing their leadership style with the shift. In the authoritarian version, all policy was determined by the leader. Techniques and activities were dictated by the leader one step at a time; thus the boys were uncertain about what would be permitted next. The leader determined as well the specific task assignment and companion for each boy. Remaining aloof from group activity except when demonstrating, the leader was dominant and was personal in his praise or criticism of member efforts.[10]

Although these club meetings involved many activities other than group discussion, there was a lot of social interaction and talk. The operational definition contrived to designate authoritarian leadership in these studies gives a good clue to the behavior characteristic of the autocratic leader in discussion. This kind of person tends to feel that ordinary members are limited in ability and cannot be trusted to manage without strict guidance and control. His leadership thus tends to be rigid and somewhat formal. He assigns the floor judiciously, discourages interruptions, expresses displeasure unless members wait for him to decide when to move forward, favors those who agree with him and is reluctant to recognize those disagreeing, and in other ways dominates the talk and the entire decision-making procedure. Where the leader insists on maximum control there is obviously minimum permissiveness. Members have little choice except submission to dictation. Such an arbitrary, autocratic dominator makes frequent direct influence attempts, retaliates by withholding privileges when members fail to agree, arbitrarily shuts off contributions that displease him, takes sides aggressively in conflicts, and in other ways operates as a combination emperor-oracle who has just received divine ordination.

Laissez-Faire Leadership

In the White and Lippitt study, the laissez-faire style granted the boys complete freedom to make group or individual decisions as they chose, with a minimum of leadership participation. The hands-off leader explained that he would answer questions about activities and work companions when asked but otherwise he took no part in the discussions of the work. He made no effort to appraise or regulate the course of events and commented on activities only when questioned.[11]

A discussion leader who behaved in this way would obviously fail to provide leadership and thus we would be confronted with leadershipless discussion unless others filled the void. Actually few such leaders can be observed. This category is worth defining primarily to fix the end of a continuum opposite autocratic leadership as a method of bracketing the democratic style.

[10] "Leader Behavior and Member Reaction in Three 'Social Climates,'" in Cartwright and Zander, pp. 527–53.

[11] Cartwright and Zander.

Designated leaders can be observed exhibiting some tendencies in the laissez-faire direction. Occasionally a leader will not have done his homework and thus will not be well enough informed to provide effective guidance. Even less frequently a member is designated chairman in a situation where the obvious and actual control is being exercised by a strong man who for some reason wants a puppet in ostensible control; under these conditions the leader at times will resemble the laissez-faire style, remaining tentative and hesitant, exercising no control, permitting anything, preventing nothing, and supplying no direction or guidance until he receives the signal from the person who is the actual dominator.

Democratic Leadership

The democratic style defined in the White-Lippitt study allowed members to decide policy through group discussion, with encouragement and assistance from the adult leader. Members could work with companions of their choice. The group divided up tasks and agreed on activity steps and objectives. The leader tried to be objective or fact-minded in praising or criticizing member achievement. His aim was to be a "regular group member in spirit without doing too much of the work."[12]

Democratic leadership style in discussion obviously lies between the extremes of autocracy and abdication. Members submit to some measure of control and guidance to provide some degree of order, efficiency, and forward locomotion. At the same time there is a minimum of restraint and a maximum of permissiveness consistent with task productivity and good interpersonal relationships. In conflicts between the leader and the group, the democratic style of leadership requires that the group have its way.

The evidence from the studies summarized by White and Lippitt is revealing. Laissez-faire leadership was the lowest in quality; the least and poorest work was done under this style. Autocracy created much hostility and aggression, resulted in discontent including some dropping out of the groups, and encouraged submissive or dependent behavior. When interviewed, the boys tended to prefer the democratic leader. In this style, there was more group-mindedness and friendliness. Authoritarian leadership produced somewhat greater quantities of work, indicating its efficiency, but work motivation was stronger under the democratic style and there was more originality.[13]

There is nothing very surprising in these results but it is helpful to have this kind of confirming clues about leadership behavior. The autocrat is preferable to the do-nothing leader, since the latter invites chaos. At worst, he is not leading at all. The authoritarian leader is at least efficient, although at times he probably does not permit interaction to operate freely enough for discussion worthy of the name to occur.

Collaborating with Bradford in another study, Lippitt reported that a

---

[12] Cartwright and Zander.
[13] Cartwright and Zander.

"hardboiled autocrat" caused resentment and stirred up incipient revolt; there was irritability and unwillingness to cooperate. The lowest morale of all in this study was brought on by the laissez-faire leader; no one knew what to do or to expect and the result was absence of teamwork and the lowest productivity. The democratic leader, who shared decision-making and explained the basis for his decisions, was met with enthusiasm; his group had the best teamwork and production in the study.[14] Fox also found positive leadership superior to negative leadership in promoting permissiveness, friendliness, and member satisfaction. Revealingly, positive leadership took twice as long before consensus was reached or members felt that further talk would be fruitless.[15]

We can visualize these three leadership styles on a continuum ranging from laissez-faire at one end to authoritarian at the other, with the do-nothing leader exercising minimum control and the autocrat insisting on maximum control. The democratic style would then be somewhere in the center:

	Laissez	Democratic	Autocratic	
MINIMUM	faire	control	domination	MAXIMUM
CONTROL				CONTROL

Permissive Leadership

On the basis of such a continuum it is possible to suggest a style of leadership occurring to the left of democratic control and closer to the laissez-faire end. We could call this style *permissive leadership*. It would be characterized by even more freedom to speak up than is usual in the democratic style. The leader would be more a "director of traffic" than a guide. He would leave to members decisions about moving forward on substantive matters.

This style encourages spontaneity and may be appropriate where groups want to be especially creative. It may be desirable also in situations where members have low motivation to remain in the group, as in some extracurricular student activities or community improvement groups. No doubt there are other circumstances where extreme permissiveness and freedom of expression would be appropriate. Perhaps groups where interpersonal relationships are much more important than the task assignment, as in many social and recreational situations, would appreciate a permissive-leadership style.

Supervisory Leadership

On this same continuum, to the right of center, we can probably identify a style of leadership that is more controlling than would be characteristic of democratic style but would stop far short of autocratic control. The super-

[14] L. P. Bradford and R. Lippitt, "Building a Democratic Work Group," *Personnel*, 22 (1945), pp. 142–52.
[15] William M. Fox, "Group Reaction to Two Types of Conference Leadership," *Human Relations*, 10 (1957), pp. 279–89.

visory style may be appealing where efficiency is crucial, as in some industrial work teams, and where opportunities for communication are limited.

Hare reports the results of studies comparing supervisory leaders, who do not take part in the discussion but who see that the group finishes on time, with participatory leaders, who "take part in the discussion and try to insure an equal chance for participation to all group members." Participatory style tends to produce greater opinion change and higher satisfaction, apparently because each member has an opportunity to give his opinion. The supervisory leader also had less influence on the group decision.[16]

It would be possible to propose many additional styles and variations of leadership but those we have identified seem sufficient to suggest the differences in leadership behaviors. We can turn now to three key questions the leader must answer in deciding on a style appropriate for particular circumstances.

DEGREE OF CONTROL

What influence should a designated leader exert in discussion? How much power should he have? In democratic discussion groups, of course, power resides in the group. He will have whatever influence and power the group is willing to allow him, but this statement must be qualified. Temporarily, a designated leader may exercise more authority than members approve of, and the group must expend time and effort to replace him or redistribute the leadership functions. A group may be lethargic, indifferent, or unalert, and simply by default allow him more power than they really intend. Then, of course, there are groups where the designated leader is arbitrarily autocratic. Such is the case when a staff appears to "talk things over" but in reality is called together to be told by the boss what is to be done.

During an interactional discussion some leadership behaviors are related to talk about the substance of the problem and others to recognizing persons to speak, allotting time for each stage, etc. The former could be called substantive control and the latter, procedural. There is some evidence that many groups may want the designated leader to exercise firm procedural control even when they would not allow him to dominate the substantive contributions.

Berkowitz sees support for this possibility in commenting on studies of seventy-two decision-making conferences in industrial, business, and government groups. The groups studied seemed to expect the designated leader or appointed chairman to exercise control and be somewhat dominant as leader. However, what they seemed to approve was procedural control; "they do not indicate that they want substantive control over what should or should not be said." Berkowitz cites Heyns' unpublished doctoral dissertation to show that

---

[16] *Handbook of Small Group Research*, p. 316.

groups may approve firmer leadership if this kind of control is expected and if the leader is successfully performing the expected functions. Under positive leadership, a member was rejected by the others if he competed with the designated leader when the leader was doing his job. In contrast, members who helped with leadership were perceived as contributing to unity and were liked under circumstances of negative leadership where the designated leader did not perform and was inactive and unhelpful.[17]

There is also a possibility that groups accept firmer leader control in a crisis or under conditions where a decision is urgent. Hamblin reports such an outcome in a study of student groups. Those exerting high influence on the others tended to have even more influence during periods of crisis than during periods of lessened pressure.[18]

The individual leader must decide what his style of leadership will be. Where a group gives him wide latitude in the amount of control they will allow, his dominance will be a function of his personal philosophy of leadership control, tempered no doubt by the way he sizes up what is appropriate under the circumstances.

PARTISANSHIP-IMPARTIALITY

Should a designated leader be an active participant in the group's substantive deliberation, contributing his own opinions and factual information? Or should he be an impartial guide, refusing to become a partisan participant and concentrating on procedural control?

This matter is controversial. Haiman advises the leader to express his ideas with restraint, but feels we should not make the chairman an "idea-eunuch," robbing the group of his "intellectual and emotional virility."[19] Other authorities, such as Utterback, have described him as a moderator who suppresses his own convictions in order to bring the will of the group to full fruition.[20] Probably the question should not be answered "yes" or "no." A reasonable answer seems to be that the designated leader's partisanship or impartiality should be a matter of degree, depending on the situation.

In small, informal committee discussions, the chairman can probably fairly and efficiently perform his guidance functions and still be a complete partisan or participant, expressing his convictions as fully and vociferously as the others do. In this situation, we would perhaps be depriving the group of its most articulate and well-informed voice if we expected the designated leader to be silent on substantive matters. He often is made chairman because he has

[17] Berkowitz, p. 683.
[18] Robert L. Hamblin, "Leadership and Crises," in Cartwright and Zander, pp. 571–85.
[19] Franklyn S. Haiman, *Group Leadership and Democratic Action*, Boston: Houghton Mifflin, 1951.
[20] William E. Utterback, "The Moderator's Function in Group Thinking," *Quarterly Journal of Speech*, 34 (1948), pp. 455–8.

the most interest in and knowledge related to the group's task function. A similar position could be taken in regard to designated leaders of small conferences, study groups, and round tables.

The designated leaders of larger committees and conferences, and of public panels, may find it somewhat more damaging to the group's productivity if they are active partisans. Especially if the group is faced with an extremely complex and controversial problem, or if members feel strong emotional involvement, the leader may be wise to concentrate most of his attention on guidance and procedural functions and participate substantively only with caution. Thus, he would contribute information only when it could not be elicited from members; withhold his opinions whenever possible; express his convictions tentatively and carefully; phrase his statements as "another view which could be taken into account"; avoid for the most part direct attempts to influence the group's decisions; and unless it was extremely important to him, avoid agreeing or disagreeing aggressively with some members in a conflict with others.

When a designated leader must strive to promote direct interaction in a large discussion, say a committee or conference of twenty persons, or in the forum period of public discussion, he has little choice about partisanship. He is so busy guiding, channeling contributions, clarifying, and distributing participation, that he has little or no opportunity to express his own convictions. Here his function is to be an impartial guide, to help the group be maximally productive under the circumstances.

There are other situations, also, in which the designated leader must be an impartial guide. One is when he serves as arbitrator of a labor–management negotiating conference. And, of course, the parliamentary chairman is expected to be absolutely neutral; his functions are restricted to guidance and control of the interaction process.

Another situation in which he must be capable of being completely impartial arises when a sharp personal conflict occurs within the group. The leader will want to restore harmony as efficiently as possible. If he is to succeed, he must not take sides, even by subtle overtones in his voice or a facial grimace which suggests where his sympathies lie. To show complete impartiality requires practice since it is easy to betray feelings by signs the speaker may not be aware of.

Where the designated leader is an impartial guide, moderator, or presiding chairman in whom bias would be particularly damaging, he must be especially careful not to reveal his opinions or evaluations. An impatient gesture or vocal inflection, an amused smile, or an unguarded retort can suggest partisan feeling that may limit the leader's effectiveness in performing his vital functions.

These differences in the extent of partisan participation are matters of degree. The designated leader must decide whether it is appropriate under the specific conditions to be more partisan than guide, less partisan than guide, almost wholly an impartial guide, or completely neutral. Further, what seems reasonable will vary with the attitudes, intentions, and values of the persons involved. Perhaps the possibilities can best be represented by a continuum suggesting the relative locations of types of discussions and the extent to which designated leaders may wish to be partisan:

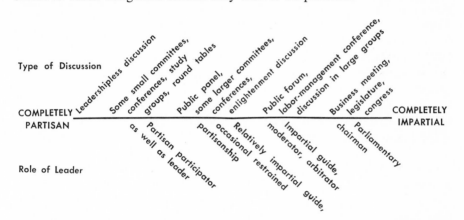

Maier believes that leaders conducting discussions with their subordinates should refrain from proposing a course of action since "solutions suggested by the leader are improperly evaluated and tend either to be accepted or rejected." In some situations the leader's suggestions may be blindly followed or they may be resented; they are not likely to be weighed as are proposals coming from others. The safest thing for the leader to do, Maier says, is to specialize in guiding the discussion procedurally, refraining from introducing views or offering judgments on the members' ideas.[21]

QUALITIES OF LEADERSHIP

We have seen that the type of leadership exerted in discussion depends on many factors, such as the kind of discussion and the situation in which it takes place; the objectives of the group; the alertness, inclinations, and attitudes of the participants; the degree of control members wish designated leaders to exercise; and the extent to which the designated leader is also a participant in the deliberation. We turn now to a final question about the personal attributes of those contributing leadership. What qualities and abilities must a person possess if he is to adjust to this wide variety of situations and circumstances? When democratic style is appropriate, for example, how is he to control without coercion and guide without goading?

To list these qualities is not to suggest that every successful discussion leader possesses a full measure of each one. A person can supply adequate discussion leadership and be deficient in some or perhaps many of them. Moreover, emphasis here is upon qualities of leadership which it is desirable

[21] Maier, pp. 251–2.

for someone in the group to supply, rather than upon the qualities of any single person. It may happen that some deficiency in the designated leader can be compensated for by others in a particular group. These are attributes and abilities that aid the designated leader in performing his functions.

Mutuality

The leader must be willing to lead—to accept the responsibilities of leadership with its consequences in energy, social relationships, and so on. In addition, there must be a mutuality of acceptance between the leader and the led. Those providing leadership must accept the leadership role and work at it; and followers must accept his guidance if he is to be effective. As Gibb says, the leader is not a leader until his ideas are communicated and he has won followers.[22]

Ability to Communicate

Obviously, the discussion leader must be a skillful communicator. He must use language accurately and expressively, making sure that he carefully defines terms that may be misleading. Also he must recognize when words used by others should be clarified.

His voice usage should be such that he is heard and understood easily, of course, and his manner and meaning should match. The most important speech skill for him, however, is the ability to express complex ideas clearly, fairly, objectively, and swiftly. When a comment is unclear, he should be able to restate it clearly, without offending the person who made it initially. He must summarize in one minute what a number of persons have contributed in ten, and do so in a way that will not overlook any important contribution. In addition to being clear, his summaries must represent fairly the collective ideas being reviewed; if the members were polled, he would want each to agree that his quick summary presented their opinions without distortion.

Listening

The designated leader should also be a good listener. This means more than hearing, or giving the speaker undivided attention, or appearing attentive. It means being actively absorbed mentally in what others say, gaining clear insight into what is meant, what is implied, and perhaps why it was expressed in one way rather than another. If the leader is really a good listener, he encourages further comment because of the way he received and accepted earlier ones, and is able to incorporate these ideas into later questions and summaries.

Quick Thinking

While participants are discussing a point, the designated leader must have the mental agility to engage in two thinking processes approximately at the

[22] Gibb, p. 89.

same time: to follow closely and in detail what is being said, and to think ahead of the group, anticipating what question he must next ask in order for the discussion to move forward. Thus he needs the ability to think quickly. To clarify confusing contributions or tangled involvements, to restate immediately what others have said, or to summarize requires rapid and alert thinking. It goes without saying that his thinking must also be of high quality.

Knowledge of the Problem

The designated leader should have a thorough understanding of the problem being discussed by the group. Ideally, of course, he should know more about it than any participant. Without knowledge of the problem and keen insight into its implications and ramifications, he cannot guide discussion on it because he will not recognize when a point has been fully covered, when the group has contributed sufficient information on which to base a decision, or when it is appropriate to move from one stage to another.

Knowledge of Group Process

The more the designated leader understands about discussion groups and the discussion process itself, the better able he should be to help a group attain its aims. Everything said in this book could be repeated here. He should know in particular about interaction—the influences of communication structure, power relationships, interpersonal relations, group size—objectivity, cooperative attitudes, possible group objectives, and his own duties in taking these factors into account. He certainly must know about discussion outlines and how to use them.

It has been noted that democratic leadership means achieving control without sacrificing permissiveness and member rights. The designated leader must understand and appreciate this delicate balance.

Respect for Others

The good discussion leader will have genuine respect for other people, for their ideas and for them as human beings. In discussion, all the members' ideas are not equally meritorious, but every member is equally worthy of respect. To respect others means more than to like them or to tolerate them. If the designated leader respects them, he will go out of his way, especially when disagreeing with them, to protect them and their feelings; he will have confidence in their statements; he will trust their judgment, and he will speak to them courteously—not only because to do so is to exhibit good manners, but also because he really wants to. To be genuinely respectful is to be eager to learn all he can about them, how they think, and why they hold the attitudes they do. For the designated leader to be respectful, to be curious about the why behind what others say, means that his reactions to them and to their contributions will be gentle rather than harsh, pleasant rather than strident, objective rather than critical.

Social Sensitivity

Related to treating others respectfully is the ability to respond sensitively to others. Discussion leadership is not often a desirable office for the crass, callous, indifferent, and insensitive. The responsible guide must be aware of "how things are going," and how members feel about the discussion. He must catch the nuances in voices that imply, "I am not happy with this turn of events," when the words spoken were, "I will accept that suggestion." It is the leader who must recognize when the members are on the verge of consensus, and when it would be a mistake to let the discussion move on without hearing more from a particular participant. He must study the participants constantly during the discussion, reading signs in their faces and posture, and reacting sensitively to their expressed and unexpressed feelings and attitudes.

This social sensitivity of the designated leader is exactly the same as the sensitivity of the good hostess. She knows when her guests are excited, content, bored, or indifferent. She suggests entertainment, changes the subject of the conversation, or rearranges the conversation groups within the room according to the signs she has read in studying the guests, collectively and individually.

Other Qualities

The list of desirable abilities could probably be extended indefinitely. Objectivity has been mentioned a number of times, and the leader who cannot be objective will have difficulty. Members might wish the designated leader to have self-control, since often his patience and forbearance are sorely tried. If he loses his temper, the group will of course flounder, at least temporarily. He needs persistence, since members are sometimes lazy and they may overestimate the quality of the work they have already done; he may need to prod them to greater effort and to stay with a point until it has been sufficiently explored. Also he must be firm, since the group may want to take the easy way out or in some similar manner dodge its responsibilities. He can well use a sense of humor, because in many cases calm and equanimity can best be restored after a storm of conflict by a relaxing bit of humor.

But as was noted earlier, it is unreasonable to expect the designated leader to be a superman possessed only of sterling virtues. The abilities and characteristics described here will each add to his effectiveness in leading the group. If a particular person has some degree of most of them, a group must be willing to settle for that, and hope that his proficiency will increase with training and practice.

SUPPLEMENTARY READING

Barnard, Chester I., *The Functions of the Executive*, Cambridge, Mass.: Harvard University Press, 1938.

Braden, Waldo W., and Brandenburg, Earnest, *Oral Decision-Making*, New York: Harper & Row, 1955, Chapter 11.

Cartwright, Dorwin, and Zander, Alvin, *Group Dynamics: Research and Theory*, 2nd ed., New York: Harper & Row, 1960, Part V.

Collins, Barry E., and Guetzkow, Harold, *A Social Psychology of Group Processes for Decision-Making*, New York: John Wiley & Sons, 1964, Chapter 11.

Haiman, Franklyn S., *Group Leadership and Democratic Action*, Boston: Houghton Mifflin, 1951.

————, "A Measurement of Authoritarian Attitudes toward Discussion Leadership," *Quarterly Journal of Speech*, 41 (April, 1955), pp. 140–144.

Hare, A. Paul, *Handbook of Small Group Research*, New York: The Free Press, 1962, Chapter 11.

Homans, George C., *The Human Group*, New York: Harcourt, Brace & World, 1950, Chapter 16.

QUESTIONS AND EXERCISES

1. How much power do you feel the discussion leader should have? Under what conditions would you feel that increased control is appropriate? Be specific.

2. Is the amount of appropriate control different for a designated leader and a leader who emerges during the discussion? Give your reasons. Which do you think will be more authoritarian: a designated leader or an emergent leader? Why?

3. Professor Utterback[23] presents three widely held views of the moderator's function: "According to one view the moderator is simply a presiding officer enforcing in informal and flexible fashion such rules of parliamentary procedure as seem to be applicable. . . . A second view is that the moderator is essentially a teacher . . . who employs question and answer. . . . A third view is that the moderator is primarily a stimulator of conversation. . . . It is the purpose of this article to suggest that all of these views of the moderator's function misconceive the nature of group thinking, that the moderator performs certain functions indispensable to cooperative thinking, and that these have little in common with the duties of the presiding officer, the teacher, or the mere stimulator of discussion." Utterback proceeds to offer a fourth view of the moderator's functions. Which of these four views, if any, is the most defensible? Which method will help a group best accomplish its task? Which method will best promote friendly interpersonal relationships?

4. Braden and Brandenburg (see Supplementary Readings) make the distinction between leaderless and leadershipless groups. Do you agree that

[23] Utterback.

a group may be leaderless even in the presence of a designated leader and that a group may have leadership without a designated leader?

5. Write a paper in which you discuss the characteristics of authoritarian and democratic leadership in the small group, as you have observed them in in discussion groups.

6. Listen carefully to a discussion. Identify and evaluate the leadership qualities displayed by the designated leader and/or others in the group sharing leadership responsibilities. Relate them if possible to the group's task productivity and social relationships.

7. Distinguish between leadership qualities and functions or duties. To what extent will the leader be handicapped in performing his functions if he does not possess the kinds of qualities described in this chapter?

Chapter 11

LEADERSHIP
FUNCTIONS

A group engaging in discussion must receive from one or more of its members some minimum amount of guidance and control in order to achieve maximum productivity and satisfaction with the outcome and to help members interact as a cohesive unit. Thus leadership functions of guidance and control are those duties most directly related to the central objectives of an inter-actional discussion group. These duties may be performed by a designated leader, or they may be distributed among several members. It is possible, too, for the responsibility to shift from one person to another as the discussion progresses.

Most of the time in this chapter we will concentrate on leadership of direct, conversational, interactional discussion characteristic of committees, small-group conferences, study groups, and public-panel discussion. What we have to say, however, should have some application to other discussion situations. When we refer to the leader, we will be talking about a designated leader or about the person in the group who at the moment is providing leadership.

Our purpose is to explore some of the duties of leadership related to group effectiveness in decision-making discussion. In Chapter 10 we considered the traits and qualities the effective leader may exhibit in fostering productivity. To talk about leadership attributes in one chapter and leadership functions in another suggests that these subjects can be divided into two separate cate-gories, but this is not true. They have been divided here for purposes of analysis and study, but they are actually not easily divisible. Traits and abilities cannot be separated neatly from duties or functions. We are talking about both abilities and duties in both chapters and there is no intent here to conceal the overlapping and repetition. When we attempt to concentrate on functions, we can never quite avoid continuing to talk about leader attributes. These two different ways of looking at qualities and functions are both part of the larger subject of the complex relationships between the leader and the led in discussion. If our consideration of leadership functions is clear enough, it should help to throw light both on leadership abilities and leadership responsibilities.

It is worth our while to concentrate on leadership functions as well as abilities because the management of discussion is extremely important in in-fluencing decision quality and member satisfaction. As Maier has observed in working with business and industrial management problem-solving groups, "the skill of the discussion leader tends to upgrade the quality of the decision."[1]

CATEGORIES OF FUNCTIONS

Possible duties that could be performed by the discussion leader may be categorized in any number of ways. It is important that we consider as fully as we can the various posssibilities, leaving to the individual leader's judgment the question of what is essential. We can begin this exploration by examining the categories suggested by two authorities, as well as those indicated by research studies and observation.

Sociologist George Homans, in his book, *The Human Group*, has done some exceptionally deep thinking about the operations of small groups. He is looking at behavior in social situations more general than group discussion, but he is including discussion as one kind of activity engaged in by groups. "The job of the leader," he says, "is twofold: (a) to attain the purposes of the group, and (b) in so doing to maintain a balance of incentives, both reward and punishment, sufficient to induce his followers to obey him." He refers to the necessity of maintaining the social system, not in a static state, but in a steadily changing state that retains this balance, a kind of "moving equilibrium." Students of discussion may not want to agree that the leader should induce his followers to "obey him," since discussion usually involves greater permissiveness than the concept of obedience suggests. Nevertheless, the basic duties visualized give insight into the essence of the leadership assignment.[2]

The leadership role as observed in many different group situations has been described in an extensive study by Hemphill. Leaders were found to perform five functions common to all the groups. They:

1. Advanced the group's purposes
2. Administered
3. Inspired greater activity or set the pace
4. Made members feel secure within the group
5. Acted without regard to their own self-interest.[3]

Both Homans and Hemphill are concerned with social situations in general. We have observed that some group activity is substantive, intellectual in content, and relevant to the achievement of the task. Other activities concern

[1] Norman R. F. Maier, *Problem-Solving Discussions and Conferences*, New York: McGraw-Hill, 1963, pp. 20–2.
[2] George Homans, *The Human Group*, New York: Harcourt, Brace & World, 1950, p. 423.
[3] See A. Paul Hare, *Handbook of Small Group Research*, New York: The Free Press, 1962, pp. 293–4.

member feelings, are emotional in content, and are related to interpersonal relationships. Where the first kind is devoted to talk about the problem and the decision, the second is designed to preserve harmony, build cohesiveness, and maintain the group as a group.

Again we must emphasize that these two activities are not unrelated. They are mutually interdependent: when the task productivity is high, this fact may contribute to positive emotional feelings in the group; and also a warm, cohesive climate may make substantive achievement easier. No doubt the opposite relationships also hold.

It should be emphasized, in addition, that a designated leader may have the skill to perform both these functions effectively. It is not necessary that two different champions emerge to promote intellectual and affective behavior. While it is true, as Cartwright and Zander write, that "everyday experience in groups provides many examples of instances where members make group maintenance their major concern to the detriment of work to be done, or where too much interest in task achievement leads to insufficient attention to group maintenance," the problem for the designated leader is to balance these two requirements of group activity.[4] Imbalance is caused when the leader is so eager to have a high-quality decision that he ignores the feelings of members, or when he has such an emotional regard for the group that he cannot insist on rigorous standards of productivity.

In discussion there seems to be a third category of functions which is purely procedural. The leader in this regard is a kind of director of traffic and administrator of group activity. The procedural duties could serve either task achievement or social harmony but in any case would be trivial compared with the other two categories.

It is interesting to recognize in passing that many group members, when they talk of leadership, seem to be thinking primarily of procedural functions. Thus when some persons say they "like a strong, forceful leader who takes command and sees that the group moves forward," they mean only that they want him to preserve order, recognize only one speaker at a time, and bang his gavel for attention. If the leader begins to interfere with their right to say what they wish about the problem, they may change their minds about desiring strong, commanding leadership.

The wide range of duties performed by the designated leader in discussion, or by several members sharing the leadership, can be organized within these three broad categories of procedural, social, and task functions. All five of the general leadership functions described by Hemphill are represented directly in these divisions. The first, advancing the group's purposes, is common to task achievement and social harmony because most discussion groups seek both to be productive and to maintain the group. The second, administration, is approximately the same category we are calling procedural. The third, in-

[4] Dorwin Cartwright and Alvin Zander, *Group Dynamics: Research and Theory*, sec. ed., New York: Harper & Row, 1960, pp. 497–8.

spiring greater activity, is clearly a matter of task productivity, while the fourth, making members feel secure, concerns interpersonal relationships or group maintenance. The fifth function listed by Hemphill, acting without regard to self-interest, is again a general one cutting across all three of the others. Moreover, it is somewhat different in kind as well as in generality, since it raises questions directly about the leader's motives, dedication, and philosophies. For these reasons we will defer consideration of this fifth one to Chapter 13, when we take up some of the larger challenges of leadership.

We can proceed now to say what we can about the duties of leadership in each of these categories, beginning with the least demanding.

PROCEDURAL FUNCTIONS

A discussion group usually assigns to one central person the functions that are merely procedural. If there is a designated leader, such as an appointed committee chairman or elected mayor, members readily defer to him as the one to take charge of the meeting. In a group meeting where there has been no assignment of leadership, some member will usually emerge or the group will draft someone to perform these essential functions.

The procedural duties serve the purpose of achieving an orderly meeting even though several people are involved. In most cases participants in discussion are articulate speakers and are knowledgeable about the problem; almost any one of them could use up the available time for talk all by himself. Further, there is usually more or less intense personal involvement in the problem and often the matter is highly controversial. Since all the members realize these facts they are willing to have the meeting conducted in a civilized fashion. Simply to be polite and considerate, they must assign to someone the responsibilities of controlling the procedures of the meeting.

These duties usually begin for the designated leader even before the talking starts. In many cases, he must check to see that the advanced planning has been carried out properly, that members have received the printed materials needed for intelligent discussion of the problem, and that the physical arrangements are adequate.

Also before launching into the discussion, the leader should try to take into account the total situation. He must review swiftly the over-all purposes of the meeting and the relationship between this small-group session and the external social system. This is true whether this is a board of directors responsible to stockholder-owners or the Security Council deciding the fate of nations, or a neighborhood coffee-break session deciding on a gift for a departing friend. If he is familiar with the members, the leader should think a moment about the nature of these persons, their tendencies to talkativeness, their involvements in the problem, and so on. By taking these and other factors into account, he can decide about the appropriate degree of formality, the probable difficulty in maintaining decorum, and other matters that should be anticipated in order to have a good meeting. Such decisions at this point will help him to set the tone of the meeting in his opening words. The way he conducts the meeting in the first few minutes or perhaps even seconds, will have an influence on the whole session. When he has thought about all these matters, he can take a deep breath and begin.[5]

Getting Started

The leader must immediately make clear what the group is assembled to accomplish, if that has been clearly decided in advance, or ask the group to agree on the agenda if the objectives are unclear or not yet specified. He cannot proceed effectively until the nature and purposes of the meeting are clear to all.

The leader who knows in advance he is to be the leader should be prepared at this initial point to suggest positively what could reasonably be accomplished in the time available. One matter he must keep in mind is that groups should not set unattainable goals for themselves, else they will be frustrated and discouraged. "Give a group too much to do," Irving Lee warned, "and, no matter how interested they are, they are in danger of bogging down in the doing."[6]

In getting started with the first few sentences, the leader should usually try also to think of the persons involved. If they are tense, he may want to begin casually and informally. If the problem is so controversial that participants are highly emotional, he may try to use humor or a light touch in the beginning. On a solemn occasion he will set quite a different tone in his opening remarks.

Controlling Communication Flow

The most critical procedural functions are related to the flow of communication during a discussion. The person "in charge" is assigned the responsibility of preserving order, preventing chaos, and keeping everyone from talking at once. He achieves orderly talk by "directing the communication traffic" as if the words of members were automobiles hurrying by. He must see that only one person at a time talks, and when two or more persons are competing for attention, he is the one who must give the nod to the participant who may talk next.

The leader must protect the person speaking from interrupters and in addition remember who had asked earlier to speak. He can then return to those who were denied the floor earlier and ask if they still wish to contribute. As controller of communication exchange, his assignment is to distribute speaking rights to all in a fair and comfortable manner.

[5] See in this connection George C. Homans' eighth rule of leadership behavior: "The leader will take into consideration the total situation." *The Human Group*, New York: Harcourt, Brace & World, 1950, pp. 433–4.

[6] Irving Lee, *How To Talk With People*, New York: Harper & Row, 1952, p. 139.

At times the leader will find it necessary to clarify what has been said or to remind members about the agenda agreed upon in order to make way for further communication. Otherwise confusion and disorder may build up and the talk may stop flowing. The leader has a larger responsibility in connection with the substance of the task where he must clarify the content of contributions, but the procedural aspects of clarification concern the statements he should make to keep the talk moving smoothly. Of course there will be overlapping between his procedural and task functions at this point but it is not important that he be able to distinguish between them. A difficulty could occur, however, if two different persons were performing these two kinds of functions and they had a problem of coordination.

In public discussion such as a symposium, lecture-forum, or debate-forum, the presiding chairman controls discussion flow through his introductory remarks, the speech of introduction (see Chapter 17).

No doubt there are other procedural matters important in a particular situation. The leader should remind the group of the direction it agreed to go and in other ways help members bear their objectives in mind. He can help them maintain the right direction by internal signposting: reviewing the ground covered and pointing the way to the next step. It is his job also to remember the time if the group is on a particular schedule.

SOCIAL FUNCTIONS

The social functions of leadership serve the purposes of promoting human relationships, developing group cohesiveness, maintaining the group as a cooperating unit, and in other ways helping members to work together in a common cause.

If the participants are unacquainted, the leader should begin at once to build positive social relationships by introducing them to each other. In many closedgroup situations, of course, members will already know the others well. Unless they do, they must be introduced gracefully and their positions carefully identified. It is helpful to place a name plate before each participant around the table until names and faces become familiar.

Creating a Permissive Climate

Interaction is easier, naturally, in a group that is cohesive. There is some evidence that task productivity is also increased in many situations when an atmosphere has been created in which all members feel permitted to speak freely, fully, and frankly. This would not hold, of course, if members become so congenial that the socializing takes precedence over task achievement. For the most part, however, one of the aims of leadership is to encourage interaction by helping to create a permissive climate.

The Michigan study of seventy-two conferences in business and government, to which we have referred so often, collected some evidence relevant to this point. When members had their self-needs "satisfied through rewarding personal interrelations within the conference itself," Collins and Guetzkow report, "there [was] a significant tendency for the group to achieve consensus, especially when intense conflict prevails." The pleasantness of meetings and a positive affective atmosphere "created a climate conducive to agreement," except "when there was little conflict in the meeting."[7]

There is also some evidence that high influencers in the group who drive too relentlessly toward task productivity may damage interpersonal relationships. The explanation may be that they "do things which alienate the affection of other group members," perhaps by failing to give them sufficient opportunity "to react, comment, or feedback their reactions to the contributions of the idea leader."[8] The evidence here is indirect and inconclusive but it may indicate that the designated leader must work hard to provide members ample time for interaction.

In opening a discussion, the leader should set the stage for permissiveness by stressing that everyone's comments are not only invited but are absolutely essential if thorough collective consideration is to be accomplished. He also suggests by his manner whether all members are *really* permitted to speak up. The boss, for example, may *say* to the staff, "We want everyone to speak his mind here," but his vocal inflections may not quite convincingly communicate the same message. Then when someone does express disagreement, if the boss frowns, flinches, or looks shocked or injured, it is clear that he did not actually intend to solicit permissive discussion.

To stimulate direct interactions, the designated leader must be sincere when he tries to establish a climate of frankness. When others talk, he must listen carefully and intently. When presenting a transitional or final summary, he must take all views into account. Otherwise, the member who was almost sure that minority views were unwelcome will be convinced that he is wasting time by contributing.

The leader must invite contributions and then wait for them. Sometimes the eager or nervous chairman asks a question, urges frank response, but then keeps talking or asks another question when there is a brief silence. Members must think hard before answering if they are to be most helpful. The leader must learn to tolerate some short periods of silence. Waiting for a contribution that is somewhat slow in formulation—meanwhile holding off other more loquacious and fluent members—will promote rather than stifle permissiveness.

Members not only should feel permitted to contribute, but ideally should actually do so. Obviously, some participants always will talk more than others, but to have a truly collective product requires some help from every individual present. The quality of the outcome is usually improved if everyone con-

---

[7] Barry E. Collins and Harold Guetzkow, *A Social Psychology of Group Processes for Decision-Making*, New York: John Wiley & Sons, 1964, pp. 109–11.

[8] Collins and Guetzkow, pp. 220–4.

tributes, assuming that groups are more productive than individuals working alone. Maier and Solem found, for instance, that discussion groups in which there was a leader who permitted the expression of minority opinions produced more correct answers to the problems posed than did groups without leaders.[9]

One of the unique values of group discussion is that the presence of others interacting orally apparently stimulates each person to think better than he does alone. Most members think of ideas that would not have occurred to them without this stimulus. Included within this larger phenomenon is the fact that the individual is roused to keener effort by his own contributions. Hence, if a member is silent, he is not experiencing a self-stimulus. By encouraging him to take an initial step, the designated leader may provide the group with later help it would otherwise be denied.

Triggering universal participation makes it more probable that real feelings, hidden purposes, and latent hostilities will be revealed. Bringing them into the open makes more likely the resolution of the disagreements they harbor. There is an old saying that "silence gives consent." In discussion, silence may mean unexpressed opposition, which will appear later as conflict or as obstacles to carrying out the group's decision. It is healthier for discussion when repressed feelings are brought out frankly. At least, the wise leader needs to sense how persons are reacting. To do so is difficult in the case of silent members, who are often enigmas. If they can be encouraged to contribute something, they will almost always give some clue to their attitudes through tone of voice or facial expression, if not through the content of their comments.

Persons who contribute to the outcome are also more likely to be committed to its support. A member can help more enthusiastically to put a policy into effect if he was one of its architects. The silent participant may later be an opponent or at least a lukewarm supporter. The group needs the benefit of his help and should have the opportunity at the time to meet his objections and perhaps thereby improve the outcome.

For the reluctant participant, permissiveness is essential. Under some conditions, the leader may be safe in drafting the silent member to comment: "Joe, would you like to add anything to what has been said?" It is a mistake, of course, to call on individuals in rotation as a teacher occasionally does in classroom recitation. Questions should be thrown out to the group for general discussion. A question should be directed to a silent member only after much patient waiting for him to respond voluntarily. Even then, the question must be carefully phrased. If the leader asks, "Joe, do you know when the trouble first started?" and Joe is forced to say, "No, I don't," then his embarrassment

[9] Norman R. F. Maier and A. R. Solem, "The Contribution of a Discussion Leader to the Quality of Group Thinking: The Effective Use of Minority Opinions," *Human Relations*, 5 (1952), pp. 277–88.

at being unable to answer will make him even more cautious about future participation. The question must be asked in such a way that he can decline to comment without accompanying humiliation: "Do you wish to comment?" or "Would you like to add something here?" He can then answer simply, "Not at this time," or "Not now, thank you," or "No." This limited response sometimes will make it easier for him to participate more fully later.

Since interaction is usually easier among persons who like each other, the leader will do as much as he reasonably can to make members personally compatible. He will encourage the sensitivity of all to the needs, personal characteristics, and backgrounds, which make each member unique and worthy of respect. He will react to others, and encourage members to react, in ways which will reduce threat to their egos and to their positions in the group. He will try to get members to respond to others objectively, on the merits of their ideas rather than on the merits of the persons expressing them.

A discussion group should be characterized by cooperation and not by competition. Interpersonal relationships can be made more cordial if members can work together cooperatively. Thus, the designated leader will hesitate to side with some members against others, or to allow avoidable division. He will recognize the compatibilities present in the group, stressing and building on signs of harmony.

The designated leader encourages future contributions if he responds to every communication with acceptance. He should not react with agreement or disagreement; he should merely let the communicator know that his message is received, with appreciation that it was offered. He should say, "Yes, that point should be considered"; or "I see what you're getting at"; or "I'm glad you brought that out." He must not say, "Oh, we couldn't consider that"; or "I disagree"; or "You must be mistaken"; or "You talked out of turn."

Homans has stressed this point even more bluntly: "The leader must not take a moral stand and show approval or disapproval of what is being said. He must accept—utterly, or, as some say, he must create a permissive atmosphere."[10] If every time a low-status member who is participating infrequently makes a comment, a high who is also a high participator pounces upon the idea, the leader should gently come to the low's rescue. He may say: "Now, wait a minute. I'd like to hear more about that idea. . ." The leader should not directly take issue with the high. What he does is show the low that his ideas have worth (if they do), are welcome, and are being received. Note that the leader does not indicate whether he agrees with the low.

Regulating Member Interaction

The designated leader should strive for balanced communicative interaction. He must realize that some members participate more than others and thus he should restrain the overanxious contributor and draw out the reluctant

[10] Homans, p. 439.

ones. Since some high participators may talk so much that they deprive others of time to interact, the leader must be sensitive to the need for redressing the balance.

When members become dogmatic and express extreme opinions, the leader may find it desirable to make a general statement about cooperative attitudes, objectivity, shared goals, and similar matters. He can invite reflective deliberation and plead for calm, unemotional discussion, but of course he should not directly chastise participants for uncooperative behavior. They are usually in the group voluntarily and can do as they please. Occasionally, a leader will propose a recess or an adjournment if his plea for reasonableness is unheeded.

Another regulating responsibility is to attempt to restore equanimity after a violent clash. The leader may stress areas, if any, in which the conflicting parties have agreed, or emphasize the group's respect for all points of view, or appeal for as much objectivity as possible, or use humor, or in some other way attempt to reduce tension and get on to the next question.

TASK FUNCTIONS

Almost always there is a reason for holding a discussion other than mere socializing. The group will want to decide something or to gain a better understanding of a problem. This task becomes the most important part of the meeting; the procedures followed and the interpersonal relationships maintained or strengthened are secondary to task productivity. Thus the task functions are the most vital responsibilities of leadership.

Members should not underestimate the difficulties encountered in group decision-making nor the demands placed upon those willing and able to provide leadership. Irving Lee has reported extensive conversations with designated leaders involved in business and industrial discussion groups. He felt that most of them were discouraged in the face of the energy they had to expend to foster group productivity. "They begrudged the amount of effort it took to get people to talk and think together," Lee wrote. "They were unhappy about the value received from the energy they spent waiting for people to come to terms with each other. Was the nervous strain worth it?"[11]

Our purpose here is not to counsel despair but to emphasize that the leader must approach his task functions realistically. He must understand what is required of him and be willing to persist in order to achieve a collective decision.

Introducing the Problem

Focusing participant attention on the problem almost at once is critical and involves stating clearly the question for discussion, presenting background information and giving the immediate cause for the discussion of this question

[11] Lee, pp. 132–3.

on this problem at this moment. The designated leader should not say so much that he stifles later interaction, nor so little that he fails to set the stage, clarify the precise problem, and stimulate members to begin discussing. A critical moment for the leader comes with the transition from his general introductory remarks to his first specific question, to which he invites response from participants. This first question must be thoughtfully planned by the leader in advance so that there is an immediate, spontaneous answer from the group. The discussion can get off to an awkward start if his first question is broad, general, or difficult to answer.

In most situations, he must not allow members to jump ahead immediately to arguments about possible decision. He must be determined to have them agree on an understanding of the problem before they rush to judgment.

Guiding Discussion on the Problem

The most important duty of the designated leader is to guide the group as it moves from problem to outcome. He must keep the discussion on the track, seeing that there is steady progress and systematic forward locomotion. His guiding must be indirect—he must suggest, not order; gently restrain, not scold; encourage, not drive; ask for cooperation, not manipulate nor threaten nor dictate.

An aid in guiding is the developmental outline explained in Chapter 12. Without a satisfactory plan, efficient guiding is almost impossible. Even with a clear outline, the designated leader must overcome many other obstacles that send the group in circles, or deflect it from a direct path to its objectives. To do so skillfully requires expertness in language usage and communication. He must tactfully stop members from moving in one direction and suggest another, the one indicated by the outline. He must see that all contributions, including his own, are clearly expressed.

Recognizing Tangents and Irrelevancies

To guide the group's discussion of a problem, the designated leader must recognize when a contribution leads in an unproductive direction. One deflection, which is especially difficult to check, is the fascinating tangent. Every complex problem has many aspects, all interesting if members are thoroughly informed. The danger is that the group will become so absorbed in examining a fascinating aspect that no one, including the leader, recognizes for a time that this tangential material is leading away from a solution to the specific problem being discussed. The alert leader will see that the topic, although related, is not directly contributing to forward progress on the question at hand, and will gracefully lead back to the planned pattern.

A similar deflection is the irrelevant fact or opinion. The designated leader must recognize it as unrelated, suggest that it may lead the group astray, and restore forward motion with a relevant question. A common example is a statement about solutions to the problem expressed during the analysis stage.

If the leader does not step in at once, the group will often switch to consideration of proposals for action.

Rebounding

When a member leads the group astray, the designated leader is responsible for helping the group bounce back without injuring the sensibilities or losing the cooperation of the wayward participant. Tactful rebounding requires, first, responding to the deflection with *acceptance* by saying, for instance: "That is an interesting point and I wish we could pursue it"; and, second, suggesting a question that leads in the desired direction: "May I ask this question . . . ?" The rebound is even smoother if the question leading back to the point can be related to and grow out of the comments made during the deflection. What must be avoided is the blunt, sharp retort: "You're off the track"; "Your comment is irrelevant"; or "You are wasting time."

Some discussion students, when advised not to tell participants bluntly they are off the track, protest and answer that the leader is only stating the bald truth. They ask if discussion requires leaders to hide the truth or sugar-coat it in order to "protect the feelings of sensitive weaklings who aren't helping the discussion anyway." They often then point out that "in the real world men look facts in the face and speak the exact, unpleasant truth." This kind of polite sweetness, they say, makes discussion a method useful only to sissies. This type of objection is a rational protest and deserves an answer. The fact is that the designated leader is not hiding the truth; he is obliged to recognize the deflection, check its progress, and put the group back on the right path. If his first tactful attempt does not get results, he must try a more blunt approach. His manner of achieving the rebound, however, is largely a matter of language choices. He can accomplish his purpose politely and keep the wayward thinker within the psychological group. He should not risk alienating him if he can avoid it, since nothing is to be gained by doing so. The leader must succeed in restoring the proper direction, but if he is skillful he can achieve the desired result without arousing resentment or feelings of failure and rejection in those who have wandered out of bounds.

Clarifying and Restating

Part of guidance is to keep clearly before the group what is being discussed at the moment, so there will be no confusion about where they are and where they are heading. If a member's statement is unclear, it is the leader's responsibility to ask the member to restate it, or to supply a clarification, or to reword it more explicitly. Obviously, the leader must choose his words carefully. He should resist saying: "Is this what you're trying to say?" or "I'm going to restate that so it will be clear this time." Instead of scolding the participant for his failure, the leader could say: "Let me see if I understand you; you are saying that. . ."

As noted in Chapter 7, a group also must frequently and fully define terms used. If the leader feels that the words employed will confuse, mislead, or deflect, he should ask members to stop and explain what they mean.

Asking the Right Questions

A difficult part of the leader's guidance function is to ask the right questions at the right time. In the words of Wendell Johnson, "The surest way to get a clear answer is to ask a clear question." In fact, the leader guides primarily by asking questions. Thus the planned outline helps him most in this respect; but the leader must sense when the group is ready to grasp the next question, what the question should be, and how it should be phrased.

Perhaps the most common error is asking a question that is too broad. Since any number of answers can properly be given, the group is sent exploring in the direction determined by whatever aspect of the broad question the first member answering happened to choose. The direction pursued in this accidental manner may not coincide at all with what the leader had in mind. Hence he must stop members and pull them back, when he could have avoided this necessity by asking a limited question in the first place.

Collins and Guetzkow report that "Chairmen of groups in high substantive conflict which ended in consensus did three times more seeking for information of an objective factual nature from members of their groups than did chairmen in groups which did not end in consensus." This result of questioning was not the same for groups in high affective, or interpersonal, conflict.[12]

The leader must decide how to ask questions to achieve many different purposes: to elicit additional information, to confirm understanding or agreement, to check on and pinpoint disagreement, to seek clarification, to resolve conflict, and so on. When seeking understanding for himself and on behalf of the others, he must be the eager searcher with unsatiable curiosity and not the cross-examiner. He should communicate his eagerness to know and to share. He should invite explanation, and he must be careful not to talk down to members by pretending to ask a question when he is actually displaying the superiority of his own knowledge. His tone and words should not imply: "I know the answer to this next question, but I am asking it to see if you dummies do." What he must do is demonstrate that he is one of the group's leading thinkers by the quality and eagerness of his questions.

Especially critical is his skill in asking the follow-up question. By gently but persistently staying with a thread of thought, through asking another question or two when the first one does not elicit a complete or clear response, the leader sets the example for thorough consideration of a complicated problem.

Offering Transitional Summaries

At the conclusion of each stage in the discussion, the designated leader should briefly summarize the agreement reached and clearly introduce the

[12] Collins and Guetzkow.

next phase, in order to show the group where they have been, where they are now, and where they are going. Careful transitional summaries are among the leader's most potent guidance techniques. They make clear the transition, or passage, from one phase to another. At the end of the definition stage, for example, the leader might say: "Are we agreed, then, that by the terms in the question we mean. . . ? And are we now ready to explore the nature of the problem facing us?"

Encouraging Creative Thought

It may be an impossible assignment to ask the designated leader to promote creative thinking because we cannot explain how to bring this happy process about. It is clear, however, that to be productive the group will want to think along new paths and to consider some creative new alternatives. The leader should make whatever statement he can think of that might encourage creative thought, and certainly he can react approvingly when new insights are expressed.

Securing Proper Evaluation of Ideas

The leader should also strive to see that ideas are tested and that the group takes advantage of all available resources for proper evaluation of suggested solutions. He will not be helping the group to capitalize on its collective effort unless he can use the talents of all to seek out fallacies, to judge new proposals against the past experiences of all members combined, and to apply the facts members know collectively.

Summarizing the Outcome

At the end of a discussion, the designated leader must summarize what has been said, state the outcome agreed upon, and give participants an opportunity to confirm or reject his summary statement. Usually, this is a controversial matter only in problem-solving discussion.

The summarizing statement should be clear. Ambiguous statements can be misinterpreted later and the intent of the group distorted. In addition, the summation must be fair; it must represent exactly, without bias or coloring, the members' decision. One way to achieve clarity and fairness is to write out the decision agreement. It can then be read as the discussion closes, and if necessary each member can be asked in turn if the statement represents satisfactorily the group's decision.

DIFFUSION OF FUNCTIONS

As we have indicated, the leadership functions need not be contributed by a single person. It is possible to distribute the various functions among members of the group.

If all the duties of leadership are to be performed by a single person during a complex discussion, he will be extremely busy; he may not be skillful enough to perform ably all his functions at the same time, and the group may therefore be deprived of his substantive knowledge and views, even though because of his leadership he often will be the most influential member of the group. If members in a particular situation wish to avoid any of these weaknesses, they can diffuse the leadership among several persons. One member may guide and recognize speakers, another regulate, and a third introduce and summarize. It is possible to divide the responsibilities even further, so that every member of a group shares some leadership function.

A recorder can be asked to keep careful notes on the discussion. He may be requested to give the introduction and the summary. Certainly he should supply the written record of the summation agreement, which is so important at the close of the discussion. The designated leader can also turn to the recorder for assistance with his transitional summaries between stages.

Another helper used by some groups is a process observer. This person is asked particularly to watch the group's progress; its efficiency in pursuing planned stages; the leader's success in regulating, and so on. At any point, the group can stop and request the process observer to evaluate what has been achieved, explain where the group is in its deliberations, and point out weaknesses. The process observer feeds back to the group what it has done, said, accomplished, and failed to do.

Whether it is better to have leadership assigned to one or a few, or to distribute this responsibility widely, is a controversial matter. As Cartwright and Zander say,

> There are those who believe that greater efficiency results when all leadership functions are concentrated in a few roles—the officers. They maintain that 'too many cooks spoil the broth.' And there is much reasonableness in the argument that if everyone has a final 'say' in running the group, chaos will result unless all want to 'say' the same thing. On the other hand, it is argued that the concentration of authority in the hands of a few undermines the motivation of the rest, thus destroying enthusiasm, morale, and creativity, and engendering conflicts and hostility between leaders and followers.[13]

In a study of six groups which held a series of three meetings, where three had an appointed leader and the others had no instructions about leadership, Mortensen found that all participants made comments that were called by observers, "attempted leadership communication." In the three leaderless groups, however, a leader had emerged rather clearly by the third meeting. In the other three groups, the designated leaders dominated leadership attempts in the initial meeting but by the third meeting, in two of the three groups, a natural leader had emerged who became more influential than the nominal leader. Mortensen advises designation of a leader in a transitory group meeting for an hour or less. Whether it is helpful to assign a leader in

---

[13] Cartwright and Zander, p. 505.

continuing groups, he feels, depends on the designated leader's ability to earn the role and on the amount of group loyalty in the situation. He concludes that "an initially unstructured group appears ideally suited for discussion groups meeting for several hours over a period of weeks to work on a task that means a great deal to its members."[14]

Cathcart makes a most convincing argument for placing responsibility more directly on the whole group by recognizing leadership as a secondary function in discussion. He feels that our stereotypes about the division of responsibility between a designated leader and the others as followers do harm to the decision-making process in which all should be actively involved. There is a danger that assignment of leadership to a single person gives him the power to push the group in the right direction.[15] Thus Cathcart would want us to emphasize that leadership responsibilities should be shared by all even if there is an appointed or elected chairman or central figure.

Regarding the matter of the effects on discussion itself of centralized compared with diffused leadership, the experimental evidence is scanty and offers little guidance. One revealing study, however, has been reported by Berkowitz in connection with the Michigan analysis of seventy-two business and governmental conference groups. Member satisfaction seemed to be higher when the chairman controlled the group's procedural behavior. Members tended to be less satisfied with the discussion when leadership was shared by others, although such groups were apparently no less productive.[16] When, on the other hand, there was a reason for members to share, as for example in the crisis of an urgent problem, cohesiveness and satisfaction seemed to increase in relation to the increasing influence of others who were thus sharing leadership functions.[17]

We should probably be cautious in making any statements about the wisdom of distributing leadership functions. What a group decides to do will depend on the nature of the task, the situation, the purposes of the group, and other factors. In any situation there are likely to be both advantages and disadvantages in any possible leadership arrangement.

ADJUSTING TO CIRCUMSTANCES

In relation to the kind of group, leadership assignments may be related to its purposes and to the length of time it will be in existence. A vocational group will be likely to have a designated leader, while a voluntary group such

[14] Calvin D. Mortensen, "Should the Discussion Group Have an Assigned Leader?" *The Speech Teacher*, 15 (1966), pp. 34–41.

[15] Robert S. Cathcart, "Leadership As A Secondary Function in Group Discussion," *The Speech Teacher*, 11 (1962), pp. 221–26.

[16] Leonard Berkowitz, "Sharing Leadership in Small, Decision-Making Groups," A. Paul Hare, E. F. Borgatta, and Robert Bales, *Small Groups: Studies in Social Interaction*, rev. ed., New York: Alfred A. Knopf, 1965, pp. 675–87.

[17] Berkowitz.

as a YMCA committee or a social club might flourish better without appointed leadership or with diffused responsibilities.

The task can vary from simple to complex, from routine to unusual, and from informational to the most difficult kind of decision-making. In many situations, groups will probably be inclined to have more centralized leadership when the assignment tends to be more complex, more unusual or perhaps when it is in the nature of an emergency, and when a difficult decision is required. It must be remembered, of course, that individuals differ in their orientations toward authority. While some persons are more equalitarian in their expectations, the evidence suggests that "authoritarians accept status-laden, strongly directive leadership, demand that others adhere to ingroup values, and interact with the leader as a person rather than as a role."[18]

To lay down rigid recommendations would be foolish, however, and in addition would take us beyond our evidence. The student is urged, nevertheless, to speculate about the circumstances in which a group would wisely centralize or distribute leadership functions. Careful observation should provide some clues.

SUPPLEMENTARY READING

Barnlund, Dean C., "The Use of Group Observers," *The Speech Teacher,* 4 (January, 1955), pp. 46–8.

Barnlund, Dean C., and Haiman, Franklyn S., *The Dynamics of Discussion,* Boston: Houghton Mifflin, 1960, Chapter 13.

Braden, Waldo W., and Brandenburg, Earnest, *Oral Decision-Making,* New York: Harper & Row, 1955, Chapters 11 and 15.

Cathcart, Robert S., "Leadership As A Secondary Function In Group Discussion," *The Speech Teacher,* 11 (1962), pp. 221–6.

Homans, George C., *The Human Group,* New York: Harcourt, Brace & World, 1950, Chapter 16.

Maier, Norman R. F., *Problem-Solving Discussions and Conferences,* New York: McGraw-Hill, 1963.

Sattler, William M., and Miller, N. Edd, *Discussion and Conference,* Englewood Cliffs, N.J.: Prentice-Hall, 1954, Chapter 10.

Wagner, Russell H., and Arnold, Carroll C., *Handbook of Group Discussion,* Boston: Houghton Mifflin, 1950, Chapter 6.

Walser, Frank E., "Diplomacy, Discussion, and the Chairman," *Quarterly Journal of Speech,* 40 (February, 1954), pp. 43–8.

QUESTIONS AND EXERCISES

1. To what extent should a recorder participate substantively in the discussion? To what extent should the process observer participate?

[18] Hare, pp. 294–5.

2. Suppose you are the designated leader of a closedgroup, problem-solving discussion to be held on the question, "What changes, if any, should be made in university (or college) regulations governing the social activities of students on this campus?" Prepare a report in which you list and explain each step you would go through in fulfilling your functions as leader, from the first thing you would do through the end of the discussion itself.

3. Write a paper on the merits of diffusing leadership functions among members of a small group during discussion, as contrasted with designating a single person to fulfill all the leadership duties.

4. Suggest a list of duties for a recorder. Prepare the instructional sheet he could be handed to explain his specific responsibilities.

5. Make a list of questions that a process observer might ask and answer in helping a discussion training group improve its deliberation. Two questions which could be raised, for example, are: In what kind of climate or atmosphere did the group operate? To what extent did members listen sympathetically to the others?

6. Under what circumstances do you believe a group would obtain better decisions with centralized leadership?

7. On the basis of the following problem cases, divide the class into pairs of students. One member of the pair will be the questioner and the other will give responses. The questioner will be attempting to ask the kinds of questions that will ascertain how the other understands the facts and then what he would do in the situation explained in the case. The questioner will thus be practicing carrying out the responsibilities of discussion leadership in this limited situation. Have observers from the class, after each interview is over, evaluate how well the questioner fulfilled his leadership role.

CASE A

Your friend, Joe, a hail-fellow-well-met, abhors more than sin attending classes regularly. He was in your political science lecture section last semester and his notes were spottier than a measled leopard. Before the big examination, he talked you into sharing your lecture notes, and then—in keeping with the axiom that a single Devil sometimes triumphs over all the angels—made a higher grade than you did.

This semester he is in your psychology class and you can see the sinister history repeating itself. He has already hinted that he will again need your sterling help.

What are you going to do?

CASE B

At ten o'clock one night, John Burnett received a call from the local police chief asking him to come to the station on behalf of his sixteen year old son, Jack. An excited householder had summoned police when he heard noises in his driveway and discovered two hubcaps missing from his car. When the police arrived, officers found Jack and two companions loitering on a street corner nearby. Jack was carrying a large screw driver—a type convenient for removing hubcaps.

When Mr. Burnett arrived at the station, the police advised him to leave Jack in their charge overnight "to teach him respect for the law." Jack told his Dad that he and his friends were coming from the opposite direction when the police stopped them, and had not been near the car.

What are you going to do?

CASE C

Tim Blankenship, a sophomore in liberal arts, turned in a term paper in History 128 which sounded familiar to Professor Simpson, but the professor was unable to find the original source from which he suspected much of the paper had been copied. Then the professor discovered on the final examination that Blankenship did exceptionally well only on those objective questions which the man sitting next to him had known the answers to. During the examination, Professor Simpson thought he saw Blankenship looking at the next man's paper, but he wasn't sure.

What do you think Professor Simpson should do?

Chapter 12

DISCUSSION
OUTLINES

If a busy man boarded an airliner in Chicago to fly to St. Louis and the plane landed in Indianapolis, then in Denver, and then in Little Rock, he would naturally ask what had gone wrong. If the stewardess explained that this particular pilot did not like to plan his flight in advance but preferred to fly happily from airport to airport as he happened to pick up a radio signal, the busy man would be justifiably furious. Yet most people spend more time in discussions than in airliners and they often suffer such a fate, traveling with discussion leaders who neglect to plan a route in advance.

Perhaps we would have a more analogous situation if we changed the comparison from flying to traveling by automobile. The wise motorist preparing for a trip plans the route he will follow. In somewhat the same way a designated leader responsible for guiding a discussion maps out a series of questions which will lead the group in the direction of the destination, or outcome. Once the trip is underway, changes must be expected. In crossing a particular bit of terrain, or stage in the outline, there will be alternative routes, each going to a similar point. Any one of these may be chosen with approximately the same result, even though one may make passage swifter and another may involve fewer obstacles and discomforts. There will be detours; the group may take brief side trips and momentary tangential excursions. Nevertheless, the map will steer the group in the desired direction and lead to the objective. It will help members proceed in a manner not possible without a planned route.

It is common to hear discussion participants talk animatedly without any sense of direction. The talk often wanders aimlessly, pursuing this tangent and that byway, sometimes traveling in great circles and doubling back over the same ground without recognizing the familiar terrain. It is not uncommon to hear a committee chairman greet his colleagues with the disquieting question: "Well, what are we supposed to talk about today?"

To attempt guidance of a discussion without a pattern would be as inefficient as taking a journey without a map. The motorist would be forced to approach each highway intersection, locate a passer-by, and call out: "Which road should we take to reach the next village?" Perhaps a similar question for the erratic discussion leader is, "Well, what shall we talk about next?"

Discussion without a planned pattern is often chaotic, wasteful of time and energy, and frustrating for everyone.

If aimless meandering were not so common among discussion groups, it would seem too obvious to suggest that productivity requires a planned outline. Apparently it is not obvious and thus we should emphasize its value in contributing to orderly forward movement. Whoever during discussion is responsible for the guidance function of leadership should work out in advance, for his own understanding if for no other use, a developmental outline that will help him in a general way to guide the discussion. As Jacques Barzun expressed it so colorfully in *Teacher in America*, "discussion must not go off in all directions like a leaky hose."

In the Michigan study of seventy-two conferences in business and governmental groups, one of the characteristics observed was the orderliness of the discussions. Collins and Guetzkow report that "Those meetings in which discussion is orderly in its treatment of topics, and without backward references to previously discussed issues, tended to end in more consensus, despite large amounts of substantive or affective conflict. When participants discussed but one issue at a time, instead of simultaneously dabbling in two or three, it was more possible for the group to reach consensus."[1]

If the guidance function consists of helping the group to discuss one issue at a time, and to be orderly in its treatment of topics, we must decide what issues or topics must be considered during a discussion, and in what order. The beginning point is easy to identify; it is the problem for discussion worded as a question: Should the City Council restrict parking on Main Street? Once Council members understand the question, they can launch into the discussion. The destination is also clear; in information-sharing discussion it is understanding of the matters discussed, and in problem-solving discussion it is a decision. Along the route from question to outcome there will be definite stages or phases of the journey and milestones which enable participants to see their forward progress. Passing a way station on the route assures them that they are not lost and holds a promise that they are nearer their journey's end.

When we speak of the developmental outline having phases, of course, we are referring to the orderly treatment of topics in directly conversational, interactional discussion characteristic of committee and small-group conference discussion.

PHASES IN DISCUSSION

We have referred briefly in Chapter 6 to John Dewey's book, *How We Think*.[2] Dewey attempted to analyze in some detail the process of reflective

---

[1] Barry E. Collins and Harold Guetzkow, *A Social Psychology of Group Processes for Decision-Making*, New York: John Wiley & Sons, 1964, p. 111.

[2] John Dewey, *How We Think*, rev. ed., Boston: D. C. Heath, 1933, p. 12.

thinking and to suggest the phases involved. Reflection, he said, requires "(1) a state of doubt, hesitation, perplexity, mental difficulty, in which thinking originates, and (2) an act of searching, hunting, inquiring, to find material that will resolve the doubt, settle and dispose of the perplexity." The reasoner first experiences a "felt difficulty." Out of this troubled, or confused situation emerges the question that clamors for an answer. This state Dewey called prereflective. The other boundary of a reflection unit is "a cleared-up, unified, resolved situation at the close." At the end, doubt is resolved. The reasoner in this post-reflective period directly experiences the satisfaction of this completion.

In between these two limits, Dewey recognized five phases or states of thinking. He emphasized that they need not occur in any certain order; that will depend on the problem and the individual. One phase may be elaborated or telescoped and new steps not included in his five could occur at any time. The phases he described are these:

1. "*Suggestions*, in which the mind leaps forward to a possible solution." If the problem is at all complex, however, the earliest suggestions usually prove unacceptable for some reason and the process continues.
2. "An *intellectualization* of the difficulty or perplexity that has been *felt* (directly experienced) into a *problem* to be solved, a question for which the answer must be sought." When an early suggestion is blocked, what has been an annoyance felt begins to become a recognized problem, "something intellectual" with definite dimensions, specific facts, and observed conditions. The reasoner intellectualizes what at first was an emotional feeling.
3. "The use of one suggestion after another as a leading idea, or *hypothesis*, to initiate and guide observation and other operations in collection of factual material." The early suggestion "pops" into the reasoner's head spontaneously. Intellectually he must then *do* something with it—reject it if it is far-fetched, consider it, or assemble facts and data that modifies, changes, expands the initial thought. It is possible, then, that a suggestion can become a supposition or a definite hypothesis.
4. "The mental elaboration of the idea or supposition as an idea or supposition (*reasoning*, in the sense in which reasoning is a part, not the whole, of inference)." Reasoning about a suggested solution changes it, elaborates it, and tests its probable value. Utilizing facts and observations, some already stored in the mind from past experiences, the individual puzzles over possible avenues and their consequences.
5. "Testing the hypothesis by overt or imaginative action." What is needed here is verification of an idea that up to this point was only a conjecture, a possibility. The individual has reasoned about the consequences but now he seeks corroboration. He learns from the failures, too, the hypotheses not confirmed. Thus he may need to retrace his steps to earlier stages and start through with another possibility.[3]

[3] Dewey, pp. 106–118.

These phases of reflective thinking as outlined by Dewey have probably had the largest influence on the conception of the discussion outline, although the stages many groups go through would not be recognizable in these terms. Dewey was attempting to describe the reflective thinking processes of an individual solving his personal problems. When a group reasons together, the first phase, suggestion, is probably not verbalized, at least not in the beginning. Usually the problem, or felt difficulty, has developed far enough to be intellectualized before the group has a reason for assembling. Stages three and four probably do not occur in this order and, of course, Dewey did not claim that they should. It is likely they are mixed together as members consider the facts, propose alternative courses of action, and then reason about the advantages and disadvantages, the consequences, the possibilities.

Dewey's fifth phase, testing, is especially interesting because he said the corroboration could be by "overt or imaginative" testing. In one sense a discussion group cannot wait for an actual trial of its recommended solution because the report of its success or failure would not be part of the discussion. In another sense, a continuing group such as a board of directors, can continue its discussion after the tests are reported months later. Groups which cannot test their recommendations through overt action should make an effort at least to think through the verification of the consequences of their recommendations. If Dewey were giving advice directly to such a group he would probably advise, as a minimum, that they regard the recommendations as tentative until they can be tested overtly.

This conception of the phases in thinking is a germinal one and is worthy of the attention it has been given over a period of many years. If the discussion student had only these ideas to help him, he could manage adequately in drawing up discussion outlines for group guidance. Fortunately, however, we have also received some additional clues about phases in group problem-solving from contemporary research.

Bales-Strodtbeck Study

Where Dewey approached the reasoning process from the view of the individual, Bales and Strodtbeck analyzed actual discussion interaction to discover the phases the groups went through in moving toward a decision. They divided each problem-solving session into three equal periods so that an equal number of interactions have occurred in each period. Analyzing each initiation and reaction using Bales' system of interaction process analysis,[4] they found each of the three phases characterized by qualitatively different types of interaction. In the first phase, the greatest emphasis was on problems of orientation, with fewer contributions involving evaluation and control.

[4] The twelve categories for classifying communications are given in Chapter 14. For a fuller description see R. F. Bales, *Interaction Process Analysis*, Cambridge, Mass.: Addison-Wesley, 1950.

Interactions occurring with highest frequency in this early period were asking for orientation, information, repetition, confirmation; and giving orientation, information, repetition, confirmation.

After the initial phase, interactions involving orientation tended to decrease and the highest frequency of communicative acts concerned problems of evaluation. This means that in the second period there were a larger number of communications asking for opinion, evaluation, analysis, expression of feeling; and giving opinion, evaluation, and analysis, and expressing feeling or wish.

In the third or final phase, problems of control reached their highest peak, while evaluation declined. Acts involving orientation continued to decline in frequency throughout the second and third phases. Problems of control at this stage involved asking for suggestion, direction, possible ways of action; and giving suggestion, direction, implying autonomy for others.[5]

Another important finding was that, throughout the discussions, both positive reactions and negative reactions tended to increase. Bales and Strodtbeck hypothesize that orientation may need to come before evaluation: "speaking to the other in evaluative terms implies previous orientation." Further, "the attempt to control the situation by joint action implies both previous orientation and evaluation." If a group under the conditions they have set up tends to move from orientation, to evaluation, to control, they feel, then as the group moves toward agreement on a decision there will be increasing strains on the group's solidarity and social–emotional relationships. The number of negative reactions seems to build to a peak near the end where disagreement over proposals must be expressed and where tension and antagonism are most apparent. But positive reactions also build up as members resolve their differences and confirm their agreement, with positive tension reduction building to a sudden peak at the very end as members accept the outcome and show the tension release and solidarity through joking, laughing, and expressions of reassurance. As the researchers write, "We note joking and laughter so frequently at the ends of meetings that they might almost be taken as a signal that the group has completed what it considers to be a task effort, and is ready for disbandment or a new problem."

Bales and Strodtbeck are careful to point out that this phase movement may not occur under all conditions. No doubt the nature of each phase would be altered by a large number of circumstances. They speculate that a serious struggle within the group for status or leadership would affect the type of communications. Phases would be changed also with different kinds of tasks and different amounts of information possessed by members, and so on.

What they have found is not too unlike the stages Dewey hypothesizes if

[5] Robert F. Bales and Fred L. Strodtbeck, "Phases in Group Problem-Solving," in Dorwin Cartwright and Alvin Zander, *Group Dynamics: Research and Theory*, New York: Harper & Row, 1960, pp. 624–38.

one assumes that a group, before it is motivated to come together, has already as individuals "felt the difficulty" and has discovered that the early, easy suggestions were not going to work out, and is ready in the beginning of the discussion to "intellectualize" the problem. Dewey's third stage is hypothesis, guiding observation and collection of information. This is similar to orientation involving asking for information and giving information, etc. Dewey's fourth phase, reasoning, concerns mental elaboration of an idea, reasoning about its values and consequences. This process seems similar to evaluation, although no doubt Dewey would want to include here also part of what Bales and Strodtbeck have classified as control, or agreeing and disagreeing about possible decisions. These two processes of evaluation and control may be virtually inseparable pieces of the same "mental elaboration" involved in deciding on a course of action. Dewey's fifth step, also, testing by overt or imaginative action, seems to involve both evaluation and decision-making.

What should be re-emphasized is that no single series of steps could embrace the way a group would reason together each time, or on all problems, or under all conditions. It probably is unrealistic to look for a simple, invariable outline for use of the person providing guidance. Instead we should suggest a series of phases that the group may proceed to pass through under most circumstances, and then stress that a designated leader or anyone contributing leadership must realize the need for flexibility. Indeed, it would probably be remarkable if we discovered any invariable set of relationships that apply under all conditions.

Scheidel-Crowell Spiral Model

We must be careful, too, not to oversimplify the unfolding of group discussion through time by suggesting that each phase is self-contained and specialized. A group does not move forward so systematically, one logical step at a time, that it never doubles back or experiences overlapping communications.

Scheidel and Crowell have successfully questioned whether the outline a group follows can be thought of "as a linear progression from a problem through the various reflective-thinking steps to a conclusion." After a study of the idea development during ten discussions, they hypothesized that while a group is moving toward a solution, it is following a circular course in which members spend one-fourth of their comments confirming statements already made and another fourth clarifying and substantiating. "This oral play on an idea and the verbalizing of concurrence," they say, "are probably the ways by which a group gets its anchoring." One member "reaches forth" with an idea which is then tested through elaboration, "clarification, substantiation, and verbalized acceptance."[6]

---

[6] Thomas M. Scheidel and Laura Crowell, "Idea Development in Small Discussion Groups." *Quarterly Journal of Speech,* 50 (1964), pp. 144–5.

These authors offer a spiraling model to replace the simpler conception of linear development in group reasoning. This notion of a spiraling development suggests that a group moves onward, in the sense that it makes progress toward a decision; and outward, in the sense that it elaborates, agrees and disagrees, and, hopefully, confirms and solidifies at the end. This conception is a reasonable one, and we must be certain not to think of the guiding outline as a simple, mechanical, stage-by-stage list of isolated activities. Rather it is a complex, developmental set of interactions unfolding spirally as the group moves forward.

Two General Phases

With guidance from Dewey's germinal thought, from the results of controlled laboratory research, and from careful observation of discussion groups in many situations, we can propose the minimum stages which seem essential in interactional discussion. We must repeat, however, that these parts do not necessarily occur in this order nor are they likely to be the only stages or even the necessary ones developed in every situation.

There seem to be two general phases: (1) an analysis phase, which asks, essentially, what are we talking about and what are the facts? and (2) a solution phase, which asks, how should we evaluate alternatives and what should we decide?

In terms of the Bales-Strodtbeck hypothesis, analysis would be concerned with orientation and the solution phase with evaluation and control. Analysis would include, from Dewey's steps, the intellectualization of the felt difficulty and the hypothesis guiding observation and collection of facts; the solution phase would involve mental elaboration, reasoning, and testing by imaginative if not overt action.

The Analysis Phase

To think of the beginning of the analysis stage as orientation fits very well because discussions often begin, after a brief introduction, with questions of definition and limitation. The group usually wishes to make sure all members are discussing the same question—they mean approximately the same things when they say these particular words. Limitation may also be important in some instances. When a group has limited time or information, members may want to spell out the boundaries of the particular question.

The bulk of the analysis phase, however, is normally devoted to seeking and giving information, to tracing the history of the problem when this background is helpful, to consideration of causes, to exploration of developments in other times and places under similar conditions, and so on.

The analysis phase is frequently assumed to supply the background information on which a group can base a satisfactory decision, and thus it ordinarily occurs first. In outline form its parts could be these, although the order is of minor importance:

I. The Analysis Phase
   A. Definitions: What does the question mean?
   B. Limitations, if any: What part of the problem do we intend to concentrate on if we cannot discuss the whole problem now?
   C. What are the important facts about this problem?
      1. What is its history?
      2. What are its causes?
      3. What has happened; is happening?
      4. What has happened elsewhere that illuminates the problem under discussion?

The Solution Phase

The "What shall we decide?" phase is somewhat more complicated in many instances. It involves listing and then evaluating each alternative course of action. Members will wish to discuss the advantages and disadvantages of every possibility suggested.

For many problems, the evaluation procedure will prove very confusing because some members will look at the proposal from one set of standards and other members in quite a different way. When this happens, there must be another subphase dealing with criteria, spelling out which set of standards is to be applied in evaluating each proposal. For example, if a student-faculty conference is held on substituting a pass-fail grading system for the present A-B-C-D-F system, the students and faculty would undoubtedly approach alternatives with different standards for judgment. The students may want a grading system that reduces student tension, motivates students to take an interest in the subject, and removes the grade-point average as the measure of an individual's worth to society. On the other hand, the faculty may feel that a grading system must reward outstanding students, give highest status to those with the most intellectual talent, and serve to identify those who can benefit from graduate school. If they take these two philosophical positions, they probably will not agree on a decision. The students may press for a major move toward pass-fail grading and the faculty for no change or a token measure such as allowing a pass-fail option for one course a semester. If they were to agree on the criterion that in designing any grading system the faculty's judgment must be given first priority, they may agree on a policy close to the faculty's position. If, in contrast, they establish as the first criterion that a grading system must serve to motivate students to learn, they may reach a different decision.

Another question in the solution stage asks, what should we decide? or what alternative is best? Of course the group could go on after that to discuss how to put the decision into effect and how to test its effectiveness. The outline of the solution stage may look like this, although the order could be different, and some parts could be left out and others added in various circumstances:

II. The Solution Phase
    A. What are the advantages and disadvantages of each alternative course of action?
    B. By what or whose standards must any decision be evaluated?
    C. What decision should we reach?

DEVELOPING OUTLINES

A developmental outline is a series of questions organized into these kinds of phases. The designated leader, or the person who expects to contribute the guiding function if leadership is diffused, thinks through this series of questions in order to help the group progress toward the outcome they wish to reach.

Kinds of Questions

In Chapter 4 we noted three kinds of questions, those asking about fact, value, and policy. These take on greater importance in some phases of a discussion than in others. In the analysis phase, questions of fact are critical. They include questions of definition which ask, "is the matter we are discussing this or that?" If we are discussing the foreign aid program, what are we defining as aid: economic, military, political, or what?

Questions of value become prominent in the solution stage, and especially in evaluating alternatives and in deciding on standards for evaluation. Questions of policy are relatively easy to identify; they tend to be most important in asking decision questions in the solution phase. Many examples of these three kinds of questions will be observed in the examples of discussion outlines given here.

Questions for the Analysis Phase

It is usually important that the group agree at the outset on the meaning of the question. Much controversy in discussion disappears when meanings are made clear. People are familiar with the sigh of relief accompanying this exclamation: "Oh, I thought you meant. . . ." Members must define specific terms in the question as worded, and also concepts implied by the question, which may be sources of misunderstanding and conflict later. Of course, any terms overlooked must be defined when they are used in later stages of the discussion.

It is also vital to agree at an early stage upon ways in which consideration should be limited. The group may wish to exclude certain matters, and unless everyone understands that these matters are not being considered, later confusion will be certain.

An illustration will make the needs clearer. This question could be discussed in a faculty-student committee on traffic and parking or in an administrative staff meeting: "Should underclassmen be denied the privilege of operating automobiles on campus?" It will be necessary to define what is meant by *underclassmen, privilege,* and *campus.* Also there are some terms implied by the question that may cause confusion, such as *other motorized vehicles,* and *student rights.* A group may wish, in addition, to establish some limitations in the beginning. Members may agree, for example, to exclude from consideration underclassmen who are married and living off campus, on the grounds that a different arrangement would apply to them. Students who live at home in the community, rather than in the campus area, may be excluded. Careful definition and limitation help to make clear precisely what problem the group will try to solve, conserve discussion time, and avoid wasted talk in later phases. Loss occurs when one person has been pressing for restrictions on undergraduates while another is opposing them if they then discover that one is thinking primarily of young, single underclassmen and the other of older underclassmen who are married and live off campus.

Following definition and limitation, the analysis phase is devoted to asking, essentially, "What are the facts?" Putting all the relevant information before the group as the basis for a high-quality decision is the central contribution of the analysis stage. In addition, there are other values resulting from a careful examination of the facts. Describing the situation is a matter of seeing the external world as it exists and analysis is not the place for bias or value judgments or opinion; hence the analysis stage promotes objectivity and, once stimulated, the members may be more inclined to be objective also in later stages where expressions of opinion and value judgments are necessary. In analysis, members can meet on neutral ground and learn to work together easily before proceeding to more difficult matters where conflict is natural; hence a carefully conducted analysis stage may contribute to the cohesiveness of the group.

We can illustrate the types of general questions that suggest the line of information-seeking in a specific situation:

Analysis
Phase   I. What is the nature of the problem?
          A. (Definitions)
          B. (Limitations)
          C. What are the facts of the present situation?
              1. How can the present situation best be described?
                  a. What is going on?
                  b. Who is involved?
                  c. What kinds of difficulties exist?
                  d. Have we presented enough factual information to make the problem clear?
              2. How serious is the problem?
                  a. Is the problem extensive?
                  b. Is a change urgent?
                  c. Why is the problem important now?

      D. What are the causes of the problem?
        1. What is the history of the problem?
        2. What conditions brought it about?
      E. What forces are at work to change the present situation?
        1. What solutions have been tried?
          a. Where have these solutions been tried?
          b. How extensive have these attempts been?
          c. How successful have the attempts been?
        2. Is there a need for additional attempts to solve the problem?
        3. What will be the probable results if no action is taken?

It should be repeated that these are general questions. For a particular problem, the subquestions must be relevant to the specific problem facing the group. The following set of questions designed to ask only, "How can the present situation best be described?" will illustrate such elaboration:

SHOULD GREEK SOCIAL SOCIETIES BE ABOLISHED ON THIS CAMPUS?

    C. What are the facts of the present situation?
      1. How can the present situation best be described?
        a. How many Greek social societies are on campus?
        b. What percentage of the student body is housed in Greek social societies?
        c. What activities, events, rituals, procedures, etc., are engaged in by members of Greek social societies which are not engaged in by nonmembers of Greek social societies?
        d. What is the nature of the conflict, if any, between members and nonmembers of Greek social societies?
          (1) When did this conflict develop?
          (2) Why did this conflict develop?
      2. How serious is the problem?

The development is sufficient to suggest the possibilities for thorough consideration. It is obvious that not all the detailed questions thought of in advance could ever be asked in a particular discussion. The objective, however, is to prepare the person providing guidance to pursue the facts in a thorough manner.

Those planning a developmental outline must think creatively about possible ways of organizing the analysis stage. The unfolding structure chosen will depend on the problem and other factors.

One place to look for alternative organizations for examining the facts of a situation is to the standard patterns of analysis, such as the chronological pattern, the space pattern, and the topical pattern. We can illustrate these three arrangements using as an example an outline for the question, "What are the essential features of the British educational system?"

The definition and limitation questions of the analysis phase would be standard and straightforward:

Analysis
Phase   I. What is the nature of this educational system?

        A. What do we mean by the question for discussion?

            1. How shall we define the specific terms used in wording the question?

                a. What is meant by *essential features*?

                    (1) Do *essential features* include types of curricula offered?

                    (2) Do *essential features* include the educational opportunities provided by admissions requirement?

                    (3) Do *essential features* include teacher preparation, compensation, and prestige?

                    (4) Do *essential features* include provisions for physical plant and equipment?

                    (5) What else is meant by *essential features*?

                b. What countries are to be considered British?

                c. What is meant by a *system of education*?

                    (1) Does this term refer to elementary schools, secondary schools, and higher education?

                    (2) Does this term refer to publicly supported schools, to private schools, or both?

                    (3) Does this term refer to academic education, to vocational training, or to all types of education?

            2. How shall we define terms and concepts implied by the question?

                a. What is meant in Britain by a *public school*?

                b. What is meant in Britain by a *modern school*?

                c. What is meant by other terms implied by the question?

        B. What limitations should be agreed upon?

            1. Should we agree to limit our examination to elementary and secondary schools?

            2. Should we exclude consideration of private schools?

            3. What other limitations should be applied?

We can make a choice in the structure of the questions to be asked next. If we feel that a chronological pattern lends itself well to the analysis we seek, the next part of the outline might be arranged in a time sequence:

    C. How can the essential features of the British educational system best be described?

(Past)   1. What were the essential features of the British educational system prior to the British Education Act of 1944?

       a. What was the nature of educational opportunity?

       b. What were the essential requirements for admission to schools of all types and at all levels?

       c. What were the essential features of curricula offered?

       d. What other essential features should be described?

(Present)   2. What are the essential features of the British educational system today as provided by the Education Act of 1944?

       a. What is the nature of educational opportunity?

       b. What are the essential requirements for admission to schools of all types and at all levels?

       c. What are the essential features of curricula offered?

       d. What other essential features should be described?

(Future)   3. What are the foreseeable future developments in the British educational system?

       a. What is likely to be the evolution of educational opportunity?

       b. What are likely to be the essential requirements for admission to schools of all types and at all levels?

       c. What are likely to be the essential features of curricula offered?

       d. What other essential features should be described?

Another choice would be to arrange this portion of the analysis phase in a space pattern, where the partition is based on spatial ordering or geographical location. In the case of this question on the British educational system, the subquestions above would ask: (1) How can the essential features of the educational system of England best be described? (2) of Scotland? (3) of Wales?

Still another possibility is to use a topical pattern. In this type of arrangement, the subdivisions are organized into natural parts according to the way a subject divides into components. This part of the analysis phase could be organized topically by considering various educational features:

1. What are the essential features of curricula?
2. What are the essential features of teacher preparation, compensation, and prestige?
3. What are the essential features of administration?
4. (Other essential features?)

Or the substages might concern the system from the view of those involved:

1. What are the essential features as viewed by the students?
2. What are the essential features as viewed by the teachers?
3. What are the essential features as viewed by administrators?

We can mention one other choice of pattern based on comparison or contrast. When two or more systems can be analyzed at once, this arrangement may be useful. The British educational system could be explained by comparing it with programs in other nations:

1. What are the essential features of the British educational system?
2. What are the essential features of the American educational system?
3. What, then, are the similarities and differences between the two systems?

Another possibility is to compare the two systems one feature at a time (here the pattern is closely related to topical development):

1. How do the British and American educational systems compare in regard to educational opportunity?
2. How do the British and American educational systems compare in regard to curricula? (And so forth)

These are only some of the possibilities for organizing the analysis phase. The particular outline selected should be the one that best fits the problem for discussion.

We should note that an outline for an information-sharing discussion could end at this point, without moving into the solution stage.

Questions for the Solution Phase

The solution phase of a developmental outline for decision-making discussion often has three parts, as we have said: (1) evaluation of the advantages and disadvantages of each alternative proposal or course of action; (2) consideration of the standards or criteria for judging any solution to the problem; and (3) discussion of the decision agreed upon. These parts may not be taken up in this order, although agreement on a decision cannot usually come until the others have been considered.

EVALUATION/ To evaluate advantages and disadvantages of proposed solutions is relatively straightforward. The alternatives must be listed and the gains and losses likely to be consequences of each one discussed as carefully as possible through mental elaboration and imaginative testing.

CRITERIA/ The criteria stage can be more troublesome, but often the group cannot agree upon a decision until it decides whose interests are to be given priority or which standards for judging a decision matter most to the group members. *Criteria are those standards arrived at after thorough examination of the problem; they must be met by any solution and are used by the group in evaluating alternative proposals.*

Perhaps we can make the criteria stage clear with an illustration. On one campus a spring carnival organized by students and held in the university armory became so popular that one year 11,000 spectators crowded into a building which the fire marshal said could safely hold only 5,000 at one time. In the same semester that the fire inspector questioned continuation of the carnival on the grounds of audience safety, the faculty-student committee on extracurricular activities became concerned about the amount of energy being expended in producing the kind of spectacular exhibits and carnival acts, complete with barkers and dancing girls, that were attracting such large crowds. The Health Service had reported high incidence of illness from fatigue in this period. Some faculty advisors had complained that fraternities were starting to work a year in advance on planning, writing, staging, and rehearsing their carnival shows. When the matter finally came before the committee on activities, the question was, "Should Spring Carnival be discontinued?" Naturally enough it was controversial. Some students argued that they needed a spring event as a time to release pent-up energy. Some faculty members were alarmed about the safety hazard and the threat to student health, as well as the competition with academic studies. The committee seemed headed for stalemate until someone suggested that members try to agree first on the criteria that would have to be met before a decision would be acceptable. After much discussion, the group agreed on these criteria and decided they were important *in this order*:

1. No spring event should require so much student energy that it seriously hampers academic studies, the primary purpose for being on the campus.
2. No spring event should require so much time that a student's health is seriously affected.
3. No spring event should create such a crowded situation in the armory that the lives of performers and spectators are endangered.
4. If the standards of study, health, and safety can be safeguarded, there is every reason for the university to encourage a wholesome spring event where students can release pent-up energy.

Once these criteria were written down and accepted, and ranked in this order, the decision was comparatively easy to reach. The group decided not abolish the carnival but to move it outside and to make the spring event a real carnival with ferris wheel, roller coaster, guessing games, etc. Students were to plan some games and to furnish manpower for operating booths, but there were to be no more elaborate shows written, produced, and performed by students. It is easy to see that the quality of the decision grew directly from the reasonableness of the criteria. Once agreement was hammered out on the standards of judgment, the wise course of action was fairly clear.

In the criteria questions on the problem of U.S. foreign aid, suggested in the outline below, the essential query concerns whose interests are to be ranked first: those of the United States, those of the developing nations, or those of the United Nations? The decision a group reaches will be structured by the order in which members consider these standards for judging the program.

DECISION/ Questions leading to a decision ask, "What shall we do?" or "What shall we decide?"

The total solution phase can be arranged in any number of ways. Instead of weighing the advantages and disadvantages of alternatives, considering criteria and then decision, a group could (1) establish criteria; (2) consider whether proposal A, B . . . N meet the criteria; and (3) discuss the decision. No matter how this phase is organized, a group will try to arrive at a decision with the most advantages and fewest disadvantages, and one that best meets the criteria. If the group wishes, it can go on to consider how to put the proposal into action and how it wants to measure future success of the policy.

The entire solution phase of a discussion on the question, "What changes should be made in the U.S. foreign aid program?" could be arranged in this manner:

Analysis
Phase A. (Definitions)
        B. (Limitations)
        C. (Nature of situation; the facts)

Solution D. How would we evaluate the alternative proposals that have been
Phase   offered?
           1. Should the present U.S. foreign aid program continue unchanged?
              a. What would be gained from such a policy?
              b. What would be the disadvantages of such a policy?
           2. Should there be an increase of U.S. aid to our allies?
              a. What would be gained from such a policy?
              b. What would be the disadvantages of such a policy?

3. Should there be a decrease in U.S. aid granted to our allies?
   a. Advantages?
   b. Disadvantages?
4. Should all U.S. foreign aid be administered through the United Nations?
   a. Advantages?
   b. Disadvantages?
5. Should the United States encourage private investment abroad in lieu of government aid?
   a. Advantages?
   b. Disadvantages?

E. What standards or criteria must be met by any proposed foreign aid program?
   1. Should a foreign aid program serve the best interests of the United States? If so, in order to serve the best interests of the United States:
      a. Should the program be as inexpensive as possible?
      b. Should the program contribute to world peace?
      c. Should the program strengthen the international position of the United States?
      d. What other criteria should a program meet in serving the best interests of the United States?
   2. Should the U.S. foreign aid program help our free world allies?
      a. Should the program help to keep our allies economically strong?
      b. Should the program strengthen the nations of the West in their conflict with the Russian bloc of nations?
      c. In what other ways should a program help our allies?
   3. Should the U.S. foreign aid program help the United Nations?
   4. What other criteria should be applied in judging any U.S. foreign aid program?
F. What should we decide?
   1. What alternative has the most advantages and the fewest disadvantages?
   2. Which alternative best meets the criteria we have agreed upon?

We should re-emphasize the tentative nature of the planned outline. Never does a designated leader get to ask questions in the orderly, logical sequence suggested in the examples given here. The value of the outline is the help it provides those guiding the group through leadership. Thinking through the phases prepares them for the rapid-fire adaptations required as a discussion group moves forward toward a decision.

Before leaving the matter of developing the outline in advance of the discussion, we should stress some other considerations that a designated leader should take into account.

An Outline Is More than an Agenda

An agenda for a meeting lists in chronological order the items of business to be taken up at a particular session. It is an important part of advanced planning, since an entire meeting should be conducted in an orderly manner. An agenda for a board of directors meeting might contain these items:

    I. Reading of minutes of last board meeting
   II. Reports of committees
      A. Engineering
      B. Production
      C. Sales
      D. Others
  III. Reports of officers
      A. President
      B. Treasurer
      C. Others
  IV. Unfinished business
      A. Salary increases for office personnel
      B. Final plans for annual stockholders meeting
      C. Other unfinished business
   V. New business
      A. Revised policy on scheduling of summer vacations
      B. Proposal for increasing the capital stock
      C. Other new business

Many of these items may be relatively simple, and discussion on them may be reasonably brief. But the proposal for increasing the capital stock may be complex; to discuss it may require careful thinking and lengthy discussion. Hence it may be necessary not only to list it on the agenda for the appropriate time, but also to formulate in advance a discussion outline, which will insure thorough and systematic discussion. In addition to an agenda, then, the designated leader will follow an outline especially developed for each item on the agenda complex enough to require one.

An Outline Consists of Questions

The planned outline being recommended here should consist only of questions which the designated leader may ask in guiding the discussion.

If members wish to be thoroughly prepared, they may also prepare as individuals the answers each would supply to these kinds of questions. During the discussion, of course, they would not give the information in this scholarly form, but would limit themselves to supplying information needed by the group at a particular moment. For use in classroom discussion, Baird has called this research document an "individual outline."[7] We could also call it a *position paper*, since the student is writing out as part of his preparation the answers he would give if he were the only participant. A debater would call this research document a brief. A sample of this kind of individual outline is given as part of the "Questions and Exercises" section at the end of this chapter.

Question of Distribution in Advance

One difficult decision for a designated leader is whether he should share with the group in advance the questions he has planned for the outline. Brilhart in an experimental study found no strong support for the recommendation that a leader should do so.[8] Members and designated leaders must make this decision according to their particular circumstances and objectives. The risk in distributing the outline ahead of time is that discussion will be rigid and prestructured. In most situations it would probably be better to let members decide for themselves individually how the discussion might unfold. The questions planned by the person contributing the guidance function would then be heard spontaneously and members could respond with fresh insights.

USING OUTLINES DURING DISCUSSION

Although anything we can say may be obvious, it seems desirable to comment briefly on the use of the developmental outline while the discussion is in progress.

The outline should be only a guide, followed flexibly rather than rigidly. It should not be a strait jacket that keeps the designated leader from asking new questions that could not possibly be anticipated. Quite the opposite result is desirable. Rather than insisting on asking every planned question, the thorough thinking in advance should prepare him for asking the spontaneous questions suggested by the interaction occurring. While he should restrain members from capricious and erratic shifting from one phase to another, and back again to the first, he must retain flexibility and adaptation from moment to moment, on the basis of what is said.

---

[7] A. Craig Baird, *Argumentation, Discussion, and Debate*, New York: McGraw-Hill, 1950, Chapter 21.

[8] John K. Brilhart, "An Experimental Comparison of Three Techniques for Communicating a Problem-Solving Pattern to Members of a Discussion Group," *Speech Monographs*, 33 (1966), pp. 168–77.

SUPPLEMENTARY READING

Baird, A. Craig, *Argumentation, Discussion, and Debate*, New York: Mc-Graw-Hill, 1950, Chapter 21.

Bales, Robert F., "How People Interact In Conferences," *Scientific American*, 192 (March, 1955), pp. 31–5.

————, *Interaction Process Analysis*, Cambridge, Mass.: Addison-Wesley, 1950, pp. 49–65.

————, and Strodtbeck, F. L., "Phases in Group Problem-Solving," in Dorwin Cartwright and Alvin Zander, *Group Dynamics: Research and Theory*, New York: Harper & Row, 1960, pp. 624–38.

Braden, Waldo W., and Brandenburg, Earnest, *Oral Decision-Making*, New York: Harper & Row, 1955, Chapter 10.

Dewey, John, *How We Think*, rev. ed., Boston: D. C. Heath, 1933.

Wagner, Russell H., and Arnold, Carroll, *Handbook of Group Discussion*, Boston: Houghton Mifflin, 1950, Chapter 5.

QUESTIONS AND EXERCISES

1. Suppose that the president of your college or university has called you, as a campus leader, to his office. He has explained to you his great concern with the symptoms of poor student attitude toward education: student enthusiasm for carnivals, stunt shows, dances, and similar nonacademic pursuits, and student disinterest in classwork, library study, and special honors for distinguished academic achievement; student interest in grade-point averages without particular concern for the acquisition of knowledge and understanding. The president has asked you to plan and lead a closedgroup, problem-solving discussion using both faculty and student participants; he has specified that he wants from this group specific recommendations for improving the situation.

   a. Draw up word for word, and in detail, the outline you would use in leading this discussion.

   b. Defend in a report the major divisions and subsections of your outline. Explain why you have chosen these questions, why you have placed them where you have, and why they are worded as they are.

2. Apparently in small group discussion, a feature of all patterns is that fact-seeking, inquiry, or analysis comes before value judgment, generalization, or decision-making. In conducting a group deliberation using formal parliamentary procedures, however, the general pattern appears to be reversed: a motion specifying an action or proposal must be presented before the matter can be talked about. Can these contradictory positions be reconciled? Are there differences between the two kinds of situations that require these opposite approaches? Which general pattern produces

better results? Can the patterns of one deliberation situation be profitably adapted in the other?

3. Write out in detail a discussion outline on a question of current significance. Then prepare a thorough, carefully documented and footnoted outline for your individual use as a potential participant in a discussion on this question. The quality of this individual outline is a reflection of the extent to which you are prepared to participate, and the stages and questions indicate your understanding of outlining in discussion. To guide you in completing this exercise, the following individual outline prepared by a student is presented.

This sample outline was prepared by Patricia Freehill; it illustrates the use of questions from the leader's discussion outline, followed by possible answer(s) to the questions. The facts here are obviously out of date, but the outline has been retained because it is such an excellent example. It is of historical interest, also, when compared with the situation today.

*TO WHAT EXTENT SHOULD FEDERAL FUNDS BE USED
AS SUPPLEMENTARY FINANCIAL SUPPORT FOR
PUBLIC HIGH SCHOOLS IN THE UNITED STATES?*

I. How shall we define the terms?
   A. What do the terms in the question mean?
      1. By *public* we mean that our discussion excludes parochial and private schools.
      2. By *supplementary* we mean that primary responsibility for schools remains in state and local hands.
   B. What concerns are implied by the question?
      1. We are concerned with the amount of aid the federal government should give to high schools.
      2. We are concerned with the manner in which the government should allocate financial aid.
      3. We are concerned with the control of federal aid.
II. What is the nature of the problem?
   A. What are the causes of public high schools' need for financial aid?
      1. Are high school teachers' salaries too low?
         a. Since 1939 teachers' salaries have on the average increased by 199 percent; this is a gain of about half that made by industrial workers (252 percent) during the same period.[9]
         b. The average male teacher receives $4,374 a year, and the average female teacher $3,932 a year.[10]
      2. Are high school enrollments increasing rapidly?
         a. Secondary school enrollment is now 9,694,193, an increase of 40 percent in 10 years.[11]

[9] H. G. Spalding, "How Can We Pay for Good Schools," *Scholastic*, 70 (May 3, 1957), p. 11.

[10] "The Status of the American Public School Teacher," *National Education Association Report*, Washington, D.C., No. 1201, 1957.

[11] "School Statistics for 1957–1958," *National Education Association Journal*, 47 (January, 1958), p. 4.

      b. Average enrollment is going up 1,000,000 per year.[12]
3. Are some communities unable to support a high school?

    a. Per pupil expenditures varied from $158 to $482 this past year.[13]

    b. "The slum regions of American education would have to levy taxes for schools two or three times as high as the New York state taxes in order to finance even a moderately acceptable school program."[14]

    c. Less wealthy states expend only a fraction as much per pupil as does New York, yet they make considerably greater tax effort to support their schools.[15]

    d. On the other hand, the federal government provides an equalization factor through its progressive tax system: it takes a larger share of the income of wealthy states than of poorer states. For example, federal taxes in one year took 19.4 percent of income payments to individuals in Mississippi and 30.4 percent of such income in New York.[16]

4. Is federal financial aid deemed necessary by any recent investigation?

    a. Recent investigation shows that one third of our youths are rejected for military service for mental, physical, and educational deficiencies.[17]

    b. In states with the poorest education, the rejection rate reached as high as 40 to 50 percent.[18]

    c. On the other hand, some evidence suggests that the failure rate in Armed Forces tests is not related to educational attainment or educational opportunity.[19]

    d. There has been no shifting in the military load between states because of failure to pass armed service tests; every state has met its draft quota since 1948.[20]

    e. The U.S. Office of Education in 1951–52 found states varying in mean annual expenditure for education per pupil from $95 to $352.[21]

B. Is the federal government giving financial aid to public high schools at the present time?

1. In the past four years more than a half billion dollars in federal

---

[12] "School Statistics."

[13] "School Statistics."

[14] John K. Norton, "The Need for Federal Aid for Education," *School and Society*, 83 (March, 1956), p. 87.

[15] Norton.

[16] Roger A. Freeman, "A New Look at Federal Aid to Education," *School and Society*, 83 (March, 1956), p. 90.

[17] Norton, p. 87.

[18] Norton.

[19] Freeman, p. 90.

[20] Freeman.

[21] H. Thomas James, "Federal Support for Education," *The School Review*, 64 (March, 1956).

financial aid has been spent on local school construction under Public Law 815.[22]

2. In the past four years, 213 million dollars in federal funds have been paid out to local school districts under PL 874 to meet current operating costs.[23]

C. What policies of federal financial assistance to high schools have been tried?

1. President Hoover's policy of 1929–31 granted aid to the states to expend as they saw fit.[24]

2. The federal government has long had a policy of financial aid to vocational agriculture and home economics teachers.

III. By what criteria must we judge any possible solution to the problem?

A. Do we accept aid to education as a responsibility of the federal government?

1. The first federal Congress in the Ordinance of 1787 recognized the inescapable relation between knowledge and the maintenance of good government and declared that "schools and the means of education shall forever be encouraged."[25]

2. The Morrill Act of 1862, making possible the establishment of an agricultural college in every state, is an example of the federal government accepting this responsibility.[26]

3. The Smith-Hughes Act of 1917 establishing vocational education in public high schools is another example.[27]

B. Should we be protected from federal control?

1. A study of federal-state programs in education reveals that federal controls over education imposed by federal statutes and regulations tend to be relaxed as the programs mature.[28]

2. On the other hand, it is likely that there can be no federal legislation in education which does not violate state and local autonomy.

C. Should federal funds be limited to integrated schools?

1. Adoption of this limitation implies enforcing compliance with the Supreme Court's segregation decision.[29]

2. We cannot adopt the limitation of federal funds to integrated schools without violation of our goal of federal aid without federal control.

IV. What are the possible solutions?

A. A possible solution would be to place the responsibility for federal

[22] James.

[23] James.

[24] Freeman, p. 90.

[25] Norton, p. 87.

[26] Norton.

[27] Norton.

[28] E. Fuller, "Criteria for Congressional Action," *Nation's Schools,* 56 (November, 1955), p. 53.

[29] I. F. Pearson, "NEA's Legislative Program," *National Education Association Journal,* 46 (February, 1957), p. 108.

control of funds in the U.S. Office of Education, removing it from a large number of noneducational federal agencies.[30]
B. The NEA proposal to the 85th Congress is a possible solution.
C. The use of federal funds to bring all schools up to a national minimum standard is a possibility.

4. Divide the class into two discussion groups, I and II. Have each member of the class consider the following problem as if he were about to become the designated leader for a committee discussion (such as a committee of the state legislature).

The question for discussion is, *"Should capital punishment be abolished or re-established in this state?"*

In the *Analysis Phase* of this discussion, members might consider questions such as these:
A. What do we mean by *capital punishment?*
B. What do we mean by *abolish?*
   1. Are we considering the elimination of all use of execution, or are we excluding the death penalty for treason?
   2. Are we limiting our consideration to abolition of the death penalty for criminal violence against the person as distinct from crimes against the state?

In the remainder of the analysis phase, what are the questions you propose for the developmental outline?

(Group I will now consider this question for 15 minutes with the class as audience, attempting to produce an outline of this section.)

In the *Solution Phase* of the outline, what are the questions you propose?

(Group II will next consider this question for 15 minutes with the class as audience.)

[30] Fuller, p. 53.

Chapter 13

THE CHALLENGE
OF LEADERSHIP

We noted in Chapter 11 the five leadership functions listed by Hemphill. The fifth function was that those supplying leadership tend to act without regard to their own self-interest.[1] Many people feel that this dimension in leadership suggests a special challenge to those who would influence discussion groups. Those providing leadership must make some sacrifices of their own personal objectives for the greater good of the group. This necessity forces such persons to examine their own motives and their concepts of service to the others involved.

The contributions of the designated leader, and of others responsible for exercising leadership functions, should be directed toward helping the group advance its purposes: to create maximum opportunity for achieving collectively the group's objectives.

The special challenge of leadership, which contributes to all these objectives at once, is to increase the "groupness" or the spirit of unity among the members. The leader who refrains from pursuing his self-interests is placing the group's welfare above his own. In so doing, he may set an example that will influence others to consider the collective welfare along with their own self-interest. When enough group-centered interest is present, members tend to develop "groupness" or unity.

We should attempt to suggest some of the ways in which members can help to increase "groupness" and in this way contribute to leadership.

Examining the Willingness to Lead

Irving Lee wrote in an insightful little book, *How To Talk With People*, of "tired leaders" who "begrudged the amount of effort it took to get people to talk and think together."[2] In many situations the talented person is tempted to do it himself. To help the group decide is often more taxing and more difficult than to act alone. But to decide alone will not achieve the same objectives; that way out alters the nature of the task, the interrelationships of the persons, and the consequences flowing from the decision.

The leader who wishes to help the group reach collective decisions must

[1] See A. Paul Hare, *Handbook of Small Group Research*, New York: The Free Press, 1962, pp. 293–4.
[2] New York: Harper & Row, 1952, Chapter 12.

examine his own motives, his own approach to the problems and persons involved and his own capacities for selflessness, and decide whether he is willing to expend the time and energy required for leadership. Homans emphasizes the need for the leader to know himself so that he can control himself: "He may be the most active member of the group, and yet he must often keep silent. He must live up most fully to the group norms, and yet he, more than anyone else, must resolve conflicts of norms. More than anyone else, he has the ends of the group at heart."[3]

If a designated leader, for instance, is willing to give leadership as well as to hold the title, he must almost by definition be willing to make some sacrifices of his personal orientation and accept many of the group's interests as his own. His willingness will be communicated at once to the members and this attitude itself, if he continues to work in this manner, will contribute to "groupness" and hence to advancement of the group's purposes. He should not, however, overlook the fact that at times this willingness will cause him inconvenience and frustration, not to mention the occasional thwarting of goals he may wish to accomplish.

BUILDING SOLIDARITY

Task achievement is enhanced when a group operates as a cohesive unit, working as a team with high *esprit de corps*, and presenting a solid front to itself and to outsiders. Those willing to help with leadership can make several contributions to this desirable end.

Stressing the Task's Importance

Unity is increased when members recognize that a discussion has significance in a wider setting. The outcome of a particular discussion is important to other persons and groups who will be influenced by it. A parent group, for example, is concerned with the deliberations of its committees; the whole corporation is affected by the board's decisions; and an entire community overhears when the city council meets. Realization that others are involved and interested prompts members of the group to try harder for solid achievement and commendable teamwork. The leader can aid such realization by his opening remarks, by gentle reminders at appropriate points when cooperation falters, and by his general attitude. Businesslike efficiency, for instance, underlines the importance of the group's task, while casual indifference or lack of enthusiasm may suggest that member effort matters little.

Enhancing Individual Prestige

If the group's task is important, then the committee or the board or the city council performs a vital function, and, therefore, the individual members deserve recognition for their contribution. If, in turn, the individual feels that

[3] George C. Homans, *The Human Group*, New York: Harcourt, Brace & Co., 1950, p. 440.

his prestige is increased by virtue of membership, then for him the attractiveness of the group is enhanced. In this way, cohesiveness is increased. Members operate more solidly as a unit.

The designated leader should not overlook any opportunity to express in words the significance of each member's contribution to the group effort. Also, he must convey his respect for each individual as a participant in an endeavor that is earning deserved recognition.

It often happens that an individual recognizes the group's quality and sees the importance of its task, but feels that his value to it is so slight that he is not, in Durkheim's words, *solidaire* with the group. The leader and other members can enhance his feeling of prestige by such measures as encouraging more active participation on his part, assigning him an important subtask, or asking him to serve as recorder at times.

A simple instance of the way this process may operate can be observed in an elementary school classroom. A deviate or isolate who is disruptive and noisy, and who seeks recognition by interfering with classwork may be assigned by the teacher to check the roll or clean the blackboards. He then often becomes a more enthusiastic cooperator in class efforts.

Emphasizing Shared Interests

Solidarity depends in part on sharing of interests. Groups form and prosper in relation to fulfillment of needs that could not be met except by collective existence. The designated leader should emphasize the objectives, purposes, and values that members cherish in common. This is the concept of community: members share a community or commonness of interests.

One of the contributions of leadership is helping a group define clearly the objectives that all accept, and which hold them together as a unit. If common objectives are not identified, cohesiveness suffers. It is also possible for a continuing group to lose sight of its common objectives. Its reasons for unity must be stated afresh and kept always in mind. This restatement often occurs, for example, when a new chairman, president, governor, mayor, or other designated leader takes office.

A dramatic increase in cohesiveness usually results when a group is attacked from outside, or when it is singled out for commendation by a highly valued source. Military units offer perhaps the clearest examples: a battle unit cut off and subjected to prolonged siege develops a camaraderie which months in training barracks does not bring about, and a Presidential unit citation for courage beyond the call of duty makes every man hold his head a bit higher. Under some conditions such regimental pride persists for generations, long after the memory of the original heroism is dim.

In somewhat the same way, a discussion group may become more unified when its work is being criticized or opposed by outsiders, or when it receives deserved praise. This phenomenon illustrates the importance of the group's shared interests; their feeling of solidarity is increased because they have suffered, or sacrificed, or achieved together, as a unit. Of course, the leader cannot create conflicts with outside groups in order to build solidarity; rather he should verbalize his group's collective responsibility for censure or praise.

Helping Members Accept Group Purposes

Members must be encouraged to work as a unified group, accepting *group* purposes. They may then operate according to what is in the best interests of all, and will be more likely to believe that collective effort will be superior to the combined efforts of each working alone.

The designated leader should help members approach the problem as objectively as possible, and to be as accepting as possible of the other persons. He can ask tactfully for clarification of loaded statements, or restate biased contributions, taking out the bias. If a member says, "A bill for reducing the *crushing burden* of the income tax on those who *invest* to make the nation *prosperous* was introduced, but the *machine politicians* of the large cities *beat it to death* in committee," the designated leader, in asking his next question, can rephrase the contribution: "You are saying, then, that a bill for *modifying* the present income tax by *lowering rates on high incomes* was introduced, but opposed by *Congressmen* from large cities; what were their arguments against the reductions?" By his example of careful, uncolored word choices, the leader can encourage others to look at the problem objectively. Occasionally, he may also wish to compliment members when they succeed in describing a situation with objective fairness.

Encouraging Reflective Search

The designated leader should do whatever he can to help members enjoy inquiry in discussion. There is real excitement in a search for information and understanding, and in discovery of a satisfactory solution. A group that can become absorbed in the adventure of investigation will be more unified than one torn by dissension, the pleadings of advocates, or the machinations resulting from thinly disguised hidden agendas. If members can concentrate on achieving the best possible group product, individuals cannot be so concerned with personal aggrandizement. A unified group is excited by anyone's and everyone's discovery; it rejoices in and takes credit for accomplishment collectively rather than individually.

The excitement of search can be intensified by a leader with a seemingly insatiable curiosity. When facts are offered, he asks about the why behind the information. He is curious about everything relevant. His eagerness for content is matched by his enthusiastic manner, and by his positive reaction when members turn up particularly significant facts or achieve a major breakthrough in thinking.

Planning Programs with Meticulous Care

A concrete contribution to cohesiveness is made by the designated leader who expends the effort necessary to plan discussion programs with care.

Members are exasperated—and there is an accompanying decline in solidarity feeling for the group—when discussions waste precious time or seem unnecessary, avoidable, or fruitless.

The responsible leader finds out in advance as exactly as possible what is to be on the program. He makes an agenda listing in order what is to happen, and prepares any needed discussion outlines. He does not wait until members are assembled to discover what should be discussed. Under these conditions, he can only try to bluff his way through the situation. Of course, the agenda cannot always be prepared in advance; in some situations the members must agree on an agenda after they assemble.

Insofar as possible, the efficient leader helps the group avoid spending time discussing matters unrelated to the group's function, those over which members have no control, those that more properly belong to other groups, and those that can more efficiently be decided by an appropriate executive.

Encouraging Interaction

By creating a climate of permissiveness, as we saw in Chapter 11, the designated leader encourages interaction. Members feel more a part of the group if they participate actively. One aspect of permissiveness is to reduce the threat felt by reluctant individuals. The leader must protect the feelings of participants; respond with acceptance, not necessarily agreement, when they do speak up; and stress any signs of congeniality being generated among members.

Norman Maier describes a "Risk Technique" for encouraging members to express opposition even in situations where the designated leader is the supervisor or boss. The leader wishing to hear complaints and objections to a proposal being considered by the company sets aside a special period within the discussion during which members are expected to talk about the *risks* that the proposed policy may introduce. In this period members feel less threatened by the situation because they are invited to express opposition, reservations, and doubts. Maier reports that criticisms often turn out to be due to misunderstandings and false assumptions, although they may result in modification of the policy. "The risk technique was developed," he says, "to aid the emotionally involved discussion leader in listening, accepting, and understanding."[4] It would also have the virtue of encouraging interaction from all participants in particularly threatening situations.

MINIMIZING EFFECTS OF POWER DISCREPANCIES

A serious problem arises in some discussion situations when the discrepancies between those high and those low in influence interfere with group

---

[4] *Problem-Solving Discussions and Conferences*, New York: McGraw-Hill, 1963, pp. 171–7.

effort. If the powerful dominate the discussion, or if the lows are intimidated, even though the highs do not wish to suppress them, the result is the same.

There may be every justification in some situations for the influential members to dominate; it is possible that the most meritorious ideas will come from them, since there is a correlation between merit and positions of high influence. Lows in these situations may want the highs to take the lead. Certainly highs must not often deprive the group of their own ideas merely to encourage lows to participate. The quality of the outcome will almost surely suffer if only low-status persons contribute. If, however, collective thinking is actively desired in a situation, then participation is required from members of all shades of influence.

What the designated leader must achieve is a condition in which highs can contribute frankly and at the same time lows are encouraged to do likewise. He must minimize the effects of power discrepancies. He should not allow the powerful to dominate without anyone in the group realizing it. It is to be misled indeed to think that the outcome was produced by the group when in actuality it was a production of two or three influential members accompanied by the passive acquiescence of those too unsure of their positions to speak up.

To minimize power discrepancies, the leader should in his opening remarks stress that all members are invited equally to participate, that ideas should be judged on their merits rather than their source, and that all contributions are equally worthy of respectful consideration. Then in his behavior, he must be sure to treat all with equal respect, listen as carefully to lows as to highs, and take the views of lows as readily into account as those of highs in his questions and summaries.

Those high in power and those who are most confident tend to address their communications to the whole group, whereas lows are inclined to direct contributions to specific individuals, often to those higher in power. The designated leader may be able to make differences between highs and lows less noticeable if he gets all members to address most of their communications to the group as a whole. His goal is to get members to operate as a group of equals, and not as highs, middles, and lows.

Further, lows are more likely to make their influence attempts nondirective, that is, to say, "Do you think it would be permissible if I suggest this . . . ," rather than, "One thing we could do is . . ." or "This would work in our plant." The group should encourage the kind of permissiveness where lows feel as free as highs to make direct suggestions, rather than feel defensive about their proposals.

Highs, of course, make more influence attempts than do lows, and are more likely to succeed in having their views accepted. The group should be made frankly aware of these tendencies, and if the highs want to promote collective effort, everyone in the group should support the designated leader when he encourages highs to be less forceful and lows to be more courageous.

The real effects of power discrepancies are usually determined less by the efforts of the designated leader than by the attitudes of highs. To guarantee equal consideration for equally meritorious ideas originating with low-status persons, highs must understand thoroughly the operation of power, remind themselves constantly of its effects, and take the initiative in overcoming its influence. For instance, highs can state their positions tentatively: "Here is a possibility to consider." They should not often say, "Here's what we should do." They must be doubly cautious, in responding to the contributions of lows, to be objective: to use language carefully, without bias or coloring; to maintain cooperative attitudes; to preserve cordial interpersonal relationships. At every opportunity, the designated leader can, of course, encourage highs to take these steps. Also, the designated leader must realize that, because of his central position in the group, he is himself a high-power figure; he must use his influence to help rather than to interfere with group operation.

RESOLVING CONFLICTS

In problem-solving discussion, the designated leader can make a vital contribution if he can help resolve satisfactorily the conflicts that so often occur. Only when there is conflict are members tested as effective discussers; then attitudes toward the group, objectivity toward the problem and other persons, and similar essentials are tried under fire. Certainly, leadership cannot succeed unless members are willing to cooperate.

There are many causes of conflict. Disagreement can occur over the accuracy, interpretation of, or the significance of facts, or over the language in which ideas are expressed. Persons may disagree about the criteria by which a proposal is to be judged. Different individuals view the world differently, embrace divergent values, and emphasize conflicting objectives. Before they can accept a common course of action, they must reconcile their values. Although most people tend to find comfort in the accustomed ways, individuals vary in the extent to which they resist change. Discord results when some members are more willing than others to experiment with untried methods. Conflict can result from a simple misunderstanding, and also it can represent differences in basic convictions which no amount of discussion can resolve. Such was the case apparently in the American Civil War, when brothers with a common language and heritage stopped talking and started shooting.

Reasons for difficulty in reaching group decisions have been reviewed by Blake and Bradford.[5] In addition to inadequate leadership and "methodological blundering" through such weaknesses as too much rigidity or laxity of control and insufficient information, groups may fear the consequences of reaching a decision and express concern with what outsiders will think. Also,

[5] R. R. Blake and Leland Bradford, "Decisions... Decisions... Decisions," *Adult Leadership*, 2 (1953), pp. 23-4.

there can be conflicting loyalties to various reference groups, conflicts of inter-personal likes-dislikes, threat, and insecurity.

The discussion group thus faces a real challenge when the time arrives for the resolution of serious conflict. The designated leader can help first by seeing whether there is a simple cause and an easy way to resolve it. Occasionally, a group has a noisy hassle over the accuracy of a fact, when the dispute can be settled by consulting a reference book. When misunderstanding is a cause, careful restatement or definition or a more accurate use of language may help members see that the discord is only a matter of making meanings and intents clear.

At times, conflict results from failure to consider a problem fully. The designated leader should encourage the group from the beginning of the discussion to consider all aspects thoroughly. All views should be taken into account. No member's ideas should be overlooked or ignored. Time spent in hearing a minority view is time well invested. A member may refuse to accept the majority view simply because he feels other proposals, perhaps including his own, were not given a fair hearing.

Help Members with Insights

More serious conflicts take more effort. If members disagree because they view the world differently, or have divergent values, they may be able to achieve some rapport only if they can obtain clearer insight into the world view or the value-system of the other. No one should pretend that this process is easy. Objectivity and careful listening contribute to an understanding of the other person's notions. For many discussion situations, such careful considera-tion within the group probably is sufficient to bring about some measure of agreement.

When differences in outlook are extreme, however, the designated leader in some discussion situations may wish to recommend role-playing, a method useful in giving persons more insight into the convictions of others. A member who has opposed integrated housing, for example, is asked to take the role of a Negro seeking an apartment in a brief, impromptu drama involving landlord and applicant. Being forced to verbalize the needs, feelings, and frustrations of the Negro denied a room usually enables the role-player to understand and appreciate more fully the views of those who had opposed him on the question of integration. In the same manner, the others will after role-playing usually understand him better. It must be kept in mind that most closedgroups cannot use this procedure. The city council or corporation board is unlikely to stop in the middle of a serious conflict and engage in role-playing. This procedure is most useful as a training device for discussion groups actively studying group process. It can also be used by those participating in public discussion as a part of the preparation stage.

Lee has reported some success with a method for getting beyond an impasse. Advocates of each conflicting position are allowed to state their positions without interruption. Then other members are permitted only to ask questions of three kinds: those requesting clarification; those asking for information concerning the uniqueness of this proposal or position; and those asking about means of investigating or verifying the speaker's assumptions or predictions. Progress toward agreement is easier after members are forced, through this careful process, to see more clearly the nature of the conflict and the bases for the positions of the others.[6]

Methods of Agreement

Whatever the cause of conflict and whatever procedures help members understand its basis, the task of leadership is to achieve some kind of concrete agreement before the discussion ends, if this is at all possible. The three methods of reaching agreement described here are taken up in the order of decreasing desirability. Ideally, a group should reach consensus; if it cannot, the leader would strive for modification of views through compromise; finally, he would try for a settlement by majority vote. These are general categories of method; there may be other variations within each. Further, there may be additional methods for agreeing in particular situations.

CONSENSUS/ The ideal way to resolve conflict in discussion is to achieve consensus, or complete agreement. The designated leader should present alternative possibilities one at a time and strive for thorough discussion of each. Members should be asked to discuss objectively the advantages and disadvantages of each. Consensus is more likely if every participant, whether for or against a specific proposal, is capable of taking part enthusiastically when the group considers both the strengths and the weaknesses of each alternative. If the habit of objectivity has been developed throughout the discussion, members should be able to recognize admitted virtues in decisions they oppose, and weaknesses in proposals they favor.

Discussing each possible solution thoroughly and fairly in this manner prepares participants to face more objectively the final, most vital question: "What should we do?" or "Which alternative should we decide upon?" Under optimum conditions, the group should choose the proposal with the most advantages and the fewest disadvantages. The leader asks for general consent: "Are we agreed, then, that we should recommend proposal D?" There is a nodding of heads and consensus is achieved.

COMPROMISE/ Often in highly controversial discussions, the ideal of consensus is unattainable. Members need not despair. The designated leader should try for the next best outcome. By compromise is meant modification of proposals that are unacceptable in their present form but that can be approved after changes or amendment. Compromise does not mean horse-trading, log-rolling, you-scratch-my-back-and-I'll-scratch-yours, or other forms of deals which have questionable reputations.

[6] Irving J. Lee, "Procedure for Coercing Agreement," *Harvard Business Review,* 32 (1954), pp. 39-45.

When no proposal that has been considered is acceptable to everyone, the group must discover which specific features are the bases of conflict. Then it may be possible to suggest amendments to one of the proposals which will remove enough objectionable features so that it can be approved by all or most of the group. Modifications must be suggested with keen insight and skill. To amend a proposal so that it meets the requirements of those previously opposed to it often calls for more than a hasty patch here or a plugged loophole there. In some situations, it is necessary for some member to see a whole new approach and offer a different proposal which combines features of several solutions and fulfills the minimum requirements each person has been seeking.

MAJORITY VOTE/ If modification fails to result in general approval or near consensus, the group may be forced to reach agreement by counting noses. In small-group discussion, a vote should be taken only when the possibilities of reaching consensus or compromise have been thoroughly exhausted, and when members of the group are almost literally exhausted! Under some conditions, of course, the method of voting must be used more freely: if reaching a decision at this meeting is imperative and time is running out, the designated leader is justified in calling for a vote. When, on the other hand, the group has time for discussion or is concerned more with member commitment and satisfaction than with speedy results, majority vote should be used only in desperation.

When a proposed decision must be put to vote, it has not yet been perfected; those who vote against it have objections to some of its features and would probably prefer further opportunity to amend it. In a vote, some members win while others lose, and this procedure is divisive as far as the group is concerned. Nevertheless, when it must be used, the method of majority vote is perfectly respectable. Members will accept it as part of the democratic process, as will outsiders affected by the decision. It is easy to employ, and the outcome is simply interpreted.

What does the designated leader do if none of these methods works? Probably the wise course in the face of deadlock, stalemate, or noisy clash is to suggest a recess, adjournment, or postponement. In some cases, delay is preferable to a decision reached by hasty compromise or vote, one which no member may support enthusiastically. The leader should be especially concerned if an attitude such as this is expressed: "Oh, let's get it settled one way or the other." This statement suggests indifference and makes the whole matter seem unimportant. If the group accepts an unsatisfactory decision just to end the meeting, it will probably fail to win cooperation from members in putting the proposal into effect. Such outcomes often have a way of becoming unsettled and unsolved, and the problem may appear on the agenda of the next meeting anyway. Delay may be preferable also if an immediate decision is not as important to the group as is enthusiastic commitment to the outcome.

It should be re-emphasized here that a certain amount of conflict is a helpful accompaniment of thorough discussion. Through disagreement, reasoning is improved, facts are more accurately applied, and decision quality is increased. The expression of hostility is usually healthy because it clears the air and makes more likely the complete examination of reservation and doubt. What is critical is whether conflict can be resolved after it develops. In this connection it may be wise to summarize here what has been reported piecemeal about conflict resolution. The Michigan study of seventy-two business and governmental conferences included an analysis of the conditions under which these actual groups reached consensus after conflict, either substantive or affective, had developed. Consensus was more likely after either kind of conflict when rewarding interpersonal relationships developed; when a positive, supportive atmosphere came about in the meetings; when meetings were characterized by an over-all pleasantness; and when members reported feeling a need for united action and "willingness to give and take." Pleasantness helped consensus, however, only when serious conflict occurred; minor conflicts did not cause the same results.

These conditions related to motives and emotions of members. Conditions relevant to task achievement associated with consensus after conflict were: orderly treatment of topics, where members took up one issue at a time; easy intelligibility of comments; and understanding of the vocabulary of others. There were still other conditions related to consensus following either substantive or affective conflict. Then, of course, some conditions did not aid consensus at all.[7]

STRESSING AGREEMENT

At intervals throughout the discussion, the designated leader should try to put into words just what has been agreed upon. Emphasis should always be upon agreement rather than difference. To make this statement is not to say that disagreement should be ignored or glossed over. Differences should be resolved, but the leadership responsibility is to discover what the members want to decide; their decisions grow out of agreement. Hence, the leader should develop the habit of identifying and expressing agreement.

When offering a transitional summary at the end of each stage in the outline, the leader should say, for example: "Are we agreed, then, that we want to define the question in this way . . . ?" It is helpful if a recorder can put this agreement in writing before the group moves on. Habitual emphasis on agreement stresses the importance of deciding together as a unified group. Consensus at the end may then become more probable. Of course, the members must not be hurried into saying that they agree before they actually do.

At the end of the discussion, the final agreement must be stated carefully, preferably in writing. If necessary, each member should be given an oppor-

[7] Barry E. Collins and Harold Guetzkow, *A Social Psychology of Group Processes for Decision-Making*, New York: John Wiley & Sons, 1964, pp. 106–19.

tunity to comment orally on its acceptability. Misunderstanding that would not be expressed until later may thus be avoided.

SUPPLEMENTARY READING

Anderson, Martin P., "The Agree-Disagree Discussion Guide," *The Speech Teacher*, 8 (January, 1959), pp. 41–8.

Barnlund, Dean C., and Haiman, Franklyn S., *The Dynamics of Discussion*, Boston: Houghton Mifflin, 1960, Chapters 3, 8, and 11.

Chase, Stuart, *Roads to Agreement*, New York: Harper & Row, 1951.

Guetzkow, Harold, and Gyr, John, "An Analysis of Conflict in Decision-making Groups," *Human Relations*, 7 (1954), pp. 367–82.

Haiman, Franklyn S., *Group Leadership and Democratic Action*, Boston: Houghton Mifflin, 1951, Chapters 9 and 10.

Lee, Irving J., *How To Talk With People*, New York: Harper & Row, 1952, Chapter 12.

———, "Procedure for Coercing Agreement," *Harvard Business Review*, 32 (January–February, 1954), pp. 39–45.

Maier, N. R. F., *Problem-Solving Discussions and Conferences*, New York: McGraw-Hill, 1963, especially Chapters 7 and 8.

Maier, N. R. F., and Solem, A. R., "The Contribution of a Discussion Leader to the Quality of Group Thinking: The Effective Use of Minority Opinions," *Human Relations*, 5 (1952), pp. 277–88.

Sattler, William M., and Miller, N. Edd, *Discussion and Conference*, Englewood Cliffs, N.J.: Prentice-Hall, 1954, Chapter 11.

QUESTIONS AND EXERCISES

1. A cartoon in *Fortune* (April, 1957, p. 147) depicted a table loaded with rumpled papers, two men leaving the meeting room, and two men standing by the deserted table, one of whom is saying: "Now that the meeting's over, let's get things settled!" To what extent has this kind of attitude toward meetings been displayed in groups in which you have been an active participant? What are the symptoms displayed by a member who feels that the group meeting could not settle the real issues? What would you as the designated leader of a group discussion do to counteract such an attitude while the meeting is in progress?

2. Write a paper in which you explain what differences one or more of the following aspects of group process make in the actions of the designated leader while the discussion is in progress; in influencing the quality of a group's decision; in influencing the group's ability to reach consensus; in influencing members to feel commitment to the decision; and in helping the group to remain a group:

   a. communication structure

b. power relationships
c. sociometric structure
d. group cohesiveness
e. cooperative attitudes
f. language skills
g. speech skills

3. Describe a small, closedgroup, problem-solving discussion situation in which you have been or might be the designated leader. Explain in a report how you would take into account what you know about the elements of group process listed in exercise 2, above, as you lead the discussion. To explain, you will need to tell what you would do and why you would do it.

4. Name some other methods of resolving conflict in addition to the ones described in this chapter. Among the other methods that may occur to you are these: chance (flipping a coin); following tradition; asking a respected authority, such as a judge, to hand down a decision; force; and coercion. What are the advantages and disadvantages of resolving conflict through discussion method as contrasted with each of the other possible methods?

5. Divide the class into groups of four and have each buzz group simultaneously consider for 15 to 20 minutes one of the cases for discussion printed in the Appendix. After the discussions are over, have the class consider these questions: At what point did the first disagreement occur? How was this disagreement and later ones resolved?

6. Do you think that cohesiveness is stronger in a decision-making group that experienced conflict and successfully resolved it, or in a group where no conflict developed during the meeting?

7. What do you feel would be the most important advantages and disadvantages of using Maier's "Risk Technique"? Under what conditions would you expect it to work best? In what circumstances would you hesitate to try it?

PART FOUR

THE STUDY
OF INTERACTION

Chapter 14

THE ELEMENTS
OF GROUP PROCESS

Up to this point we have examined the procedures involved in defining, using, preparing for, participating in, and leading discussion. It is now time to emphasize that individuals can engage in small-group communication, and often do so effectively, with little awareness of what is actually happening. Participants may be unable to explain, for example, why one discussion succeeded while another was a disastrous failure.

Some part of the explanation, of course, will involve factors we have considered in previous chapters: preparation, information, reasoning, language and communication abilities, participation, leadership, etc. The interaction process is extremely complex, however, and the careful student will want to go beyond the procedures to an explanation of other subtle forces in operation during a discussion. This closer examination will be the purpose of Part IV.

Since we are practitioners of discussion, learning to use communication effectively in small-group decision-making, the logical place for beginning was with the procedures treated in the first three parts of this book, and these remain the proper place for our major emphasis. Now, however, we must take a closer look at the operation of the discussion group as a form of interacting social system. We want to consider in some detail what changes take place in the various elements as members discuss; how particular parts affect and are affected by the multitude of other elements; and what occurs as a result of the interaction.

Above all, we should try to explain why one group is successful and another unproductive; why some participants are satisfied with the results of their work and others disgruntled; and why individuals modify their attitudes because of their participation in one situation while in others, where the circumstances seem much the same, they increase their hostility. We would like to be able to specify what elements in the system should be altered to produce positive rather than negative outcomes. While human beings are too complicated for us to expect the discovery of simple, systematic relationships, there should be some consistent lawfulness to the ways people behave in discussion. The purpose of social research is to discover this lawfulness wherever possible.

Although there is much we do not yet know and much we are not very certain about, the reader should seek out what has been learned so far in research. He must keep in mind that all the hypotheses are tentative, partial, and must be considered as open-ended statements to build upon. Only if he understands the basis for the hypotheses about interaction can he begin to grasp the complexities of discussion. Participants and leaders alike need an appreciation for the subtle demands of various sets of circumstances if they are to be capable of the adaptation required from moment to moment and situation to situation. A study of group process will also give a better understanding of the relationships encountered in social situations other than group discussion.

Fortunately, the reader has available a range of resources which will help him understand this fascinating province of human interaction. Ideally, he should take a course in social psychology or sociology of small groups before enrolling in a discussion course. If this is impractical, as it often is, there are a number of books recently available that offer insightful syntheses of the research literature on small groups. Much research in the last decade or two has dealt explicitly with our primary interest—decision-making discussion. These sources have been helpful in preparing this part of the present book and some of them are listed as supplementary reading following Chapters 14, 15, and 16.

The complexity of group process should not cause the student to despair. Few studies are as rewarding as the study of the small human group. What it should lead to is a healthy respect for the vast amount there is to learn. No one should assume that he knows all about groups from studying this book— or from taking a few courses in college, for that matter—since few of the social psychologists or sociologists who are experts on small groups would be brash enough to claim they know "all about groups." What should be hoped for is that careful study here and in other sources and courses, wide reading, alert observation, and broad experience through the years will be rewarded finally with the beginning of wisdom in understanding groups. What can be achieved immediately is some insight into some kinds of discussion behavior in some kinds of group situations. If this view seems unnecessarily cautious and pessimistic, let it be said that it is a thousand times better in this instance to claim too little than too much.

What we can do here in Part IV is to introduce the basic concepts and interrelationships. The student can then pursue these matters more fully on his own or in additional courses.

In this chapter, specifically, we will examine the elements that are operating in this limited kind of social activity. In doing so, we must re-examine from a different perspective some of the aspects discussed earlier in the book and add some new ones.

An Interacting System

We can think of the operating discussion group as a system in which (a) certain inputs (b) are modified by a number of intermediate and dynamic interactional processes (c) leading to particular outputs.[1]

The individuals who make up the group, with their personal characteristics, are the first elements of input. They manifest attitudes, goals, personalities, roles, and status positions. The group itself, with its standards, expectations, goals, and other characteristics, is another element of input. Then there are such inputs as the situation, the nature of the group's task, and group size. In addition, there are many inputs of the kind already considered in the first thirteen chapters of the book, such as the question for discussion, the background and information each individual brings with him into the group, and the talents of reflective thinking, reasoning, communicating, and so on.

These inputs change in complex ways while the discussion is in progress. Individuals initiate communications that may restructure attitudes toward the problem and alter images of each person in the perceptions of the others. A particular climate of permissiveness and interpersonal attraction is created and modified throughout the session. The phases of the discussion outline introduce differences through time, as do the shifting influences of leadership and of power relationships. A kind of equilibrium is achieved from moment to moment in balancing the demands of task and social functions. There are still other dynamic interactions taking place, too many to describe swiftly.

When the discussion ends, there are particular outputs resulting from the interactions. One is a task outcome, such as a decision. Closely related outputs may be attitude change and learning. Another type involves individual feelings about the outcome. These may be measured in terms of satisfaction with the discussion, reward perceived by participants, and commitment to a decision. Still another kind of output is the degree of group harmony, "groupness," or cohesiveness after the discussion is over.

This conception of the interactions among inputs, intermediate processes, and outputs is helpful in visualizing the operation of group process. It makes clear that all the elements are dynamically interrelated rather than discrete, static, and isolated. If we can specify the parts of the system and if we can say

---

[1] McGrath and Altman have suggested this kind of analysis in calling for systematic research to fill gaps in our knowledge about performance effectiveness: "We need a better understanding of the sequential linkages that begin with inputs in the form of member, group, and task characteristics, that become *manifested in* intermediate interactive processes, and that culminate in a performance output." They ask also for further exploration of the performance relationships among behavior, situation, and task. Joseph E. McGrath and Irwin Altman, *Small Group Research*, New York: Holt, Rinehart and Winston, 1966, p. 65.

something about their interrelationships, we should be in a better position to explain why some discussions are more pleasant and productive than others.

INDIVIDUAL CHARACTERISTICS

Groups are made up of individuals and the kinds of persons who happen to be present obviously help determine what the discussion will be like. The individuals, as we have said, become the first element of input. A committee with an obnoxiously aggressive member will not be the same as it would be without him.

Also, individuals bring to groups unique talents, abilities, and interests; various combinations lead to varied group functioning. The person who has the most information on the financial condition of the organization, for example, will be a high participator when money and costs are being discussed and, other things being equal, his knowledge will cause him to have high influence in deciding financial matters. Other members may have high credit-ability because of a reputation for broad understanding of and specific information about the organization, or for speaking effectively about its problems, or for a peacemaker role, or for encouragement of others, and so on. Individuals vary almost infinitely: in talkativeness, closed-mindedness, empathy, sensitivity, energy-enthusiasm, ambition, knowledge, willingness to do their homework, self-confidence, ways of evaluating the world, etc.

Individuals join groups to satisfy some of their needs. They work in vocational groups in part because they must make a living, social groups because they need the companionship of others, and certain clubs for reasons of prestige. The frequency and liveliness of their communication in group meetings probably vary directly with the relevance of the proceedings to their vital interests. Thus we would expect livelier talk in the committee that is concerned with earning a living than in the recreational group. Some individuals feel more need for joining than do others. Some take an active part in every discussion of every meeting of the many organizations to which they belong, while others may say little or nothing even when their vital interests are at stake. One member may be content to let "George" do his talking where another would be miserable if left off a single committee roster. Some are more motivated than others to contribute, to achieve, to be a part of things.

Some members also feel more compelled to promote their self-oriented needs. This concentration on self may be revealed as a striving to dominate others, to have a prominent position, to be reassured by others, to compete rather than cooperate, or to express hostility or aggression.

A further complication is the fact that human beings are changeable. A group member who almost monopolizes the discussion in objecting to one proposal may say nothing at all when a similar matter is brought up 10 minutes later. A person in a relaxed, friendly mood may accept ideas he would disown noisily while feeling hostile or dejected.

In groups that continue over a period of time, members bring into meetings their previously acquired attitudes toward the persons involved. While attitudes can be modified during interaction, it should be noted that impressions of others are built up from hundreds of minute interchanges and nuances of feeling; thus attitudes toward people change slowly and may not be much affected during a one-hour discussion. The cold, unbending participant who suddenly in one meeting turns warm and reassuring need not expect others to drop immediately the caution they have learned to exercise in reacting to him. Even when participants are strangers, they will bring to a discussion certain general expectations about the behavior of particular kinds of persons.

Roles and Status

While individuals are almost infinitely individualistic and changeable, social interactions are not completely chaotic and unpredictable because particular individuals fulfill roles and occupy status positions that are relatively easy to identify or to learn quickly. These roles and status positions carry with them certain expectations of social behavior that help others predict what such persons will say and do, and also how others can appropriately respond.

It is these expectations that help us to define and identify a role. The designated chairman of a committee is expected to behave in particular ways; for example, he is the one who should call the meeting to order. We produce through experience a definition of the role of committee chairman that applies to the position, irrespective of the personality of the individual holding the particular chairmanship or the nature of the committee and its task assignment. In the same sense, the treasurer of a board of directors can be expected to fulfill certain role functions in talking about money, and so on.

In addition to roles brought into the group because of outside responsibilities, functional roles related specifically to a particular discussion group may quickly be identified when members spend time together. One man may become the task-expediter and another the feeling-soother, as we saw in Chapter 9. Of course, these roles are not formalized and they constantly fluctuate.

Groups seem to be more successful when the role differentiation is clear and well defined. Apparently members can communicate more effectively with each other if everyone knows in general who is expected to perform various functions. This may be another way of saying the obvious: that members are more productive after they have worked out a way of working together. Specialization of role does not prevent members from taking advantage of substitutability of behavior. When a subtask is performed by one person it does not have to be repeated by another. When one member says approximately what a second intended to say, the latter need not speak. Specialized roles help listeners grasp more quickly the meaning being communicated from that role position.

A stable and somewhat predictable group structure is not only a matter of role differentiation. Certain roles and individuals occupy status positions in a group hierarchy, which also help members understand what communication is appropriate and when. The chairman of a committee is assigned higher status than the secretary: greater prestige attaches to the position of chairman. Status may come from outside positions, as in the case of the president of the company, or from the reputation gained over a series of meetings by a person who has earned the position of best informed, for example.

Discussion groups almost always develop quickly some kind of status distinctions. In addition, a great many groups have a strict hierarchical structure built into them. A military staff is an example of a rigid rank-order system. The board of directors of a corporation will have an easily identifiable "pecking order" of status positions based on the official job held in the company, the amount of stock owned, or both. The structure of the hierarchy influences directly the communication flow in discussion. Groups immediately develop notions based partially on the group structure about how business should be conducted, which members should be listened to most intently, who should be responsible for what, and so on. Even in groups having a brief existence, members tend to be influenced by the prestige others bring with them from outside, and the group often proceeds as the individuals have done in similar situations. In continuing groups it is easier for members to become differentiated in the amount of status and influence they have. Although influence over others is a flexible rather than a rigid matter, every member over a period of time becomes aware of these differences and could probably estimate rather accurately who has high prestige within the group.

GROUP CHARACTERISTICS

The character of the group as it assembles for a discussion could be considered a second major category of input elements. These are the group properties that exist collectively in the members gathered together, and in the particular circumstances, at the moment before their interaction begins. Some of these are the nature of the group; shared goals and attitudes; norms, standards, and expectations; the situation; the task assignment; and group size.

Nature of the Group

A group is more than a collection of individuals assembled in the same place. A dozen people sitting in a railway station waiting room do not constitute a group. They may become a group, however, under certain emergency conditions. Suppose, for example, that these dozen people suddenly discovered that they were trapped in the building, and that all the exits were blocked. If they start working cooperatively together to plan an escape, they would become a group. In changing themselves from a collectivity into a group, they have added three characteristics: (*a*) The individuals have accepted as their own a common goal of the group—escape—and the action of the group fulfills a need in each individual—self-preservation. (*b*) The accomplishment of the group task has involved interaction. (*c*) In most cases there will be a third characteristic, which is most important for those interested in group discussion—there will be oral communication, a specific type of interaction.

Cattell has defined a group as "a collection of organisms in which the existence of all (in their given relationships) is necessary to the satisfaction of certain individual needs in each." This definition is broad and general, but it is adequate for the group in the railway station. They may engage in minimum interaction and, conceivably, they might not talk at all. Cattell gives the example of three swimmers far from shore, who say nothing to each other— and yet have the need for security satisfied by the presence of the others.[2] Whether or not this definition is satisfactory for groups in general, it is not adequate for the purpose of defining a group in the discussion situation. It only implies interaction in a most general sense; and it leaves out communication.

Homans defines a group as "a number of persons who communicate with one another often over a span of time, and who are few enough so that each person is able to communicate with all the others, not at second hand, through other people, but face to face."[3] Klineberg feels that the concept of interacting "over a span of time" places too restrictive a limitation on the definition; he says "if two or more individuals are together briefly, but interact and influence one another, they constitute, if only for a time, a real group."[4] Klineberg's statement seems to have a common-sense fit; there is often a situation in which persons are together for a single meeting, conference, or public discussion, and yet surely constitute a group for that short period. Of course, many closedgroups and a few public discussion groups interact over a long period. With this exception, Homans' definition moves closer to concepts useful to the discussion student, since it suggests the notions of direct, communicative interchange, and of interaction in a face-to-face situation.

Bales offers a definition that agrees for the most part with what has been said here so far, and that introduces the concept of individual awareness of other persons:

A small group is defined as any number of persons engaged in interaction with one another in a single face-to-face meeting or a series of such meetings, in which each member receives some impression or perception of each other member distinct enough so that he can, either at the time or in later questioning, give some reaction to each of the others as an individual person, even though it be only to recall that the other was present.[5]

[2] Raymond B. Cattell, "New Concepts for Measuring Leadership, in Terms of Group Syntality," *Human Relations*, 4 (1951), pp. 161–84.
[3] George C. Homans, *The Human Group*, New York: Harcourt, Brace & World, 1950, p. 1.
[4] Otto Klineberg, *Social Psychology*, rev. ed., New York: Holt, Rinehart and Winston, 1954, pp. 438, 474.
[5] Robert F. Bales, "A Theoretical Framework for Interaction Process Analysis," in Dorwin Cartwright and Alvin Zander, *Group Dynamics*, New York: Harper & Row, 1953, p. 30.

According to this definition, then, participants in a public panel may be a group, but the listening audience can not; they cannot become aware of each other person if the audience is at all large. The entire student body of a school could not be a discussion group, if this definition were accepted, but committees of the student senate could be, and the whole senate could conceivably be, although when groups are large, obviously, clear perception of each other individual becomes difficult.

Kelly and Thibaut feel that even in groups created experimentally, "a collection of individuals . . . becomes a group as the members accept a common task, become interdependent in its performance, and interact with one another to promote its accomplishment."[6]

With the addition of these components, it is possible to construct a definition satisfactory for our purposes. To have a group in group discussion:

(1) Individuals must interact, primarily through oral communication, directly enough that each individual is aware of each other as a person.

(2) Individuals must, as in all groups, accept the common tasks and aspirations of the group as their own; that is, accept the group's goals. The accomplishment of the group's goals, of course, will lead to the satisfaction of certain needs of each individual. Groups then develop norms, accept roles providing for expected behaviors, and build interpersonal feelings. Thus, members become interdependent.

The individuals may become a group during one meeting or many. In fact, it is helpful to think of groups, not in static, it-is-a-group or it-is-not-a-group terms, but in terms of a growing, developing set of relationships. Some groups have more "groupness" than others; a small group working intimately together for years would obviously exhibit the characteristics of "groupness" to a greater extent than strangers meeting for a two-hour conference.

One other statement must be made to complete the definition. There is no group entity, no group mind apart from the discrete individuals who are present. The difference between a group and the same persons as separate, isolated individuals is that individuals when they become a group interact and become interdependent.

Kinds of Groups

Each individual belongs to many groups in which discussion occurs. Some of these are formal organizations or clubs. The same person may be a member of Rotary, the Moose, the First United Church, the Tri-City Organists Guild, and the East Side Stamp Collectors Club. Each person also holds membership in groups that are not formally organized: an office work force, the gang that meets for coffee each morning, the bridge-playing set, the golf foursome, the group assembled by accident within the same classroom.

[6] Harold H. Kelley and J. W. Thibaut, "Experimental Studies of Group Problem Solving and Process," in Gardner Lindzey, ed., *Handbook of Social Psychology*, Volume II, Cambridge, Mass.: Addison-Wesley, 1954, p. 735.

Groups can be differentiated on the basis of their acceptance of common goals, the quality of their interaction, and the extent of their interdependence. If we observed carefully several meetings of different groups, it would be instructive to attempt to classify them on these three dimensions, as suggested in Table 1. A board of directors of some large corporations would be composed of busy persons, some of whom would have interests in other enterprises. They would share such goals as earning a profit and the intensity of their interaction would be directed to this end. Their interdependence would not be extremely great, however, because their involvement would be limited to major policy decisions. The executive committee responsible for the day-to-day operations in that corporation, in contrast, undoubtedly would develop a high degree of interdependence as they counted on each other for the specialized skills and knowledge necessary to a successful industry. They would also share common goals and their interaction should be high in quality and quantity. We should be able to observe these manifestations during their meetings. A different example could be found in a discussion course or a course using case study method where a subgroup is assigned a topic to investigate and then discuss with the class as audience. This subgroup would share limited goals in common, such as cooperating well enough to earn a satisfactory grade. Their interdependence would probably be low, since their course success would depend on much activity outside this subgroup, and the liveliness of their interaction would depend on a number of factors and would need to be observed to be classified. A report of our observations could take the form represented in Table 14.1.

Kind of Group	Apparent Acceptance of Common Goals	Intensity of Interaction	Extent of Apparent Interdependence
Board of Directors	High	High	Fairly High
Executive Committee	High	High	Very High
Classroom Subgroup	Fairly High	?	Low

Table 14.1 Differences Observed in Three Kinds of Groups

PURPOSE/ Another way of differentiating groups is to classify them according to their purposes. The following list suggests only a few functions of groups and gives some examples:

Vocational groups: business conferences, teachers' association, the executive committee of an industrial plant.

Instructional groups: members enrolled in the same course, campus clubs, study group.

Governmental groups: city council, school board, student senate.

Religious groups: church, boards and committees of the church, YMCA, YWCA.

Fraternal groups: Elks, Moose, social fraternities and sororities.

Recreational groups: golf foursome, baseball team, bowling club.

Social groups: coffee hour, cocktail party, bridge club.

Most individuals will belong to two or three groups within each of these and other categories.

PERMANENCY/ Another distinction among kinds of groups involves the length of time they exist. Some groups are temporary, or momentary. Examples are a one-meeting conference, a summit meeting of heads of states, and a public panel using experts for a single, special program. At the other end of this continuum are continuing groups, meeting regularly over a long period of time. Congressional committees exist for a session of Congress, and with some changes in personnel for much longer periods. Membership of a corporation's board of directors or an executive's staff may be stabilized for several years.

INTIMACY/ Groups vary also along what may be called an *intimacy* dimension. At one end of this continuum lies what Charles Cooley called the *primary group*; he viewed these as "characterized by intimate face-to-face association and cooperation. They are primary in several senses, but chiefly in that they are fundamental in forming the social nature and ideals of the individual."[7] This label may be assigned to groups that are small, interact frequently—probably daily—over long periods, develop deep awareness of each other as an individual, satisfy the individual's most basic needs, and are the important developers of each person as a social being. The family is, of course, the best example. At the nonprimary end of this continuum are groups that do not interact intimately, with membership being voluntary and easily withdrawn. An example on a college campus might be a language club that students enrolled in language courses are asked to join, which meets occasionally to discuss academic matters related to foreign language study, which members attend irregularly—perhaps primarily when they feel attendance will improve their standing with an instructor—and where interaction is possible but unflourishing.

The importance for us of this dimensional concept lies in comparing the relative primariness of two groups. For the vice-president in charge of sales, the executive committee that controls his corporation is usually more primary as a group than is the board of directors of the country club of which he may also be a member.

MEMBERSHIP AND REFERENCE/ One important distinction is not of the same order as those already discussed. This is the distinction between membership groups and reference groups. Membership groups are simply those to which an individual belongs. He may or may not belong to his reference groups. In Klineberg's words:

> We often pattern our behavior and our attitudes in terms of standards laid down not by the group to which we belong, but by a group which serves as our frame

---

[7] C. H. Cooley, *Social Organization*, New York: Charles Scribner's Sons, 1909, p. 23.

of reference. Such reference groups may be our membership groups as well, but not necessarily; they may be groups to which we aspire, or groups that we use as a reference point in making evaluations of ourselves or others.[8]

The relationship between kinds of groups and the quality of discussion occurring therein can be easily suggested. Generally speaking, most members are probably more motivated to prepare in advance for and to take part vigorously in discussions within their vocational groups than within casual social groups. Interaction should be easier, in general, within continuing, intimate groups than within momentary, formal groups. A violent disagreement within a board of directors might be incomprehensible without the knowledge that the two men clashing have different reference groups; for example, one may have as a reference group those who wish to make large profits regardless of legality and morality, while the other may be guided by the ethical standards of quite a different group, such as a church.

Group Goals and Attitudes

As we have observed, groups form because they are instrumental in satisfying member needs. Any discussion group has expressed or unexpressed goals, and the group will probably be healthy and productive to the extent that individual members feel they can embrace the group's goals in relation to their individual needs.

The existence of, acceptance of, and changes in group goals are not simple matters. They are more than the sum of individually held motives and aspirations for the group. While individuals have their own personal goals which may coincide or conflict with group goals, a group to be successful requires some goals shared and internalized by the members. A corporation executive committee, for example, may have the general goals of earning the largest possible profit, building the best products in the field, and contributing to the welfare of the community. The first general goal is to some extent in conflict with the third: the more they spend on community welfare, the less profit the firm will realize (unless the contributions are deductible). The group must decide how the general goals are to be interpreted and ranked in importance before it can make day-to-day decisions. One thing it does is to establish operational goals more specific than these general ones. It may not be able to reach goal number two because there may be no way to tell who makes the best products in the field. The committee may be forced to set an attainable goal by striving for achievement of one major improvement a year in each product.

Individuals in this group will also have personal goals. The vice president for sales may want to become executive vice president, for example, and his contributions at board meetings will be affected by this ambition.

Members usually vary in their attitudes toward working for the common

[8] Klineberg.

good. Some persons seem to have little difficulty developing a cooperative relationship to the group and internalizing the group's goals as their own. Others seem unable to keep their personal motives from competing with the group's activities. Successful groups probably have a greater proportion of members who can endorse group goals and work for the common welfare.

It is, of course, difficult to generalize about the objectives of all group discussions. However, most discussion groups will usually have three group goals:

1. The group strives toward a group product—or outcome—of high quality, arrived at efficiently. The product in information-sharing is understanding—understanding by the participants in closedgroup and by the listening audience in public discussion. A public panel group discussing the guaranteed annual wage, for example, would wish to achieve at the end understanding of the problem on the part of listeners; the measure of its success would be the information and insights communicated. The product in problem-solving discussion is a decision or policy. In closedgroup discussion, the decision is a basis for action if the group has power to act, or a recommendation if the group is a recommendation group. In public discussion, the outcome is a recommended decision for consideration by the audience, and part of the participants' goal is to stimulate the audience to consider it.

Note the relationship between the group's goal and the satisfaction of individual needs. Members of a corporation's board of directors have an economic motivation to reach high-quality decisions, because the prosperity of the firm relates to their income, security, self-preservation, and maintenance of home and family. Members of a city council may strive for good decisions because, among other reasons, they derive satisfaction from the approval of their constituents.

2. The group also seeks to win individual commitment to the group product. This means member satisfaction with the outcome, the group, and the discussion itself. Proponents of discussion, as Sheffield said years ago, "realize that a decision will be carried out far more satisfactorily if the minority against it have been brought into some adjustment toward it, instead of merely beaten as a faction."[9] One of the factors that leads to commitment is the opportunity to participate in the discussion and to influence the outcome. One study of conferences points in this direction; it found that high satisfaction with the discussion was related to the feeling that members were free to talk and not to how much they actually took part.[10]

In information-sharing discussion, commitment means individual satisfaction with the understanding achieved. In problem-solving discussion, com-

[9] Alfred D. Sheffield, *Joining in Public Discussion*, New York: George H. Doran, 1922, p. x.
[10] Roger W. Heyns, "What Makes a Conference Tick?" *Adult Leadership*, 5 (1956), pp. 83–7.

mitment means individual willingness to defend and to carry out the decision, if the group has power to act, or to recommend the action to those who have power to execute it if the group is a recommendation group. A listener to a public problem-solving panel would show commitment, for example, if he wrote his congressman to recommend the proposal agreed upon by the discussion group.

3. In most cases, a third goal is to maintain the group as a group, to promote harmonious interrelationship that will be lasting, and to prevent dissolution of the group. This goal applies most importantly to continuing groups, and is less vital in momentary groups. The aim here is to develop unity, solidarity, and cohesiveness.

Norms, Standards, and Expectations

Closely related to the existence of individual roles and status positions that give a group structure are the norms, standards, and codes of acceptable behavior in social situations. Standards of productivity, acceptable communication patterns, methods, and procedures thus are group approved. In group situations, loyal members tend not to violate the norms. Group pressures may even enforce rigid conformity upon members.

An impressive number of studies show that individuals tend to conform to the standards established by the group. Apparently members choose not to deviate from the norms because it gives them solidarity with the group. In the famous Bennington study, Newcomb showed that through their college years, students moved in the direction of commonly held liberal attitudes, if they accepted the college community as a dominant reference group.[11]

Sherif demonstrated the establishment of a group standard in judging an ambiguous physical stimulus. He showed persons in a dark room a point of light that was stationary, suggested that they would see it move, and asked them to estimate the distance of movement. (The apparent movement is the "autokinetic effect.") As they make estimates of the distance, individuals in this unstructured situation establish a range of estimates and a norm or reference point within that range. When several individuals who have established such judgments alone are placed with a group that observes the light together, "the ranges and norms tend to converge."[12]

The strength of group pressure in enforcing conformity was also demonstrated by Asch. Subjects were asked to look at a vertical line on a card and report orally which of three other vertical lines was most nearly equal in length to the first line. Then subjects were asked to make an incorrect response; that is to call out "line x" when it was clearly evident that "line y"

[11] T. M. Newcomb, *Personality and Social Change*, New York: Holt, Rinehart and Winston, 1943.
[12] Muzafer Sherif, "A Study of Some Social Factors in Perception," *Archives of Psychology*, 1935, no. 187.

was the correct answer. At this point, one new, uninstructed subject was brought into the room. He then heard all the other subjects reporting an answer that his perception told him did not square with reality. The experimenter's objective was to discover how many such subjects would conform to the almost unanimous judgment, even though it was incorrect. Approximately one-third of the uninstructed subjects did conform, apparently so that they might be in harmony with the group.[13]

If some individuals can be thus influenced when the subject matter is in the realm of physical reality, which can be verified by the senses, it is reasonable to speculate that there is even more pressure on individuals to conform to group opinion on subjects where the right answer is anchored in social sanction. Some light is thrown upon this matter by the studies showing that individuals feel they are more nearly in harmony with group opinion than is actually the case. In an early investigation, Travers asked persons for their opinions and for estimates of the percentage of others in the group who would agree with them. Subjects had a marked tendency to believe that their opinions corresponded to the majority view.[14] Gordon concluded after a similar study that "individuals tended to conform to their conception of the group norms when giving their public [that is, publicly expressed] opinion. The typical pattern is for the individual to compromise between his private opinion and his conception of the group opinion when expressing his public opinion."[15]

Group enforcement of conformity is a great danger to effective discussion. While the development of standards gives system and stability to a discussion group, blind obedience to sanctioned norms can lead to rigidity and sterility. Members should not allow the acceptance of traditional ways of proceeding, managing, and interacting to stifle suggestions for innovation and improvement. The powerful should not enforce upon newcomers and those low in prestige a conformity of silence. Otherwise the group is deprived of talents it needs. Paulson has pointed out that discussion can be improved by encouraging clear expression of the minority view, by taking advantage of the improved thinking resulting from the conflict of ideas, and by protecting individualism and nonconformity.[16] In a study of disagreement in group decision-making, Torrance found that disagreement was impeded by status or power discrepancies among members and by some leadership techniques that failed to give members' views consideration. He concludes that "task-

[13] Solomon E. Asch, *Social Psychology*, Englewood Cliffs, N.J.: Prentice-Hall, 1952, pp. 450–501.

[14] R. M. Travers, "A Study in Judging the Opinions of Groups," *Archives of Psychology*, 1941, no. 266.

[15] R. L. Gordon, "Interaction between Attitude and the Definition of the Situation in the Expression of Opinion," *American Sociological Review*, 17 (1952), pp. 50–8.

[16] Stanley F. Paulson, "Pressures Toward Conformity in Group Discussion," *Quarterly Journal of Speech*, 44 (1958), pp. 50–5.

oriented disagreement is almost always 'good' " and that "willingness to disagree is a major characteristic of the aces—the high achievers," even though, alas, "too often the greatest rewards are for conformity."[17]

On the other hand, standards of appropriate behavior enable members of groups to anticipate more clearly what is expected of individuals, including those who hold particular status positions and fill certain roles. Members conserve energy when they avoid explaining what is appropriate.

Individuals form groups but in a real sense groups also form the individual and tell him "who he is." A society is built on group organization and could not function at all efficiently without being able to depend on certain institutionalized operations. Standardized expectations about group communication thus are often helpful to effective decision-making. In our culture, for example, we expect that one central person in the group will at least perform certain procedural functions such as calling on speakers, urging one person to speak at a time, and so on. We expect to be productive in some way, or at least to have something to show for the time spent. In fact, our attitudes toward time wasting control a number of communication expectations. We expect a minimum level of good manners, politeness, and consideration; the avoidance of shouting except under extreme provocation; and so on.

The Situation

The situation existing at the moment a discussion begins is an element of input that obviously influences the nature of the talk and the decision reached. The matter of who is present will immediately affect participants, whether friends or strangers, powerful or unknown, etc.

If the chairman of the board is a visitor at the plant executive committee meeting, the discussion will be altered, as it would be from other shifts in the power relationships among participants. The presence of expert consultants or important observers may influence participation. The accidental absence of key members because they are out of town or busy elsewhere is a frequent cause of disrupted discussion.

When time is short, members tend to make allowances, foregoing as thorough a discussion as is customary and sometimes compromising more readily on decisions. Discussions held at certain times of the day or week may also change the communication flow. A meeting on financial planning held just before the budget deadline may operate under a similar urgency.

The time of the meeting may be significant in another way if a discussion occurs when there are impending external events that will have an impact on the problem being discussed. For example, if a college plans to announce tomorrow the choice of the new dean, a meeting of a faculty committee this afternoon for the purpose of considering staff promotions will be a rather

---

[17] E. P. Torrance, "Group Decision-Making and Disagreement," *Social Forces*, 35 (1957), pp. 314–18.

cautious affair. Indeed, the members may well postpone their meeting. If a group must make a decision today, however, knowing that an outside event may cancel their effort, the discussion today is unavoidably affected.

As we noted in Chapter 4, physical arrangements of members around the table may affect communication.

Even the locale of a meeting may be a situational factor important in structuring some discussions. A conference involving two nations may be held on neutral ground in a third so as not to give one even an imagined advantage. Recent presidents of the United States have provided other examples. On occasion the President has invited labor-management negotiators who are locked in a serious dispute to move their negotiating sessions to the White House. This location often has hastened agreement and certainly has pointed up the seriousness of the dispute in relation to the national welfare.

It is interesting to note that situational factors are sometimes manipulated by shrewd executives to influence purposely the course of a discussion. Since a shortage of time may hasten agreement, it is possible to postpone a meeting until the last possible hour before a decision must be made, or to stretch out an agenda so that the group has only 15 minutes of the meeting left for the most important decision of the session. Meetings called for four o'clock on Friday afternoons are often poorly attended or they may be more perfunctory than is usual; members may not discuss problems as fully under this kind of pressure. The chairman who wants a favorable decision on an unpopular matter may wait to call the meeting until he has a joyous piece of news to announce, hoping that the members will be less critical after his announcement. If he has stalled as many weeks as he can a proposed reform he wants the group to defeat, he may invite the members to his home for cocktails, "to discuss this decision in a relaxed manner," hoping members will be too relaxed to insist on a stern decision.

Such manipulations immediately raise questions of ethical propriety. The student should consider them along with the problems of ethics examined in Chapter 8.

The Task

The nature of the task is another element of input. Some continuing groups, such as the President's Cabinet, must consider problems of great complexity and seriousness. In contrast, a committee planning a fraternity dance is not burdened with frightful responsibilities. Even here, of course, generalizations are somewhat risky. Decisions in the fraternity committee could quickly become more stressful if a student were injured or killed putting up decorations.

At any rate, the seriousness of the problem will affect the length and formality of discussions. Other differences in the group's task assignment will likewise influence discussion. A parent organization may be pressing a committee for a quick answer on an extremely difficult question and the truncated discussion possible under the circumstances may not do the problem justice. A problem beyond the resources and talents of the group may result in unsatisfactory decision-making. In such circumstances the groups may bring in resource persons.

The complexity and quantity of problems discussed will be related to a whole range of other matters: time required, information needed, importance of experienced leadership, and so on. Congressional committees must employ a large staff of lawyers, investigators, and other workers to keep up with the large volume of serious and complicated questions they must regularly face.

Group Size

A final element of initial input we will mention is the size of the discussion group. The number of persons assembled to talk about the problem has a clear effect on the interaction that takes place.

Discussion requiring direct, conversational interchange becomes more difficult for members as group size becomes large, but how many members constitute a large group depends on the circumstances. Particularly important to small-group discussion, as we have seen, is the fact that each person must be aware of and be able to react to each other individual. This kind of interaction becomes improbable when a group contains, say, fifteen or twenty persons or more.

James studied the size of a number of important groups and found they averaged from 4.7 to 7.8 members. Forty-six subcommittees of 11 U.S. Senate committees ranged in size from 2 to 12 and averaged 5.4 members. House of Representative groups were larger; 111 subcommittees of 14 committees had a range of 3 to 6 and averaged 7.8 members. Ninety-six state of Oregon executive, legislative, and judicial boards, departments and commissions ranged from 2 to 14 and averaged 5.7, while 19 Eugene (Oregon) city committees and boards, with a range of 3 to 11, averaged 4.7 members, smallest in the study. Twenty-nine subgroups of officer and board of director organizations of 4 large corporations averaged 5.3 members and had a range of 3 to 9. The secretary of a large bank, James reports, wrote that their action committees were smaller than nonaction groups, where objectives were to hear points of view and to test reactions.[18]

A question often asked is, how large should a committee be? Obviously it cannot have very many members if interaction is to be easy, although a maximally efficient number would depend on many complex factors. One study conducted by Slater involved groups ranging in size from two to seven. Members were asked when the group seemed too large or too small. Fewest complaints were received from groups of five:

> Groups larger than size four were never felt to be too small and groups smaller than six were never felt to be too large. Size five emerged clearly, therefore, as

[18] J. James, "A Preliminary Study of Size Determinant in Small Group Interaction," *American Sociological Review*, 16 (1951), pp. 474–7.

the size group which from the subjects' viewpoint was most effective in dealing with an intellectual task involving the collection and exchange of information about a situation, the coordination, analysis, and evaluation of this information, and a group decision regarding the appropriate administrative action to be taken in the situation.[19]

After studying interaction in many small groups, Bales recommends committees smaller than seven and larger usually than two or three.[20]

Larger groups have more resources. A greater number of persons represent a pool of skills available to the group and more different ideas can be expressed. Larger numbers, on the other hand, have an adverse effect on communication. As group size increases, there seem to be increasing restraints against communication, individuals report more feelings of inhibition and threat, and those least active in smaller groups tend to communicate even less. Whereas in groups of four or five each individual feels permitted to talk, only the forceful members may have the opportunity to speak when numbers are large.

As group size increases toward eight or twelve, there is increasing difference between the high participator and the next highest participator in the number of communications initiated. Even in groups of eight there are more persons who talk infrequently than in groups of three or four. In larger groups, some persons are inclined to be anonymous; they can remain silent without calling attention to themselves.

Not only do a few persons do more of the talking while many say little in larger groups, but also there is a tendency for persons when they do speak to make longer speeches. Participants may store up several matters to comment upon while waiting for an opportunity to contribute, and then talk for a longer time than they otherwise would because they feel they may not get the floor again. Another factor may be a result of the large group situation; the presence of many persons may suggest a public meeting, which calls for a public speech rather than a conversational effort. Whether from the monopolizing of talk by one or a few, or the length of speeches, or both, members of larger groups are more likely to feel that they have not had sufficient time for discussion.

More disagreement is expressed in groups of eight or ten than in groups of three or four. Slater has hypothesized that very small groups may inhibit aggressiveness. Disagreement may seem somewhat impolite, at least until some intimate group harmony develops. Slater feels that "physical freedom" is restricted in larger groups as members compete for the talking time, but that "psychological freedom" is increased in groups as large as ten because speakers can ignore some comments, be more forceful, or even "withdraw from the fray without loss of face." He proposes an "inhibition index" to

---

[19] Philip E. Slater, "Contrasting Correlates of Group Size," *Sociometry*, 21 (1958), pp. 129–39.

[20] R. F. Bales, "In Conference," *Harvard Business Review*, 32 (1954), pp. 44–50.

measure restraint against alienating others in the group. As the size increases, he feels, "the consequences of alienating a single member become less and less severe."[21]

This freedom to pursue controversy in groups larger than three or four may help explain why some persons feel that larger groups are disorderly and wasteful of time. On the other hand, if a designated leader supplies centralized control members tend to report dissatisfaction with the structure. Even in groups of seven as compared with those as small as two members, the larger groups were described in one study as too hierarchical, centralized and disorganized, and the members as aggressive, impulsive, competitive, and inconsiderate.[22]

As group size increases beyond seven, members have a multiplying number of interpersonal relationships to maintain and less time to maintain them. There seem to be fewer friendship choices and decreasing cohesiveness under these conditions. The evidence is ambiguous, however, as to whether members are less satisfied with the discussion and the decision in groups as large as ten. Members clearly report less opportunity to participate and some studies have found decreased satisfaction in larger groups. In groups of four or five, members usually are more satisfied with the discussion and their part in it. Larger groups are less stable and apparently place members under greater stress.

Thus, it is not safe to say that groups of four or five are necessarily more effective in decision-making. Larger groups may make a more thorough examination of the problem, but communication is more evenly distributed when members have opportunity to talk in smaller groups. More variety of suggestions and opinions and more resources are available in larger groups but group harmony may be better in smaller groups. The size group that is best depends on the thoroughness of discussion wanted, the importance of cohesiveness, and other factors. One guide may be to have the smallest number of persons who represent all the talents and resources needed, who can explore the problem fully, and who can produce the kind of harmony required.

When it is necessary for a designated leader to attempt to achieve direct, conversational interchange in a large group—of twenty or forty persons, for example—it is certain that his difficulties multiply rapidly. There is some evidence that in groups as large as twelve, groups are more likely to reach consensus if the leader is skillful in leading the discussion. Also, leaders in five-man groups have more influence on what the group decides than do leaders in the larger groups.[23] It is possible that leaders in twelve-man groups are busier controlling discussion, calling on participants, and guiding, and hence do not have as much time to contribute substantive remarks as do

---

[21] Slater.
[22] Slater.
[23] A. Paul Hare, "Interaction and Consensus in Different Sized Groups," *American Sociological Review*, 17 (1952), pp. 261–7.

leaders in groups of five. The larger the group, the more serious each of these problems is almost certain to become. Each of the leader's functions is likely to be more difficult. Apparently it is harder to maintain an orderly discussion, perhaps because speakers make several points when they get to speak, since opportunities are fewer, and because by the time a member is recognized, the comment he wishes to make is not as relevant as it was earlier.

Hemphill asked subjects to recall a group they had participated in and to evaluate its leadership. Their judgment was that, for superior leaders, as groups became larger than thirty-one members, there were greater and more numerous demands made upon the leader, but that tolerance for leader-centered direction of the group increased.[24]

In larger groups there is some tendency for groups to break into cliques, with spokesmen emerging as high participators. These spokesmen seem often to speak for others in addition to themselves. It is not uncommon to see others whispering suggestions to the spokesman for his next comment. It is certain that in very large groups—say forty or more—that a few individuals communicate most while many others contribute nothing. It is possible that within the large group there are smaller subgroups with similar notions that are communicated by one or two persons who represent the whole subgroup (see Chapter 18).

These, then, are the elements of input going into the interacting social system as the discussion gets underway. During the talk, these forces interrelate dynamically in what we can call intermediate interactional processes. These interactions could themselves be thought of as inputs, of course, but we are separating them from inputs here for purposes of analysis and orderly explanation.

INTERMEDIATE INTERACTIONS

These intermediate interactions are processes in which the input elements are modified and new ones generated during the discussion. The individuals and group characteristics are present to begin with, but the leadership patterns and the communication networks emerging can be thought of as new elements. The important fact is that the elements become interrelated throughout the period of the discussion in dynamic and ever changing ways. The interactions are complex and reciprocal.

These interactions will be enumerated here but will be discussed in Chapter 15. There are two reasons for developing them in a separate chapter on interaction. First, these matters are the elements in discussion most subject to control. That is, here the conscientious group member or leader can make the most difference through diligent study, careful application, and expenditure of energy during the discussion. While the individual may in some cases

---

[24] J. K. Hemphill, "Relations between the Size of the Group and the Behavior of 'Superior' Leaders," *Journal of Social Psychology*, 32 (1950), pp. 11–22.

be able to control the size of a discussion group, he can make more difference in the climate and the nature of the communications.

Second, the interaction processes have the most influence on the communication flow, which is one of our major interests, and is the first of the intermediate interactional processes.

While there are any number of interactions taking place during discussion, there seem to be four major ones that should be singled out for emphasis. They must be mentioned in this chapter in order for us to have a fairly complete picture of the major elements involved in group process.

1. The first is communication flow itself, which includes the networks of talk connecting each individual to the others. This element also includes patterns of participation such as the contribution of information, use of language and reasoning, offering of suggestions, asking for information and opinion, and so on.

2. Differences among members in their power and personal influence are a second element of interaction. It is obvious that some members have more influence than others and that the patterns of power relationships keep changing during discussion.

3. A third interactional element involves interpersonal relationships, including both the social climate and the task climate. Some of the dimensions here are sociability–hostility and harmony–conflict related to the persons as people; and the permissiveness created and maintained in allowing members to talk freely about the task. Another is the degree of conformity–creativity. Others are the agreement–disagreement and the cooperation–competition dimensions. Resolution of substantive conflict is an additional part of the task climate.

4. The contributions and shifting requirements of leadership constitute a fourth element. As we have observed in Part III, leadership is not a single, simple function of guidance but a many-faceted complex of influences coming from many sources. It can have remarkable impact on the direction and the results of discussion.

OUTCOMES

We have seen that individual and group characteristics are inputs to the interacting social system. These are modified by intermediate interactional processes, which in turn can be thought of as inputs. Both categories of initial and intermediate inputs lead hopefully at the end of decision-making discussion to outputs emerging as a result of the interactions. The major outputs of the system are (1) the decision; (2) member satisfaction with the decision; and (3) the resulting cohesiveness or group harmony. The first of these is related to the task assignment of the group; the second to the interrelationships between the task and the persons involved, taking into account their personal goals, aspirations for the particular discussion, and other factors of the individual's relationship to the group; and the third to the social functions of maintaining and perhaps solidifying the group as an operating social unit.

We will try to suggest here some of the results which are due to the elements of initial input. In this chapter we will deal only with the possible effects of the individuals involved and the group characteristics existing at the moment discussion begins. We will defer until the end of Chapter 15 an examination of the output resulting from the intermediate interactional processes.

It is impossible, of course, to trace a particular outcome back to a specific cause. Discussion is much too complex a set of interrelationships for simple explanations. At best, with our present evidence, we can only point to tendencies and probable influences. It is important for us to keep these limitations in mind when we attempt to make evaluations, but at the same time it is important that we make the attempt because only in this way can we begin to explain how leaders and participants should conduct themselves in order to produce desirable outcomes.

The Decision

Most of the time it is easy to tell when and whether the group has reached a decision, although it is not so easy to specify whether it is of high quality. We must remember that a decision is not ordinarily a final solution to a complicated problem and hence the decision may come to nothing within a short time. Nevertheless groups ordinarily strive to reach operationally defined decisions, which contribute to a solution of the larger problem.

Cartwright and Zander define a group goal as a location the group wishes to reach. Progress in the direction of the location can be thought of as locomotion toward the goal. Success of the discussion, in these terms, could be estimated by measuring the distance at any moment from the desired location. Completion of the task would consist of arriving at the location.[25] Since a single discussion group can have two or more goals, any one of which may compete with the others, this way of looking at the decision is helpful. Evaluating the group's productivity on the task is not a simple matter of saying whether the members did or did not agree on a decision.

Explaining why the group reached or failed to reach its task objectives is also a complex undertaking. There seems to be a relationship between task productivity and the quantity of information and other resources members have available. Participants who are cooperative and concerned for the group's welfare seem to reach agreement more readily, as do members who are friends or who have supportive interpersonal relationships.

[25] Dorwin Cartwright and Alvin Zander, *Group Dynamics: Research and Theory,* sec. ed., New York: Harper & Row, 1960, pp. 345–63.

When members are compatible they tend to be more productive than are participants who differ markedly. Close friends in groups seem to have higher morale, tend to influence each other more, and in some situations are more productive. In some studies, however, groups that were more heterogeneous tended to be more productive. The ambiguity in these outcomes may be due to variations in the kinds of studies and to difficulties in controlling the complex variables involved. Caution is necessary at any rate in drawing conclusions.

Groups having a clearly established and accepted structure of roles and status positions appear in general to be more productive, although the evidence is not plentiful as applied directly to discussion groups. Undoubtedly, however, it is easier to concentrate on the decision when members share expectations of acceptable communication behavior and at the same time are problem-oriented in the sense that they suppress their biases, do not allow conformity pressures to prevent thorough discussion, and bring much information to the group.

Continuing groups probably learn to be more efficient in discussion than do temporary groups, working out effective ways of proceeding. Experience with problem-solving should lead to higher productivity, just as does practice in other activities. Training in the procedures should increase effectiveness.

The acceptance by members of the group's goals also should mean better and easier decision-making although the relationship here is not likely a simple one. Members of discussion groups probably have an easier time working for common goals than do individuals in some other social situations. Ordinarily members of a discussion group come together because of the existence of some commonly held objectives or problem. Thus they often begin with the advantage of a common interest.

As we have seen, several factors in the situation affect the decision, including the time available, the location of the meeting, and the physical seating of participants. In general, task productivity is probably increased when members have adequate time for thorough consideration of the problem under favorable conditions of location and seating: a situation in which members are comfortable, can see and talk with each other easily, and feel that they can say openly what must be said about the problem for discussion.

The complexity and difficulty of the task assignment obviously influences the productivity. Groups can be more effective in discussing concrete, limited questions suited to member talents, resources, and outlook.

Group size affects decision quality indirectly as it restricts communication flow. A small group, ideally five to seven, can usually best reach a decision effectively, other factors being constant. As size increases, communication becomes more unbalanced, and other factors such as power structure, friendship cliques, and dominating communicators can exert disproportionate influence on the outcome. When the group is too large for interactional discussion, the decision must usually be reached by majority vote and automatically the minority will point to imperfections in the decision.

Satisfaction-Commitment

If a group has clear goals and achieves them efficiently, members naturally tend to be satisfied and to have high morale. If, on the other hand, a member's personal objectives are in conflict with the group goals, he will likely report dissatisfaction with the discussion. It is possible, also, to accept the general direction but to become dissatisfied with the means for reaching the objectives.

A relatively small group and the presence of persons who like and accept each other influence satisfaction indirectly, as is the case with productivity itself, by helping to increase the ease and quantity of communication. One basic ingredient for accepting the decision is the opportunity to talk fully about the problem as it is being discussed.

Cohesiveness

A third output is cohesiveness, the attractiveness of the group for the members. A particular group may gain in solidarity, or interpersonal relationships may deteriorate during discussion. Members who are attracted to each other communicate more and do so less aggressively and defensively. They are also more likely to emerge from the discussion with more harmonious group feelings, and to perceive others as doing well on the task performance. Whether productive groups foster harmonious relationships is unclear. In general, high productivity is rewarding and approved; there may well be in many situations a positive relationship between success on the task and personal attraction to the group.

Groups pursuing shared goals seem to develop "groupness" more easily than do groups in conflict, as do groups with a small proportion of members with self-oriented needs. Interpersonal relationships are probably strengthened when members accept the role structure and behave in expected ways.

Individual characteristics such as cooperativeness, maturity and being an accepting person tend to help cohesiveness and friendliness, while striving for prominence or being a suspicious, nonaccepting person may inhibit unity.[26] Naturally, groups are more attractive if members feel secure in them, attain prestige from membership, and enjoy social approval during interaction.

It is probably easier to increase social harmony when the group is small and homogeneous. Increasing size may mean the formation of cliques, which makes solidarity across the whole group more difficult. Whereas heterogeneous groups have more resources to apply to task productivity, members who are more alike tend to be more compatible and their groups more unified.

While the initial elements of input influence group cohesiveness to some

---

[26] William Haythorn, "The Influence of Individual Members on the Characteristics of Small Groups," A. Paul Hare, E. F. Borgatta, and R. F. Bales, *Small Groups: Studies in Social Interaction*, rev. ed., New York: Alfred A. Knopf, 1966, pp. 287–97.

extent, much of the effect of discussion on "groupness" is mediated through the operation of the intermediate interactional processes, to which we turn next in Chapter 15.

SUPPLEMENTARY READING

Asch, Solomon E., *Social Psychology*, Englewood Cliffs, N.J.: Prentice-Hall, 1952, pp. 450–501.

Barnlund, Dean C., and Haiman, Franklyn, *The Dynamics of Discussion*, Boston: Houghton Mifflin, 1960, Chapter 9.

Cartwright, Dorwin, and Zander, Alvin, *Group Dynamics: Research and Theory*, sec. ed., New York: Harper & Row, 1960.

Collins, Barry E., and Guetzkow, Harold, *A Social Psychology of Group Processes for Decision-Making*, New York: John Wiley & Sons, 1964.

Eisenson, Jon, Auer, J. J., and Irwin, J. V., *The Psychology of Communication*, New York: Appleton-Century-Crofts, 1963, Chapters 14 and 15.

Hare, A. Paul, *Handbook of Small Group Research*, New York: The Free Press, 1962.

———, Borgatta, E. F., and Bales, R. F., *Small Groups: Studies in Social Interaction*, rev. ed., New York: Alfred A. Knopf, 1966, Part III.

McGrath, Joseph E., and Altman, Irwin, *Small Group Research*, New York: Holt, Rinehart and Winston, 1966, Chapter 6.

QUESTIONS AND EXERCISES

1. Make a careful listing of the many groups of which you are a member. This list will be more extensive than the roster of formal organizations to which you belong. Classify these groups by locating each along these three continua: (a) formal to informal; (b) cohesive to uncohesive; (c) primary to secondary.
2. Can you distinguish between your own membership groups and reference groups? Are they identical?
3. In your observation, does specialization of function and the emergence of differentiated roles for members of the group help or hinder a discussion? Can there be overspecialization?
4. Discuss the implications of the pressure in a group to conform for both the discussion participant and leader. Refer to the studies cited in this chapter.
5. Name several examples of momentary and continuing groups.
6. Observe a group discussion. Try to record from direct observation evidences that the members are interdependent.
7. Observe a discussion and be prepared to make a 2-minute oral report in which you explain any indications you observed of cohesiveness or lack

of it within the group. Explain whether it increased or decreased during the discussion, and why.

8. Attend a meeting where a small-group discussion occurs. See if you can tell from observing and listening the real goals of the discussion; to what extent each member accepts the group's goals as his own; and the symptoms of conflict between group goals and individual goals and needs. Report your findings to the class.

9. Can you think of other elements of initial input going into the interactional system visualized in this chapter? If so, what effects do you believe they have on outputs?

10. Write a critique of the conception introduced here of the discussion group as an interacting social system. What are the advantages and disadvantages of analyzing discussion in this way? What risks do we take by using this analogy with more concrete and mechanistic technological systems?

11. Can you list expectations about appropriate communication behavior common to our society and culture other than those named in this chapter? In what ways do such expectations differ in other societies and cultures?

12. Observe a discussion in a group of twenty; try to find a situation where the group is large enough that interactional discussion is difficult but small enough that the group is attempting to use discussion rather than parliamentary procedure. Write a paper explaining the problems introduced by group size and the differences between discussion in this situation and discussion in a group of five to seven.

13. We have had space here to give only limited treatment to the effect which the pressure of majority opinion has on the minority. Make a study of the relevant literature on this matter and write a paper explaining how this pressure operates in discussion.

14. Write a paper similar to the one assigned in 13 above on the differences between expressions of opinion when the meeting is private and when the statements involve a public commitment.

Chapter 15

INTERMEDIATE INTERACTIONS

Now that we have taken a look at the elements of group process and their interrelationships, we should examine in some detail the intermediate interactional processes which also influence the outcomes of discussion. We have considered the small-group discussion as an interacting social system where individual qualities and group characteristics are initial inputs. During discussion these inputs are modified by a number of intermediate processes which are instrumental in determining whether a group is productive and harmonious, or inefficient and hostile. These intermediate interactions are also vital because of their relationships to communication flow. Communication, the most important facet of interaction, is central to the whole process of decision-making by group effort.

While considering these factors, we must keep in mind that interaction is neither simple nor easily predictable. It is possible to explain some of the tendencies within groups, but it should be emphasized that these are tendencies, not invariable relationships. It is unwise to attempt to form generalizations applicable to every discussion situation involving every type of person. What we can do here is to examine the four major interactions occurring while a discussion is in progress: communication flow itself, power relationships, interpersonal relationships, and leadership. There are other interrelationships, of course, but these seem to be the key influences on outcomes. Our purposes are to explain what happens during discussion, and, if possible, why it happens and with what results.

COMMUNICATION FLOW

It is important first to make clear the difference between interaction and communication. Social interaction is the more general process and involves all behavioral manifestations occurring when two or more persons relate themselves reciprocally. They see each other, they take each other into account, and they may or may not communicate by sending and receiving intended messages. Communication is one kind of interaction, probably the most important and frequently encountered kind. It occurs in discussion when members initiate messages consisting of words, gestures, facial expressions, etc., intended to elicit meanings and responses in the others.

Some communication is consummatory: it expresses an emotional state such as joy, anger, or hostility and may serve to reduce the tensions of the speaker rather than further the purposes of the group. The communication we are interested in, however, is instrumental. It is initiated because it contributes to the group's task achievements or to interpersonal relationships, which become rewarding to the individuals communicating. Some consummatory expressions may contribute to interpersonal relations but these are minor in importance.

In studying communicative interchange among group members, there is constant risk of oversimplification, but we must analyze the process by breaking it down into components. Most of the communicative interaction in discussion can be examined by answering the key question: Who says What to Whom? During interaction, communications are initiated by individuals in the group; we can ask who initiates messages when, how often, why, etc. What is said is also vital; what kinds of messages are being communicated with what intent? A third aspect is the destination to which messages are addressed, the extent to which messages are directed to individuals, to certain persons more than others, and to the group as a whole.

This key question also suggests a definition of communication structure; it is the pattern, over a period of time, of the communicative interchange, or the continuous matrix of who says what to whom.

As we have observed in several other places earlier, communication is important to discussion in many ways. It is the medium through which members affect the views of others. Without talk, there would be virtually no modification. Communication allows the group to move toward greater uniformity of opinion through the use of information and reasoning, the testing of argument, and the application of judgment and experience. Through the feedback made easy and simple by small-group communication, accuracy and quality of decisions can be improved. Through practice in communicating together, continuing groups shorten the time needed to reach decisions and also to increase decision quality.

One general aspect of the operation of communication involves the study of communication networks. These consist of positions in a hierarchy and the interconnecting channels that provide open pathways for messages. Many theoretical structures have been studied, such as the circle, chain, Y, wheel, the all-channel, and the two-level hierarchy, shown in Figure 15.1.

The research on networks is more applicable to a hierarchy in a military organization or an industrial corporation than to small face-to-face discussion groups. In a corporation where department heads report to division chiefs, chiefs to vice-presidents, etc., the Y network or a combination of the Y and wheel may represent the channels of communication. The findings from this research may give us some clues about communication in discussion, however, since some of the studies have included the all-channel network characteristic of direct interactional discussion. In such a network, every individual is free to talk with every other, without relaying messages through intermediaries.

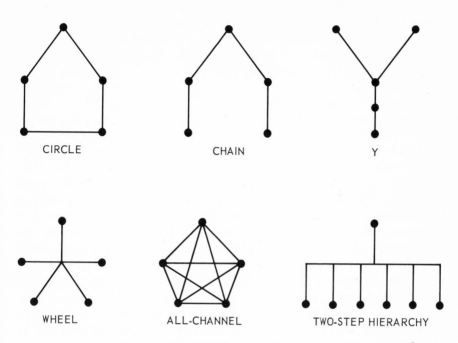

CIRCLE   CHAIN   Y

WHEEL   ALL-CHANNEL   TWO-STEP HIERARCHY

FIGURE 15–1   *Some experimentally created communication networks.*

Even here, of course, most of the data was collected in studies where notes were passed or some communication channel was used other than direct face-to-face conversation. We must keep these limitations in mind when considering the network studies.

These studies have shown that the positions and the channels open in a network affect the amount, flow, speed, and efficiency of communication transmission. The more central positions, those closest and most open to the other positions, tend to be best in promoting rapid and accurate communication. Members have often reported being better satisfied when they occupy a central rather than a peripheral position, although the findings are not consistent. Rigid leadership control is more possible in the wheel or the two-step hierarchy than in the looser arrangement of the circle, where each member may communicate only with the person on either side of himself. However, circle members seem to send more information, give more answers, provide more feedback, and correct more of their errors than some of the more organized networks. Members seem to have higher morale in the circle than in the wheel. Thus the wheel may provide efficiency at the cost of morale while the circle may mean higher satisfaction and more communication but some loss in control and some confusion. There is some indication in the studies that the all-channel network may enjoy a medium position between the wheel and circle, having some of the virtues of both and fewer of the disadvantages. Until we have additional studies and clearer theoretical explanation of what is operating in a network, however, we must refrain from drawing any conclusions.

We have somewhat better information about the initiation, content, and destination of communications in discussion.

Initiation of Communications

Some members of a discussion group communicate markedly more than do others. Which persons tend to talk most? For one, a designated leader is in a position to be a high participator. Those who are in central locations tend to initiate more contributions. Other high participators may be those who have the largest amount of information relevant to the problem being discussed. Obviously, also, some individuals are personally more talkative than others or less inhibited by the presence of others.

The gradient of rate of participation often falls sharply from the high participator to the lowest. There are some indications that individuals have a characteristic level of contribution that they tend to attain in different situations, although there is also some evidence that a low participator may talk more than is his habit if placed in a position of centrality. Of course, as Bales says, it is desirable to have a gradient of participation.[1] A group composed entirely of high participators or of low participators would have some obvious difficulties.

More communications tend to be initiated when the subject for discussion is important to the functioning of the group. Schacter experimented with discussion groups in which the group task was relevant or largely irrelevant to the group's purposes. There was clearly more pressure to communicate in the groups where the problem was related to the functioning of the group.[2] Attempts to encourage participation from low participators should be made in the areas of concern to them; otherwise persons are unmotivated to take part.[3]

More communications are initiated when the group is highly cohesive. A study by Back varied the attractiveness of groups in various ways. The results suggest that the more cohesive groups engaged in more intensive rates of communication.[4]

Previous acquaintance of members and the presence of friends within the group may lead to increased communication. There is some evidence that friendship reduces communication barriers, and observation suggests that it is easier to talk with friends. Hence, members of friendly continuing groups may tend to initiate more communications than do those in momentary groups.

[1] R. F. Bales, "In Conference," *Harvard Business Review*, 32 (1954), pp. 44–50.
[2] S. Schacter, "Deviation, Rejection, and Communication," *Journal of Abnormal and Social Psychology*, 46 (1951), pp. 190–207.
[3] Leland P. Bradford, "A Fundamental of Democracy," *Adult Education*, 2 (1952), pp. 146–9.
[4] Kurt W. Back, "Influence Through Social Communications," *Journal of Abnormal and Social Psychology*, 46 (1951), pp. 9–23.

The smaller the group, the more communications each person will initiate, simply because, in a given time, there is more individual opportunity for communication. As group size increases, the rate of member contribution may decrease because there is usually a limited number of alternative solutions to any problem and the likelihood increases that some member has already said what other members intended to contribute. Bradford points to the anonymity phenomenon as groups get larger. On the other hand, in a large group there will be more diversity of opinion and a wider variety of ideas.[5]

The larger the group, the more marked tends to be the differential rate of participation between the highest and the second highest participator, while the rate of participation of members other than the high participators tends to be more nearly equal in large groups than in small groups. Often in groups of thirty or forty, many persons will say nothing at all.

What Is Communicated

Kinds of content communicated—what members say—may be classified in one manner as Robert F. Bales has done. After extensive research and elaboration of his system, he has arrived at a classification of communications into twelve categories:[6]

A. POSITIVE REACTIONS	1. *Shows solidarity*, raises other's status, gives help, reward 2. *Shows tension release*, jokes, laughs, shows satisfaction 3. *Agrees*, shows passive acceptance, understands, concurs, complies
B. ATTEMPTED ANSWERS	4. *Gives suggestions*, direction, implying autonomy for other 5. *Gives opinion*, evaluation, analysis, expresses feeling, wish 6. *Gives orientation*, information, repeats, clarifies, confirms
C. QUESTIONS	7. *Asks for orientation*, information, repetition, confirmation 8. *Asks for opinion*, evaluation, analysis, expression of feeling 9. *Asks for suggestion*, direction, possible ways of action
D. NEGATIVE REACTIONS	10. *Disagrees*, shows passive rejection, formality, withholds help 11. *Shows tension*, asks for help, withdraws out of field 12. *Shows antagonism*, deflates other's status, defends or asserts self

[5] Leland P. Bradford, "Leading the Large Meeting," *Adult Education Bulletin*, 14 (1949), pp. 38–50.

[6] Reproduced from Robert F. Bales, *Interaction Process Analysis*, Cambridge, Mass.: Addison-Wesley, 1950, Chart 1, p. 9. Used by permission of the author.

Communications are either questions or answers, or positive or negative reactions. Within these four major groupings, there are subdivisions which specify in greater detail the type of message. Bales and his colleagues use this system for recording during a discussion the communications sent; of course, the system is much more elaborate than the part reproduced here may suggest. It is possible to indicate, after making such an analysis, whether there were more positive or negative reactions, more questions than attempted answers, and many other facts about the discussion. This Bales proposal for interaction-process analysis is only one method which has been devised for classifying kinds of messages.

Bales and his colleagues have found that only about half of a group's communication time is taken up with substantive matters, the other half being used for questions and positive or negative reactions. Scheidel and Crowell confirm this finding using their own system of interaction recording. About half the time is spent on feedback, substantiating what has already been said, clarifying, repeating, etc.[7]

What is communicated tends to change as the discussion proceeds. Early in the consideration of a problem there are more communications asking for information, clarification, and orientation. As the discussion proceeds, information seeking decreases and opinion giving and expressions of agreement increase.

Strong friendship ties among members may contribute to the communication of non-task-related and socially oriented contributions. In a study of industrial work groups, Horsfall and Arensberg found that the least productive groups indulged in the most social activity.[8]

The content of communications initiated may be affected also by the abilities of the participants as these are related to the needs of the group at a particular moment. For example, individuals in the group may develop specialized roles by developing reputations for being dependable clarifiers of complex points, for having the facts, for reconciling conflicts, or for reducing tension through the use of humor, etc.

Minority views tend to get communicated more often if the leader supplies encouragement to persons expressing them. Maier and Solem found that the presence of a leader in discussion increased group productivity: groups with leaders reached a correct solution to a mathematical problem more often than did leaderless groups—largely because the leader influenced the group to listen more carefully to minority opinions. In this experiment, involving sixty-seven groups, the initial majority view was wrong and the minority opinion was right enough times to make a substantial difference in the final outcome. In the groups that had an observer but no leader, the group did not change as

[7] Thomas M. Scheidel and Laura Crowell, "Idea Development in Small Discussion Groups," *Quarterly Journal of Speech*, 50 (1964), pp. 140–5.

[8] A. B. Horsfall and C. M. Arensberg, "Teamwork and Productivity in a Shoe Factory," *Human Organization*, 8 (1949), pp. 13–25.

often in the direction of the minority view, even though it was affirmed later as the correct one.[9]

Notice that the recording of who says what to whom says nothing about the quality of contributions. An evaluation of the worth of each communication would be useful additional information. In terms of what is communicated, it is safe to say that some individuals make contributions of higher quality, supply more relevant information which the group needs at a particular moment, and offer more new alternatives for action.

Destination of Communications

To whom are communications directed in discussion? The available evidence suggests that high participators and those high in power tend to direct more contributions to the group as a whole than to specific individuals. In contrast, low participators and those low in power tend to direct more contributions to other individuals than to the group as a whole. Limited evidence indicates that about half the communications in some kinds of discussion are directed to the group as a whole. Obviously this proportion would be affected by a wide range of variables.

In many situations, more communications are directed to the designated leader than to other members. Those high in power may also be recipients of more than average amounts of communications. Bales and his colleagues found that, in small groups, those who initiated the most communications also tended to receive most.[10]

Communications tend to be directed to a deviate—one who disagrees with the others—until the group decides that his views cannot be reconciled with the group view. Then the deviate is rejected and communications to him decrease or stop entirely. Festinger and Thibaut found a disproportionately large number of communications addressed to those taking nonconforming views. A majority of the communications—from 70 per cent to 90 per cent— were directed to those who had expressed opinions divergent from the majority. As the deviate's views moved toward the majority position, communications addressed to him decreased rapidly.[11] Schacter obtained similar results and discovered that nonconformists who resisted group influence tended to be rejected. He planted persons in groups with instructions to disagree with the majority and stay with their divergent position no matter what the others said. Members tended to "throw this person out of the group" —figuratively. As members recognize the deviate as a person who is not a member of the group, or who does not wish to be, or if members do not

[9] Norman R. F. Maier, and A. R. Solem, "The Contribution of a Discussion Leader to the Quality of Group Thinking: the Effective Use of Minority Opinions," *Human Relations*, 5 (1952), pp. 277–88.

[10] R. F. Bales *et al*, "Channels of Communication in Small Groups," *American Sociological Review*, 16 (1951), pp. 46–8.

[11] L. Festinger and J. Thibaut, "Interpersonal Communication in Small Groups," *Journal of Abnormal and Social Psychology*, 46 (1951), pp. 92–9.

wish him to be a part of the group, communications to him tend to decrease.[12] On the other hand, members increase their communications to the deviate if they feel they can influence him to change in the direction of majority opinion.

Members may address more communications to those seated opposite, although the influence of seating positions is not clear from the limited evidence.[13]

POWER RELATIONSHIPS

A second intermediate process in interaction is the operation of the power some members have over others. As we examine this and other aspects of interaction, it will be obvious that we are still talking primarily about communication. Communication structure was treated separately above because of its particular importance, but that was not intended to suggest that any part of interaction can be described without including consideration of communication.

Students of discussion must understand the influence of power relationships upon communication patterns during discussion, and, hence, upon group productivity and member commitment to the outcome. The interrelationship between power and group process is exemplified in the meetings of industrial leaders. For example, in attempting to train executive- and middle-management men for better planning and conducting of meetings, one industrial group reported:

> Bridging communication gaps between different management levels was a major problem. The seminars revealed, for instance, that lower-level managers had been afraid to speak up firmly to their superiors. Because top executives were listened to more closely, they tended to participate vigorously in any discussion. Lower-level managers, however, sat on the sidelines in most meetings simply because their opinions carried less prestige weight. A full awareness of this problem was the first step in solving it.[14]

Definitions

Power in discussion means simply the capacity to influence the work of the group and of the individuals present. Influence attempts may be direct or power may operate indirectly. The basis for influence may be the attractiveness of the person or the fact that he is liked, is respected and esteemed. The influencer may have power because of his expert knowledge or because he has authority over members and can give or withhold rewards.

One kind of indirect influence is behavioral contagion, which occurs when

---

[12] Schacter.

[13] Bernard Steinzor, "The Spatial Factor in Face to Face Discussion Groups," A. Paul Hare, E. F. Borgatta, and R. F. Bales, *Small Groups*, New York: Alfred A. Knopf, 1955, p. 348.

[14] "Reform in the Conference Room," *Dun's Review and Modern Industry*, 69 (1957), p. 64.

an individual's behavior is imitated by others without any conscious intent on his part to lead the others to copy him. When a popular sorority girl adopts a new hair style, other girls in the house may soon appear with the same style. In discussion, one person's suggestion may be taken up by the group spontaneously.

Power relationships are the lines or networks of influence within the group during the discussion. These may also be referred to as the power structures. There may be several different grids of attraction, expert power, authority, and other kinds of influence operating at the same time.

Sources of Power

There seem to be two important and general kinds of power operative in discussion groups, springing from different sources.

One kind we can call *positional power*, which comes from the individual's position within a set of hierarchies recognized by the group. Examples are numerous. The holder of a particular title or job will have high status with some groups and he may use this status as a source of power. He may be chairman of the board of directors or president of the company; he may be a professor meeting with a student group or the president of the university meeting with a faculty group; he may be the mayor within a city council or the prime minister in a summit meeting. Seniority is another type of positional power; a man may have power within an industrial group if he has been with the company since it was founded; the alderman with thirty years service may have high status in the city council; the elders on a church board have power there. The person of wealth may have power in some groups: he may be the member of the board of directors who owns the largest bloc of stock in the company; he may be the member of the YMCA board whose grandfather owned the land, built the building, and endowed the institution, and who is the wealthiest supporter and the best potential source of financial aid. Still another source of positional power comes from social standing. In some groups a person of influence may be a woman who lives "in a big house on the hill" and who speaks for those who have social prestige in the community, or the member of a student committee who represents the best—that is, the most prestigious fraternity on the campus.

A position may give its holder high influence if he has authority over others. The boss has legitimate power over employees and influences them because he can confer or withhold rewards. An assignment as designated leader within a group itself may be a source of positional power.

A second kind is called *earned power*, which comes from the individual's behavior in the past or during the discussion, when he earns a reputation for having certain abilities. This kind of power is particularly important in continuing groups. For example, an individual may have status because he is educated or competent, or he may earn a reputation for being honest and frank. Another may have prestige because of his ability to restate and clarify complex points. An individual may consistently contribute proposals for action which later prove sound. In other ways he may gain in influence because of past successes in or out of the group. Another member may exercise power because he has helpful insights and contributes ideas that lead to break-throughs. Others may have influence because of friendship ties. In many situations, of course, power due to competence or knowledge of the problem will be tied to the problem. Those who are influential may thus shift from time to time within a discussion and from meeting to meeting of continuing groups.

Whether a member makes direct influence attempts, or affects others through contagion, the extent to which the group follows may depend, among other things, on the initiator's positional or earned power within the group. Of course, different groups will react to power figures in different ways.

Measurements of Power

It may be useful at times to have a measuring device for estimating the extent of influence being exerted by an individual.

Goldhamer and Shils propose that power in a group be measured by the ratio of the number of successful power acts to the number of direct influence attempts:[15]

$$\frac{\text{number of successful power acts}}{\text{number of attempts made}}$$

Lippitt et. al. suggest two measures. The first is an index of attributed power, obtained by asking each member of the group to estimate the extent to which each other member has influence over the other fellow. Thus, the index is a measure of the influence attributed to others. The second is an index of manifest power, which measures the "behavioral success the member has in attempting to influence others." This second index is similar to the Goldhamer and Shils' ratio.[16]

Consequences of Power

What is important here is the effect that power discrepancies within the group have on interaction during the discussion. Ultimately, the student of discussion must decide what leaders and participants can do to increase group productivity, given the kind of power relationships that exist within a particular group.

Highs tend to make more influence attempts than do lows. Strodtbeck in a study of husband-wife discussion pairs discovered that the member of the

---

[15] H. Goldhamer and E. Shils, "Types of Power and Status," *American Journal of Sociology*, 45 (1939), pp. 171–82.

[16] Ronald Lippitt *et al*, "The Dynamics of Power," Dorwin Cartwright and Alvin Zander, *Group Dynamics: Research and Theory*, 2nd. ed., New York: Harper & Row, 1960, pp. 745–65.

pair who exerted more influence on the outcome after discussion was also the one who talked more. He compared husband–wife discussions among Mormons, Navahos, and Texans in the Southwest. Husband and wife were asked to make independent judgments on a problem and then to reconcile their differences through interaction. Among the Mormons, the husband generally had more influence than the wife; the opposite outcome occurred more often among the Navahos. Among the Texans, husbands and wives were dominant about an equal number of times. Strodtbeck relates his findings to the fact that the man is the dominant partner among the Mormons, while the wife has more influence in Navaho culture. Thus, the person with greater power had more influence on the decision.[17]

A study in a boys' camp revealed not only that highs make more frequent influence attempts, but also they are more likely to be successful. This study also suggests that the group is more likely to be influenced by high-power members both through behavioral contagion and through direct influence attempts. Bass and Wurster, in a study of leadership performance of oil refinery supervisors in small groups, found that high-ranking company supervisors usually had more influence than did average- or low-power members. This influence seemed especially effective when the problem for discussion was related to the company and to situations in which the company hierarchy was recognized as relevant.[18]

Whereas highs are more likely to make direct influence attempts, average- and low-power members are more likely to make nondirective influence attempts. That is, highs are more likely to say, "We should do this," while lows tend to say, "Do you think we might consider this as a possibility?" or "One company tried this solution, but I don't know whether the rest of you think it would work here."

Average- and low-power members tend to exhibit deferential behavior in their relations with highs. A number of studies have found that low-power members often direct their communications toward persons with higher status. One explanation offered is that persons low in status who wish to improve their positions tend to use upward communication as a substitute for being able actually to move upward in the hierarchy. Hurwitz, Zander, and Hymovitch found that "group members occupying low-status positions will perceive and behave toward high-status members in an essentially egodefensive manner, i.e., in ways calculated to reduce the feeling of uneasiness experienced in their relations with highs." Both highs and lows, they discovered, generally like high-status persons more than they do lows; both want more to be liked by highs. Highs feel freer to talk and talk mainly to other highs, while lows communicate less, and when they talk, address their remarks mainly to highs.

[17] F. L. Strodtbeck, "Husband-Wife Interaction over Revealed Differences," *American Sociological Review*, 16 (1951), pp. 468–73.

[18] B. M. Bass and C. R. Wurster, "Effects of the Nature of the Problem on LGD Performance," *Journal of Applied Psychology*, 37 (1953), pp. 96–9.

Lows tend to exaggerate the extent to which highs like them. "*Lows* will be liked less than *highs* by *highs* and *lows* alike; there will be less of a desire among all group members to be liked by *lows*, and fewer communications will be directed to them."[19] Thus in some groups there is a tendency for the highs to form cliques within the larger group.

While lows seem to behave in self-effacing ways in the presence of highs, this reaction is lessened for lows who have the active support of other low-influence persons. In a discussion, the backing of even one peer may enable a low-power member to resist conformity pressures, to challenge the fallacious reasoning of a high, or in other ways to operate more nearly as a high would.

Highs are influential in directing the behavior of members lower in power but they themselves tend successfully to resist being influenced by others. For similar reasons high-power figures can violate group norms with less fear of reprisal.

There is some evidence that persons low in power are more likely than highs to communicate messages that are not relevant to the group's task, such as complaints or criticisms of the task and the group. "The more unpleasant is a position in a hierarchy," Harold Kelley reports, "the stronger are the forces on a person to communicate task-irrelevant content."[20]

For obvious reasons, persons holding high-power positions feel more satisfied and more rewarded when they occupy such positions.

There is some indication that the existence of stable power relationships recognized by the group increases group productivity and member satisfaction. Heinicke and Bales created temporary discussion groups and observed them for four sessions. In some groups, the power relations became standardized and members recognized the stable status positions. In others, the power relationships fluctuated and there was disagreement among members as to which persons exercised greater influence. The results of the study suggest that the groups which recognized stable power relations were more satisfied with the outcome and reached agreements more efficiently. Apparently members in the unstabilized situation consumed some energy fighting for position and trying to discover the lines of influence, while the settled group spent a greater proportion of its energy on the task.[21]

Low-power members apparently feel threatened when the power structure is ambiguous, perhaps because it is not clear who can withhold rewards or can influence what the group decides.

When the power hierarchy is clear, a larger number of communications are

[19] J. Hurwitz, A. Zander, and B. Hymovitch, "Some Effects of Power on the Relations Among Group Members," in Dorwin Cartwright and Alvin Zander, *Group Dynamics: Research and Theory*, 2nd ed., New York: Harper & Row, 1960, pp. 800–809.

[20] H. H. Kelly, "Communication in Experimentally-Created Hierarchies," *Human Relations*, 4 (1951), pp. 39–56.

[21] C. Heinicke and R. F. Bales, "Developmental Trends in the Structure of Small Groups," *Sociometry*, 16 (1953), pp. 7–38.

directed to highs than would otherwise be the case. In fact, directing communications to highs may be socially rewarding to lows and may be an extension of the finding that lows behave deferentially toward high-power members. If the power structure is unclear, as is the case in leaderless discussion among comparative strangers, persons who aspire to high power may direct more of their communications to lows than they would if a clear structure existed or if they were not interested in raising their influence potential.

The available evidence on power relationships enables Cartwright and Zander to suggest the following effects on group discussion. They propose that an observer may be able to identify a vice-president and a junior executive of a company during discussions because of the differences in their behavior:

> The man whom you believe to be the junior executive addresses the majority of his remarks to the man you believe to be the vice-president. Moreover, he chooses his words with care in order that he not seem to imply any criticism of the other man or appear inadequate. He listens carefully to what the vice-president has to say and is usually ready to see the reasonableness of the arguments made by him. He is friendly toward the boss, ready to tell a joke or talk about his family, and to copy some of the older man's mannerisms.
>
> In contrast, the vice-president talks pretty much to the entire group. He freely offers information, advice, and even criticism to others. He seldom makes critical remarks about himself. Nor is he nearly so ready as the younger man to listen to statements made by the rest of the group. He is more likely to defend his own position than to see the value in the points made by the staff. And on the whole he is less inclined to idle talk than is the junior executive.
>
> You may come away from the meeting feeling that the two men acted the way they did because they had quite different personalities, and you would undoubtedly be correct—in part. If, however, you were to see the junior executive in a meeting with *his* staff in which he is now the boss, you would probably be surprised to see how different he behaves. Now it is likely that you would find the young man acting toward others in a way very similar to that shown by the vice-president in the earlier meeting.[22]

Zander and Cohen describe a classroom demonstration in which two strangers were introduced into the group and identified as a Dean and a freshman. Toward the one perceived in a high-power role, members of the class appeared "attentive and appreciative," while they were "less interested in one to whom they assign little power."[23] This description confirms what anyone can observe in a social group. For effective discussion the problem is to minimize the restricting effects of such power discrepancies.

[22] Dorwin Cartwright and Alvin Zander, *Group Dynamics: Research and Theory,* New York: Harper & Row, 1953, p. 415. Used by permission of the publisher.

[23] Alvin Zander and A. R. Cohen, "Attributed Social Power and Group Acceptance: A Classroom Experimental Demonstration," *Journal of Abnormal and Social Psychology,* 51 (1955), pp. 490–2.

INTERPERSONAL RELATIONSHIPS

Another vital influence on interaction is explainable in terms of interpersonal relationships among members. Given two individuals to whom we attribute equal amounts of power, we may feel relaxed in the presence of one and quite tense interacting with the other. With one we may enjoy communicating, and with the other we may be constantly on our guard. In a situation of free choice, we may seek out one and avoid the other. One we may find stimulating and the other difficult to listen to carefully. One's suggestions may usually seem reasonable and acceptable, while we may find ourselves dissecting hypercritically the suggestions of the other. One we like and the other we dislike.

Definition

Interpersonal relationships are those aspects of interaction that affect the way each individual reacts to each other individual in the group as a person.

Our reactions to other persons are extremely complex and involve all the attributes of whatever it means to be human and to interact within a group which is part of a society that has developed particular cultural patterns. It is impossible to consider here all these complex relationships. Instead, it is feasible to examine the dimensions of personal reaction that seem especially important in group discussion, and attempt to explain some of their effects on interaction. These dimensions overlap, of course, and are different views of much the same phenomena.

Interpersonal attraction is related to the way each individual estimates his own and others' attitudes, status, and power as these are affected by interaction in the discussion situation. Some group discussions are more satisfying, rewarding, and productive than others; hence attractiveness of the other individuals present will be altered. Persons who are pleasant, help the group, or have power to reward others are more attractive. In turn, these attractive individuals respond by liking those who obviously like them. Thus interpersonal relationships have a reciprocal, circular quality leading toward friendliness and harmony or toward increasing hostility or at least caution in interacting.

The Like-Dislike Dimension

To put the matter simply, we like some persons in the group more than we like others. For us explain why we like or dislike a certain individual, and how much, is more difficult. It is an easy reaction for us, nevertheless, to record which members of the group attract us most as persons.

To record such reactions, individuals are asked to make sociometric choices, as first suggested by J. L. Moreno in his book, *Who Shall Survive?*[24] Members of a limited group—each person is able to react to every other individual—

[24] Washington, D. C.: *Nervous and Mental Disease Monograph*, No. 58, 1934.

are asked to choose an unlimited number of other persons in the group with whom they would prefer to be associated in some specific social situation. Preferences of each individual are then represented schematically on a sociogram. This diagrammatic representation indicates which individuals are chosen by many others. These are called *stars* by Moreno. It also shows which persons make mutual choices (indicating a paired or triangular relationship), and which neither prefer anyone nor are preferred. Those in the final category are called *isolates*; some researchers have designated as isolates the underchosen as well as the unchosen.

To diagram like-dislike preferences in a discussion group, it would be possible to ask each person to respond to the following request:

> Assume that you and the members of your immediate family are planning to take a long automobile trip during your vacation next summer, and that you have room in the car for one more passenger. List the members of this group in the order in which you would prefer to have them accompany you on this trip.

Research with young children usually involves simpler questions, such as, "which members of the group would you most enjoy playing games with?"

The sociograms derived show which persons like whom. This procedure is not feasible, of course, in most actual discussion situations, and leaders and participants must learn to estimate the like-dislike network by subtler methods.

Interaction is easier among persons who are attracted to each other. One of the most helpful studies in this area is the one by Deutsch, in which he created cooperative and competitive groups. Observers who rated the discussions reported "significantly fewer communication difficulties" in cooperative than in competitive groups. Since apparently there was more friendliness in the cooperative groups, this finding seems to apply indirectly to the like-dislike dimension.[25]

Other things being equal, we probably communicate more freely to those we like and to those we perceive as liking us. Thus communication rate increases in the group when interpersonal relationships are harmonious. When members talk with friends or other accepting, approving persons, they tend to exhibit less defensiveness and aggressiveness, and, in turn, are more attentive when others talk.

Studies of rumor transmission offer evidence that communication barriers are reduced among friends, and this finding may help to explain communication rates in the discussion situation. Husband found that pairs of close friends completed tasks involving communication more rapidly than did pairs of strangers.[26] In Deutsch's study, cooperative group members tended to learn somewhat more from each other than did competitive group members. There was more "mutual comprehension of communication" in cooperative groups.

[25] Morton Deutsch, "The Effects of Cooperation and Competition Upon Group Process," *Human Relations*, 2 (1949), pp. 129–52, 199–231.

[26] R. W. Husband, "Cooperative Versus Solitary Problem Solution," *Journal of Social Psychology*, 11 (1950), pp. 405–9.

Discussion participants tend to be influenced by persons they like. Deutsch asked his subjects, "How did you react to the ideas or suggestions of others?" and "How frequently was your own thinking or reaction affected by what the others were saying?" Those in the cooperative groups reported that they were affected by the ideas of others significantly more than were those in competitive groups. Further, cooperative group members "were markedly more agreeable and acceptant toward the ideas initiated by others."

A study of a discussion workshop showed a strong relationship between the tendency to agree with an assertion and the tendency to like the asserter. Moreover, members perceived that persons they liked were more apt to agree with their assertions.[27]

When interpersonal relations are pleasant and supportive, members report higher satisfaction with the discussion and perceive the group as more successful and productive. Again, this development is reciprocal. Seeing the group as successful often leads to better relationships and makes a high-quality, acceptable outcome more likely. However, these interactions are not yet clearly confirmed in the experimental literature. Congenial, harmonious groups are not always more productive. The variables accounting for effects here have not yet been identified specifically enough to explain all the variation occurring.

The Social-Sensitivity Dimension

Some persons in their interactions are more sensitive than others in at least two ways: they are more sensitive to the ways in which another individual is reacting; and they are more sensitive to what is appropriate in a particular social situation. This awareness of others' reactions and of the situation can be called *social sensitivity*.

If he is a person of high manifest power in the group, the socially sensitive person may, by his behavior, alter his influence. For example, he may express modesty and humility when making positive suggestions. He may be especially tactful and kind in reacting to the contributions of others. He may listen respectfully when others contribute. He may encourage others by receiving their contributions with enthusiasm when he can sincerely do so.

The sensitive person may consider the backgrounds, biases, and publicly stated convictions of others when he contributes or reacts to contributions. For example, he may choose his words carefully so as not to criticize unnecessarily. He may preface his remarks with a recognition that others differ in bias and background.

Interaction is probably easier among persons who are sensitive to the needs, personal characteristics, backgrounds, strengths, and weaknesses of others. Individuals who are intimately acquainted have more information about common experiences. There are difficulties in carrying on a conversation with a complete stranger. We probably feel less tension in talking with someone who already knows our weaknesses and habits, especially if we are confident that they are not likely to embarrass us by bringing them up.

The Threat Dimension

Another crucial aspect of interpersonal relations is the extent to which an individual considers each other person in the group a threat to his ego, self-respect, position in the group, or esteem in the eyes of others. For example, if a member sees that each time he contributes, his remarks will be attacked or criticized by a particular individual, his reaction to the critic will be altered. The perceived threat may cause him to be more careful in future communications, or to decrease his contributions.

In contrast, some other individuals in discussion are more objective. They examine each contribution on its merits, point out its strengths and weaknesses, and make every effort to dissociate the contribution from its author. This objectivity has been described as "shooting at the idea rather than the man."

Threat is decreased in discussions where a permissive atmosphere is created. Also, there is less threat in groups with democratic leadership than in groups with autocratic leadership. Under such conditions as these, interpersonal relationships are likely to be more cordial and supportive.

Interaction is often easier among persons who react to each other in ways calculated to reduce threat. Deutsch, in the study cited earlier, found that during discussion of one kind of problem, "a greater percentage of encouraging or rewarding remarks was made in cooperative groups, and a significantly larger proportion of aggressive remarks was made in the competitive groups."

A study by Haythorn suggests that "mature, accepting persons facilitate, while suspicious, nonaccepting persons depress group characteristics indicative of smooth functioning."[28] Heyns reports that individuals who felt their discussion groups were unified, who felt accepted, and those who were actually accepted were "significantly more satisfied with the group's decision" than were their colleagues.[29] Gibb's results are similar: "the number and quality of solutions produced were found to be significantly greater" under conditions of reduced threat, whether the group had two, twelve, or ninety-six members.[30]

The Cooperation–Competition Dimension

Closely related to the problem of threat is the dimension of cooperation–competition. Each individual will react differently to other persons when group members are cooperatively rather than competitively interrelated.

[28] William Haythorn, "The Influence of Individual Members on the Characteristics of Small Groups," *Journal of Abnormal and Social Psychology*, 48 (1953), pp. 276–84.
[29] R. R. Heyns, "Effects of Variation in Leadership on Participant Behavior in Discussion Groups," Unpublished Doctoral Dissertation, University of Michigan, 1948.
[30] J. R. Gibb, "The Effects of Group Size and of Threat Reduction upon Creativity in a Problem-Solving Situation," *American Psychologist*, 6 (1951), 324 (Abstract).

Good interpersonal relationships are harder to establish and maintain in competitive groups. Moreover, some evidence suggests that interaction is easier when members are in a cooperative, rather than a competitive, relationship.

A study of pairs of children who were "strong" friends showed that cooperative behavior increased and conflictive behavior decreased when the subjects were placed in a frustrating situation. Pairs of "weak" friends showed no significant changes.[31]

After reviewing a number of studies, Kelley and Thibaut observe that "the interdependent relationship in which cooperation is rewarded seems to lead to strong motivation to complete the common task and to the development of considerable friendship among the members . . . a cooperative relationship among members seems to be more conducive to high productivity with regard to the group task than does a competitive relationship."[32]

Members with strong self-oriented needs may be more competitive than those who find it easier to pursue group interests. Discussions with a minimum number of self-oriented persons tend to be more harmonious and productive.

Although there is a need for more detailed understanding of the effects of interpersonal relationships, it is clear that positive personal reactions make interaction easier. Hence, we would expect favorable interpersonal relationships to contribute to the ultimate goals of the discussion group.

The Equilibrium Problem

A discussion group must be concerned with a climate that encourages task productivity and also one that promotes social harmony. Some leaders concentrate on creating one kind of atmosphere at the expense of the other. This difficulty is what Bales has called the "equilibrium problem."[33] A group must somehow balance the demands of task productivity and of social relationships. Energy devoted to the decision cannot also be spent reducing tension or keeping members satisfied.

This problem is intensified because members are not generally as sensitive to the social climate as they are to the task assignment. Productivity is at the center of everyone's attention. The prevailing spirit in most discussion situations is: "Let's get on to the decision we gathered here to reach." Yet successful achievement, and commitment to the decision, are directly influenced by interpersonal relationships.

Those contributing leadership must prevent the members from ignoring the social climate in groups where there is strong motivation to reach a decision,

[31] M. E. Wright, "The Influence of Frustration on the Social Relations of Young Children," *Character and Personality*, 12 (1943), pp. 111–22.

[32] H. H. Kelley and J. W. Thibaut, "Experimental Studies of Group Problem-Solving and Process," in Gardner Lindzey, ed., *Handbook of Social Psychology*, Volume II, Cambridge, Mass.: Addison-Wesley, 1954, pp. 754–55.

[33] R. F. Bales, "The Equilibrium Problem in Small Groups, A. Paul Hare, E. F. Borgatta, and R. F. Bales, *Small Groups: Studies in Social Interaction*, rev. ed. Alfred A. Knopf, 1966, pp. 444–76.

and from neglecting the task assignment where socializing seems more appealing than work. Actually the two activities can be coordinated quite skillfully and harmoniously if members and leaders are aware of both aspects and give both the close attention they must have.

LEADERSHIP

We have had much to say already about discussion leadership, but it must be included here as an important factor influencing interaction. The same participants discussing the same question will interact quite differently in response to different styles of leadership. From the moment a meeting begins, the leadership exerted will have as much effect on the discussion and the outcome as any other influence. In fact, leadership is so pervasive and its impact so complex and important that it is almost impossible to state generalizations about how it influences discussion. Any statements must be offered tentatively and cautiously.

As we have seen, the leader who is authoritarian may inhibit communication and thorough consideration of a problem, while the democratic leader may be able to encourage participation, create a warm social climate, build a permissive atmosphere, and inspire group loyalty. The authoritarian may feel that he must control, command, and maintain rigid compliance. The group-centered person, in contrast, may hesitate to direct or guide at all. A dominant personality in a leadership role may take up a large proportion of the communication time, and a submissive person is likely to become more aggressive than is his habit. Compared with the dominant person, however, he is likely to be retiring and timid. We cannot predict how leadership will operate in a particular discussion nor do we yet have sufficient evidence to explain how leadership style affects productivity. Nevertheless we can be sure that the leadership exerted will have a profound effect.

What we have said here is that each intermediate interactional process affects reciprocally each of the other processes and that each is dynamically changing all the time the discussion is in progress. Four of the most important of these interactions are communication flow, power relationships, interpersonal relationships, and leadership. Together with the attributes of the individuals engaged in a discussion and the group characteristics existing when the discussion begins, these interactional processes can be considered inputs of an interacting social system. These inputs in turn exert the major influences on outputs of the system.

OUTCOMES

The intermediate interactions make a major impact on the communication taking place as well as on the outputs resulting from discussion. These outcomes are, hopefully, a decision, satisfaction with the decision, and cohesiveness or group solidarity.

The Decision

In general, discussion productivity is higher when communication is thorough and members are well informed, reason logically, and use language and communication skillfully. Increased feedback from receivers to speakers tends to improve the accuracy of messages and group judgments, making more likely the elimination of fallacious reasoning and the choice of better alternatives. Although full and free discussion requires additional time, the group with good ideas and reasoning power will produce a better decision than one talking superficially about a problem. The majority, when it has sound arguments well supported with evidence and effectively expressed, tends to win supporters among the minority and to help the group choose a good alternative. This outcome depends on effective communication. However, it is impossible for a group to say everything that should be said and to take into account all the available evidence. Thus there is a limitation to the contribution communication can make.

Productive groups seem to be more efficient in following orderly steps in the problem-solving process. When the group is well organized, members may try harder to be productive because the role differentiations and the results expected from each member are clear. The gain in productivity when the group hierarchy is clear may be due in part to the fact that such groups need not spend time on a struggle for status. They also may have a better procedure worked out for moving toward a decision.

Leadership contributes to higher quality decisions when it prevents power discrepancies from stifling communication of low-influence persons, when it encourages creativity and full examination of the problem, and when it fosters orderly movement toward the outcome. Style of leadership affects decision quality but it is not a simple matter to specify how this influence operates. Autocratic leadership seems to increase efficiency of decision-making. It may, however, reduce quality, restrict thorough consideration, and discourage members. Democratic leadership is more time-consuming but may result in better decisions and interpersonal relations in many situations. There is clearly higher productivity when the leadership is skillful and when leaders have had the advantage of leadership training.

Where a good social climate develops and is maintained during discussion, interaction is easier and communication more complete. When conflict develops it is more likely to be resolved if a pleasant social atmosphere has already been created. On the other hand, friends may feel they must defend each other's positions rather than evaluate their proposals fully.

Satisfaction-Commitment

Apparently there is a positive relationship between the amount of satisfaction a group member feels at the end of the discussion and the rewards received as he views them. The relationship, however, is not a simple one, because it is not easy to know what the individual will consider rewarding under particular conditions. Collins and Guetzkow warn that the industrial conference participant does not automatically feel rewarded by task productivity:

> The individuals may be completely indifferent to the amount of work accomplished or the quality of the decision. Their concern may lie more with 'keeping one's reputation clean,' 'impressing the boss,' or 'showing you can stick with your friends. . . .' Leaders who stress productivity and quality may make *management* happy, but—in many cases—the conference *participant* 'couldn't care less.'[34]

A member may be satisfied with the rewarding remarks directed to him by the leader and dissatisfied with the knowledge that he actually contributed little to the discussion or was dominated by an overbearing participant. To assess satisfaction it is necessary to know what each individual found reassuring in terms of his own perceptions and aspirations for the group effort.

Participants enjoy being part of a successful group effort. High task achievement most of the time is socially rewarding and members of discussion groups are probably more satisfied with high-quality decisions, although this relationship is by no means invariable, as we have seen. Further, participants seem more committed to supporting the decision if they have taken part in its formulation.

Cohesiveness

This dimension of output involves the attractiveness of the group, the development of friendship ties, group unity, harmony, and pleasant interpersonal interactions. It can be thought of as a desired result or outcome of discussion, since group maintenance is one of the commonly held objectives of cooperating groups. We should note, however, that cohesiveness could also be thought of as an input, since members begin discussion with some degree of harmony and group attraction. Further, it could be observed as an intermediate interaction and indeed we have included interpersonal relationships as one of the four major intermediate processes. We have said that all the group process elements interact with all the others in mutual and reciprocal interdependence. What we need to say here is that cohesiveness, or harmony, or solidarity is the most mutually reciprocal of all the elements. Since people are people wherever and whenever they discuss, since they are people when they communicate, since only as people can they tackle a task assignment, etc., we can expect to encounter the interpersonal relationship problem at every turn. In a sense we are seeking to identify in this section the conditions —leadership, communication, power relationships—that lead to interpersonal solidarity.

A student might become confused because cohesiveness and interpersonal

[34] Barry E. Collins and Harold Guetzkow, *A Social Psychology of Group Processes for Decision-Making*, New York: John Wiley & Sons, 1964, p. 193.

relationships are not quite the same. Cohesiveness is a matter of the attractiveness of the group for the individual, while interpersonal relationships involve feelings of members for each other as persons. These concepts are related, however, and all contribute to the social climate and the individual's orientation to his relationships with the others as persons.

Groups are more cohesive, and personal relationships warmer, when members find participation rewarding in terms of prestige and approval from others. Cooperative attitudes and ample opportunities for communication are important to unity. In contrast, solidarity declines if the task assignment conflicts with members' personal goals, if competitive interrelationships develop, if prestige is threatened, etc.

Attractiveness of the group depends on its goals, programs, and position in the community, etc., as these are related to the individual's needs for the affiliation, recognition, etc., that the group can satisfy. Highly cohesive groups display more "we" feeling, more friendliness, greater loyalty, less friction, fewer disruptions, and, in a business organization, less worker absenteeism and turnover. Some of the causes of disruption are aggressiveness, personal dislikes, rivalry for position, and dissatisfaction with procedures.

Relevant here is the research of Stock and Thelen and their co-workers at the University of Chicago, who have extended the interesting concepts of W. R. Bion. The designation "work" is given to activity directed toward goal-achievement; it is "sober, reflective, and orderly; members listen to one another." There is, however, a wholly different manner of group operation going on at the same time; this state, identified by strong, personalized feelings, disorder, and failure to listen, is called *emotionality*. At different moments, then, groups can be expected to exhibit varying qualities according to the momentary supremacy of work or emotionality. According to this conception, there are four kinds of emotionality, one of which may be predominantly enmeshed with work at any moment, although all four may be present. One emotional state is dependency; the group operates " 'as if' [it] exists in order to find support and direction from something outside itself—the leader, external standards, or its own history." Another is pairing, in which members show more personal regard for each other and the group finds "strength from within its own peer group." A third emotional reaction is fight; here members express hostility and aggression. The group or some persons within it act "as if its purpose is to fight something or someone." A fourth state is flight, in which the tendency is to avoid the problem, to go off on a tangent, or to withdraw or run away from the group.[35] The outcome for the group in terms of cohesiveness may be related to the kind of emotionality developing during discussion.

Interaction itself appears to contribute to a smoothly functioning social system by giving members information as to how they are being perceived

[35] Dorothy Stock and Herbert A. Thelen, *Emotional Dynamics and Group Culture,* New York: New York University Press, 1958.

by others, allowing them to monitor the appropriateness of their behavior and increasing their feeling for the group. This outcome seems especially likely if at the same time members are receiving positive re-enforcement and approval from the others. Those unable to contribute effectively to the group may tend to be rejected and the attractiveness of the group for them will decrease unless other forces intervene, such as the satisfaction of strong needs or the failure to find a more satisfying group.

Perhaps we should close this analysis of group process and intermediate interactions by emphasizing once more the circularity of a social system. We can identify inputs and outputs but at least some of the elements operate at the end of discussion as they do in the beginning. In some cases we produce harmony by beginning with and maintaining harmony. A successful discussion is more likely to be successful! Members are satisfied with the discussion if the discussion was satisfactory! These circular statements are not so much idle double talk as they are recognition of the fact that these elements are truly interactional.

SUPPLEMENTARY READING

Bales, Robert F., *Interaction Process Analysis*, Cambridge, Mass.: Addison-Wesley, 1950.

Cartwright, Dorwin and Zander, Alvin, *Group Dynamics: Research and Theory*, sec. ed., New York: Harper & Row, 1960.

Collins, Barry E., and Guetzkow, Harold, *A Social Psychology of Group Processes for Decision-Making*, New York: John Wiley & Sons, 1964.

Hare, A. Paul, *Handbook of Small Group Research*, New York: The Free Press, 1962.

————, Borgatta, E. F., and Bales, R. F., *Small Groups: Studies in Social Interaction*, rev. ed., New York: Alfred A. Knopf, 1966.

McGrath, Joseph E., and Altman, Irwin, *Small Group Research*, New York: Holt, Rinehart and Winston, 1966.

Scheidel, Thomas M., and Crowell, Laura, "Idea Development in Small Discussion Groups," *Quarterly Journal of Speech*, 50 (1964), pp. 140–5.

QUESTIONS AND EXERCISES

1. What intermediate interactional processes have you observed operating in small-group discussions other than those mentioned in this chapter? To what extent do these processes interrelate? Are there actually only one or two fundamental processes here, with the various aspects explained in this chapter being different views of the same thing?
2. To what extent is communication "the most important facet of inter-action?" Can you suggest some operational definitions that will make clear the differences between interaction and communication?

3. To what extent have you observed the use of consummatory communication in discussion?
4. Propose a method for adding to the Bales analysis of communicative interaction a qualitative evaluation of the communications.
5. Select a topic for discussion in which the participants feel maximum involvement. For example, students belonging to fraternities and sororities should feel strong personal involvement in the question, "Should fraternities and sororities be outlawed on this campus?" If this topic is used, the group should consist of two or three loyal members of such organizations and two or three who do not belong and who oppose them. Once topic and group are chosen, hold a discussion. Observers should look for ruptures in interpersonal relationships; for outbursts of temper or resentment; for conflict; and for ways in which conflicts become resolved and personal breaches healed.

    Participants can be asked to write papers explaining their feelings and reactions to a situation where interpersonal clashes were probable. They should be asked to answer such questions as these: (a) What were your personal feelings throughout the discussion? (b) How did you react to the subject matter and to the other participants as persons? (c) What, if anything, occurred to rupture interpersonal relationships? (d) What, if anything, happened to resolve conflicts and reduce interpersonal tensions?
6. Select a small, continuing group to which you belong and whose members you know and have worked with intimately. In three separate operations, spaced in time at least a day apart, perform these three tasks: (a) Rank the members of the group in the order in which you feel they have helped the group accomplish its mission(s); (b) Rank the members of the group in the order in which you feel they should be depended upon to provide leadership in a future group undertaking; and (c) Rank the members of the group in the order in which you like each of them. Then look at your three sets of rankings. To what extent is there a relationship between your respect for their abilities as group members and your liking of them?
7. A study by a sociologist showed that husbands talked appreciably more than their wives in actual recordings of family discussions. What characteristics of the individuals involved, the situations, and the whole cultural milieu can influence this finding? Under what conditions would you expect the mate who talks more to have more influence on family decisions?
8. To suggest in a mild way the effect of power relations on discussion, choose four members of the class to put on a demonstration of role-playing in which they discuss with the class as observers The Case of the Chicago Chemical Company, printed in the Appendix. After they are well into the case have a member of the class enter the room, interrupt them, and announce that he is president of the union involved and that he is going to sit in on the discussion. When he has been with them for a time, have him withdraw. Then have another person enter, interrupt, and announce

that he is Chairman of the Board of the Toledo Chemical Company and that he wants to join them. Stop the role-playing shortly thereafter and have everyone discuss the differences, if any, introduced by the presence of the new members who were in positions of influence relevant to the problem and to the men discussing it.

Chapter 16

EVALUATING DISCUSSION

Evaluation of discussion is important in a number of ways. The discussion student should learn to judge group and individual performance, assessing achievements on the criteria of excellence. Awareness of the requirements for high-quality performance should help the learner improve his own participation. In nontraining or real groups, participants wish to estimate the effectiveness of the group. While they do not often use rating scales or other paraphernalia of evaluation, they certainly should be capable of making judgments about the group's performance, efficiency, and production. They may, for instance, ask and answer such questions as, "How efficiently did this group use the time available, compared with other discussion groups of this kind?" Evaluation is important also in helping to explain effects; if a group fails to reach agreement, the explanation must be found in examination of earlier components, such as: Were members well informed? Did they have cooperative attitudes? Was the leadership adequate?

Emphasis in this chapter must be upon evaluation by the student who is learning to use discussion method. He must (a) identify the components that are vital to discussion and that become the criteria of judgment; (b) design rating scales and running record charts for making and recording evaluations of each criterion; and (c) learn to make accurate judgments while observing discussion with rating scales in hand. The quality of his judgment is determined by comparing his evaluations with other judges who have observed the same discussion. Confidence in the criteria and the judges is increased when there is high inter-observer agreement.

Judgments should be made in a large number of different situations. At least four general elements should be evaluated: (a) the group product, including the efficiency of the group's productivity; (b) the group, including collective interaction and cohesiveness; (c) the contributions of individual participants; and (d) the contributions of leadership, in most cases a designated leader. A different set of criteria may be appropriate when the discussion being evaluated is closedgroup or public, and when its purpose is information-sharing or decision-making. Thus, evaluation charts could be devised for rating group productivity in closedgroup, problem-solving discussion; in closedgroup, information-sharing discussion; in public problem-solving discussion; and in public information-sharing discussion. Scales could be designed for rating leadership in public information-sharing discussion; in public decision-making discussion; in closedgroup information-sharing discussion; and so on and on. Judging charts could be further subdivided by designing separate scales for committee and conference types of discussion within closedgroup, problem-solving discussion.

A number of options are available to a learning group wishing to practice discussion evaluation. It is possible to have structured evaluations, making use of the expert critiques of the instructor, and of evaluations by student observer teams. It is also useful to have unstructured evaluations in which the participants themselves report how they feel about the success of a discussion.

Another choice is not to have all evaluations given as end-of-discussion reports but to allow interruption of the discussion for an evaluator or participant to call attention to a good feature or a weakness. Permitting interruptions probably should depend on the group's purposes. Interruption calls attention more clearly to the problems of managing group process, while exclusive use of end-of-discussion reports permits the group to concentrate more directly on the problem being discussed.

There is no attempt in this chapter to suggest a ready-made rating scale for use in every possible situation. Instructors and students must design the evaluations they wish to use to achieve the purposes they set for themselves. In this chapter, instead, the general problems of evaluation are introduced and some examples of criteria are presented. Running record charts and rating scales are illustrated. The student must decide for himself what elements should be evaluated in a particular situation and he must be able to design rating scales that will produce satisfactory agreement in judgment. Later in real groups he should be able to make dependable estimates of discussion quality without filling out specific rating sheets.

EVALUATING GROUP PRODUCTIVITY

The most important evaluation of all is to decide the worth of the product or outcome. In information-sharing discussion the essential question is relatively simple: How much understanding resulted? Evaluation of problem-solving discussion is much more complicated. The central question is: How good is the decision produced?

The ideal evaluation of a discussion outcome can be obtained only after the passage of time, when the product can be judged by the actual results it produced. An international conference called to prevent a war should have its decision evaluated by this practical criterion: Did the conference preserve peace? At the infamous Munich Conference in 1938, Britain, France, and Italy gave Hitler's Germany a slice of Czechoslovakia and announced they had purchased "peace for our time." A year later World War II began. This conference was a dismal failure, obviously, but the negative judgment could not be pronounced definitely until the year had passed and subsequent events had forced the evaluation. At the time, there was violent disagreement about the conference outcome. Some leaders felt it had been a great success; Winston Churchill and some others disagreed.

Of course, this wait-and-see method, though ideal, is not a practical kind of discussion evaluation. The group needs to make some estimate of discussion quality at the time of the discussion. Also, later events do not always make clear the quality of an earlier discussion; the group's decision may not be successfully carried out because of new events that could not be foreseen. Moreover, participants need to have some notion of outcome quality so they can relate it at the time to the group's performance. They should ask themselves such questions as, "Did we reach a better decision when everyone participated?" In this way, members improve as participants from one experience to the next.

Hence, two types of evaluation are needed in the immediate discussion-training situation. First, during the discussion, there should be some kind of running record kept which indicates performances related to group productivity. Related running records should also be supplied in connection with evaluating the group, the participants, and leadership. Second, at the end of the discussion, there should be an estimate of outcome quality, and member commitment-satisfaction. These evaluations can best be made by observers who take no active part in the discussion, although as has been said participants must be constantly aware of such judgments and should be able to estimate quality for themselves. Obviously, those actively involved cannot judge as objectively as can detached observers.

Running record of productive efficiency

During the discussion, observers might seek answers to questions such as these:

1. What proportion of the group's time was spent on matters unrelated to the problem for discussion?
2. To what extent were some members responsible for taking the group off on tangents?
3. To what extent did members help the leader keep the discussion on the track?
4. How adequately did the group analyze the problem?
5. How many different alternative solutions to the problem were proposed?
6. Which members were responsible for the alternatives proposed?
7. How thoroughly was each alternative solution discussed?
8. How much time was spent discussing each alternative?
9. Which members contributed most to discussion of each alternative?

Some of these questions can only be answered subjectively, and observers may wish to take notes related to them while the discussion is in progress. Others can be answered more objectively by tabulating proposals and responses on a chart designed especially for this purpose. One possibility for recording answers to some of these questions is the chart suggested in Figure 16.1. The student should practice designing his own running record charts for various purposes.

Number of Times Each Participant:

Participants	Introduced topic unrelated to discussion	Helped leader keep on track	Proposed new solution to problem	Made contribution relevant to Proposal A	Made contribution relevant to Proposal B
Jim	I	I	I	ЖL I	III
Fred	III			II	
Mary		II	I	IIII	I
Bert	I		I	ЖL II	II
Ann		I	III	ЖL	I

FIGURE 16.1 *Running Record of Efficiency of Group Productivity*

Evaluation of outcome

At the end of the discussion, there should be a judgment of the group product, involving answers to such questions as these:

1. How good is the decision reached?
2. To what extent does the final decision represent the substance of the entire discussion?
3. To what extent are members agreed on the decision?
4. To what extent are members satisfied with the decision?
5. To what extent are members committed to put the decision into effect?
6. To what extent are members committed to defend the decision in later talks with others?

It is obvious that an observer cannot answer all these questions with any certainty. It would be more satisfactory to ask the members whether they agree and to what extent they feel satisfied and committed, wherever this is possible. Where it is impossible, as it is in most situations other than training sessions, the evaluator must make the best estimate he can, based on his observation of member reactions. An example of a rating scale for this purpose is presented in Figure 16.2.

QUALITY OF DECISION REACHED

5	4	3	2	1
Superior	Above Average	Average	Below Average	Poor

EXTENT TO WHICH DECISION WAS BASED ON SUBSTANCE OF ENTIRE DISCUSSION

5	4	3	2	1
Decision reflected substance to superior extent	Decision reflected substance to above average extent	Decision reflected substance to average extent	Decision only partially reflected substance	No relation between substance and decision

EXTENT OF MEMBER AGREEMENT

5	4	3	2	1
Apparently unanimous agreement	Some disagreement but near consensus	Group divided, with majority for decision	Majority disagreed	Almost all disagreed

EXTENT OF MEMBER SATISFACTION-COMMITMENT

5	4	3	2	1
Almost all highly satisfied	Most members satisfied	More than half satisfied enough to support decision	Fewer than half-satisfied enough to support decision	Almost no one committed to carry out decision

Directions: Check continuum at point representing your judgment

FIGURE 16.2 *Rating Scale for Evaluating Group Decision*

EVALUATING THE GROUP

The next element to be evaluated is group operation as a unit or team. This evaluation is important, as it is related to high-quality productivity and also to the other discussion objectives of member satisfaction-commitment and group maintenance. Here, again, two types of evaluation are appropriate: a running record, and a final estimate of group functioning.

Running Record of "Groupness"
The questions to be answered concern such elements as these:

    I. To what extent does the group climate promote free, permissive talk?
      A. Is the atmosphere informal rather than rigidly stiff?
      B. Does every member participate?

C. Do members react to contributions in ways that encourage the communicator to talk again later?

D. Do high-power members react to contributions in ways that encourage lower-power members to talk again later?

E. Are the physical surroundings pleasant and conducive to enthusiastic talk?

F. Do members seem enthusiastic about the importance of discussing the problem and do they consider participation worthwhile?

II. To what extent are members compatible?

A. Are members friendly to each other?

B. Do members seem to like each other?

C. Do members seem to enjoy talking with each other?

D. Do members smile occasionally as they talk to others?

E. Do members behave in ways which generally minimize the threat to other's egos?

III. To what extent does the group operate as a cohesive unit?

A. Is there mutual helpfulness among members?

B. Do members seem to be dependent upon each other for support?

C. Do members seem eager to hear the group's reactions rather than proceeding on their own?

D. Is there effort to bring deviates back into agreement with the group?

E. Do members seem more concerned with group interests than self-interest?

F. Do members seem cooperative rather than competitive?

G. Do members seem pleased when other members are congratulated for superior contribution?

IV. To what extent is there efficient communicative interaction?

A. Which members contribute most and which least?

B. Which members' contributions are most helpful to the group?

C. What kinds of information-opinion are contributed by each member?

D. To which members are most communications directed?

E. What proportion of communications are directed to the whole group?

F. Are members attentive listeners?

G. Do contributions relate to and build upon earlier contributions?

There is obviously much here to evaluate and no one observer can possibly judge all these elements at once. Each must choose some aspect of the whole process to concentrate on. For example, one could make a running evaluation of permissive climate, as suggested by the chart in Figure 16.3. Another could judge compatibility (Figure 16.4), and a third, cohesiveness (Figure 16.5). Similar charts could be designed for evaluating the group on each of the subquestions raised in connection with climate, compatibility, cohesiveness, and communicative interaction.

One method for recording communicative interaction is a simplified adaptation of Bales' interaction process analysis (see Chapter 15). Who initiates each contribution is indicated by making a mark in the row on which the participant's name appears, as illustrated in the chart presented in Figure 16.6.

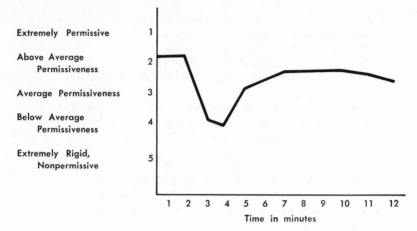

FIGURE 16.3 *Running Estimate of Permissive Climate*

What he communicates is indicated by making an entry in the column representing positive reaction, attempted answer, question, or negative reaction. The person to whom the communication is directed is designated by recording his number; a communication directed to the group is recorded as a zero. For example, in the record illustrated in Figure 16.6, Marvin has communicated only questions; the first and third were directed to the whole group, the second to Tom, and the fourth to Barbara.

After the discussion, it is possible to represent schematically the information contained on the recording analysis sheet. Figure 16.7 shows a line graph of the nature of the communications initiated in each period and for the total discussion. To construct such a graph, count the total number of communica-

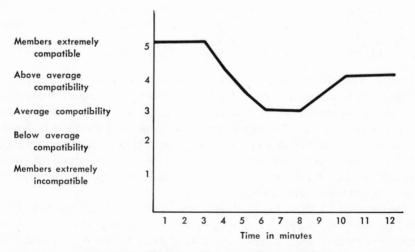

FIGURE 16.4 *Running Estimate of Compatibility*

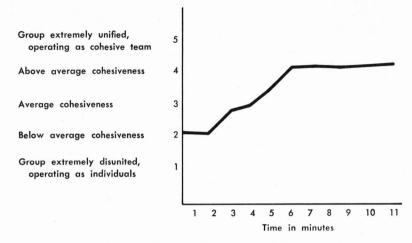

FIGURE 16.5   *Running Estimate of Cohesiveness*

tions, and calculate what percentage of the total consisted of positive reactions, attempted answers, questions, and negative reactions. Figure 16.8 presents a similar graph of the nature of communications initiated by each participant, while Figure 16.9 gives the proportions of contributions directed to each

Record of_____*3rd*_____ Period of_____*20*_____ Minutes.
　　　　　　(1st) (2nd) (etc.)

Directions:　Every contribution of each participant is to be recorded by making an entry in the horizontal row opposite his name. Record in the appropriate column the number of the recipient of the communication. If the communication is addressed to the group as a whole, or if the recipient is indeterminate, record the symbol "O" in the appropriate column.

NATURE OF COMMUNICATION:

Participant Communicating:	Category 1 Positive Reactions	Category 2 Attempted Answers	Category 3 Questions	Category 4 Negative Reactions
1. Marvin			0304	
2. Lloyd	50011100	14530033	5005000110l	011011
3. Tom	011	4454000500001	4	2112
4. Barbara	001333	30000330	0210	25
5. Jane	0230	2232	3110	4401120044

FIGURE 16.6   *Running Record of Communicative Interaction*

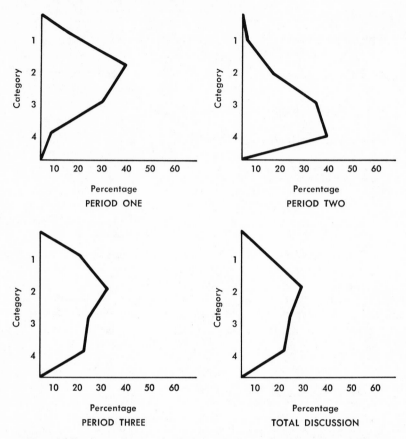

FIGURE 16.7 *Percentage of Communications by periods, which are: Category 1, Positive Reactions; Category 2, Attempted Answers; Category 3, Questions; and Category 4, Negative Reactions*

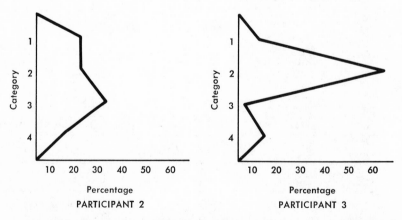

FIGURE 16.8 *Percentage of Each Category of Communication Initiated by Each Participant*

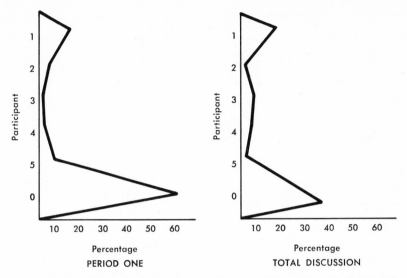

FIGURE 16.9   *Percentages of Communications Directed to Each Participant and to the Group as a Whole*

participant and to the group as a whole. A graph giving the percentages of
total contributions initiated by each participant is illustrated in Figure 16.10.

These recordings of communicative interaction are helpful for evaluation
purposes, and the graphs demonstrate at a glance the characteristics of the
discussion. At the same time, these recordings supply quantitative information
only; they leave out any qualitative estimate of the worth of particular contributions to the discussion. The efficiency and effectiveness of the interaction

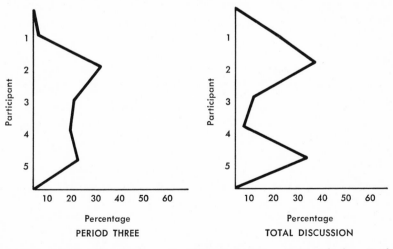

FIGURE   16.10   *Percentages   of   Communications   Initiated   by   Each
Participant*

Each Period is ___3___ Minutes

Directions: Record each member's contribution in the row opposite his name. For each contribution, enter one of the following symbols to represent the quality of that contribution:

+ Contribution above average in helpfulness to discussion.

0 Contribution of average helpfulness.

— Contribution below average in helpfulness to discussion.

? Contribution irrelevant to discussion.

Participants	Period One	Period Two	Period Three
Harold	O O + O	+ +	O – O ?
Edna	? O	O –	? ? O O
Sam	O O O +	O ? O	+
Marie	+ + O —	+ +	O + O
Gilbert	O ? ? O	? O – –	– ? O

FIGURE 16.11 *Running Record of Communication Quality*

Directions: Record one mark in the appropriate participant's column for each contribution in the categories described.

Contributions Containing:

	Harold	Edna	Sam
Information needed by group at moment contributed	THL	II	III
Information not needed by group at moment contributed	I	III	I
Opinions contributed when relevant	IIII	THL I	III
Opinions contributed when irrelevant	I		II
Questions that helped clarify or advance discussion	II	THL II	II
Questions that did not help clarify or advance discussion	I	I	IIII

FIGURE 16.12 *Running Record of Communication Quality*

must not be judged by quantity alone. A single, short comment may help the group more—if it supplies just the needed information at just the right moment—than a whole series of contributions such as, "I agree," "You are right," and so on.

There are a number of ways in which qualitative judgments of interaction can be recorded during a discussion. The Bales' type of interaction recording just described can be used by inserting above each recorded interaction an additional symbol estimating quality of the contribution. A plus sign above the number could indicate high quality, a minus sign, low quality, and no mark, average quality. Other possibilities are to record only qualitative symbols for each participant's contributions, as suggested in Figure 16.11, and to tabulate contributions falling in each of several qualitative categories of communications, as suggested in Figure 16.12.

Evaluation of "Groupness"

After the discussion, observers can judge the achievement of "groupness" on such scales as these:

PERMISSIVE CLIMATE:

5	4	3	2	1
Extremely permissive	Above average in permissiveness	Average in permissiveness	Below average in permissiveness	Extremely rigid, nonpermissive

COMPATIBILITY:

5	4	3	2	1
Members extremely compatible	Group above average in compatibility	Group average in compatibility	Group below average in compatibility	Members extremely incompatible

COHESIVENESS:

5	4	3	2	1
Group extremely unified, operating as cohesive team	Above average in unity	Average in unity	Below average in unity	Group extremely disunited, members operating as individuals

COMMUNICATIVE INTERACTION:

5	4	3	2	1
Extremely good interaction	Above average interaction	Average communicative interaction	Below average interaction	Extremely poor interaction

Similar scales could be designed for each of the subquestions that was asked about climate, compatibility, cohesiveness, and communicative interaction.

EVALUATING PARTICIPANTS

In judging group productivity and "groupness," some evaluation of individual participants occurs. It is important some of the time, however, to concentrate on judging the effectiveness of each person, since it is the individual who must attempt to improve himself as a discusser. The criteria on which he should be evaluated are drawn from everything that has been said about participation:

I. Does he have cooperative attitudes?
    A. Does he display objectivity toward the problem?
    B. Does he display objectivity toward others?
    C. Does he cooperate as part of the group?
    D. Does he discuss enthusiastically?
II. Does he make substantive contributions to the discussion?
    A. Is he well informed?
    B. Is he mentally alert?
    C. Does he answer rather than evade questions?
    D. Does he contribute information when needed?
    E. Does he reason adequately?
    F. Does he check for fallacies?
    G. Does he build on others' reasoning?
    H. Is he thorough?
III. Does he use language adequately?
    A. Is his language clear?
    B. Is his language accurate?
    C. Is his language appropriate?
    D. Is his language fair to others?
IV. Does he speak adequately?
    A. Does he speak intelligibly?
    B. Does he speak naturally?
    C. Does he speak interestingly?
    D. Does he speak efficiently?
    E. Does he listen "behind the statement"?
V. Does he help the leader?
    A. Does he heed the pattern?
    B. Does he help the group stay on the track?
    C. Does he refrain from usurping the leader's functions?
VI. Is he ethical?
    A. Does he refrain from pretending to understand more than he really does?
    B. Does he refrain from distortion and deception?
    C. Does he refrain from channeling talk for his own purposes?
    D. Does he use language and reasoning fairly?

A rating scale that provides a final evaluation of each participant on each of these criteria, as well as a running estimate during successive time periods of the discussion, is illustrated in Figure 16.13. This scale should be completed for each individual participant, and one observer usually cannot adequately evaluate more than a single member during any discussion, especially if he must make a judgment on all six criteria during each short period of time.

Name of Participant: *George Winters*

Directions: Assign the participant for each criterion during each period of ___4___ minutes one of the following ratings:

    5 Superior

    4 Above Average

    3 Average

    2 Below Average

    1 Poor

| | RATING | | | |
CRITERIA:	Period I	Period II	Period III	Over-all Rating
Attitudes: Objectivity; contribution to groupness	4	3	5	4
Substantive Contributions: Knowledge of problem; reasoning ability; contributing when helpful; thoroughness	5	3	4	4
Language Usage: Clarity; accuracy; appropriateness; fairness	3	3	2	3
Speaking: Intelligibility; naturalness; interestingness; efficiency; listening ability	3	4	2	3
Helpfulness to Leader: Heeding pattern; helping others stay on track; cooperativeness	3	2	2	2
Ethical Conduct: Fairness; refraining from exaggeration, distortion, deception, unfair manipulation	3	3	4	3

FIGURE 16.13 *Participant Evaluation Report*

EVALUATING LEADERSHIP

It is obvious that special scales must be designed for evaluating the designated leader or leaders. Here, too, the criteria are suggested by what has already been said about leadership (see Chapters 10 to 13).

Does the designated leader, or those carrying the leadership responsibility:

I. Have an adequate knowledge of group process?
   A. Understand interaction?
   B. Understand the influence of power relationships?
   C. Understand the influence of interpersonal relations?
   D. Understand the influence of group size?
   E. Understand the nature and types of leadership?
   F. Have ability to be impartial?
II. Have an adequate knowledge of the problem?
   A. Have sufficient information?
   B. Recognize when a topic has been adequately discussed?
III. Have adequate reasoning abilities?
   A. Have the ability to think quickly?
   B. Check for fallacies?
IV. Have respect for others?
   A. Have social sensitivity?
   B. Display tact?
V. Have adequate language and speech skills?
   A. Express complex ideas swiftly and clearly?
   B. Summarize objectively, fairly, and quickly?
   C. Take all views into account?
   D. Listen adequately?
VI. Introduce the discussion adequately?
   A. Introduce participants skillfully?
   B. Introduce the problem skillfully?
VII. Guide the discussion adequately?
   A. Follow an orderly pattern systematically?
   B. Keep discussion on the track?
   C. Rebound from tangents skillfully?
   D. Clarify and restate to assist forward movement?
   E. Give transitional summaries to assist forward movement?
   F. Ask for definition?
   G. Ask the right questions?
VIII. Regulate the discussion adequately?
   A. Preserve order and prevent chaos?
   B. Restrain overeager participants and encourage low participators?
   C. Encourage cooperative attitudes?
   D. Build cohesiveness-solidarity?
   E. Encourage permissiveness-interaction?
   F. Minimize effects of power discrepancies?
   G. Resolve conflicts?
   H. Stress agreement?

IX. End the discussion skillfully?
 A. Stop the discussion when it is finished?
 B. Summarize fairly?
 C. Accurately assess and state the extent of agreement?

Any number of running records and rating scales could be designed for the purpose of making observer evaluations of these nine leadership criteria. The one illustrated in Figure 16.14 is similar to that suggested for evaluating participants.

Directions: Assign the designated leader for each of the first seven criteria during each period of _20_ minutes one of the following ratings: 5, Superior; 4, Above Average; 3, Average; 2, Below Average; and 1, Poor. At the close of the discussion, assign an over-all rating on each of the first seven criteria, and on the final two criteria.

RATING

	Criteria:	Period I	Period II	Period III	Over-all Rating
1.	Knowledge of Group Process	4	4	3	4
2.	Knowledge of Problem	3	4	3	3
3.	Reasoning Ability	5	3	4	4
4.	Respect for Others	5	5	5	5
5.	Language and Speech Skills	4	4	5	4
6.	Guiding the Discussion	2	3	2	2
7.	Regulating the Discussion	2	2	2	2
8.	Introducing the Discussion				4
9.	Ending the Discussion				3

FIGURE 16.14 *Leadership Evaluation Report*

The student should remember that the charts and scales illustrated in this chapter are suggestions only. They are by no means the only evaluation devices which could be designed. These can be as simple or as elaborate as the observer cares to make them. The contents of a scale depend on the criteria the judge considers crucial. What is important is that the discussion student understand the criteria by which a discussion can be judged; that he be capable of designing his own charts and scales in ways he is able and willing to defend; and that he be proficient as an observer and evaluator.

Further, the student must keep in mind that special discussion situations require evaluations that have not been mentioned in this chapter. To evaluate leadership for interactional discussion with a group of thirty persons, for example, would call for some extensive modification of the rating scale suggested for leadership under general conditions. There are also differences between discussions in closedgroup and public situations which should be reflected in the special charts and scales designed. A thorough understanding of discussion and group process, together with some ingenuity and imagination, will lead to production of ample evaluation devices for any discussion situation.

SUPPLEMENTARY READING

Bales, Robert F., *Interaction Process Analysis*, Cambridge, Mass.: Addison-Wesley, 1950.

Beal, George M., Bohlen, Joe M., and Raudabaugh, J., *Leadership and Dynamic Group Action*, Ames: Iowa State University Press, 1962, Part III.

Braden, Waldo W., and Brandenburg, Earnest, *Oral Decision-Making*, New York: Harper & Row, 1955, Chapter 16.

Brandenburg, Earnest, and Neal, Philip A., "Graphic Techniques for Evaluating Discussion and Conference Procedures," *Quarterly Journal of Speech*, 39 (April, 1953), pp. 201–8.

Crowell, Laura, "Rating Scales as Diagnostic Instruments in Discussion," *The Speech Teacher*, 2 (January, 1953), pp. 26–32.

Howell, William S., and Smith, Donald K., *Discussion*, New York: Crowell-Collier and Macmillan, 1956, Part IV.

Thompson, Wayne N., "A Study of the Factors Considered by Students in Evaluating Public Discussions," *Speech Monographs*, 20 (November, 1953), pp. 268–72.

Torrance, E. Paul, "Methods of Conducting Critiques of Group Problem-Solving Performance," in Hare, A. Paul, Borgatta, E. F., and Bales, R. F., *Small Groups: Studies in Social Interaction*, rev. ed., New York: Alfred A. Knopf, 1966, pp. 692–9.

QUESTIONS AND EXERCISES

1. Explain and defend the criteria you would use in evaluating (a) closed-group discussion; (b) public discussion; (c) participation; and (d) leadership.
2. Design and defend your own rating scales for evaluating the performance of participants and of leaders in the various types of discussion situations.
3. What are the important differences between evaluating the discussion performances of individuals and of the group as a whole?
4. Plan and hold a series of discussions in the classroom situation. Appoint observers to evaluate each discussion. Each observer should listen and evaluate as an individual. Then he should write a paper presenting his evaluation of one (or more) of the following aspects of the discussion:
   a. The quality of the group decision.

b. Group cohesiveness.

c. Interpersonal relationships.

d. Attitudes toward the discussion.

e. Communication structure.

f. Language and communication skills.

In assessing the aspect(s) chosen, the observer should consider the influence, if any, of the following: quantity and quality of information; discussion outline; analysis; sociometric structure; power relationships; leadership; and size of group.

5. Listen to a public or closedgroup discussion and make a simplified Bales analysis of the communicative interaction. Write a report in which you:

a. Present in graphs the percentages of communications in each category; the percentages of communications initiated by each participant; the percentages of communications directed to each participant; and the nature of communications initiated by each participant.

b. Analyze what you have learned about the interpersonal relationships and the power structure of the group from the communication analysis.

PART FIVE

DISCUSSION
IN LARGER SETTINGS

Chapter 17

PUBLIC
DISCUSSION

Public discussions occur when meetings are held, not in private situations, but for the benefit of a larger group of listeners. We must consider now the differences introduced into discussion by the presence of an audience.

A city council wrangled for months about the problem of automobile parking on Main Street. Some members felt that the existing system of diagonal parking created a danger when cars backed out into the stream of traffic; so they proposed a change to parallel parking. Others objected to this because it meant fewer parking spaces and fewer customers for the stores on Main Street. The decision rested with the council and its committees, and discussion was used extensively in these internal meetings. However, public interest in the problem was keen, particularly among the store owners. A member of the council then organized a public meeting at which representatives of the city government discussed the problem; citizens attending expressed opinions. This meeting external to the council could not result in a decision; only the council had power and responsibility for action. The use of discussion in the public hearing, however, helped crystallize opinion and made it easier for council members to proceed intelligently.

In reaching the public, groups frequently utilize radio and television. For example, the League of Women Voters wished to further public understanding of our constitutional form of government and its origins. The means they chose in one locality was a series of six televised panel discussions in which prominent citizens from several communities discussed the bases of our freedoms.

RHETORICAL ELEMENTS OF PUBLIC DISCUSSION

When a listening audience is involved in a discussion, rhetorical elements are introduced. Rhetorical aspects refer to the ways in which auditors are influenced by speakers. Public discussers must be concerned with audience response to them as communicators. All phases of a public presentation— preparation, planning, messages communicated, content, language, manner of delivery—are modified in terms of possible influences on the audience.

Three characteristics distinguish a public program from closedgroup discussion: (a) An audience is listening. They may be facing the discussers directly in the same room, or they may be invisible to participants using the mass media. Occasionally, public discussers have both a studio audience and unseen auditors. (b) Participants are communicating to and for the benefit of listeners. Here is the key distinction. In closedgroup discussion, communication is addressed to other participants. In public discussion, if the public were taken away, the discussion would be pointless. If the television equipment were to break down just before broadcast of a public panel, for example, the discussion would be cancelled or postponed. Members would not go through the motions for their own benefit. It is only the listening audience that supplies impetus for the discussion. It is this key distinction, also, that introduces the rhetorical elements. Since the discussion is a presentation for their benefit, listeners must be taken into account. (c) In many cases, auditors become communicating participants at some point.

Because an audience is reacting, questioning, and evaluating, participants are subjected to greater pressures. Communicators are naturally concerned with the image they present to others, with how ably they appear to perform. No person is indifferent to his impact on other people in a public situation. Each is more aware than in closedgroup situations of his personal relationships with others, including the other communicating participants.

As has been emphasized, any discussion group must be concerned simultaneously with task functions and social functions. In closedgroups, members usually can concentrate on task functions more than social functions, whereas in public discussion the emphasis is reversed. This difference can be suggested with two continua:

	Emphasis on social-functions		Emphasis on task-functions
Closedgroup:		A	

	Emphasis on social-functions		Emphasis on task-functions
Public:		B	

In a particular closedgroup discussion, point A may represent the relative distribution of emphasis between social and task-functions, while in a certain public discussion, point B may suggest the relative emphasis.

EFFECTS OF THE AUDIENCE

Increased awareness of social functions in an audience situation has some specific effects on the discussion, the communicating participants, and the designated leader. For the most part, effective communicative interaction is more difficult in public than in closedgroup discussion. It must be recognized, of course, that generalizations applicable to all discussion situations are hazardous and difficult to defend; what is said here seems reasonable in general, but may not be descriptive of every specific set of circumstances.

Public Discussion Tends to Be More Formal

Whereas most closedgroup discussions can be held under conditions of easy, relaxed informality, public discussions tend to be more formal. Members are more reserved, more careful about remarks addressed to others. They are more likely to call other participants by their last names and to use official titles, for example. Even formality of dress is affected.

Permissiveness Is Harder to Develop

Participants in public discussion feel increased restraints against communicating. Because everything they say is being judged not only by the other participants but also by a listening audience, they may refrain from communicating as much as they would otherwise. If someone else has said approximately what they want to say, they may be unwilling to add remarks or even to indicate their agreement, whereas in closedgroups they would almost certainly do so. Hence, a permissive atmosphere is more difficult to create. Restraints can be seen in extreme form during broadcast discussions when an inexperienced participant is affected by "mike-fright."

Effective Speech Is More Difficult

Participants in public discussion have increased difficulty utilizing effective language and communication skills. Language must be adapted to a wider audience, and in mass broadcasts, the audience is unseen, largely unknown, and hence a somewhat fearful element. Words must be chosen more carefully, and hence fluency may become a problem. Any doubts of the speaker about his own effectiveness as a communicator are magnified, and he may find it harder to be heard and understood easily. It is much easier to talk to four fellow members of a committee than to address a potential audience of thousands or even millions through television. The contrast between these two cases is extreme, but these difficulties become real in some measure when the audience consists only of a few listeners in the same room with the discussers.

Participants Are More Cautious

The cooperative participant tries to be objective and to modify his ideas if he hears better ones, but modification is more difficult before a listening audience. Once a participant has taken a public stand, he feels more obliged to defend it than to modify it. Even if he wants to abandon it in favor of another position that appears more reasonable to him, he is restrained by fears that the audience will judge him inconsistent, vacillating, or short on convictions. There is greater temptation to remain silent than to embrace the new proposal. When he reacts, he is more likely to approve it tentatively, with reservations, and to re-emphasize virtues in his initial position.

Cohesiveness Is Less Likely

In public discussion, there is less likelihood that the group will succeed in functioning as a cohesive unit. Since communicative interaction and objectivity are more difficult, it is harder for participants to work together as a unified group. They are more conscious of themselves as individuals. Each must consider the relational lines that tie him to each member of his audience, and this awareness competes with his efforts to develop group involvement with those who are also his fellow participants. It is possible that he thinks of the other discussers as part of the mass that makes up his audience rather than as members of an interacting discussion team of which he also is a part. Of course, cohesiveness may also be less important here, since many public discussions take place in momentary rather than continuing groups.

Leadership Is More Difficult

Most leadership responsibilities are more difficult to discharge in public than in closedgroup discussion. The designated leader, too, finds it harder to communicate effectively and to use language skillfully. He is under greater strain. He, too, is concerned with how the audience is reacting to him as well as to the discussion. It is harder for him to create permissiveness, promote easy interaction, elicit spontaneous contributions, encourage thorough discussion of each point, and develop cooperative group spirit.

Productivity Is Lessened

The outcome of a public discussion is likely to be lower in quality than that which would result under closedgroup conditions. Because of the restraints on communication and group cooperation, participants usually do not succeed in illuminating the problem as clearly for the audience as they could for each other, or in producing in public problem-solving discussion a decision that is as fully thought out, tested, and improved as it would be if the audience were not listening.

Of course, problem-solving public discussions do not usually lead directly to action. Their purpose is most often to stimulate listeners to decide what policy should be adopted by those responsible for a decision. Hence, the quality of the particular proposal recommended by a public panel is not as critical as that of the decision of a corporation's board of directors in closedgroup discussion.

These influences of the listener combine to make ideal interactional discussion more difficult. On the other hand, there are two effects of the audience in public discussion that make the designated leader's task easier.

Systematic Forward Movement Is Easier

The designated leader's guidance functions are less difficult to perform in public than in closedgroup discussion. Whatever systematic outline he chooses to follow in guiding the public group from problem to outcome, participants are not likely to interfere. In closedgroups, alert members may suggest modifications, often urge the leader to move on to another stage before he is ready, and occasionally usurp his guidance functions altogether. They will probably do none of these things in public discussion. Restraints against embarrassing the leader, or themselves if their leadership attempt fails, usually prevent them from interfering. In fact, they would not often take over guidance even if the leader followed no outline at all. This analysis suggests that able leadership is even more important in public than in closedgroup discussion.

Harmonious Interpersonal Relationships Are Easier

It is easier in public discussion to maintain harmonious interpersonal relationships, at least superficially. Members in public groups are more likely to be courteous and polite to each other, to suppress emotional outbursts, and to refrain from attacking persons as well as ideas. This personal cordiality may exist only on the surface, while the audience is listening. Hostility may be repressed but nonetheless present.

It is clear that there are special problems in presenting public discussion. Rhetorical elements must be understood and carefully considered by those planning, participating in, and leading public discussion.

Leadership planning functions are detailed in Chapter 4. The student should review these responsibilities in planning for public discussion. One additional responsibility in the public situation is publicizing the discussion in advance.

PARTICIPATING IN PUBLIC DISCUSSION

Everything said about participation in Chapter 9, and earlier in this book, is applicable in public discussion. Panels, and to some extent, forums, require interactional communication similar to that of closedgroups. The public participant has similar duties but usually finds each more difficult to perform. He must take the audience into account at every turn. He should try to anticipate how listeners will respond to a comment before he utters it. Words should be chosen more carefully because they must be instantly clear to many persons, each with unique background experiences, and free of distortion, slanting, and bias.

Interactional panel discussion demands that participants work harder to achieve unified group effort. Members must try to interact freely, in spite of increased restraints against communicating. They should strive to be objective and to contribute to group cohesiveness and to an informal, relaxed, permissive atmosphere. By being well informed and by discussing every point thoroughly, they should produce the highest quality outcome possible. Here, too, they should help the designated leader rather than stand in his way.

Public discussion puts more demands upon the participant as a speaker. Especially in symposium, he is a public speaker delivering connected discourse. The principles of public speaking cannot be reviewed here; whoever would be an effective public discusser should make a special study of public speaking. He should beware of misinterpretation: he is not to deliver bombastic, dramatic pronouncements *ex cathedra*. Whether he talks for 45 seconds at a time while seated in panel, or for 5 minutes while taking his turn in symposium, he utilizes the same principles of direct, natural, informal communication. His purpose should be clear; what he expects to accomplish by the contribution is adapted to what the audience wants and needs to know. The message should be clearly organized. Chaotic, disordered, repetitive discourse confuses more persons than it enlightens. He should sound like himself, speaking as naturally and easily as he does in conversation, while at the same time projecting to all the audience. He does not shout into a microphone, since electronic amplification is more efficient than he, nor does he speak inaudibly when required to reach two hundred people in an auditorium. He is enthusiastic and shows awareness of the meanings of words as he speaks them. He looks directly at his listeners. His facial expressions, gestures, and bodily actions are animated and consistent with his meaning.

LEADING PANEL DISCUSSION

Leadership challenges of the public panel are similar to those of all interactional discussion already explained in earlier chapters. The designated panel leader must understand and practice all these skills and more; he must do whatever he can to promote, in spite of the more difficult obstacles characteristic of the public situation, informality, permissiveness, cooperative attitudes, cohesiveness, and high-quality productivity.

Informality-Permissiveness

Discussers about to participate in an important public panel will, of course, feel the strain imposed by the approaching audience situation. The designated leader usually should try to assemble members for a short, informal session just before they step in front of audience, microphone, or camera. Such a prediscussion meeting is particularly important if they are unacquainted. They must have an opportunity to get each others' names, positions, and affiliations fixed firmly in mind. To have the best effect, this session should take place in comfortable, relaxed surroundings. It should be held in the same building in which the discussion is to take place, so there is no last-minute rush to studio or auditorium. An ideal setting would be a lounge with overstuffed furniture, where coffee could be served. In a closedgroup discussion, the chairman emphasizes the importance of the meeting and the group's efforts in order to stimulate maximally cooperative endeavor. In this prepublic relaxing session, however, his contribution is to communicate calm reassurance by his own casual manner and by his words. He may want to assure them that they will all do well, and that the fate of the world is not being decided during the approaching discussion. They need no reminder to do their best; usually their tension results from the extreme pressure they feel to do precisely this. The leader must decide from observing their behavior and from his knowledge of their previous training and experience in public situations just how much and what to say. Members can decide at this meeting whether to use first or last names, and formal titles, such as doctor, dean, or whatever. Using last names and titles increases formality, of course, but is necessary in some circumstances.

Perhaps the designated leader's best opportunity for encouraging informality and permissiveness comes in his introduction of the problem for discussion. He creates the atmosphere, sets the tone, and suggests by his meaning and manner what is expected of the participants. If he is tense, unsmiling, and cautious in referring to group and problem, members are likely also to proceed with precisely proper and dignified formality. Obviously, this kind of restraint may be appropriate in some situations. If the group wishes to achieve spontaneous, informal, permissive interaction, however, the leader must launch the discussion in such a manner. He should exhibit warm, friendly, relaxed informality. His opening statements should emphasize that every member is invited to speak up at any moment without waiting for recognition from the chairman; that the reaction of all to each comment is solicited; and that members are urged to speak frankly.

Throughout the discussion, the leader must retain this relaxed, easy approach. If members ask permission to speak next, he should respond with a nod and smile, rather than formally announced assignment of the floor. He should not ask a new question after each comment. Rather, he should wait for others to respond to the previous contribution or add something to it himself which will trigger further response. His vocal inflections and emphases when asking questions are important; a question asked stiffly, in an official-sounding manner, invites a formal speech in reply.

In maintaining permissive informality, the leader's most serious difficulties arise if clashes occur. When members' ideas are challenged and they feel obligated to defend them, formality almost certainly increases and the easy, relaxed atmosphere may disappear. Members are put on guard and choose what they say more cautiously. The leader should do whatever he can tactfully to defend the person attacked, to turn the challenge aside, or to move into other areas as swiftly as he can do so gracefully. Of course, conflict often makes the discussion lively and spirited, and if everyone freely enters into the clash, the leader may not have a problem at all, so long as the conflict is concentrated on the merits of ideas and not on personalities.

Attitudes

In a prediscussion meeting, the leader should emphasize tactfully the purpose and philosophy of public discussion: a public panel is usually designed to stimulate the thinking of the listening audience, to give listeners insight into various approaches to a problem, and to encourage the audience to decide how the problem may best be understood or solved. Discussers are obliged to give all views a full and fair hearing, and to explore the problem thoroughly. They are not often expected to air only their own convictions without regard to other participants. They should at least stimulate a process of collective exploration or decision-making.

With this emphasis, the leader can perhaps increase the likelihood that members will have cooperative attitudes. He will have succeeded if he can influence participants at least to express during the discussion an attitude such as this: "I cannot agree with you, but I am pleased that we can bring out fully as many views of the problem as possible so that our listeners can judge for themselves."

Throughout the panel, the leader should remind members of the value of objectivity with such reactions as these when unpopular points are stated and pounced upon: "Let's hear him out"; "Don't we want to explore all possibilities fully?"; and "Let's look at all sides of the question." He can also ask for rewording and careful definition when biased language is used.

Cohesiveness

Whether or not members of a public panel operate as a cohesive unit usually depends on the participants selected, their interrelationships prior to the discussion, and their preexistent attitudes toward the problem. If a televised discussion on national labor legislation has as participants two presidents of international labor unions and the presidents of two large corporations, it should come as no surprise when the group does not develop high cohesiveness. To say this is not to suggest that these persons should not be selected; this group could present a profitable and stimulating public discussion on this problem. To select them means that cohesiveness is not considered as important a criterion here as some other excellent qualities contributed by such a group.

Even in this situation, however, the leader should do what he can to get members to discuss as a unified team. He should stress areas of agreement and outlook—that both labor and management want to operate in the best interests of the public, for example—and encourage members holding either view to explore both advantages and disadvantages of proposals partisan to either side. The leader can insist on a fair, full, and courteous hearing for everyone. At the end, he will hope that all participants can endorse some statements of common position, even if they are relatively neutral statements about the public welfare.

Productivity

Naturally, the designated leader wants the panel to produce a high-quality outcome, in spite of the restraints within the public situation. One of his most effective contributions in this respect is made through having a clear, sensible outline, which guides the group systematically and efficiently, and which prevents tangential meandering. He must promote thorough discussion of the most relevant points. He must not allow the group to become so embroiled within one area of disagreement that no further forward progress is made. He must keep the group marching steadily to the final objective: a statement of the maximum agreement possible.

The presence of the audience restricts the leader's frankness in dealing with unproductive lines of thought. He cannot often say bluntly: "We're off the track; let's get back to the point." Instead, he must try patiently and indirectly to achieve forward movement. If his participants are strong-minded—and persons competent enough to take part in an important public panel often have such an attribute to some degree—his subtle efforts may not be completely successful. His success may be more directly related to the rapport he has established with them earlier, including his prediscussion relationship and his general reputation and ability. Certainly the designated leader of an influential panel must have knowledge of the problem and of group discussion, and experience as a chairman in public situations. It is helpful if he also enjoys the respect of the participants. This is no assignment for the shy, untrained beginner.

LEADERSHIP IN SPECIAL SITUATIONS

The duties of leadership in public discussion can be as varied as the kinds of public situations. The effective leader must understand what is expected of him in different circumstances. His functions in leading a forum period or in presiding at a symposium are not the same as those in a public panel. No complete guide to all situations can be presented here, but brief mention should be made of some special problems frequently encountered. Some of the suggestions in Chapter 18 related to discussion in large groups may also be helpful in this connection.

Presiding as Chairman

The designated leader for a symposium, lecture-forum, or debate-forum is more properly called a *presiding chairman*. His task is to control the meeting without being dominant; that is, he presents the problem and the speakers, but remains unobtrusively in the background. The audience assembles to hear the speakers; the chairman is an instrument for their efficient presentation and is more concerned with the mechanics of the meeting than with its substantive content. He influences substance in his introduction of the program, in any transitional statements between speakers, and in a final summary.

At the beginning, the chairman should introduce the problem for discussion by giving a brief sketch of the background, the immediate cause for the discussion, and an explanation of the way the program will be conducted. His other important duty is to introduce each speaker. In doing so, he should explain briefly the speaker's topic, and his background and experience, which make clear why he deserves to be heard with respect on this problem and on this occasion. He should announce clearly and accurately the speaker's name, titles, if any, and present position. Finally, the speaker should be presented in some simple yet graceful manner: "It is a pleasure to introduce to you Dr. William James." The speech of introduction should be short and efficient; if the speaker is to talk for 5 minutes, the presentation should take closer to 30 seconds than to 3 minutes. After one speech in symposium or debate-forum, the next speaker should be introduced in a similar manner, except that the chairman should attempt to relate the forthcoming speech to preceding ones. This statement, too, should be very brief. Of course, some chairmen avoid this problem by introducing all the speakers before anyone speaks. This procedure may have merit in some informal situations, but more important occasions usually demand that speakers be presented as their turn to speak arrives.

When all the speakers have been heard, there is usually a forum period. Before the forum begins, the chairman should attempt to summarize the speeches, briefly pointing up areas of agreement and conflict. Perhaps the word *summarize* is ill-chosen; he should not repeat what the audience has just heard. His intent should be to interpret similarities and dissimilarities in the speeches.

One other situation requiring a presiding chairman is the film-forum. Here the chairman's duties are somewhat different. Experts in the discussion of films say that intelligent responses are unlikely unless viewers are given in advance some suggestions about what to watch for. The chairman should preview the film and in introducing it explain briefly what the audience is about to see. Then he is usually wise to conduct a brief discussion involving the whole audience, in which agreement is reached on what parts of the film's contents are going to be most important to the group, ways in which the film is to be analyzed and evaluated in the forum period, and so on.

Leading a Forum Period

In a forum period it is usually wise to require contributors to stand so that they can be heard easily. With very large audiences it may be necessary to have members of the audience move to a microphone before speaking. Often the leader must restate or at least repeat the question or comment if it has not been made clearly or if it has not been heard distinctly by everyone.

The leader should try to spread participation from the audience as widely as possible. Apparently in large groups only a few persons are willing to participate at all. Among these, there are often two or three individuals who would be pleased to monopolize the rest of the evening. The leader must endeavor as gracefully as possible not to "see" these persons after their second or third contribution, but rather to encourage participation from others. Keeping track of the source of comments and questions is difficult in large groups. The leader can mentally divide the audience into sections and try not to recognize speakers from any one section until other areas have been heard from.

There are three types of contributions most often offered in forum periods: questions directed to the speakers just heard; substantive comments expressing a point of view; and consummatory communications in which the speaker from the audience uses this occasion to put into words some feeling important to him. The chairman must listen intently to the type of communication and decide what will be the appropriate response.

When questions are directed to speakers on the platform, the leader should suggest that questions be addressed to a specific speaker. Otherwise, there is the awkward problem of asking which member of the panel is willing to answer. A further advantage of having questions directed to individuals is that the leader can then encourage listeners to distribute questions among various members of the participating group. It often happens that most of the questions are aimed at one or two speakers; this imbalance soon becomes painful to the overworked answerer and to the other speakers, who wonder why their remarks did not stimulate equal amounts of interest. Actually, this imbalance just as frequently indicates that the overworked answerer gave a biased or unsound presentation which the audience then assails delightedly although, usually, ever so politely.

If there are personal attacks or insults directed at speakers, it is the leader's responsibility to protect the feelings of his panel members. To do so, he must be clever and must have a keen sense of the mood of his audience. He is aided immeasurably by a sense of humor. If a question is asked that the leader considers too personal, inappropriate, or unfair, he can sometimes turn the questioner aside with a remark such as this: "If we ask Mr. Jones to answer that question, it might break up the meeting. Is there another question?" The leader must be sure, however, that the majority of the audience also senses that the questioner is being unfair. Unless the leader keeps the audience with him, there will be more and more critical questions, and he may lose control of the situation altogether.

Consummatory comments should have a polite hearing and then they should be ignored if possible. Unless the contributor insists on a response, the chairman should move on to another question or comment. Whereas the substantive comment usually deserves a response of some kind from one of the earlier speakers on the program, the consummatory contribution often is puzzling and unclear. To answer may make matters worse instead of better. Of course, one problem for the presiding chairman is to differentiate between substantive and self-expressive communications.

Every audience situation is uniquely and excitingly different from every other, and the leader must learn, largely through experience, what is appropriate and effective under the circumstances. Most audiences are civilized, restrained, considerate, and polite. In general, they are sympathetically aware of the leader's difficult position. Rarely does a leader blunder to the extent that the audience rebels and the speakers regret their presence on the program. If he can remain calm and exercise reasonably good judgment, he will usually sense what actions he should take to end the meeting successfully.

SUPPLEMENTARY READING

Howell, William S., and Smith, Donald K., *Discussion*, New York: Crowell-Collier and Macmillan, 1956, Chapters 1 and 11.

Lasswell, Harold D., "The Clarifier of Public Discussion, *Quarterly Journal of Speech*, 34 (December, 1948), pp. 451–4.

McBurney, James H., and Hance, Kenneth G., *Discussion in Human Affairs*, New York: Harper & Row, 1950, Chapters 20 and 21.

Sattler, William M., and Miller, N. Edd, *Discussion and Conference*, Englewood Cliffs, N.J.: Prentice-Hall, 1954, Chapter 17.

Wagner, Russell H., and Arnold, Carroll C., *Handbook of Group Discussion*, Boston: Houghton Mifflin, 1950, Chapter 9.

Zelko, Harold P., *Successful Conference and Discussion Techniques*, New York: McGraw-Hill, 1957, Part IV.

QUESTIONS AND EXERCISES

1. What differences would you expect to observe between public and closed-group problem-solving discussion in (a) attitudes of the participants toward other participants; (b) contributions of the participants; and (c) behavior of the leader during the discussion.

2. What procedures could be used during a forum period to stimulate audience participation?

3. Write a paper in which you explain and illustrate the differing conditions under which you could most effectively use one rather than another of the forms of public discussion: panel, symposium, dialogue, film-forum, lecture-forum, debate, and the hybrid forms.

4. To illustrate something of the differences between closedgroup and public discussion, divide the class into small buzz groups and hold multiple, simultaneous discussions for 10 to 12 minutes on one of the cases printed in the Appendix. Then choose a representative from each buzz group and

put this demonstration group in front of the class to hold a public panel discussion for 15 minutes. After the demonstration, have the whole class consider the differences observed between closedgroup and public discussion.

Chapter 18

DISCUSSION
IN LARGE GROUPS

Some especially difficult problems confront those attempting to achieve effective discussion among large numbers of participants. Two types of closed-group situations are of primary concern here. The first occurs when a large group wishes to use direct, conversational, interactional discussion in spite of the fact that many members are present. Unfortunately, for employing inter-actional discussion, fifteen or twenty persons constitute a large group; for a larger group of forty or fifty, direct interchange becomes extremely difficult. Problems met on such occasions are similar to those occurring in the forum period in public discussion.

A second situation of importance is the large conference or convention, in which a hundred or a thousand or even more delegates assemble for consider-ation of shared interests.

In any large group, the leadership challenge is to secure involvement of every individual through active participation, overt or covert. Whether or not each person contributes overtly, a climate must be created in which each member feels he has had the opportunity to communicate.

INTERACTIONAL DISCUSSION IN LARGE GROUPS

Interactional discussion in small groups involves direct, free, easy inter-change; members speak up without waiting for recognition by the leader; each communicator is aware of every other as a person and of his reactions. It is easy to see why the situation is altered when there are forty persons interacting rather than five. To be aware of every other member is difficult; each com-municator tends to consider his listeners a mass of others, an audience. He is less likely to feel that he is talking directly to a few separate individuals. Yet this kind of direct interaction is desirable in many large group situations. A staff, city council, board, civic group, or club often feels the need to talk things over as a whole unit, even though there are forty or fifty members.

On such occasions, leaders and participants must understand the differences introduced by large size. They can then proceed to achieve the maximum interaction possible under the circumstances.

Large-Group Obstacles to Interaction

In any group some persons talk more than others, and in large groups this discrepancy is magnified. This phenomenon occurs because some members feel increasing restraints against communicating as the group increases in size. These same silent and semisilent members would talk animatedly in a committee of five. If they were asked why they contributed little or nothing in the large group situation, they would offer explanations such as these:

1. "I didn't want to expose my ignorance in front of all those people." ("All those people" may be only eighteen others.)
2. "I felt others were more qualified than I to speak on this problem."
3. "I didn't think what I had to offer would make any difference in the outcome."
4. "Someone else had already said just about what I wanted to say."
5. "A member who is much more influential in the group than I am had already talked and I didn't want to go against him in front of everybody."
6. "I don't mind expressing in a committee what may be judged a foolish idea, but I didn't want to appear a fool in public." (Notice that the larger group seems "public" while a committee is perceived as a private situation.)
7. "I didn't think all those people would want to take valuable time to hear my ideas, which probably aren't very good anyway."
8. "I knew that time was limited and I thought it was more important to hear the ideas of others."

These comments indicate the defensiveness of the semisilent communicator, and they suggest the pressure placed upon the member by the presence of a sizeable audience.

Also, in larger groups some individuals become accustomed to being passive, immobile listeners. This role is comfortable, secure, and minimally threatening. The communication is largely one way, from the high participators to the mass of others. When the group is large enough to take on the characteristics of an audience, some members feel they can be anonymous and remain undetected as part of the passive mass.

An obvious obstacle to lively interaction in large groups is lack of time. If unlimited time were available, there would almost surely be some participation by many members. If a group of 30 spends 30 minutes discussing an important matter, however, there would be only one minute of speaking time for each, even if the time were divided equally, which can almost never be done. Members may be extremely sensitive to the shortness of time, and may hesitate to use time that, they feel, might more profitably be taken by others.

Minimizing Effects of Large Size

If interaction is to be achieved in larger groups, participation must be spread to as many persons as possible. The designated leader's role becomes much more important. He must create a permissive climate and stress that wide participation is imperative if group understanding is to result. He should emphasize each individual's responsibility to feel involved in the discussion. He must restrain the eager participators after they have spoken two or three times, and draw out the silent members. He can do so with frequent questions, if necessary directing them to "those of you we have not yet heard from."

The leader can remind the group frankly that discussion is more difficult in larger groups, and urge them to cooperate in achieving balanced communication and permissiveness. He can try to persuade them to spend as much time as is necessary to accomplish thorough discussion of an important problem. If it becomes obvious that two or three persons have dominated the discussion, and that the outcome will represent their influence rather than group consensus, he can call attention to this fact and recommend additional time, postponement of final decision, or some method of securing wider participation, as suggested in the following section.

As group size increases, the degree of interaction occurring seems to be a function of the designated leader's skill. He should realize that he must work harder than in small groups to build a permissive atmosphere, to emphasize the common interests of the whole group, and to get members to think together as a cohesive unit.

In small groups, the leader usually can choose whether he wishes to be an active, partisan participator as well as leader, or to be an impartial guide and moderator. In larger groups, he has no such choice. He cannot often offer substantive comments. He must give all or most of his mental energies to guidance and control functions. Permissiveness, cohesiveness, consensus, and member satisfaction with the discussion almost always result directly from the leader's success in promoting balanced participation, systematic forward movement, and so on, in spite of large numbers and minimal time.

SECURING PARTICIPATION-INVOLVEMENT

When groups are too large for direct interaction, or when in a group of thirty or forty wide participation is not forthcoming, several methods can be employed to secure universal participation and involvement. The method of direct interaction allows only one person to speak at a time—all the others become for the moment passive listeners. If a particular individual does not become a communicator at all, his involvement is usually indirect, as part of an audience. The essence of obtaining universal participation-involvement in large groups is to have several persons talk at the same time—in different groups, of course—and to secure increased covert response.

Buzz Groups

The buzz session is the most familiar method for allowing everyone in a large group to talk within a short period of time. Developed by J. D. Phillips and often called "Phillips 66"—where subgroups of 6 discuss for 6 minutes—

this format has the virtue of great flexibility.[1] After hearing a presentation, or after general discussion by a whole group, or even prior to a program, the large group is divided into units of six or eight persons. Each of these buzz groups is asked to consider some specific question. All the small groups may be answering the same question, or each may have a different problem. Each group selects a leader and/or a recorder and decides what it will report to the whole assembly. At the end of the allotted period, the large group hears from each small unit through its leader or recorder. In this way, every individual takes an active role in deliberation, even though his contribution is filtered through the reporter for his buzz unit. Member satisfaction is almost certainly increased by this process and usually there is a noticeable increase in interaction within the large meeting following a buzz session.

Success of this method depends largely on the quality of questions assigned to each small unit. They must be limited in scope so that a short discussion is fruitful rather than frustrating. They must create spontaneous interest. Their relation to the problem facing the whole group must be instantly apparent. Buzz groups must be small and if they are there will be no problem of animated talk and universal participation, even in a situation where the designated leader failed to get a single comment in the large meeting. The time allowed for discussion in the buzz units should be as short as possible, consistent with the problem given them, to create a sense of urgency and importance.

Multiple Role-Playing

Maier has coined the term "Multiple Role-Playing (MRP)" to designate a method of universal participation in large groups, which combines "Phillips 66" with role-playing. He uses MRP in training sessions to allow supervisors to experience the feelings of employees. Members of the large group are divided into small units and each member is given a specific assignment. One is the supervisor and each of the others plays the role of a particular employee. In one of Maier's training sessions, each small unit was a crew of repairmen; its problem was to decide which employee was to be assigned a new truck. After the MRP session, each small group reported how the "supervisor" handled the discussion, and who received the new truck.[2]

Other Methods

Bradford suggests three other methods for increasing audience participation and covert involvement in large group situations. Members can be organized before a presentation into "audience listening teams." Each team is asked to

[1] J. D. Phillips, "Report on Discussion 66," *Adult Education Journal*, 7 (1948), pp. 181–2.
[2] Norman R. F. Maier and L. Zerfoss, "MRP: A Technique for Training Large Groups of Supervisors and Its Potential Use in Social Research," *Human Relations*, 5 (1952), pp. 177–86.

listen for different things, such as how this information can be applied to this organization or what other ideas might have been explained. After the presentation, there may be forty or sixty members of each listening team, who are then divided into buzz groups to decide what they wish to report to the entire assembly in connection with their listening assignment.

Another method is to select individuals from the audience for service on an "audience representational panel," which interacts with the speaker in responding to the program, and to the reports of buzz groups or listening teams. The representational panel asks the questions and makes the comments for the other members of the audience.

A method used by Bradford and others to encourage individual involvement covertly, where there is little opportunity for overt expression, is the "post-meeting reaction sheet." Members of the audience are asked to evaluate the program and make suggestions for improvement.[3]

These and similar methods can also be employed during general sessions of complex conventions.

THE LARGE CONFERENCE-CONVENTION

Almost any type of large meeting may be labeled by its sponsors a conference or convention. The term *workshop* has also become a popular designation for a certain type of large meeting. The distinguishing features which properly place these events in such a general category of conferences-conventions-workshops are that large numbers of persons are involved—occasionally fewer than a hundred but often more than a thousand—and that usually there are multiple meetings occurring simultaneously at least some of the time. The kind of discussion used, if any, can only be determined by examining specific sessions. A corporation may call all its salesmen to the home plant to explain a new policy or demonstrate a new product and present the communication in a one-way audience situation without using discussion at all. Allowing a forum period after the presentation introduces a discussion feature, but this event has little similarity to a multiple-meeting conference or convention.

The extent to which discussion is used usually depends on the purpose of the large meeting. One purpose is information-sharing. College teachers of history or geology from all over the nation may gather in a Chicago hotel during the Christmas holidays to hear new ideas from scholarly research and teaching. Members of the American Medical Association may assemble to learn about new techniques and discoveries. Another purpose is stimulation. A life insurance company may call its salesmen into conference with the primary aim of sending them home determined to sell more insurance. A third purpose is decision-making, or its corollary, attitude change. The nominating conventions of the political parties meet to choose presidential candidates.

[3] Leland P. Bradford and S. Corey, "Improving Large Group Meetings," *Adult Education*, 1 (1951), pp. 122–37.

Most large conferences, however, do not have such a specific decision-making function. More often a purpose of this sort is restricted to attitude change; the state association of parents and teachers hopes that local PTA's will push harder for additional local money for schools, but at its state convention programs advocating this policy may be presented without asking the delegates to do more than decide for themselves when they return home.

Actually, most conferences-conventions do not have a simple, single purpose, as these statements suggest. The aim of information-sharing, stimulation, or attitude change may be primary, but often all three will be pursued at different sessions during the convention. At the national convention of history teachers, for example, there may be a general session which aims to stimulate members to become inspired teachers of history, dozens of smaller sessions designed to give information, and a business session which makes decisions on dues, future meetings, and similar matters.

Planning

Months of work and careful planning must be invested in any successful conference-convention. Since one of the most important leadership challenges is to secure member involvement through active participation and through understanding of the common aims of the meeting, letters to members should emphasize its importance and its purposes. Often members can be involved in initial planning by being asked by letter or questionnaire to indicate what kinds of aims and programs they would prefer.

Convention management is an art in its own right and the details cannot be discussed fully here. Planners must arrange for meeting rooms; registration, housing, and perhaps entertainment of delegates; presiding chairman; speakers; discussion leaders; timing and control of sessions; and many other matters. Interest here must focus on discussion chosen for various purposes in different sessions, on member participation-involvement, and on communication problems.

Opening Sessions

Most conferences-conventions open with a general session for all members. The purpose is to stimulate. Emphasis is on the importance of the organization and this particular meeting, the aims shared by all members, and the values to be derived from participation. The usual program format is to have a presiding officer, often a high-ranking officer of the organization, who presents a keynote speaker. This speech may be a presidential address or it may be a message from a respected outsider. A national meeting of teachers of speech, for example, may have as keynoter a congressman who not only is a successful practitioner of political speaking but who is also a former professor of speech.

The keynote speech, whether given by the presiding officer, the president, or an outsider, must establish the desired atmosphere or climate for the conference. Some persons consider such a speech of stimulation corny, but members need to be reminded of what the organization stands for, what it has done for them and promises to do for them in the future, and how ineffective it would be without their participation, support, and loyalty. To encourage member enthusiasm for the conference, the keynote speech must be delivered dynamically and vigorously, worded strikingly, and designed to help listeners visualize the potential values of the meeting and their vital role in it.

The opening session sets the tone for the entire conference. Members must be moved to feel involved and motivated to participate actively. At the same time, they must be stimulated to see the relationship between this meeting and their home situation, where they must apply whatever benefits are derived. Benne and Demorest have compared the attendees to travelers in the "strange land of conference." One kind of response is to feel like a tourist who is just sight-seeing, or passing through, and who can take it or leave it but would rather leave it. He resists involvement and views the proceedings with curious detachment. He does not want new ideas to upset him in his settled ways back home. Another equally undesirable response is that of the expatriate, who is so enthusiastic and accepts the new ideas of the conference so uncritically that he is ready to abandon his accustomed adjustments at home and live in the exciting new world being applauded at the meeting. This response is unrealistic since the value of the convention is to improve rather than to replace established methods. The conference adjustment Benne and Demorest recommend is that of the learner who recognizes his dual belonging in the conference and the home situation, and who resolves to incorporate at home whatever new concepts seem valuable and applicable after careful consideration. The opening session in particular and the whole conference in general should be designed to stimulate this kind of rational and personal involvement on the part of each member.[4]

Methods used in the opening session depend on aims and on the ingenuity of planners. Probably maximum member involvement will not result from a single speech utilizing one-way speaker–audience communication. Buzz groups, role-playing or case conference demonstrations, multiple role-playing, audience reaction teams, or other devices can be used to achieve universal participation or to heighten the feeling of individual association in the purposes of the conference.

PRESIDING OFFICER/ The presiding officer for a general conference session performs much the same function as does the presiding chairman at a public symposium or lecture-forum (see Chapter 17). He must remain in the background, so to speak, but his decisions and actions exert tremendous influence on the success of the session. He must analyze carefully what is appropriate in the situation, taking into account the purposes of the meeting, the nature of the organization and membership, and the planned program

[4] Kenneth D. Benne and C. K. Demorest, "Building the Conference Community," *Adult Leadership*, 2 (1953), pp. 8–12.

format. He must say precisely the right things, and no more, by way of welcome and stimulation. Within these limitations, he should in introducing the program be sincerely enthusiastic about the cause the conference represents, stimulate members to be enthusiastic about it, point with pride to past accomplishments and aims, and subtly attempt to build loyalty to and solidarity of the group.

He must deliver competently the speeches demanded by the occasion, such as speeches of introduction, of inspiration and stimulation, of presentation of gifts and awards, and of acceptance of gifts and awards on behalf of the organization.

Multiple Meetings

The spade work of most conferences-conventions is done in small meetings held simultaneously in different rooms. Those members with special interests separate into groups sharing common aims. The national convention of the Speech Association of America, for example, whose members are teachers of speech, has sessions on British and American public address, discussion, debate, interpretation, personal and social psychology of speech, and similar topics. An industrial conference may have small group meetings on sales, marketing, industrial design, and cost accounting. These multiple groups may each hold four or five morning and afternoon sessions during the conference-convention.

In other conferences, the small groups may all be engaged in the same activity. Suppose, for instance, that a life insurance company holds a national meeting for representative agents from each district. The single subject for consideration may be how to increase sales. In order to secure universal participation and involvement, the four hundred delegates may be divided into fifty working groups of eight. The task of each group is to discuss ways of selling more life insurance. At a later general session, each group can share its conclusions with the others.

Whether or not such multiple meetings accomplish the purposes of the conference obviously depends on what goes on at them. Those responsible for planning must be certain that these groups utilize the discussion format that can most effectively achieve results. Here, too, the possibilities are almost endless and what can be done is limited largely by the ingenuity of planners. It is of course impossible to specify generally what should be done in all situations, since appropriate methods are determined by factors peculiar to a specific conference and sponsoring organization. Some of the possibilities, however, can be suggested:

1. If the purpose is to inform members with special interests about new concepts, research, and techniques, then a useful format is information-sharing symposium-forum or lecture-forum. Multiple meetings at a convention of history or of speech teachers use this form. Speeches are given by persons with special competence who have engaged in some research or investigation of

interest, and these are followed by forum periods. Frequent weaknesses are that communication is one-way, too many speeches are scheduled within the limited time available, and the forum period is brief and unproductive. Sufficient time for thorough discussion should be provided, and member involvement can be increased by utilizing buzz sessions, audience representational panels, or reaction sheets as a functional part of the forum period.

2. If the purpose is to acquaint members with the thinking of persons of special competence in an area that has not yet been subjected to specific research and investigation, then a possible format is informational panel-forum. An industrial conference on industrial design could be devoted to probable future developments in the design of household appliances. Rather than listen to individual presentations, participants may prefer to invite specialists to interact in a panel, hoping that the resulting stimulation will produce new insights in what is essentially a creative process. The shortcomings in such sessions usually result from unwise selection of participants or leader. Unless they have some new ideas and have prepared thoroughly for this presentation, little stimulation for listeners will result. One of the tragedies of the panel method is that some participants feel they need not prepare in advance or bring any special information to the situation. Since responsibility is shared by five persons, each may feel that his neglect can be somehow compensated for by the others. A properly planned and conducted panel, however, can be extremely productive and the forum period a time of creative thinking.

3. If the purpose is to increase understanding about ways of approaching and investigating a new problem in which all members are involved, a fruitful form is the round-table, more often called in the conference situation a *workshop*. The multiple groups are small so that all members can participate in interactional discussion throughout the entire session. Success of the work group usually is a function of the topic for discussion, since it must be a subject that can be profitably explored by a group; of the leadership supplied, since such a session can easily get off the track and waste its time; and of the quality of participant preparation, since uninformed members sharing nothing will emerge as empty headed as they entered.

4. If the purpose is to help members decide about new policies and procedures, possible forms are policy-determination symposium-forum, panel-forum, and debate-forum. If no clear proposal for action has emerged, but if there are a number of available alternatives, the symposium format is best, since each speaker can advocate the proposal he feels is superior. If the problem has been long discussed, however, and a particular proposal is being considered for adoption, the debate form is more appropriate. Speakers for and against the proposed policy can help crystallize member thinking. Panel is best when concrete proposals have not yet crystallized. In planning such programs, the most important criterion is fairness; each proposal must be given equal and rational consideration.

There are many other variations of programs using discussion methods. These possibilities suggest some of the basic forms. In some conferences, much more emphasis is placed on member participation through role-playing, buzz sessions, and other devices. Some small group meetings make more use of visual aids, questionnaires, and reaction sheets.

Discussion Leaders

It is obvious that much of the success of multiple meetings is related to the skill possessed by the leaders in charge. It is a responsibility of those planning the conference to choose and often to train the leaders who will supervise the sectional groups. If discussion leaders and presiding chairmen are unskillful, and if they do not understand their mission and the relationship between the small meeting and the whole conference, the quality of program certainly will be lessened.

Resource Persons

Much is made in many conferences of the resource person or resource leader, who is supposedly an expert on the subject the group is discussing and a storehouse of knowledge to be tapped when members need a fact. He may be especially useful in a workshop.

If the resource person is indeed an expert, he can be worth thrice his weight in garden-variety members. Facts are an indispensable ingredient of effective discussion; most members attend conferences primarily to gain new insights and happy is the conferee who learns genuinely new and useable facts from a resource leader.

A word of caution may be appropriate, however. Resource persons must be chosen with extreme thoughtfulness. Many jibes are hurled at experts—an expert, for example, is a man fifty miles from home—and some are justified. Unless the resource leader has some special competence and knowledge, the group is better off struggling through the problem on its own. There is a danger that members will defer to the resource person, or that he will actually take over the leadership of the group, which is not his function. If he is used for strengthening the resources available to the group, if he contributes only when members ask for help, and if he can supply desperately needed information when facts are not otherwise forthcoming or are being distorted, then he can be a most valuable addition to a discussion.

Closing Session

Just as the opening session sets the tone and stimulates member interest, a closing session usually summarizes the proceedings and emphasizes values derived. The importance both to individual members and to the organization is stressed. The most vital contribution of the closing session in many conferences is to demonstrate application in the home situation. As individuals prepare to depart, their thoughts are most often on uses they may be able to make of conference learning. Here is another opportunity to secure member involvement and participation. Usually included in closing events is a request for evaluations of the conference and suggestions for future improvements.

THE PARLIAMENTARY MEETING

A specialized kind of large meeting is the parliamentary assembly. Many organizations hold business meetings in connection with an annual convention-conference. The national political nominating conventions spend most of a week in parliamentary session selecting candidates for president and vice-president, and drafting a platform.

A meeting using parliamentary procedures is not using discussion except in the most general sense, although such a group can go into "committee of the whole" and employ what is essentially informal, large-group, interactional discussion.

For efficiency, a group must utilize parliamentary methods when (*a*) large numbers of persons are involved in reaching decisions on (*b*) several complex problems (*c*) in a limited time. The chairman, called a *speaker* in the House of Representatives and the British House of Commons, *president* in the U.S. Senate, and addressed as "Mr. Chairman" in ordinary organizations, must have special training in parliamentary procedures. He must demonstrate his ability to conduct the meeting competently, fairly, and efficiently. He is granted certain powers by the assembly in order to control the meeting, to prevent chaos, to provide orderly debate, to determine majority will, and to protect the minority's right to be heard.

The parliamentary chairman, it must be repeated, should have a thorough understanding of procedures if he is to conduct this kind of meeting successfully. Only some of the minimum essentials can be sketchily presented here in order to suggest the type of knowledge the good chairman must have. Members of the assembly, too, should understand the rules if they are to participate effectively.

Classification of Motions

There are four classes of motions. *Main* motions propose action or substantive policy: "I move that dues be raised $1 a week," or "I move that this organization contribute $100 to the Community Chest." *Subsidiary* motions relate to the substance of the main motion and can serve one of three purposes: to alter wording of the main motion (to amend); to control discussion (limit debate, end debate); or to postpone immediate consideration of the main motion (lay on the table, postpone to a definite time, refer to committee, postpone indefinitely). *Incidental* motions arise in the conduct of business and relate to the machinery of operating the meeting; they are unrelated to the substance of the main motion. Examples of incidental motions are to appeal the chair's decision, to ask for division of the house (another vote), to suspend the rules, and a point of order. *Privileged* motions relate to convenience and privileges of members and the welfare of the organization. A motion to adjourn or to recess is a privileged motion.

Presenting and Disposing of Motions

Business is conducted in a parliamentary assembly through the consideration of motions. In principle, a member can say nothing except in response to a motion or to offer a motion. There are eight essential steps in presentation and disposal of motions:

1. The member rises and addresses the chairman: "Mr. Chairman" or "Mr. President." If a woman is presiding, the proper greeting is "Madam Chairman."
2. The member waits for recognition from the chairman. He does not have the floor until he is recognized. The chairman should say, "Mr. Brown," or "The chair recognizes the member in the back row," or he may merely nod.
3. The member states his motion: "I move that. . . ." He then resumes his seat.
4. The chairman asks if there is a second to the motion. It is not necessary to rise and be recognized to second a motion; a member merely calls out: "Second."
5. The chairman states the motion: "It has been moved and seconded that. . . ." Technically, the motion is not before the assembly until the chairman has so stated it. At this point, the chairman asks, "Is there discussion?"
6. The assembly discusses (debates) the motion. Any member may speak to the motion by obtaining recognition. Debate must be germane (relevant). Debate continues until no one wishes to speak, or until there is a motion to end debate which receives a two-thirds vote. When debate has apparently stopped, the chairman may say, "Is there further discussion? Are you ready for the question (that is, to take a vote)?"
7. The assembly now votes on the motion. In putting the question, the chairman says, "As many as are in favor of the motion, say 'Aye.' Those opposed say 'No.' " This is voting *viva voce* (by the living voice). It may be necessary for the chairman or the secretary to re-read the motion before the vote if there is confusion about it. After a voice vote, if there seem to be an equal number of "ayes" and "noes" the chairman or any member may ask for a division of the house. The vote will then be repeated, with members raising hands or rising. The affirmative vote must always be taken first, and the negative vote must always be called for even if everyone seems to have voted affirmatively.
8. The chairman announces the result of the vote. He says, "The 'ayes' have it, and the motion is carried." Technically, the motion is not carried or lost until the chairman announces that it is.

Precedence

It is not enough that the chairman know the kinds of motions and ways of handling them. While one kind of motion is on the floor, others may be offered. If he does not understand which motions can properly be considered while others are on the floor, the meeting will soon be in a hopeless snarl. The priority of motions is dictated by *precedence*. Each motion has its own precedence, priority, or rank. When one motion is on the floor, another with higher precedence must be considered while the initial motion waits right where it is in suspended animation, in much the same way that an army general takes priority over a junior officer because of his higher rank.

Only one main (substantive) motion may be considered on the floor at one time. If someone has moved that the organization contribute $100 to the Community Chest, no other member may move that it sponsor a children's party until the Community Chest motion is disposed of. However, while the Community Chest motion is being considered, any other motion which has a higher precedence than a main motion is in order. For example, member B may move to amend by striking $100 and inserting $75. This now becomes the business before the house, because the motion to amend has precedence over a main motion. While debate on the amendment is in progress, member C may move to lay the motion on the table, and before a vote is taken on the motion to table, member D may move to adjourn, because each of these motions has a higher precedence than the one preceding it. Thus, there are four motions on the floor at the same time: main, to amend, to table, and to adjourn. If the motion to adjourn is defeated, the next order of business is the motion to table, and so on, according to the ranks of the motions.

A clearer idea of precedence can be obtained from careful study of the chart of motions presented here. This chart includes only those motions used most often.

Interrupting the Speaker

For the most part, the member who has been granted the floor is allowed to finish his remarks without interruption by other members. In some organizations, members are allowed to ask the chairman if the speaker will yield so that they may ask a question or comment briefly. There are a few matters, however, that deserve to come to the assembly's attention immediately, even if another member is making a speech. For these special purposes, a member is allowed to *interrupt the speaker*. Examples of motions that may interrupt are questions of rights and privileges, call for orders of the day, point of order, and objection to consideration.

Requiring a Second

Most motions require a second before they can be considered. This requirement simply means that at least two members must be interested in considering a motion before it can claim the time and attention of the assembly. If the chairman hears no second he says, "The motion is lost for want of a second." Motions not requiring a second concern questions of privilege, the orders of the day, point of order, division of the house, rise for information, and object to consideration.

CHART OF MOTIONS

Down to the Main Motion, the higher the motion on this chart, the higher its precedence.

PRIVILEGED MOTIONS	May Inter- rupt	Must Sec- ond	De- bat- able	May Amend	Vote
Rights and Privileges of Members					
Fix Time for an Adjourned Meeting		Sec		Am	Maj
Adjourn (main motion if qualified)		Sec			Maj
Take a recess		Sec	Deb[1]	Am	Maj
Question of Rights and Privileges	Int				no[3]
Call for Orders of the Day	Int				no[3]

SUBSIDIARY MOTIONS					
Alter wording, control discussion, avoid immediate consideration					
Lay on the Table		Sec			Maj
End Debate		Sec			⅔
Limit or Extend Debate		Sec		Am	⅔
Postpone to Definite Time		Sec	Deb	Am	Maj[4]
Refer to Committee		Sec	Deb	Am	Maj
Amend		Sec	Deb[2]	Am	Maj
Postpone Indefinitely		Sec	Deb		Maj

MAIN MOTION (Substantive: pro- posal for action)		Sec	Deb	Am	Maj

INCIDENTAL MOTIONS					
Arise in conduct of business: relate to machinery of meeting					
Precedence: Take priority over the motion to which they relate; must be disposed of at once.					
Division of the House					no[3]
Point of Order	Int				no[3]
Rise for Information	Int				no[3]
Appeal the Chair's Decision	Int	Sec	Deb[2]		Maj
Suspend the Rules		Sec			⅔
Object to Consideration	Int				⅔

[1] Length of recess is debatable.

[2] If motion it applies to is debatable.

[3] No vote required; chair rules.

[4] 2-3 vote if special order.

Amending

A motion may be amended if its wording may be improved, or if it can be changed to better serve the interests of the majority. Main motions are the ones most frequently amended. When an amendment is offered, an amendment to the amendment is in order, but this is as far as the amendment process may be carried; there can be no amendments to the amendment to the amendment. When an amendment is proposed, it must be voted on and disposed of before another amendment can be offered, although an amendment to the amendment may be proposed while the motion to amend is still on the floor. If member A moves that the organization sponsor evening classes in history, member B may move to amend by striking the word *history* and inserting the words *wood-working*. The amendment has precedence and debate must now be confined to the amendment. Member C may now move to amend the amendment by striking the word *wood* and inserting the word *metal*. After the amendment to the amendment passes or fails, the business before the house is the amendment, to change history to wood-working (or metal-working if the amendment to the amendment carried). When the amendment is disposed of, the business on the floor is the initial main motion, as now amended (if any amendments carried).

Debate

Debate is allowed on motions in which the presentation of information and the sharing of opinion would help the assembly reach a wise decision. The best example is the main motion, where debate is the right of the members in a democratic society. Debate is not allowed on those motions where delay or talk would not be helpful. The motion to end debate is undebatable, for example, since talk about it would defeat the purpose, which is to get an immediate vote. Debate would also use up time which members want to save by voting to end debate.

Vote Required

A majority vote (one vote more than half the votes cast) is required to pass a main motion and most of the other motions. Some motions require a two-thirds vote. These include motions that end debate, limit debate, prevent consideration of a question, change the regular order of business, or suspend rules that the absent member may reasonably assume will be followed. Some motions do not require a formal vote, but may be decided by the chairman, subject, of course, to an appeal from his decision. An example is the point of order. On other occasions, the chairman need not put a motion to vote if there seems to be general consent. He may ask, "Is there objection to incorporation of this word into the main motion?" Silence indicates general consent. If there is objection from a single member, however, he must put the matter to vote.

By following these and similar procedures, the parliamentary chairman may conduct orderly deliberation in this specialized kind of meeting.

SUPPLEMENTARY READING

Beal, George M., Bohlen, Joe M., and Raudabaugh, J. N., *Leadership and Dynamic Group Action*, Ames: Iowa State University Press, 1962, pp. 271–85.

Benne, Kenneth D., and Demorest, C. K., "Building the Conference Community," *Adult Leadership*, 2 (1953), pp. 8–12.

Bradford, Leland P., "Leading the Large Meeting," *Adult Education Bulletin*, 14 (1949), pp. 38–50.

Bradford, Leland P., and Corey, S., "Improving Large Group Meetings," *Adult Education*, 1 (1951), pp. 122–37.

Lasswell, Harold D., "The Clarifier of Public Discussion," *Quarterly Journal of Speech*, 34 (December, 1948), pp. 451–4.

Maier, Norman R. F., and Zerfoss, L., "MRP: A Technique for Training Large Groups of Supervisors and Its Potential Use in Social Research," *Human Relations*, 5 (1952), pp. 177–86.

Phillips, J. D., "Report on Discussion 66," *Adult Education Journal*, 7 (1948), pp. 181–2.

Robert, Henry M., *Robert's Rules of Order Revised*, seventy-fifth anniversary edition, Chicago: Scott, Foresman, 1951.

Sattler, William M., and Miller, N. Edd, *Discussion and Conference*, Englewood Cliffs, N.J.: Prentice-Hall, 1954, Chapter 18.

Simons, Herbert W., "Representative versus Participative Patterns of Deliberation in Large Groups," *Quarterly Journal of Speech*, 52 (1966), pp. 164–71.

QUESTIONS AND EXERCISES

1. Write a paper in which you describe a group discussion involving thirty or forty persons. Explain how you would proceed if you were the designated leader and precisely what you would do, in trying to help the group to be productive, to take into account the fact that, "as group size increases, the degree of interaction occurring seems to be a function of the designated leader's skill."

2. Visit several different sessions of a large convention. Classify the kinds of discussion being employed in the various meetings, and describe the differences. What kinds of leadership are used in connection with each of the types of discussion?

3. *Robert's Rules of Order*, according to one source (Bert and Frances Strauss, *New Ways to Better Meetings*, New York: Viking Press, 1952, p. 4), "have functioned for years to stymie meetings. The *Robert's Rules* have made it possible for a few to take control and impose their convictions on those others not quite so ready to spring to their feet, not quite so able to phrase emphatically what they want to say." Is this evaluation accurate? Under what conditions is it most likely to be true or untrue? How can a parliamentary chairman avoid conducting this kind of meeting? Can any of the characteristics of informal small-group discussion be made to apply in a parliamentary meeting? Why or why not? If so, which characteristics?

4. Set up a practice session in the classroom where a member attempts to

follow the traditional parliamentary procedures for conducting the meeting, and at the same time tries to develop a permissive climate, promote easy interaction, and encourage widespread participation. After the demonstration session, hold a class discussion on the success of the demonstration observed.

5. Read the article by Herbert W. Simons listed above. Observe a large-group discussion and then write a paper in which you describe the interaction, specifying what was Representative and what Participative.

APPENDIX

CASES
FOR DISCUSSION

THE CASE OF MARY MILLER

GROUP: The State Pardon and Parole Board.

SITUATION: Mary Miller is now serving a life sentence for murder. She is not eligible for parole but it is possible for the Governor of the state to grant her a pardon. At today's meeting, the Pardon and Parole Board is to consider Mary Miller's petition for a pardon, as one of many cases on the agenda.

PARTICIPANTS: Prominent citizen, Chairman.
Three other citizens also appointed by the Governor.
State Director of Prisons.
Psychologist who is consultant to the Board.

THE CASE

Mary Miller graduated from Western Tech in 1933. Her parents are well-to-do and highly respected. Her early marriage ended in divorce within a year. In 1939 she went to a nearby city. A promised modeling job never materialized, but she stayed in town, backstopped by a generous allowance from home and occasional work as a chorus girl. Soon she had fallen in love with and was living with good-looking, slick—and married—John Thompson, whose business was extorting jewels from wealthy women.

Thompson crashed society parties seeking married women with valuable jewels. He would get acquainted, date a woman a few times, and then ask to have a closer look at her jewelry. At this point he would pocket the gems and threaten to tell the woman's husband they were having an affair if she reported the theft. The method was successful for a long time.

Mary struck up an acquaintance with Mrs. Ada Willis, who was wealthy. Thompson and an accomplice, Morris Clindinen, decided that Mrs. Willis was fair game. They rented an apartment in a hotel and a woman, whose voice was identified at the trial as Mary's, made a luncheon date at the same hotel with Mrs. Willis. When Mrs. Willis reached the apartment, she was met by Thompson and Clindinen, who took her diamond ring, tied her up, and left her in a closet. When discovered later, she was dead of suffocation.

Mary and the two men were convicted of first-degree murder. The jury recommended mercy for the girl. Thompson and Clindinen went to the electric chair; they maintained to their deaths that Mary was not involved. Mary testified that she knew nothing of Thompson's business and had taken no part in it. A court psychiatrist said that Mary had never grown up, and was a natural and easy victim of these unscrupulous characters since she was a country girl deposited in a complex metropolitan setting. The judge, however, sentenced Mary to prison "for the rest of her natural life," and specified that she was never to become eligible for parole.

Mary has been in prison since 1940. Today, her friends and relatives feel that she is ready for release and should be given a chance to return to her family. They maintain that the sentence given her, even under the sordid circumstances, was unduly harsh in a day of enlightened penology.

A prison psychiatric report says that after years of discipline and unvarying routine, Mary has become mature, possesses good reasoning powers, and has a sense of realism about life. In prison she has been stable, busy, and useful. She has attended prison church services regularly for years and all three chaplains have recommended her release.

The prison director has said: "People are sent to prison because they are a danger to society. While they are in custody, it is our job to help them see what got them into trouble. We try to make them realistic and responsive. They can fake, but they rarely fake consistently for years. When prisoners demonstrate constantly these changes, it is both a waste of the state's money and a waste of human life to keep them behind bars any longer."

The prosecuting attorney has replied that criminals are sent to prison because they must pay a debt to the society they have injured by their own voluntary acts: "If rehabilitation were the only criterion, the state could justify releasing most of the prisoners now behind bars. The judge and jury determined at the trial that Mary was sane and rational; mere evidence now that she has mature reasoning powers does not establish her right to release. She received a fair trial and the jury was convinced 'beyond a reasonable doubt' that she was guilty of first-degree murder. Moreover, the experienced judge who sentenced her ordered explicitly that she is never to be paroled. It is unwise and unfair to ask the Governor to pardon her under these circumstances."

The question is, "Should the Pardon and Parole Board recommend to the Governor that he pardon Mary Miller?"

THE CASE OF THE CHICAGO CHEMICAL COMPANY

GROUP: The Executive Committee of the Harvey plant of the Chicago Chemical Company.

SITUATION: The Executive Committee responsible for operations of the Harvey plant must decide whether to award a day's wages to workers who missed work because of false information. Whatever the Executive Committee decides will be a recommendation to the Board of Directors of the entire Company since several thousand dollars are involved.

PARTICIPANTS: Executive Vice President in Charge of the Harvey plant, chairman.
Comptroller.
Vice President for Sales.
Vice President for Production.
Assistant to the Executive Vice President and Secretary of the Executive Committee.

THE CASE

On Thursday, one week ago, there was a crippling snow storm in south Chicago. By 5:00 AM, the snow was 3 feet deep, with drifts up to 14 feet. Buses were unable to operate; cars were imbedded in driveways. The Chicago radio stations were relaying messages from superintendents of schools and other agencies that schools and other buildings would not be in operation that day. One radio station announced that the Harvey plant of the Chicago Chemical Company would be closed for the day. Officials of the company later denied that any such announcement had come from any responsible administrative officer.

The plant did, in fact, operate on Thursday, although it was necessary to reduce operations since about 40 percent of the labor force did not report for work. Those who did report were for the most part those who lived within walking distance of the plant.

The temperature rose during the day and by Friday morning the plant was able to return to normal operations.

At a meeting of the labor union on the following Monday evening, the question was raised whether workers who were unable to get to the plant because of the storm, and who made no attempt to report to work because of the radio announcement that the plant would be closed, should be paid for Thursday, just as if they had been on duty. On Tuesday, representatives of the union reported to the executive vice president that the union had voted to ask that employees who missed work on Thursday be paid.

The union claims that employees missed work through no fault of their own, that they would have made an effort to report to work except that the radio had instructed them otherwise, and that the employees should not be penalized for circumstances beyond their control.

The contract with the union states clearly that the company shall not be responsible for paying employees for work not performed.

THE CASE OF FREE MEDICAL CARE

GROUP: A Labor-Management Negotiating Committee of the Beltex Manufacturing Company.

SITUATION: The labor union representing workers in this plant has decided not
to ask for increased wages in the contract now being negotiated but
to ask instead for a company-financed medical care plan for all
employees. Negotiations on the new contract are deadlocked and
apparently there will be a strike unless the disagreement about the
medical care plan can be resolved. The question the Negotiating
Committee must answer is, "what should the clause in the contract
dealing with employee medical care specify?"

PARTICIPANTS: Two representatives of management: the senior vice president and
the director of industrial relations. Two representatives of the
union: the president of the local union, and a staff officer representing the International Leatherworkers' central office. (No one
is designated as chairman.)

THE CASE

The Beltex Company manufactures leather, rubber, and plastic belts
for industrial machinery, and employs approximately one thousand
workers. The workers are organized into a local of the International
Leatherworkers Union. The present contract expires on the last day of
this month, and the union has served notice of a strike at midnight of that
day if a new contract has not been agreed upon by that time.

The present contract provides an average wage of about $3.70 an
hour; paid vacations, the length of which is related to length of service
with the company; a pension plan, contributions for which are shared
equally by employer and employee; and one day of sick leave for each
year the employee has served the company.

For the new contract, the union has proposed no additional increment
in wages but has asked for a company-financed medical-care plan for
all employees. In asking for the new plan, they have called attention to
similar arrangements in other industrial plants: some companies provide
a medical staff on company premises; some pay premiums for all workers
in Blue Cross, White Cross, or other medical insurance systems; and
others allow employees to be treated by a physician or hospital of their
own choice, with the medical bills paid by the company. Union representatives have stated their willingness to accept any of these systems so
long as the plan is paid for completely by the company.

The company claims that the wage rate being paid under the present
contract is above the prevailing rate in the area for similar work, that the

fringe benefits already being provided are a strain on the resources of the company, and that the company is not financially able to take on the costs of such a medical program at this time.

The union feels that the employees' needs for medical care are related to their service to the company, and that provision of such medical care is a responsibility of the company. They point to the extensive precedent for such responsibility in the existence of company-financed medical plans in other industrial plants.

The company feels that the provision of medical care is a personal responsibility unrelated to work performed for the company, and that workers should pay their own medical bills out of wages earned.

THE CASE OF JUDITH SCOTT

GROUP: College Committee on Student Discipline.

SITUATION: The rules of this college require co-eds to be in their campus residences by 11:00. Judith Scott has been reported by her residence hall counselor for violating this rule. The Committee on Student Discipline must decide whether she is guilty and, if so, fix the penalty to be assessed.

PARTICIPANTS: Professor of Spanish, Chairman.
Asst. Professor of Geology
Asst. Professor of English
Student: President of the Student Body
Student Chairman of the Interfraternity Council
Student Chairman of Independent Women's Association

THE CASE

The college has a rule that women students must be in their dormitories by 11:00 P.M. on nights before school days. The dormitory in which Judith Scott, a junior, resides also has a practice of requiring girls to sign out in a book kept at the door when they leave the house in the evening. In the sign-out book they are required to specify where they are going, who is accompanying them, how they are traveling, and when they expect to return. Signing the book does not relieve a girl of the responsibility for being back in the dormitory by closing hours.

On Tuesday evening, Judith Scott wrote in the sign-out book at 7:45 P.M. that she was going to Springfield, 50 miles away, to spend the night at the home of an aunt; that she was being accompanied by Tom Crawford, a senior; that they were traveling in his car; and that she would return to the house at 7:00 A.M. the next day.

When Judith returned to the dormitory at 7:00 next morning, her counselor informed her that she was being reported to the committee on student discipline for staying out all night without permission. Judith protested that she had explained clearly in the sign-out book what her plans were. She further pointed out that she had had her mother's written permission to spend that night with her aunt in Springfield. The fact of having her mother's permission was subsequently confirmed. The counselor wrote a letter to the committee on student discipline in which she said: "The fact of having her mother's prior permission does not excuse a student from conforming to college and dormitory regulations."

When questioned later by the committee, Tom Crawford reported that he had driven Judith to her aunt's home in Springfield, had returned to his own rooming house on the campus, and early the next morning had driven back to Springfield to bring Judith to the campus. An investigator for the committee could find no resident of Tom's house who remembered whether or not Tom had spent the night in the house.

The chairman of the committee on student discipline had stated, in connection with an earlier case in which a woman had remained away from her house all night without permission, that the next woman involved in such a situation would be expelled from the college.

THE CASE OF STUDENT HOUSING

GROUP: Ad-hoc Committee of University Administrators, faculty, and representatives of the Student Government.

SITUATION: An ultra-liberal organization in the state has threatened to bring suit against the state university for allowing certain student houses to restrict their membership to students of one religious faith. Students who live in these houses say they will boycott classes if the University changes the system. Parents have been putting pressure on the University's Board of Trustees and the Board has passed an ultimatum to the President of the University: get a faculty-student group together and work out a decision that everyone can accept.

PARTICIPANTS: President of the University, Chairman
Dean of Students
Chairman of Faculty Committee on Student Welfare
President of the Student Body
Vice President of Student Government
President of a house which accepts only
members of his religious group.

THE CASE

At the present time, dormitories under control of the University accept students on a first-come, first-served basis.

Some houses on the University campus, however, especially those sponsored by religious foundations, restrict membership to students who belong to a particular religious group. Two of the largest houses are sponsored by the Baptists and Methodists. There are also Catholic and Jewish houses. One house organized last year is restricted to students who refuse any religious affiliation.

There has for a long time been pressure from some people on the campus to require such houses to abolish restrictive clauses from their regulations or to close their houses. Other persons feel that a private association has a right to choose members on whatever basis it pleases.

Recently an organization in the state has started a campaign to prevent restriction in housing on this basis. They have appealed to the Board of Trustees to end what they consider a violation of civil rights. They have threatened to bring suit to force compliance. In response, students who live in the twenty-four houses affected threaten to stay away from classes if the University takes away their privilege of choosing their own residents.

The Ad Hoc Committee has been told by the Board of Trustees to work out a solution at once.

THE CASE OF MOTORCYCLE REGULATIONS

GROUP: Faculty-Student Committee on Traffic and Parking

SITUATION: An alarming increase of injuries sustained by students in motorcycle accidents has caused the Committee on Traffic and Parking to consider establishing regulations for the control of motorcycles on campus.

PARTICIPANTS: Four faculty members appointed by the Executive Vice President: a professor of history, chairman; an associate professor; and two assistant professors.
Three students elected by the Student Government: a senior and two juniors.

THE CASE

In the last two years there has been a sharp increase in the number of motorcycles, motorbikes, and motorized scooters being operated on streets in the campus area. While there are no rules at present concerning speed limits for motorcycles, there have been numerous complaints from faculty members, student groups, and local citizens about excessive speeds of these vehicles on crowded campus streets. There have been a few complaints about noise made by these motorized vehicles.

A year ago one student was killed when his motor scooter hit a truck after he lost control. This fall a student was critically injured when struck by a bus at an intersection. The hospital reports an average of twelve injuries a day—some of them serious—involving the operation of motorcycles and scooters.

In the last six months there have been suggestions from various groups that the University should impose stricter regulations concerning the operation of such motorized vehicles. At the present time there are rules covering operation of motor vehicles and others for bicycles, but none for motorcycles.

Present rules for motor vehicles require that cars be registered with the University: that the driver be licensed by the state; that the owner have liability insurance for the vehicle; and that the vehicle be operated in accordance with state and community traffic regulations. Students are warned in the regulations that they are subject to monetary fines by the University discipline committee for unauthorized operation of a motor vehicle or for violation of traffic regulations.

Bicycle regulations require that bicycles be registered with the University; be equipped with brakes, a warning horn or bell and, if operated at night, a light; and be parked only in authorized areas. Bicycle operators are required further to obey all motor vehicle traffic laws. They are warned also that violators may be assessed monetary fines by the discipline committee.

The Executive Vice President has now asked the Committee on Traffic and Parking to consider whether regulations specifically for motorcycles should be added to the rules at this time; and to make whatever recommendations the Committee deems desirable.

THE CASE OF NEWTON ROCKWELL

GROUP: The New Ordinances Committee of the Oldtown City Council.

SITUATION: Newton Rockwell was arrested in Oldtown during an argument over playing a religious recording on the street, but was released because the City Attorney could find no ordinance that he had violated. A group of irate citizens are putting pressure on the City Council to adopt an ordinance which would outlaw the playing of religious propaganda on city streets. The Council expects at its next meeting some kind of recommendation for its New Ordinances Committee. The Committee must decide whether it wishes to propose a new ordinance and, perhaps, whether the Newton Rockwell incident is sufficient cause for taking action.

PARTICIPANTS: Alderman with twenty years on the Council, Chairman
Three other aldermen
The City Attorney, Consultant to the New Ordinances Committee.

THE CASE

Newton Rockwell is an ordained minister of a religious group, Jehovah's Witnesses. One afternoon in an Oldtown neighborhood, he was going from house to house selling religious materials. He carried a bag containing books and pamphlets, a portable phonograph, and several records. When a person answered his knock, he asked permission to play a phonograph record. If the householder responded favorably after hearing the record, he tried to sell a book or pamphlet containing information similar to that on the recording.

The neighborhood in which he was working on this particular day is heavily populated; about 90 percent of the residents are Roman Catholics. One of his phonograph records, called "Enemies," contained an attack on the Catholic religion. This recording condemned all organized religions, but it condemned Roman Catholicism in particular and it did so in language which would probably offend not only persons of that faith but also anyone who respects the religious views of others.

As Rockwell was leaving one house, he met on the street James Johnson and Timothy Morency, both of whom are Roman Catholics. He asked them if he might play a phonograph record for them. They gave their permission and Rockwell played the record, "Enemies." When they had heard enough of the record to perceive its intent, Johnson and Morency shouted for Rockwell to stop the record. He replied that they had agreed to listen. As the three men continued to shout, other persons from the neighborhood were attracted to the altercation, including a policeman. Rockwell was arrested for inciting others to a disturbance of the peace.

A state statute provides that any person who shall disturb or threaten the peace, or who shall provoke contention by threatening, quarreling with, or challenging another, shall be fined not more than $500 or imprisoned for not more than one year, or both.

On the other hand, the First Amendment to the Constitution of the United States says that the federal government shall make no law respecting an establishment of religion or prohibiting the free exercise thereof. The Fourteenth Amendment has established the same prohibition against the state governments.

INDEX